Uncanny
Encounters

Uncanny Encounters

*Literature, Psychoanalysis,
and the End of Alterity*

✦

John Zilcosky

NORTHWESTERN UNIVERSITY PRESS
EVANSTON, ILLINOIS

Northwestern University Press
www.nupress.northwestern.edu

Portions of some chapters have appeared earlier in different form: "Unheimliche
Begegnungen: Abenteuerliteratur, Psychoanalyse, Moderne," in *Literarische
Entdeckungsreisen: Vorfahren—Nachfahrten—Revisionen*, ed. Hansjörg Bay
and Wolfgang Struck (Weimar: Böhlau, 2012); "Savage Science: Primitives, War
Neurotics, and Freud's Uncanny Method," *American Imago* 70 (Fall 2013); and
"Hermann Hesse's Colonial Uncanny: *Robert Aghion*, 1913," *New German
Critique* 41 (Fall 2014). Permission to reuse this material is here acknowledged.

Printed in the United States of America

10   9   8   7   6   5   4   3   2   1

Library of Congress Cataloging-in-Publication Data

Zilcosky, John.
Uncanny encounters : literature, psychoanalysis, and the end of alterity / John
Zilcosky.
    pages cm.
    Includes bibliographical references and index.
    ISBN 978-0-8101-3210-8 (cloth : alk. paper) — ISBN 978-0-8101-3209-2
(pbk. : alk. paper) — ISBN 978-0-8101-3211-5 (ebook)
    1. German literature—20th century—History and criticism. 2. Uncanny, The
(Psychoanalysis), in literature. 3. Travelers' writings, German—History and
criticism. I. Title.
    PT405.Z54 2015
    830.90091—dc23

                                                          2015031421

For Rebecca, Charlie, and Nora

CONTENTS

ILLUSTRATIONS

ACKNOWLEDGMENTS

It gives me great pleasure to sit back and think of everyone who has helped me over the years of writing this book. For financial support, I thank the Social Sciences and Humanities Research Council, the Alexander von Humboldt Foundation, the German Academic Exchange Service, Victoria College (University of Toronto), and especially the National Endowment for the Humanities, which provided me with a year free of teaching, most of which I spent in Berlin finishing this manuscript. My host there, Joseph Vogl, offered me an academic home away from home and many lively conversations, which, even when not related to this book, inspired me in surprising ways. I am grateful also to Stefan Willer, who brought me into the community of the Zentrum für Literatur- und Kulturforschung, to Uwe Schwersky, who gave me a work space at the Berlin Staatsbibliothek, and to Annette Vowinckel, who joined me for always engaging coffee breaks at the Staatsbibliothek. I thank my friends at the KiK Berlin Judo Club, especially Oliver Pittelkow and Thomas Linck, who forced me to think about things other than my book for two nights a week, and also Rainer Börner, whose insights on German politics reminded me of the broader implications of my work.

I am grateful to the colleagues who, over the years, have provided me with *Denkanstöße* about this project: Hansjörg Bay, Cathy Caruth, Stanley Corngold, Wolf Kittler, Malte Kleinwort, Jean-Michel Rabaté, Lou Rose, Robert Stockhammer, Wolfgang Struck, and David Wellbery. I thank also Suzan Alteri, curator of the Baldwin Library of Historical Children's Literature at the University of Florida, for offering expert advice about maps from early editions of *The Swiss Family Robinson*. Closer to home, I think of Manda Vrkljan from the University of Toronto's Kelly Library, who tirelessly and cheerfully tracked down articles and books for me from around the world. Olga Bazilevica, Marlo Burks, and Anna Stainton located high-quality images and obtained the rights for them. I am especially grateful to my longtime research assistant, Lara Pehar, who combed early drafts of this book for stylistic and logical infelicities, unearthed countless hard-to-find sources, and compiled the entire bibliography; it was wonderful having an assistant who is already such an accomplished scholar herself. Finally, while writing, I often thought of my long-ago mentor, Charles Bernheimer, and I hoped that even small traces of his analytic acuity and literary grace would appear in this book.

I thank my mother and father for being so generous with their time and attention, and for being proud of me; this still gives me confidence, even after all these years. And I thank Charles Hanly, who showed me how to loosen knots that kept me from writing; memories of his calm wisdom resonate with me almost daily. My greatest gratitude goes to my wife, Rebecca Wittmann, who loves our gravel road as much as I do and, more than this, knows exactly how to write a great book, so was able to help me at every turn. She makes everything possible. I dedicate this to her and to the new bodies that we belong to: Nora Kathryn, who likes to sit on my lap and help me type, and her big brother, Charlie, whose astute questions in my office the other day spurred me finally to finish this book. "Papa, are you writing different stories each day? Or always the same one?"

ABBREVIATIONS AND NOTE ON TRANSLATIONS

The following abbreviations are used throughout the text and notes to refer to frequently cited sources:

A	Hofmannsthal, Hugo von. *Andreas*. Trans. Marie D. Hottinger. London: Pushkin, 1998. German in *SWK*.
DV	Mann, Thomas. *Death in Venice*. Norton Critical Edition. Ed. and trans. Clayton Koelb. New York: Norton, 1994. German in *FA*.
FA	Mann, Thomas. *Große kommentierte Frankfurter Ausgabe*. Ed. Heinrich Detering et al. 38 vols. Frankfurt am Main: S. Fischer, 2001–.
FLF	Freud, Sigmund. *The Complete Letters of Sigmund Freud to Wilhelm Fliess, 1887–1904*. Ed. and trans. Jeffrey Moussaieff Masson. Cambridge, Mass.: Harvard University Press, 1985.
FW	Musil, Robert. *Five Women*. Trans. Eithne Wilkins and Ernst Kaiser. Boston: Godine, 1999. German in Musil, *GW*.
Freud, *GW*	Freud, Sigmund. *Gesammelte Werke: Chronologisch geordnet*. Ed. Anna Freud et al. 19 vols. London: Imago, 1940–87.
Musil, *GW*	Musil, Robert. *Gesammelte Werke in neun Bänden*. Ed. Adolf Frisé. 9 vols. Reinbek bei Hamburg: Rowohlt, 1978.
SE	Freud, Sigmund. *The Standard Edition of the Complete Psychological Works of Sigmund Freud*. Ed. and trans. James Strachey. 24 vols. London: Hogarth Press and the Institute of Psycho-analysis, 1953–74. German in Freud, *GW*.
SW	Hesse, Hermann. *Sämtliche Werke in 20 Bänden und einem Registerband*. Ed. Volker Michels. 21 vols. Frankfurt am Main: Suhrkamp, 2001-2007.
SWK	Hofmannsthal, Hugo von. *Sämtliche Werke: Kritische Ausgabe*. Ed. Rudolf Hirsch et al. 42 vols. Frankfurt: S. Fischer, 1975–.

Throughout this book, I cite from standard translations of German (and some French) works—emending these when necessary (marked as "trans. rev."). In the cases where I do not refer to an existing translation, the translation is my own.

Uncanny
Encounters

Introduction

✦

Uncanny Encounters

When I was a boy, I loved maps. I touched them and dreamt of places far from my small-town Pennsylvania home, especially in the East Indies and the Caribbean, the settings of my favorite novels: *The Swiss Family Robinson, Treasure Island,* and *Robinson Crusoe.* I could of course never find these novels' islands; they didn't exist outside of the stories. But I did discover maps of them within the books themselves because each included a chart of its own fictional territory (Robert Louis Stevenson even drew his "Treasure Island" map before inventing the plot). I got to know these maps better than the "real" ones I kept in my room. I imagined passing Shark's Island on my way up Jackall's River into the Swiss family's settlement, with its mysterious Flamingo Marsh and dazzling array of flora that never could have grown in one climate zone: cotton, acorns, cabbage, cocoa palms (figure 1). And Treasure Island's map taught me how to get from Captain Smollett's mighty schooner, *Hispaniola,* to Spyglass Hill, Skeleton Island, and the three crosses that marked the treasure—their veracity all vouched for by Billy Bones's signature scrawled at the bottom (figure 2). Crusoe's Island of Despair similarly revealed the site of the castaway's hut, a river disappearing tantalizingly into a lush interior, and the dreaded cannibals dancing behind thickets on the island's far end (figure 3).

Despite the obvious differences between Daniel Defoe's early-eighteenth-century map[1] and the later ones in Johann David Wyss's and Stevenson's books, the three shared something essential to all maps: incompleteness. Crusoe's overproduction of childlike sketchings—hills, rivers, and dancing natives—expresses the pre-Enlightenment cartographer's *horror vacui*: he covers over blank spaces to hide how little he knows. Although the early nineteenth-century chart for New Switzerland (1812–13) gives us a better sense of how to get about—a detailed coastline's rivers leads to the farm and to named marshes and woods—its eastern edge reveals only an enigmatic terra incognita. Treasure Island's map (1883) likewise leaves some blank spaces and, more important, gives the impression of being crafted in a rush, without precision, by a pirate on the run. The torn sheet lacks even the obligatory neat line to demonstrate its own limits. When my younger

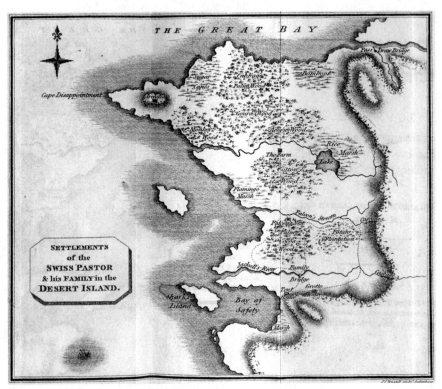

Figure 1. Map of the family's settlement from the 1816 English edition of *The Swiss Family Robinson* (close likeness of the map from the original 1812–13 German version)—dubbed "New Switzerland" in later editions

brother and I began mapping the park near our childhood home, the Treasure Island chart was our model: we sketched a compass rose and a scale on a scrap of paper, drew paths dividing up exotic regions ("Elbow Tree Turn," "Luce's Pass," "Dead Man's Hill"), and left the remainder blank. Our map did what all maps do, even the ones that claim to be complete: it made our world seem more mysterious than it actually was. Like the map of Treasure Island, it showed us how much was left out. Our familiar park became foreign.

As a teenager in the 1970s and 1980s, I collected more maps and began coloring lines on them to mark my own travels, as if to render visible my burgeoning sense of self. I drew routes outward from my childhood home along the East Coast into the Southern states and, eventually, throughout Europe. As satisfying as this was, I sensed that I was just tracing existing lines and not, as in my boyhood, inventing worlds along with my heroes. I was drawn back to the more obviously incomplete maps, and eventually to ones created long

Figure 2. Map of Treasure Island, from the first book edition of *Treasure Island* (1883)

Figure 3. Map of Crusoe's Island, first published in *Serious Reflections During the Life & Surprising Adventures of Robinson Crusoe*, a 1720 sequel to *Robinson Crusoe* (1719)

before the invention of modern cartography's insistence on a sharp divide between fiction and reality: the Babylonians' first map of the world, with its outlying islands where the "horned bull dwells and attacks the newcomer"; the Greek maps based partially on Odysseus's fictional journeys to the caves of the Cyclopes, Ogygia (Calypso's island), and Scheria (the land of the Phaeacians); and the medieval charts that depicted the "Garden of Eden" far to the East, just past the Ganges River delta. Here, again, my imagination had free reign. And I soon realized that I did not need to go so far back in history to find such inviting incompletion. Over dinner one night, an older friend of my parents told me that his own father had studied geography precisely because he was drawn to the last white spots on maps. Excited by this possibility, I began perusing the late nineteenth-century charts the man gave me, and I watched how, as the maps progressed over the next few decades, their open spots were filled in. The fringes and interiors of the world came into relief: the North and South poles, the Himalayas, and the hearts of South America and Africa.

How did these maps—no older than my own grandparents!—turn so quickly into the "complete" ones that I now knew?[2] Looking at maps of Africa, for example, I saw that they had remained relatively unfinished from the Babylonian era through to the Enlightenment. Ancient cartographers had called the entire continent "Libya" and depicted it as about half its actual size, missing its still unknown southern part. By the Renaissance, the coastline began to take shape, but the center was still blank. Like Crusoe,

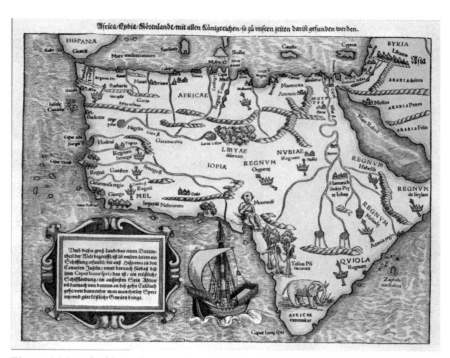

Figure 4. Map of Africa, whose emptiness is filled with an elephant, exotic birds and a Cyclops (from Sebastian Münster's *Cosmographia* [1544])

cartographers filled this blankness with imagined rivers and lakes, as well as with elephants, crocodiles, lions, monkeys, exotic birds, and even Cyclopes (figure 4; figure 5).[3] Eighteenth-century mapmakers erased these creatures in the name of the Enlightenment: no one should fear the *horror vacui*, and only proven geographic phenomena should be documented. The result was the relatively open, blank center of Africa we see in maps from the mid-eighteenth through the mid-nineteenth century (figure 6). These white spaces achieved exactly what they were supposed to: they encouraged new scientific expeditions. But this process moved slowly, gaining crucial momentum only in the second half of the nineteenth century, when colonizers conquered more regions, and new cartographic technologies allowed for improved accuracy.[4] By the end of the nineteenth century, scientific travelers, especially surveyors, eclipsed the touring gentlemen as the paradigmatic European voyager.[5]

The chronological concentration of the maps' development struck me: what had remained terra incognita since the Babylonians was now "discovered" and mapped in the space of forty years. Consider this historical condensation beginning in the 1870s: Henry Morton Stanley, among others, searched for the source of the Nile in the 1870s and, in the 1880s, explored

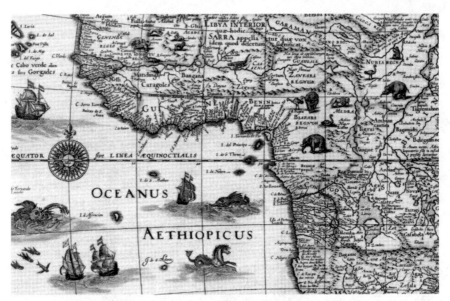

Figure 5. Section of Willem Blaeu's "Nova Africa" map (1617), featuring lions, elephants, a monkey, a crocodile, and, along the coast, fabulous sea creatures

the Congo;[6] in 1882, the British occupation of Egypt opened the "scramble for Africa"; in the late 1880s and again in 1896, 1903–05, and 1911–13, the German explorers Karl von den Steinen and Theodor Koch-Grünberg traveled farther up the Amazon than any European ever had; Robert Peary came within a few degrees of the North Pole, perhaps even reaching it, in 1909; Roald Amundsen planted the Norwegian flag at the South Pole in 1911; and the British launched their intensive Mount Everest expeditions in 1921, culminating three years later in George Mallory's fatal climb toward the summit. In this relatively short period, from roughly 1875 to 1920, explorers reached all of the goals of which they had, for centuries, only dreamt.

And they quickly made maps. Whereas an 1875 map of Africa is only slightly fuller than a 1750 one, maps from the late 1890s reveal an African cartography nearly as detailed as today's. A comparison of an 1875 map with one from 1899 demonstrates this starkly. In just over two decades, the cartography of Africa developed from being as sketchy as that of Stevenson's Treasure Island—the mapmaker simply wrote "*unerforscht*" (uncharted) across central Africa in 1875—to being almost as complete as today's (figure 7; figure 8). History may indeed tend to repeat itself, but the blank spaces on the earth were mapped for the first time only once—and this in an astonishingly short period of about twenty years. Abruptly and irrevocably, the earth came into relief.

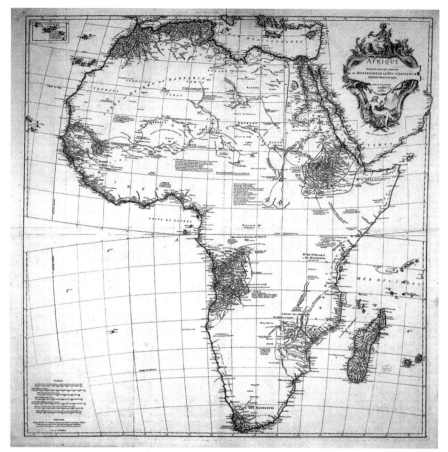

Figure 6. Typical Enlightenment map of Africa (1749), with the interior left blank (by Jean-Baptiste Bourguignon d'Anville)

Uncanny Adventures: Germans in the Jungle

This unique historical moment led to the pressing question of my book: How did this apparently final mapping of the earth affect the European imagination?[7] How did Europeans' fantasies about themselves and their world change when these apparently virgin territories disappeared? As I discovered while reading travel writing from around 1900, Europeans experienced this new global world as a shocking series of "uncanny encounters." At the ends of the earth, they found not primitive savages but "civilized" natives or, even worse, European doppelgängers: "Dr. Livingstone, I presume," but as a frightening surprise. Robert Scott, for example, traveled all the way to the South

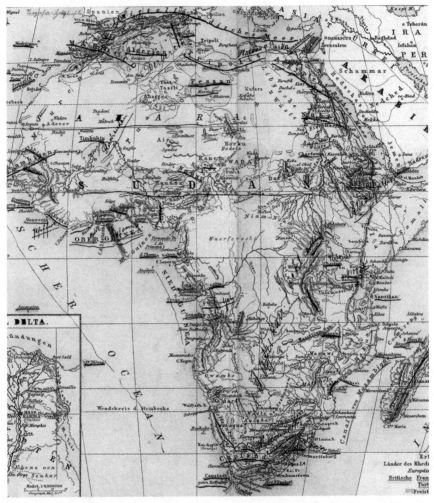

Figure 7. An 1875 map of Africa, where the middle is still relatively blank—marked "*unerforscht*" (uncharted)

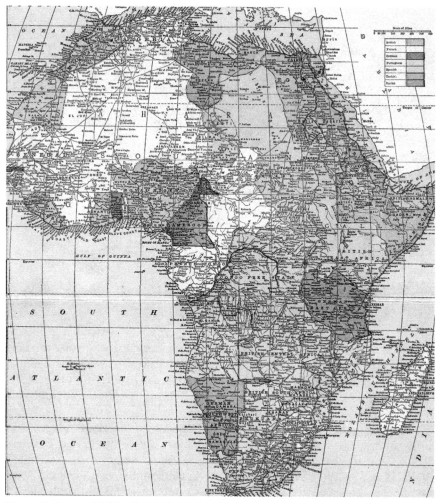

Figure 8. A map of Africa from only twenty-four years later (1899), almost as complete as today's maps

Figure 9. Roald Amundsen's black flag, as discovered by Robert Scott within a few miles of the South Pole (sketched by a member of Scott's party, Dr. Edward A. Wilson, in January 1912)

Pole in 1911–12 expecting to be the first. But when he arrived at 89°42′ S, just a few miles from the Pole, cold, hungry, and exhausted, he saw the horror before him: Roald Amundsen's flag, blowing next to a camp that had just been abandoned by the Norwegians. "The worst has happened," Scott writes in his diary (which, unlike its author, survived the journey), "Great God! This is an awful place" (figure 9; figure 10).[8]

Scott's "awful" encounter with his European predecessor dogged less famous travelers, too, as this brief sampling from my first two chapters illustrates: the geographer-explorer Georg Wegener traverses the "immense" Pacific Ocean in 1900, eventually landing in German Samoa to find not "colorfully screaming and swarming" natives but rather shockingly "orderly" German civil servants.[9] The hero of Norbert Jacques' popular 1911 *Heißes Land: Eine Reise nach Brasilien* (*Hot Land: A Journey to Brazil*) similarly discovered a series of German colonies deep in the Brazilian rain forest, each already eerily named after a German city. And Stefan Zweig describes his anxious quest for alterity while visiting the Indian city of Gwalior in 1909: "the wanderer always searches for the other, the foreign, and does not want to rediscover Europe in India."[10] But fin de siècle European, especially German, travelers were in fact always discovering Europe everywhere, resulting in a new kind of fear, *not of difference but of similarity*, and also a new, uncanny way of talking about this fear—years before Freud published his *The Uncanny* in 1919. By examining these popular travel texts as well as so-called high literature and Freud's psychoanalytic works,[11] I aim to show how these three types of writing expressed a related anxiety and how, in the age

Figure 10. Amundsen's tent at the South Pole, the Norwegian flag flying on top

of the apparent end of alterity, they pointed toward a new source of modern violence: not in the oft-cited fear of difference, but in the dread of uncanny recognition.

For this reason, early twentieth-century psychoanalytical theories of *Unheimlichkeit* (uncanniness) are better tools for understanding these texts than late twentieth-century postcolonial theories, which either neglect unconscious motivations (Said's *Orientalism*) or examine these primarily through the lens of "difference" (Homi Bhabha). Bhabha's theory at first seems fitting because it, too, views the colonial world's mixture of sameness and difference— its "hybridity"—as upsetting to the European traveler; but Bhabha ultimately sees this fear as issuing from the residue of difference, which the colonizer attempts to "disavow."[12] The fin de siècle German-speaking traveler, however, was frightened by the opposite situation: he searched precisely for this difference and discovered instead the *unheimlich* "long familiar" (Freud), which shocked him and led to attempts at denial.[13]

My book opens with Jacques' *Hot Land*, which concludes in a way that we can best describe as uncanny, in this Freudian sense of something "known of old" now unexpectedly returning (Freud, *SE* 17:220). After surviving the requisite excitements of contemporaneous travel fiction—the stormy sea passage; the love affair with the beautiful dark-skinned girl; the malaria; the violent confrontation with the natives—the protagonist complains that Brazil and its inhabitants have become too European. He thus ventures deeper into the jungles of Brazil, farther from familiar territory, searching for the "limits of the world" (Jacques, *Heißes Land*, 201).[14] Getting closer to the mysterious mountain range he calls the "Range of Wonder [*Wunder*]," behind which hides "virgin land," he looks for the longed-for, un-Europeanized natives (207). But after pushing his way through one last thicket, he finds only—Germans. They are living in horrible conditions, often at the verge of death, in villages that weirdly bear the names of familiar metropolises: "Berlin, Hamburg, Bremen, and so on" (222). The heart of the Brazilian darkness, it seems, is German.

Because this encounter is paradigmatic for popular German adventure writing at the beginning of the twentieth century, it is worth taking a closer look—especially at its two primary features. First, there is the meeting itself: the unsettling confrontation with one's mirror image in a world that ought to contain wondrous, inscrutable strangers. Then comes the second stage: the disappointed, angry reaction to this surprising sameness. The hero detests his German predecessors for "taking for themselves the virginity of the beautiful, old, untouched soil" and, more than this, for turning the jungle into "a brutal little Europe." The fact that Germans traveled thousands of miles only to transform the tropical forest into Europe shows that they are "foolish and crude" (*Heißes Land*, 221–22). In a telling earlier scene, the narrator journeys to a remote Brazilian brothel, only to discover there, of all things, a German prostitute. Her foreign-familiarity shocks him; he flies into a rage and slanders her with such "brutality" that she goes mad (174). This mini-narrative—in which fright is followed by anxious aggression—forms the microcosm of my thesis about fin de siècle German travel writing: that it is *uncanny*, and that this uncanniness spawns violence.

I say "fin de siècle" and "German," but do not overlook the facts that there were uncanny encounters long before the turn of the twentieth century and that travelers from other European nations recorded them as well. In fact, one could argue that there was always *only* the uncanny encounter: contrary to Levi-Strauss, the "native" was never without writing; the tropics were always *tristes*.[15] More specifically, James Clifford describes the "Squanto-effect" registered by British pilgrims traveling to the astonishingly wild New World in 1620 (when you could smell the pine trees fifty miles from shore). They discovered that their Indian helper, Squanto, had just returned from England and spoke better English than many of them.[16] Stephen Greenblatt likewise documents the informants, middlemen, and go-betweens appearing in sixteenth-century Spanish, British, and French accounts of the New World. But, as Greenblatt stresses, these uncanny figures did not overturn the master trope of Renaissance travel writing: the "wonder" of seeing the marvelous for the first time.[17]

When does wonder give way to what I am calling uncanniness? The shift had already begun in the Age of Discovery; both terms were prominent in Romanticism; and wonder survived the turn of the twentieth century. Despite this gradual and overlapping process, I maintain that uncanniness gained conspicuous importance around 1900. Whether we choose as a starting point the 1880s (the "scramble for Africa," the Berlin conference to partition Africa, and the exhibits of "primitive" peoples in Europe), the 1890s (Alfred Penck's proposal for an International Map of the World), or the 1900s (the races to the poles), fin de siècle developments reinforced two ways of thinking about non-Westerners that had been undermining wonder for a long time. First, Europeans now understood the extra-European world primarily in *real-politische* terms: as spheres for gaining resources and staging unforgiving national interests, not as spaces for possible wondrous encounters with non-Europeans;[18] imperialism's well-published atrocities—the British in India, the French in North Africa, the Belgians in the Congo, the Germans in South-West Africa—cemented this demystification. Second, turn-of-the-century travelers realized that there was no more virgin soil on which to tread, even as this insight made them long for it even more; as adventurers mapped the earth's final frontiers, the average traveler found himself disappointed by a world where there was nothing new. These two developments—the spending of colonialism's remaining utopian credit and the penetration of the last untouched territories—left wonder wanting. As Ali Behdad argues, the fin de siècle traveler realized that he was tragically "belated": an uncanny double destined to arrive only where others had gone before.[19]

But why should this apply especially to German travelers? Does it not equally affect, for example, the French and the British, as demonstrated by Scott's diary? Behdad and Chris Bongie claim that the "age of colonial dissolution" was the era when *all* European travelers discovered themselves to be repeats (Flaubert in Egypt; Segalen in China; Conrad in Africa).[20] Many British and French adventure novels followed the uncanny narrative of *Hot Land*, notably H. Rider Haggard's best-selling Victorian lost-world tales, which eventually appeared in Freud's dreams (see my chapter 3). It is fair to say that there was a general European anxiety about belatedness around 1900, but, as I argue, this feeling was heightened for German travelers. Consider just a couple of additional examples from my first chapter: the popular German actor, writer and globetrotter Hanns Heinz Ewers traveled all the way to rural India in 1910 only to discover a maharaja who spoke perfect English, wore a tuxedo, and played Wagner on his gramophone.[21] Three years later, the Expressionist painter Emil Nolde found in the jungles of German New Guinea, to his dismay, uncannily familiar natives who sported "haircuts and clothing just like our own."[22]

As I discuss in chapter 2, a "brutally Europeanized" Indonesia likewise greets Hermann Hesse in 1911: gramophones play upper Bavarian yodel music; street fronts copy "the most tasteless" German small towns; and Malaysians dress in European suits and speak better English than Hesse.[23] Hesse attributed this contamination to his German predecessors and also to the British and the Dutch, demonstrating how German travelers felt themselves to be *second-level repeats*: following other Germans and the adventurers from the primary colonial powers (England, France, Portugal, Spain, and the Netherlands). This doubled antecedence amplified German travelers' already nervous sense of repetition, rendering them the most extreme case study for what is otherwise a generally European uncanny encounter.

As Hesse reveals in *Robert Aghion* (inspired by his Indonesian journey), arriving in an already Europeanized colonial world gave German travelers a perspective that the earlier British and French travelers lacked. Hesse, like other Germans, saw before him a landscape filled with Westernized natives and European doppelgängers, on whom he trains his eye. He documents the uncanny effect when Europeans meet other Europeans: specifically, when belated Germans discover their English "cousins," whom the Germans both mimicked and threatened in the colonies.[24] Hesse demonstrates how this ambivalent colonial family romance (Queen Victoria was Kaiser Wilhelm II's grandmother) breaks down categories based on the colonizer/colonized dualism, including Bhabha's "hybridity." Instead of exposing the European traveler's fear of the other's difference, Hesse reveals a world full of globalized "natives" who are almost indistinguishable from Westerners, and, more devastatingly, of European doubles. His protagonist longs for the difference that Bhabha says he should fear—finding instead only ubiquitous mirror images. These images produce the same *unheimlich* returns that Freud will describe six years later: of ancient narcissisms, primitive beliefs, and repressed infantile ideas.

A psycho-linguistic element further renders the German experience unique. As Freud and, later, Martin Heidegger demonstrate, German is the only language where the unsettling confusion between being at "home" (*Heim*) and "away from home" appears in one word: *heimlich*, which originally meant "of the home," "familiar," and "cozy" but shifted, around 1800, into signifying "dreadful," "strange," and "creepy." *Heimlich* thus transformed into its opposite. It became *un-heimlich*, also in its lexical history, at the precise moment when "*unheimlich*," too, took on its modern psychological register of "fear-provoking" (Freud, *SE* 17:224–26).[25] Containing its converse within it, *heimlich* turned into a "strange" and "dreadful"—*unheimliches*—lexeme. For this reason, German speakers were more attuned, if only unconsciously, to the uncomfortable familiarity of early twentieth-century travel. This helps to explain why the word *unheimlich* appears so often in popular accounts and also why this term was first theorized in German-speaking lands.

Uncanny Thinking: Savage Freud

Just as the change from wondrous to uncanny travel developed slowly, over centuries, so too did the concept of the uncanny, as I discuss in chapter 3. Uncanniness only became theoretically possible in the modern era, specifically after René Descartes' seventeenth-century attempt to bracket an irrational world that in its strangeness interfered with the subject's ability to reason.[26] Descartes did not, in the end, succeed in creating a more familiar cosmos. Rather, he, like many of the Enlightenment thinkers to follow, constructed a differentiation between the mind and the body—the self and the non-self—that could not be sustained. John Locke, for example, attempted to manufacture a "horizon" that would finally set "the bounds between the enlightened and the dark parts of things."[27] But because such a boundary was untenable, it materialized only in an impossible prohibition that ultimately heightened the power of the strangeness that Locke had wanted to banish. The strange and the familiar inevitably mixed. When they did, this mixing seemed illicit, unnatural, and significant. The stage was set for the uncanny to be born.

But even if the Enlightenment produced the uncanny's philosophical conditions, it does not follow, as Terry Castle argues, that the eighteenth century invented the uncanny—and certainly not as a concept.[28] "*Unheimlich*" was hardly even used before 1800, and, when it was, then either to describe neutrally things "outside the home" (in the Late Middle Ages) or to signify witches and ghosts (in the sixteenth and seventeenth centuries).[29] *Unheimlich* only gained its modern connection to our emotional lives—our feelings of fright—after the eighteenth century had passed. The Grimm dictionary reports the first isolated uses of *unheimlich* as "dreadful, ghastly" in the years just before 1800; this sense became common only in the first decades of the nineteenth century, at the same time that *heimlich* was turning into its opposite.[30] It was also at this point that *unheimlich* entered into general usage.[31]

In the course of the nineteenth century, German-speaking philosophers began thinking of *unheimlich* conceptually, albeit only in the margins of their work. Schelling's 1830s definition of the uncanny as "the name for everything that ought to have remained secret, hidden, latent, but has come to light" seemed to echo the Romantic sense that something horrible lurked beneath civilization's façade.[32] Marx then claimed that capitalism thrived on a similar suppression of two uncanny—invisible yet hauntingly present—entities: "commodities" and "capital." Commodities were ghostly "sensuous-supersensuous entities" ("phantasmagoria"), and capital, the return of "dead labor," lived "like a vampire sucking up living labor"; it flourished "all the more, the more it devour[ed]."[33] Near the end of the century, Nietzsche proclaimed nihilism to be "that uncanniest of all guests," a phrase that would eventually open his *Will to Power*.

But such nineteenth-century remarks remained unsystematic. The conceptualization process only gained crucial momentum in 1906, when the psychiatrist Ernst Jentsch discovered the uncanny's importance for psychology, defining it as a feeling of "psychic uncertainty" about whether the objects surrounding us are animate or inanimate.[34] The psychoanalyst Otto Rank repeatedly referred to the "double" as *unheimlich* in his 1914 "Der

Doppelgänger," which strongly influenced Freud's *The Uncanny* (1919). In 1917, the eminent theologian Rudolf Otto further prefigured Freud by claiming that religion itself was *unheimlich*: because our monotheistic gods remind us of religion's animistic roots, they appear as "ghostly" embodiments of "the uncanny-terrifying" (*des Unheimlich-furchtbaren*).[35] The psychoanalyst Theodor Reik, building on Freud and Otto, similarly argued in 1923 that religious feeling was *unheimlich*: all gods seem uncanny because they remind us of ancient animistic beliefs and repressed infantile fears (circumcision = castration; communion = cannibalism).[36] In 1927 Heidegger proposed that, more than just religion, modern life itself was *unheimlich*. Contrary to Otto, Freud, and Rank, Heidegger did not see uncanniness as issuing from a return (whether to childhood or animism) but rather from the modern world's uprootedness. The technologized global world created a perpetually "uncanny" state of "being not-at-home" (*Nicht-zuhause-sein*)—of being "*Un-zuhause*." Within this anxiety, Heidegger writes, "one feels *unheimlich*."[37]

In the midst of this flurry of conceptual activity in Germany and Austria, Freud wrote his famous 1919 treatise. Beginning with the ambivalence inherent in the word *heimlich*, Freud—like Jentsch, Rank, Otto, Reik, and Heidegger—undermined the Cartesian separation of the familiar and the foreign: even within *heimlich* itself, he insisted, the "not-homey" haunted the "homey" and vice versa. But unlike Jentsch and Heidegger, Freud emphasized the familiarity of the *unheimlich*. Jentsch concerned himself with the unknown, and Heidegger stressed the uncanny's move *away* from the "homely" (*Heimlichen*), beyond the "customary, familiar [*heimischen*] limits" of everything that we consider "familiar" (*des Heimischen*).[38] Freud conversely argued, like Rank, Otto, and Reik, on the uncanny's recognizability. It was precisely the "*heimlich*"—that which "is known of old and long familiar"—that was frightening, especially when it appeared where not expected (*SE* 17:220).[39]

Theoretical enquiries into the uncanny thus were ongoing when fin de siècle travelers wrote about their encounters in faraway lands, but the concept was far from satisfactorily formulated, and it would be wrong to say that a philosophical discourse of the uncanny prescribed these stories.[40] It is more likely that the opposite was true: that the recurrent reports of uncanny encounters in the age of colonial dissolution contributed to stimulating the conjectures by Jentsch, Rank, Otto, Freud, Reik, and Heidegger.[41] As Anthony Vidler points out, *Unheimlichkeit* was born out of two intellectual watchwords that had been gathering steam throughout the nineteenth century: "estrangement," produced by workplace industrialization and mass migration to the cities, and "homelessness," generated by wars and an increasingly inequitable distribution of wealth.[42] These domestic causes combined with external ones during the heyday of imperialism (foreign-familiar things brought back from colonial adventures; strangely hybridized "natives") to trigger further interest in the concept, whose usage increased rapidly in the two decades preceding Freud's *The Uncanny*.[43] As my book demonstrates, this context affected Freud's conceptualization directly: through the travelogues, colonial stories, exotic novels, and ethnographic folklore that he read, including an explicitly "uncanny" Haggard novel about Africa and a popular story about the New Guinean colonies—"Inexplicable"—that appears in *The Uncanny* (Freud, *SE* 17:244). Such writings about the exotic, primitive world led Freud to theorize the uncanny initially not in his eponymous 1919 essay but in his 1912–13 study of disconcertingly similar "savages": *Totem and Taboo: Some Resemblances between the Mental Lives of Savages and Neurotics*.[44]

Given the current trendiness of "the uncanny"—we use it to describe everything from a David Lynch film to the 9/11 attacks[45]—why has no one attempted a historicization of the concept's birth years?[46] A possible answer lies in the era when Freud's *The Uncanny* was rediscovered. Neglected after Freud's death by psychoanalysts and cultural theorists alike, this essay first reappeared on the scholarly scene in 1970, when Jacques Derrida mentioned it in three of the most momentous footnotes in modern literary criticism. These notes produced a series of 1970s readings that all viewed *The Uncanny* as an exemplarily self-deconstructing text.[47] Signifying both itself and its opposite, the "uncanny" seemed to unravel itself and, in so doing, demonstrate the instability at the heart of all concept-making. This interpretation has had remarkable staying power, guiding readings through the 1980s and 1990s and even into the twenty-first century, when the first monograph on the uncanny appeared (Royle's *The Uncanny*). As sophisticated as these interpretations have often been, accepting them would mean limiting our study of *Unheimlichkeit* to one text by one author (Freud) and, what is more, forgetting that uncanniness, like all concepts, has a birth and, presumably, a death. As Samuel Weber wrote in 1973, it is high time that we historicized this concept.[48]

My book is, in part, an answer to this call, which has gone unanswered now for over forty years. I place the uncanny in a philosophical tradition beginning in the nineteenth century and, for the first time, reposition it within the fin de siècle events that helped to shape it. Tucked away in Freud's theorization of the *unheimlich* in *Totem and Taboo* and, later, *The Uncanny* are echoes of their own uncanny global moment: adventure stories about the frightening familiar tropics; anthropological theories about strangely similar savages; and the shaking bodies of ghostly "primitive" neurotics returning home from World War I's faraway fronts. My purpose is not to explain uncanniness through contextualization but rather to perform an important act of cultural recovery: to disclose the uncanny's surprising social-political richness, particularly in relation to the fear of the end of alterity around 1900—a fear that, I argue, remains with us today.

As I demonstrate further in chapter 3, Freud borrows from adventure writing not just themes but also style and form. In *The Interpretation of Dreams*, *Totem and Taboo*, and *The Uncanny*, Freud employs the popular late Victorian lost-world structure[49]—portraying himself as an "adventurer" into an untouched realm that turns out, especially in *The Uncanny*, to be not so strange after all.[50] Because Freud uses this adventure trope, his writings are stories at the same time that they are theories for interpreting stories. They are "secondary" and "primary" texts at once, and I allow them to perform this double duty in my book: they guide me theoretically at the same time that they are objects of my analysis. On the one hand, I adopt Freud's definition of the uncanny as the unexpected return of the familiar and so employ psycho-analysis as an analytical tool to better understand the shock of recognition felt by travelers around 1900. On the other hand, I show how Freud's story-like essays were shaped by these travelers' writings. Freud's essays are also stories among stories, and all of these narratives, I argue, worked together to produce a way of speaking that we now call uncanny.

In fulfilling this double duty, Freud's writings are paradigmatic for my book: they illustrate how, when dealing with the uncanny, we cannot sepa-rate literature from theory, or fiction from science, just as we cannot separate "popular" from "elite" culture. Freud makes this point in *Intepretation of Dreams*, *Totem and Taboo*, and, especially, *The Uncanny*, through his own literary performance: he demonstrates through a series of first-person "adven-ture" anecdotes how fantasy can never be expunged from science (Freud, *SE* 17:237). Even psychoanalysis itself is not immune from art's supersti-tions, fears, and delusions. As Freud well knew, any admission of his fledgling science's fantastical nature threatened its legitimacy, and this explains the elliptical, often defensive, nature of his admissions. But at the same time, Freud sensed that psychoanalysis's awareness of its own contamination by fiction was also its strength. Psychoanalysis's self-consciously "uncanny" structure produced its inimitable advantage over that other fin de siècle sci-ence of man: anthropology.

Uncanny Modernism: Exotic Europe

Beyond their formal and thematic similarities, popular travel writing and psy-choanalysis agreed on a major specific point: that the distance between Europe and its other had shrunk to the point that Europe's identity was threatened. The travel writers reacted with uncanny, anxiogenic fictions about doublings in far-off realms, while Freud posited the unsettling theory that primitiveness can never be expunged from "us." This preoccupation with the Europeaniza-tion of the jungle and, conversely, with the jungle's permeation of Europe is remarkably similar in these literary (yet conceptual) travel books and Freud's scientific (yet literary) essays. These two genres keep circling back to the same site of self-recognition. This demonstrates uncanniness's discursive prominence and, what is more, its effect on the genres themselves: adventure literature and psychoanalytic writing begin to resemble one another.

So-called high modernist literature shares this thematic obsession and formal slipperiness, as I argue in chapter 4. Here, too, the primitive and the civilized become frighteningly indistinguishable. The Dark Continent migrates into the European psyche; the aboriginals populate "our" minds.[51] And here, too, popular and theoretical languages blur. Consider the eloquent ape, Red Peter, whom Kafka borrowed from circus and adventure stories. He speaks in a scientific tone, only ultimately to be frightened by the "half-trained chimpanzee" that returns him to his wild—and pulp fiction—past.[52] There are many other examples of modernist tales in which a civilized European discovers an exotic other without ever leaving his home: in cities (Hesse's *Steppenwolf*, Kafka's *Metamorphosis*, Brecht's *In the Jungle of Cities*); in valleys nestled within Europe's internal Himalayas, the Alps (Musil's *Grigia* and Hofmannsthal's *Andreas*); and in Europe's exotic south, a markedly backward Italy (Mann's *Death in Venice*).

With these similarities between travel writing, psychoanalysis and modernism in mind, I argue that we need to reconsider the trope of *Unheimlichkeit* as it extends across not only genres but also registers. I disagree with Andreas Huyssen's classic argument that modernism separates itself from popular culture, and maintain instead that travel writing, psycho-philosophical theory, and modernism conjoined to create uncanniness as we know it today.[53] Just after travelers bemoaned the end of alterity along the Amazon and the Ganges, modernism and psychoanalysis made the reverse—but uncannily the same—claim: the exotic other was alive and well, infiltrating Mann's Venice, Hofmannsthal's and Musil's Alps, Kafka's Central European city, and Freud's consulting room. By announcing that there was nothing new in the jungle, adventure literature forced high culture inward. The external exotic journeys of the nineteenth-century Bildungsroman now discover the foreign at the hearth. Shortly after reading a boys' book about disappearing "Red Indians," Kafka created one vanishing across shorn plains, and then replaced this Indian with Gregor Samsa, the outsize alien insect who creeps across Europe's living-room floors.[54]

Until the early twentieth century, Europe's longing for alterity had, like Kafka's "desire" to become an Indian, moved primarily centrifugally. Although the Romantics did sometimes turn the quest narrative inward and even discovered the stranger within, they did so while maintaining an equal fascination for the stranger without.[55] Consider the magisterial travel writings of Humboldt, Goethe, Cook, Forster, and Herder, as well as Rousseau's philosophical musings on savages. The modernists had no such cadre, at least partially because they lived in a globalized world where nearly everyone had access to these primitives, who therefore became less interesting. The modernists understood well Bronislaw Malinowski's lament following his 1914–18 expeditions to Melanesia: ethnography was "tragic[ally]" discovering its object at the moment when it was disappearing.[56] Sensing that the indigenous peoples were either already dead or disappointingly too much like "us," the modernists discarded travel as a major mode of discovery. They traveled much, but their resultant notes were only literary training grounds, not distinct experiments for discovering "the new (the really new)."[57] There is no modernist equivalent to the eighteenth and early-nineteenth century travel classics: Goethe's *Italian Journey*, Sterne's *Sentimental Journey*, and Humboldt's *Voyage to the Equinoctial Regions of the New Continent*. The centripetal replaces the centrifugal; travel becomes internal.[58] In a marked change from the preceding century, travel writing lands in the trash heap of *Trivialliteratur*.[59]

At this moment, the modernists elected to travel at home, to anthropologize Europe. They rejected travel writing while borrowing its methodology, its *ethnographic eye*.[60] Freud turned this eye on his fellow Viennese, asking his patients to reveal their internal primitiveness.[61] And various modernist writers attempted miniature anthropologies of Europe. I think of Kafka and Max Brod's expedition through *Mitteleuropa*, fictionalized as *Richard and Samuel: A Short Journey through Central European Regions*; Hofmannsthal's journey into Germany and then back through Austria (in "Letters of a Returnee"); and Walter Benjamin's diaries from Russia. Even in the great modernist novels, the characters experience their homes as if they were foreign towns: Leopold Bloom's Dublin, Joseph K.'s nameless Central European city, Septimus Smith's London, Marcel's "Combray," and Ulrich's Vienna. Similarly, Mann's Gustav Aschenbach travels within a Europe that uncannily recalls the "warm swamps of the Ganges delta"; it requires the sensibilities of an anthropologist.[62]

Although British and French modernists also anthropologized Europe, one could argue that Austro-German modernisms did *only* that.[63] I think of Mann's Italian proletariats and Polish boys; Hofmannsthal's Carinthian *Mädchen* and Italian virgins; Musil's exotic Tyrolean peasant women; Kafka's and Freud's *Ostjuden*, as well as their Czech and Galician servant girls. All borrow the general Conradian structure of penetrating a heart of darkness, except that this heart is now in Europe. And, what is more, this Europe appears even more uncannily "*fremd vertraut*" (foreign-familiar) than did Conrad's Congo.[64]

Whereas the Austro-German modernists combine exoticist and domestic investigations, the British and French modernists are still, for the most part, divided into two camps: those who write primarily about faraway regions (Conrad, Forster, Segalen), and those who describe the local realm (Proust, Woolf, and Joyce).[65] This separation is not surprising, considering that England's and France's "foreigners" lived almost exclusively in non-contiguous lands (with the exceptions of Scotland and Wales),[66] whereas Germany's and Austria's outsiders inhabited contiguous realms to the immediate east and south (the exception being the short-lived extra-European German colonies). This *mitteleuropäische* proximity between "Occident" and "Orient" led to confusions, persisting to this day, about where the imperial homeland ended and where the East began. Because home itself was unsettled, one never knew where the Occident ended and the Orient began. The schoolbooks pointed to the Caucasus and the Bosphorus, but wasn't this line actually closer? Near to today's ever-changing European Union borders? Perhaps somewhere near Königsberg (Kaliningrad)? Or just east of Pressburg (Bratislava)? Or just south of Laibach (Ljubljana)? This muddied geography caused Germany and Austria, as we will see, continually to reinvestigate Europe's parameters, and, in so doing, unsettle the difference between "motherland" and "colony" in ways that were superfluous to Britain and France—as well as to the postcolonial theory that sprang from their realms.[67] Mann pressed precisely this point when he decided *not* to send Aschenbach to his longed-for "tropical swamp, under a vapourous sky" and instead to an apparently exotic space within Europe: the Venetian *porta Orientis* (DV 5).

This Austro-German modernists' tendency to search internally for alterity issued not only from geography: the peculiar belatedness of their countrymen's travel experiences also led them to turn inward. Hearing how these travelers were always arriving too late to have a first-contact encounter, German and Austrian modernists looked for strangers closer to home, even in the psyche. But the stranger they found there, like the one their popular-culture colleagues found in Brazilian jungles, was not as strange as they had imagined. This stranger is chillingly recognizable, somehow already known and "long familiar." Consider just the examples from the exemplary modernist texts I will discuss in chapter 4: the frighteningly recognizable old man from Pola on Aschenbach's boat (in *Death in Venice*); Andreas's terrifying Austrian alter ego, Gotthelf (in Hofmannsthal's *Andreas*); and the Germanic "primitives" caught outside of time in Musil's Alpine valley (*Grigia*). These dreadful amalgams of the foreign and familiar within Europe create the same effect as did the Westernized native and the European doppelgänger in the jungle: they frighten the "normal," "civilized" Western observer. My aim in chapter 4 is to document this disturbance as it makes its way into the heart of Europe. In my epilogue, I argue that these literary descriptions presciently elucidate the fears of the West during the world's first globalization—and, what is more, predict our violent reactions to this fear both at the fin de siècle and today.[68] To describe this specifically modern form of aggression, I coin the term "uncanny violence."

Before embarking on this journey, I would like to address a question posed to me when I first introduced this project in public. A listener asked me whether I was exaggerating when I spoke of the uncanny "end of alterity" around 1900. Were there not, he asked, still *some* spaces undiscovered by Europeans? And do some not remain even today? Other lecture guests told me of spots in Mongolia, the Amazon River basin, and on a southern Pacific island where they were far and wide the only Westerners. One even directed me to the website of Survival International, which claims that there are still now, in 2015, over 100 "uncontacted tribes," including an apparently newly discovered one in the Amazon basin. Brazilian government aerial photographs show half-naked men in war paint aiming arrows at the surveillance plane.[69]

In a similar vein, cartographers have taught me how the map of the world was certainly not complete in 1900, just as it is not complete today. The 1891 project for an International Map of the World, at a scale of 1:1,000,000, was never finished.[70] And even in the unlikely case that all nations had released and combined their maps, including secret military ones, this would not have produced a "complete" map; the nagging question of scale remained. Is a map at 1:1,000,000 complete? Would we not have to magnify the scale to the rare 1:10,000? Or to the unheard of 1:1,000? Or even to Borges's impish 1:1, a map the same size as the earth itself?[71] And even if Google Earth reaches its present goal of covering most of the earth at 2.5 meters per pixel, there is still no absolute resolution: the minimum size of a pixel necessarily inflates tiny streams, paths, or divots.[72] And even if the pixel problem were somehow solved, the inevitable time-lag between picture-taking and map-viewing still separates representation from reality—most obviously in the stitching together of photos that are inevitably taken non-simultaneously. Are these gaps in our self-representation, listeners asked me, not the cartographic equivalent of "uncontacted tribes"? The world will not let go of its mysteries, I was told. Am I not attempting to disenchant them prematurely?

The answer is that my book is indeed about disenchantment, even though I do not reject this possibility of "blank spaces," whether around 1900 or today; the globe's vastness, combined with the temporal and spatial impossibilities of ordering it, guarantee terra incognita. But I do insist that this terra incognita shrank significantly around 1900 and, more important, that this shrinking generated new anxieties. These anxieties revealed themselves sometimes in the reports about uncanny European doubling I describe in chapters 1 and 2, but sometimes also in the shrewd defensive tactics I outline in these same chapters. As the map's white spaces shriveled, the desire for them increased. Travelers who could not find white spaces or pure natives often deliberately cropped signs of Europe from their reports in order to maintain their fantasies. Is not the same thing happening now—in the aftermath of the second (post-1989) great globalization—when, even more than around 1900, the entire world seems to be open to us? When we discover remote spaces overrun by tourists and industrialization and, for this reason, find every marker of alterity more significant and precious? Did the listener who claimed to be the only Westerner in rural Mongolia not see *some* sign of his predecessors—as all of us do in our own attempts to get off the beaten track? Did he, too, not crop his forerunners' markers, however unconsciously, from his story? And even if he really saw no Westerners, who were these apparently uncontaminated natives he remembers? Did they bear no signs of intermarriage or intercultural exchange? Were there no go-betweens, mediators, or middlemen? Who translated for this traveler? And even if this world seemed to be utterly "uncontacted," how could the traveler ever know for sure?

The modern tourist is plagued by such uncertainties. Even if he can get past the obviously touristy "front spaces," he never knows whether he has reached a real "back space" or a simulated one. When a "native" brings you into his home, for example, is this home perhaps just another stage, to which he leads every tourist?[73] Such insecurities are writ large in Walker Percy's *Message in the Bottle*, where an American couple watches a "ritual dance" in Mexico but can't be sure whether it is authentic; they only become certain when a Western anthropologist appears through the woods and reassures them.[74] The controversy surrounding Survival International's recent discovery of the new "uncontacted tribe" aiming their arrows at a plane brings up similar questions: How can we be certain of a lack of contact? Has no outsider ever been there, even centuries before? What constitutes an outsider? Must he be "Western," whatever that connotes? And what do we mean by contact, or, better, lack of it? Can this negative ever be proven?[75] Does not the proof of non-contact always also prove contact, thus confirming Malinowski's melancholic 1922 claim that ethnography is that most tragic of endeavors?

More important than all of these questions is one lying behind it: Why is it important to prove first encounters at all? What is at stake in purporting that there is still a tenaciously blank space out there somewhere, waiting for me? Renato Rosaldo sees in this the paradoxical nostalgia of imperialism: we industrialize Europe and then search for our pure childhood homes in faraway lands. We destroy our own environment and then worship nature in Africa.[76] And imperialism offers further paradoxes: we Europeanize a faraway land and then hope to retrieve there our own pre-industrial, European home. This self-delusion sometimes works. Like the best-selling German writer Waldemar Bonsels in India in 1903–4, we can imagine that our old home was never really lost but only hidden on an alternate grid of time and space: "in other historical periods and other cultures, in purer, simpler lifestyles."[77] Bonsels claims, astonishingly, to have found the village from his childhood—from his own "German *Heimat*"—in the middle of this Indian countryside (*Indienfahrt*, 217).

But such nostalgia promises more than just a sentimental cure for homesickness: it opens realms where the traveler can commit violence without repercussion. Long before Kafka's 1914 "In the Penal Colony," the colonies were places where Europeans broke into fits of cruelty so inexplicable that they caught the attention of medical researchers, who went so far as to invent a diagnosis: *Tropenkoller* ("tropical rage").[78] This rage was often sexual, explaining the metaphor of virgin territory that runs through fin de siècle travel descriptions. This male sexual violence also explains the lack of travel accounts by women in this book, even though there would have been plenty from which to choose.[79] The penetration of untouched spaces was a powerful male fantasy, and this generated much of the European travel energy at the turn of the century. Like the rapacious leader of the colony in *Hot Land*—the "Wolf"—the male traveler believes that the female genitalia *are* his jungle: they belong to him, as does the "virgin" rain forest. With this in mind, we see the danger within the sentimental fantasy of the blank spot: it is the traveler's nostalgic pre-industrial European home but, at the same time, the space where he can take out his anger at having this home stripped from him.

In documenting this uncanny violence, I move methodologically from literary and cultural analyses to a psycho-sociological diagnosis of globalization's aggressions, especially in its fin de siècle heyday. When the first globalization around 1900 produced the familiar-foreign encounter, it also created fears about identity: How was the traveler to know who he was when the "other" also spoke his language, wore his clothes, and listened to his Bavarian music on a gramophone? Who, the European asked, am I not? The problem was not the world's homogeneity—it was not fully homogenous in 1900 just as it is not today—but rather its uncanniness: the world had become simultaneously foreign and eerily familiar, whether the European was at home or away.

The "good" traveler's unease with his feelings about the uncanny other manifested itself then, as now, in an *anti-colonial exoticism*.[80] "We" decide to save the "native" from extinction because, apparently, we love him and want to defend him from the forces of evil: the imperial Dutch logging companies that Hesse hates, as well as international corporations and foreign armies. But this love hides a strategy that explains the widespread preference for saving "uncontacted tribes" over, say, the "untouchables" in the Third World's slums. We need the unadulterated savage to tell us who we are not. If the native does not hold onto his precious alterity, our identity wavers, and it is not long before our aggression appears: first toward the "bad" colonizers (the English, the French, and the Dutch around 1900 or, today, the Americans), who have taken the virgin territory for themselves, and then toward the hybridized native himself—the "pants-wearing nigger" (*Hosennigger*). Bonsels slaps such a "mixed-breed" in Mangalore; Jacques' narrator beats an Itajahian prostitute who seems neither German nor Brazilian; within Europe, Musil's miners brutalize the "foreign-familiar" German-speakers whom they discover in an Alpine valley. As I will discuss in my conclusion, this psychology pertains also to other failed assimilation processes within Europe around 1900; we see here disappointed exoticism lurking behind the great domestic brutalities of the twentieth century.

The violence proceeding from this identity confusion does not pertain only to "bad" Westerners. It is, rather, endemic to the modern encounter. As psychoanalysis, ethnography, and literature all claimed around 1900, there was no safe position outside of this uncanny disarrangement. Freud, for example, asked the same essentially *ethnographic* question as did Malinowski and the modernists: how do I write about (other) people? Like the ethnographer and the novelist, the psychoanalyst needs to "translate himself" into this other in order to begin to comprehend him and even share his fantasies (Freud, *The Uncanny, SE* 17:220). But he also needs to find a way back out. If not, he will become hopelessly displaced, disarranged, and even mad, as suggested by the German word "ver-rückt."[81] Can the observer ever fully extricate himself and reclaim the differentiated position of the analyst? Especially when the "other" turns out to be uncannily similar? How many of "his" fantasies are already within "me"? Many of these questions struck me while writing this book. I recognized myself in many of the travelers I studied; their fantasies of penetrating a virgin territory resonated with ones that I knew from my youth, when I first dreamt of going beyond "New Switzerland." For this reason, I was simultaneously the analyst and the patient during the writing process. The pages that follow do more than diagnose global *unheimlich* encounters around 1900. They also record, tacitly, my own attempt to gain some distance from an "other" who was uncannily too close for comfort.

Chapter 1

Germans in the Jungle

Hot Land and Tales of Adventure

I first picked up Norbert Jacques' *Hot Land: A Journey to Brazil* to grasp better what Freud and the German-language modernists—Kafka, Hesse, Mann, Musil, Benn, Schnitzler—found so intriguing about exoticism.[1] If the modernists were fascinated by the *Exotik*, I needed to see what this looked like. What better place to start than with a popular travelogue published in 1911, the same year that some of these better-known authors began writing their own works about the exotic world: *Amerika, Out of India, Death in Venice,* and *Totem and Taboo.* But as so frequently happens, the supporting material insisted on its own leading role; "context" asserted itself as "text."[2] Based partially on Jacques' own journey to Brazil, *Hot Land* was a mixture of travel report and Expressionist novel that inspired younger writers.[3] More than this, I discovered that *Hot Land* had contentions of its own that were not so different from modernism's. It, too, investigated the frightening dissolution of the European subject, and it, too, presented the search for an "other" against which this subject could delimit itself.

Unlike the more famous modernists, though, Jacques employed primarily a map of the world, not of the psyche. At the same time that Freud searched for the "aboriginal population of the mind" (*psychische Urbevölkerung*) in the unconscious, Jacques, the literary anthropologist, traveled to South America looking for real aboriginals (Freud, *SE* 14:195; *GW* 10:294). But the two projects had similar goals and, more important, similarly upsetting results. Both aborigines—the "psychic" and the "real" one—proved difficult to pin down. Neither the unconscious nor the "savage" was static but always in a state of flux, presenting the investigator with different versions of itself. Beyond this, both remained silent or dissembled, requiring complex decoding. And, most disturbingly, both seemed to mimic the interrogator—whether the ego or the anthropologist—such that both became almost indistinguishable from their inquisitor. Instead of providing the embattled European self with its defining opposite, this primitive third person—Freud's "it" (*Es* or

29

"id")—infected the investigating "I" (*Ich* or "ego"). The "aboriginal" became civilization's doppelgänger.

By discovering this uncanniness in the exotic world, popular travel writing foreshadowed modernism—thereby challenging modernism's claim to separateness from popular culture[4] and to exclusive access to a theory of the uncanny. Writers like Jacques rendered exoticism philosophical and, in so doing, caused "high" and "low" to bleed into one another. Jacques deserves our attention not least because he—together with other popular fin de siècle exoticists—demonstrates how popular exoticism developed theories of the uncanny that influenced Freud, Kafka, and Mann. Only after travel literature had uncovered the end of alterity along the Amazon and the Ganges did modernism make the converse, but, according to the logic of uncanniness, the same claim: the exotic other infiltrated Mann's Venice, Hofmannsthal's and Musil's Alps, Hesse's unnamed European city, Kafka's bedroom, and Freud's Viennese study.[5]

Born in Luxembourg, Jacques emigrated to Germany after high school and, as a writer, exemplified the fin de siècle generation of German exoticists that wrote literature both "high" and "low" (figure 11). This group included Max Dauthendey, Robert Müller, Waldemar Bonsels, Hanns Heinz Ewers, and Stefan Zweig, who all authored popular travel books and also literary novels, and were much closer to the famous modernists than we realize today. They often published in the same journals as Mann, Musil, and Kafka (*Hyperion*, *Die neue Rundschau*, *Die weißen Blätter*, etc.), and gained acclaim and interest from these same writers. Thomas Mann praised Jacques and Bonsels; Walter Benjamin wrote an essay about Dauthendey; Kafka owned a copy of Jacques' second adventure book, *Pirath's Island*.[6] What is more, these "trivial" writers' popular works were often formally modernist: Jacques experimentally pasted together travel memoir and short-story styles; Dauthendey peppered an internally rhymed epic with Baedeker-like banalities, prefiguring Eliot's *The Waste-Land*; and Müller acted as a Conradian mediator, posing as the editor of a dead traveler's found manuscript. In terms of content, too, these writers were modernist: they investigated how ego and other—the "I" and the "it"—blurred, thereby heralding a modernist obsession.

Working centrifugally (toward the ends of earth) instead of centripetally (toward the psyche), these popular writers performed the field work for the geography of the modern uncanny. They arrived on the fringes of the globe and discovered hauntingly familiar pieces of Europe. Bernhard Kellermann is shocked in 1907 to find masses of Western-made objects in a Japanese small town: "German sewing machines, French clocks, American bicycles."[7] The hero of *Hot Land* similarly encountered, in the middle of the Brazilian rain forest, German colonies bearing the names of German cities. Zweig described the anxieties surrounding this search for alterity during his 1909 visit to the holy city of Gwalior: "the wanderer always searches for the other, the foreign,

Figure 11. Norbert Jacques in Brazil

and does not want to rediscover Europe in India."[8] But German travelers *were* discovering Europe everywhere, not least because, as discussed in my introduction, this was the era when the last cartographic blank spots disappeared: the formerly white spaces of the North and South poles, the summits of the Himalayas, and the Greenland glaciers were now covered with rivers, paths, and mountains. Maps of central Africa, once graced only with fantastical sketchings of lions, elephants, and giraffes, likewise gave way to European cartographic order.[9] This ordering conspired with the colonial Westernization of non-Europeans, the arrival of tourists into previously untrodden territory, and post-Darwinian evolutionary theory to produce a new kind of fear, not of difference but of similarity, and, with this, a new, uncanny way of writing about this fear. This *unheimlich* perspective appeared first here, in popular travel writing, years ahead of Mann's, Hofmannsthal's, and Musil's comparable modernist breakthroughs—and well before Freud published *The Uncanny* in 1919.

Hot Land

Based on Jacques' first, 1907 journey to Brazil, *Hot Land* begins as did Joseph Conrad's modernist masterpiece from the preceding decade, *Heart of Darkness*: late at night, on a small boat in a European port. The discourse of uncanniness creeps in already here, when the nameless protagonist's little vessel shoves off toward the great "*heimlich*" ocean liner that will carry him onto the "foreign" (*fremd*) seas.[10] Before considering the plot of *Hot Land*, let us first notice Jacques' decision to begin his book with a *heimlich* experience, thereby mirroring Conrad, who insisted that, when the Romans first dropped anchor in England, it too was filled with "darkness" and "utter savagery."[11] Stemming from the word for home—as Freud emphasized a few years after Jacques—*heimlich* originally meant "familiar" (of the home) and only later transformed into "secretive" (covert within the home) and finally into "mysterious" or "foreign" (outside the home). *Heimlich* therefore grew over centuries to signify its own opposite—*un-heimlich*—and so become an uncanny word itself. This lexemic uncanniness is apparent already in this image of the "*heimlich*" ship: overtly, *heimlich* signifies the modern meaning of "mysterious," but hidden within this is also the older sense of "homey," for this ship in the German harbor is the last piece of home the protagonist expects to encounter on his trip to the *Fremde*. He proves to be wrong— "home" turns out to be disturbingly omnipresent in Brazil—but precisely because of the *Heimlichkeit* of his ship and of colonialism in general. As in *Heart of Darkness*, the ever-presence of home in the colonies becomes what makes them so frighteningly *unheimlich*.

Following this opening image, this mixing of the familiar and the foreign appears to disappear, replaced by the fin de siècle's standard clichés of pure strangeness: the dangerous sea passage; the love affair with the dark-skinned girl; the malaria; and the violent clash with the natives. But hidden within these colorful stereotypes is a persistent homeliness, suggested by Jacques' obsessive repetition of *heimlich* (at least twenty-eight times) in a dizzying array of meanings: foreign cities; a Brazilian woman's naked arm; dock workers in Santos; the "Negro" who steers Jacques upriver; the greenish evening light; dust before a Creole woman's eyes; houses in palm gardens; sand on an Itajahi street; a mysterious door in the jungle; a jungle river's sheen; the breaking of glass; and even the hopes of the forlorn German colonists at the end.[12] Explicitly signifying only "mysterious," these usages nonetheless mobilize *heimlich*'s uncanny familiarity, if only through their sheer repetition. Lurking beneath Brazil's exciting kitschy exoticism, Jacques' diction tells us, are the uncanny ghosts of home. Things are not as strange as they appear.

Heimlich's hidden homeliness finally breaks into the open in the final third of the book, when the protagonist has an overtly uncanny experience: the unexpected return of "something known of old and long familiar" (Freud, *SE* 17:220). He enters a remote coastal town, Itajahi, where he imagines having another titillating exotic experience: the town's "outlandish" name seems to promise this. In this utterly alien world, however, he stumbles across something recognizable: a group of German men. These countrymen offer a journey to prostitutes in Itajahi's "*heimlichen*" houses (*Heißes Land*, 167). This nighttime trip takes the group outside of the town, away from civilization, over dirt roads and "unrecognizable" tangles of undergrowth toward ramshackle bamboo-covered huts. The men bang on one particularly dilapidated hut until a half-naked overweight old "Negress" opens the door and leads them into a red-lit room (169). They see, first, a naked black man—her son—and then a girl with thin blonde hair and green eyes: a German girl, it turns out, named Elsa. After the narrator and his friends whip the black man with a riding crop, they harass Elsa, ordering her, under threat of whipping, to sing German folk songs: "Zu Straßburg auf der Schanz." But she refuses and seems not even to understand German anymore, after her years in Brazil. The narrator berates her for sleeping with "black men"; he speaks with such "brutality" that Elsa suffers something like a nervous breakdown (171–75). The men are eventually cursed by the Negress as "brutal Germans" and chased away by her son, who turns out to be Elsa's pimp. The Germans flee back to their lodgings, drink themselves into oblivion, and mull over the "frightening truths" that have appeared to them (177–79).

How is this encounter with the German prostitute uncanny? And how are its "frightening truths" paradigmatic for *Hot Land* and for popular German fin de siècle adventure writing in general? As mentioned in my introduction, this paradigm features two essential stages. First, the encounter itself: the shock of seeing someone familiar—Elsa—in a world that ought to contain wondrous, unfathomable strangers. The narrator's road to the mysterious (*heimlich*) houses has led him to something uncannily (*unheimlich*) recognizable from his own home. His experience presages that of many of Freud's patients, who, a few years later, repeatedly dreamt of exotic spaces of which they said, "this place is familiar to me, I've been here before." Before considering Freud's famous interpretation—that this "place" is the mother's genitals, "where each one of us lived once upon a time and in the beginning"—it is worth simply asking why his patients kept having this same dream (Freud, *SE* 17:245). Various other narratives could just as easily have served as neurotic dream-displacements of their Oedipal traumas. But why do these dream-stories seem to come right out of *Hot Land*? Were Freud's patients—like Ernst Jünger's 1913 hero from *African Diversions* (*Afrikanische Spiele*), Herbert Berger, and Freud himself—reading too many "bad books" about "adventurers"?[13] Were these infecting their dreams? And not only with the promise of "blank spaces" but also, as in *Hot Land* and *African Diversions*, with the eventual withdrawal of this promise?[14] Does the unconscious fear of returning to the mother issue from the adventure encounters instead of the other way around? Does the dream reproduce a geographic uncanny encounter that is already taking place? A journey to a feminized "dark continent" that turns out to be uncannily like the vagina we knew from home?[15]

Following this discovery of Brazil's *Unheimlichkeit*, Jacques' normally mild-mannered protagonist breaks into a rage—the second stage of the uncanny encounter. He bullies Elsa out of what appears, at first, to be a fear of difference: he hates the debauched German woman and the black man who has sullied her. But a closer reading suggests an underlying fear of similarity. As the narrator later makes clear, he despises his countrymen for violating Brazil's "virginity" (*Jungfernschaft*) before he arrives: in Itajahi itself; in Itajahi's most remote brothels; and in this prostitute's body, which was neither virginal nor exotic to begin with (even before the black man slept with her). How many expatriate Germans have already had sex with Elsa? And, before that, how many Portuguese and Euro-Brazilians (Elsa now speaks primarily Portuguese) (*Heißes Land*, 221, 172–74)? The narrator is ultimately only superficially upset about black blood contaminating white blood; he worries more about the reverse trajectory. His enemies in the struggle for virginity are not the German whore and the black pimp, but the German and Portuguese men who reached Brazil's jungles, and its dark women, ahead of him.[16] Uncanny here is not absolute difference (black blood or, for Freud's dreamers, female genitalia) but similarity: the white phallus, prefiguring Freud's oft-neglected statement that the *male* genitalia, when "doubl[ed] or multipli[ed]," are also uncanny.[17] These genitalia are already everywhere, hidden in the most unlikely of places, contaminating every nook of exotic purity with their "frightening truth."

This almost-sameness haunts the protagonist for the rest of his journey, beginning with the subsequent chapter, when he steams for the first time into Brazil's interior and enters the first of his five concentric circles of uncanniness. In the midst of the jungle, he hears German words, springing "abruptly out of the night, as if through a metamorphosis" (*Heißes Land*, 184). He has entered the largest German colony in Brazil, Blumenau, whose inhabitants greet him with beer, music, and newspapers. After enjoying a moment of camaraderie, he longs again to "be rid of Europe!" and so ventures on horseback deeper into the jungle, farther again from recognizable territory (202).

He enters here the book's second concentric circle: the "limits of the world," the mysterious mountains in the range known as Serra do Mirador ("Range of Wonder"), behind which lurks "the virginal cradle of primordial times [*Urzeit*]" (*Heißes Land*, 201–2). Like Itahaji, however, this landscape reveals itself to be uncannily familiar. A tiny German village appears out of nowhere, complete with a Director—the "Wolf"—who preys on the village's women. A German "Kurtz" in the heart of the Brazilian darkness, this "uncanny white man" denies God, worshipping instead the Range of Wonder, and he seduces a different man's wife each evening.[18] Post-coitus, he drinks until inebriated and then shoots his revolver before going to bed. Even though this Wolf is German—not Afro-Brazilian, like the pimp—the colony's pastor treats him as if he were racially impure: the Wolf goes from house to house like "the plague," "contaminating" the village's women. The pastor promises to fight this Wolf "*bis aufs Blut*"—meaning "mercilessly" but literally "on the blood." The pastor's struggle over *Blut* becomes clearer in his final confrontation with the Wolf, when the pastor accuses him of generating "bastards," echoing the term used in fin de siècle colonial discourse primarily for children of mixed race (211, 214).[19]

Why should sex between two Germans be contaminating? Because, as for the narrator in Itajahi, the fear of racial/sexual alterity is a screen for a deeper contaminating fear: of similarity, introduced by the European man who has beaten him to the tropics. This underlying fear of similarity explains why the pastor transports "othering" colonial language onto the German Wolf and why the narrator replaces his dread of his male predecessors with his hatred of the female German prostitute. As becomes clear in the Wolf's village, the sexuality of the prostitute in Itajahi is uncanny not, as Freud would have it, because she recalls the sexual mother.[20] She is uncanny because her non-virginity produces a phantasmagoria of other men. Again turning from Freud's famous statement to his lesser-known one, *the man's* genitalia become uncanny. Like the snakes on Medusa's head, the phallus doubles and triples.[21] It moves with the Wolf "from house to house" as a "ghost" (*Spuk*), lying in the other men's beds while they are away (*Heißes Land*, 211). These men long only to lie with their "willing wives" but return instead each night to find them "raped." Most troubling is what always lies next to each of them: the "disgusting Wolf," who takes the travelers' place, both in the jungle and in the woman's body, causing fears of detachment and castration. These latecomers now become "shy," "anxious," and "utterly"—totally "afraid" of their phallic predecessor (214, 215, 216, 211).

Through this castrating double, Jacques prefigures not only Freud but also a second "Jacques"—Lacan—who likewise claims that "uncanny" castration anxieties stem from the phallus appearing where it ought not to be: from the lack of a "lack," from a "*horror plenitudinis*." For both of these "Jacques," the male subject fears castration when he sees too many phalluses, not too few. And, for both, the doubled phallus belongs not to the "good" law-making father (the Name-of-the-Father) but to the "bad," punitive, libertinous one (the "father-jouissance").[22] Norbert Jacques' "Wolf" breaks laws and punishes violently anyone who interferes with his orgasms. He kicks the pastor's lantern into the night, threatens everyone near him with his physique, his riding whip, and his revolver, and grotesquely displays his promiscuity. He cuckolds leisurely while the village men, including the affected husband, protest weakly outside of the house. His phallus is obscenely overexposed, a white "spook" that reminds the others of what they already knew: that his member precedes them in the jungle, even if it is not only his (which it never is). Because Jacques places this phallus in every swamp, hut, and bush in South America, he takes Lacan one step further. He sends his characters into a parodic Lacanian nightmare: a supposedly womanly jungle that is filled with men's genitalia.[23] By the time Freud exoticizes the female genitalia and even situates female sexuality in the "dark continent," travel literature had long maintained the opposite. And it had turned this into a bitter joke. The problem with the faraway world was not its feminine inscrutability but its masculine overexposure: the phallus was everywhere.

When the narrator prepares to leave this village, he has a violent dream about a "fist in the back of [his] neck" and wakes up feeling as if he—like the village women—has been "raped" (*Heißes Land*, 220, 221). This repetition of "raped" (*vergewaltigt*) shows that the violation once reserved for women can also be turned on men. In Jacques' uncanny, invaginated world, everything is reversible, such that even the homology of "vagina = jungle" loses its hold. The entire hetero-system of exotic difference implodes into homogeneity; every hole becomes equally unsacred.

Upset by this homo-topography, the protagonist flees, in the final chapter, even deeper into the jungle, toward what he hopes will be the final frontier of difference: the "limits of the earth." He begins speaking again, symptomatically, about the possibility of virginity—returning to his hetero-fantasies of purity. He rails against his predecessors who, like the Wolf, have taken for themselves Brazil's "virginity" and, more than this, turned the jungle into "a brutal little Europe." The fact that Germans traveled thousands of miles in order to transform the tropics into Europe shows only that they are "foolish" and "crude." As he pushes onward, he senses that this homogenization might continue all the way to the ends of the earth: he still finds Germans, even here, in the deepest jungle, living in horrible conditions in colonies that weirdly bear "the names of large German cities . . . Berlin, Hamburg, Bremen, and so on" (*Heißes Land*, 221–22).

But the narrator's hopes of an exotic heterotopia do not die easily. As the paths grow narrower and rockier, he gazes up at the Range of Wonder, whose "brutal beauty" resembles a woman's body: its "lapidary flanks" rise in the "foams of heaven"; behind it, he insists, lurk the mysteries of the "primal wilderness" (*Urwildnis*). The protagonist's whole journey was "nothing other than this": an attempt to reach this erotic world of absolute difference, which promises the "protoplasm of a new life, 'the' life without preconditions, the life of great, succulently fresh events."[24] What a brilliant insight, he exclaims, that the inhabitants named these mountains at the end of civilization "Wonder"! Inspired, he keeps moving, getting ever closer, spotting now only one or two more sparsely populated colonies. He sees everywhere, to his delight, "virgin" (*jungfräuliches*) land pushing up against the colonists' tiny clearings, even against the doors of their houses; the jungle appears unconquerable (*Heißes Land*, 222–23).

Working his way through the last one of these thickets, the hero arrives at the narrative's third concentric circle: the "last outpost." Here again, however, he does not find the elusive, pure native. As before, he discovers a German. This time it is a loud-mouthed trader, who tries to sell souvenirs to him: otter hides, a jaguar pelt, a giant arrow. This jungle's back space again proves to be a false back space: contaminated by a European phallus in the form of a salesman holding out this "ghastly" two-meter-long sharpened Indian bamboo (223).

Because *Hot Land* is structured as a topographical *mise en abyme*, the story does not end here. The trader takes the narrator into a fourth concentric circle: the back room of a hut whose only window looks out promisingly onto the ever-encroaching "virgin forest" (*Urwald*) (223). The narrator discovers here an old crate containing snake skins, toucan feathers, and armadillo shells. After taking these out piece by piece, he comes across, at the bottom, a yellowed book with a tattered cover. It is written in German. As he leafs through it, he finds, inscribed on the first page, a name that has been effaced by two strokes of a pen. This effacing, it turns out, has a real-life counterpart: the previous owner had been a "crazy" (*verrückt*) German who had come to the jungle and held outlandish, long-winded speeches, only one day to sell everything and disappear into the *Urwald*. The well-educated narrator is both moved and upset by this encounter with his intellectual doppelgänger: this second German Kurtz in Brazil's murky core. The vanished man achieved what the protagonist cannot. He went crazy, but through a salutary form of travel for which the hero longs. He got completely off of the beaten track, became displaced, "disarranged" (*ver-rückt*), and radically "lost without a trace" (*verschollen*) (224).

Only one generation before the protagonist, men succeeded at this, as evidenced by the very book he now holds in his hands: Wilhelm Raabe's *Abu Telfan* (1868), the story of a heroic, adventurous voyage to Africa's blank spaces that occurs immediately before the scramble for Africa and the mapping of its interior. As Raabe writes stirringly in his preface, neither Abu Telfan nor "Turmukieland" can be found on any map of Africa. But such an adventure is impossible for Jacques' narrator because of his crude contemporaries *and* his "*ver-rückte*" adventurous predecessors: the vanished man and, before him, *Abu Telfan*'s protagonist. In a second level of uncanniness, the European doubles surrounding the narrator are themselves already doubles of their predecessors—both fictional and real. This twice-doubled narrator now stands in the middle of a South American jungle reading a book about a successful version of himself.[25] Like Jünger's Berger, he gets from adventure books what the real journey cannot supply, but the very existence of these books keeps him from ever really getting what he wants. Even the past is overpopulated with his doubles. And even this past is not spared the degradations of repetition. *Abu Telfan* is lying at every corner of the globe because its narrative, like the protagonist's, has been swallowed into a homogenizing consumerism that knows no borders. The protagonist eventually gives in and purchases *Abu Telfan* from this "scammer at the edge of the universe" (*Heißes Land*, 224).

Like the earlier examples from Itajahi and the "Wolf's" colony, this encounter describes the traveler's shock and then anger at discovering compatriots at the other end of the world, but it also emphasizes an additional, third feature: stubborn hope. Despite this latest uncanny encounter, the protagonist constructs again, on the final page, another hetero-fantasy: of a native still living, untouched by Europeans, on the other side of the "Range of Wonder." Looking up from *Abu Telfan* toward this range—this fifth and last concentric circle—he imagines himself once more in the role of the hero. He sees himself tramping toward this mountainous haze of "hidden [*heimliches*] blood." This *heimliches* mist, he concludes, is all that separates "us" from those "who are still animals." Behind it, he hopes, lurks the virgin jungle: that exotic, erotic, feminine wonder that will receive gratefully his "painful, foaming ecstasies" (*Heißes Land*, 225). This narrative—with its shock, rage, and stubborn hope—forms the uncanny encounter paradigm for *Hot Land* and, what is more, for most early twentieth-century German travel writing. It describes the surprise, anger, and melancholic delusion of travelers encountering the eerily familiar where they expected the spectacularly foreign.

How German Is It?

As discussed in my introduction, I say "early twentieth-century" and "German," but in so doing do not deny that there were uncanny encounters long before then and that voyagers from other European nations chronicled them too. Despite this, I maintain that uncanniness asserted a discursive prominence by the end of the nineteenth century and that this was heightened for German-speaking travelers. Consider just a few examples beyond those already mentioned in the introduction. In fin de siècle Mexico, Max Dauthendey's protagonist repeatedly encounters the ghosts of Spanish colonial crimes, and a mysteriously familiar Dutch woman keeps crossing his path. Hermann Keyserling stumbles across European brothel tourists on the other end of the world in 1912 Kyoto. And Jünger's Berger sets off for Africa in 1913 dreaming of "white spots on the map," only to encounter everywhere familiarity: African rocks from which a golden snake should slither turn out to be as banal as those "in the Lüneburger Heide"; a "most African" "wild jungle" is, in the light of day, an artichoke field cultivated in "orderly rows"; and a dream-like exotic mussel bed ends up being a commonplace pile of coals.[26] A volunteer in the Foreign Legion, Berger sees everywhere fellow Europeans who, in this setting, become eerie to him. In prison, he comes across German wall-graffiti: "Heinrich Huke, Braunschweig, Akazienstrasse 17, 4th floor." And a Dutchman becomes explicitly "uncanny" (*unheimlich*) because he reminds Berger, here in faraway Africa, of home—of those foreign-familiar things "that one imagines seeing in the semidarkness of old dusty hallways" (Jünger, *Afrikanische Spiele*, 191, 147).

I think also here of the 1913–14 South Seas journey of the Expressionist painter Emil Nolde. Part of an official German ethnographic expedition, Nolde traveled overland through Russia to Korea, Japan, and China, then by ship via the Philippines to Kaiser-Wilhelmsland in German New Guinea. Nolde first sees New Guinea's wild coastline from the sea, and its radical foreignness thrills him; his heart "skips a beat" (*Welt und Heimat*, 56). But this exotic frisson is quickly frustrated. He lands in the colony's administrative center, Friedrich-Wilhelmshafen, where he sees only Europeans—just as Jacques' protagonist did when arriving in Brazil. Nolde walks past the "Europeanized" apartments of German civil servants and the souvenir stores that hawk decorated skulls to "globetrotters" (57). Disgusted, Nolde travels onward, this time in a boat filled with natives toward an island deeper in the archipelago. On board, he sees "cannibals," whom he twice calls "*unheimlich*," both times in the conventional sense of dreadful: their stares are "uncanny" as is, he insists, the "concept" of cannibalism itself (57). After landing in the next port town (Rabaul), Nolde uses "*unheimlich*" for a third time—witnessing a group of Europeans pouncing on a raw beefsteak like "beasts of prey"—and hints at why cannibalism is uncanny in general. Cannibalism apparently marks the native's unqualified difference from "us," but it also signifies his uncanny similarity. Even if Nolde never mentions this, he knows that these meat-eating Europeans also eat men—the body of Christ; the thought of a New Guinean tribesman eating another man is not only foreign but also uncannily familiar (61).[27]

Just as these Christ-eating Europeans eerily resemble the New Guineans, the converse is also true: the inhabitants of Rabaul are "too Europeanized." Nolde longs powerfully for something "other" (*anderem*) and so travels now into the interior, as did Jacques' protagonist, toward a "native village" (*Welt und Heimat*, 66). But as in Rabaul, everything here is turned upside down. The aborigines—again called "*unheimlich*"—appear civilized, smoking Western cigarettes, while the nearby Germans act like savages, hunting down rebels with "ruthless severity" and shooting them on the spot (67–68). This second uncanny encounter leads Nolde to plunge even deeper inland, along rough jungle paths and through swamps toward the "middle of the virgin forest" (*Urwald*) (72). But here, too, Europe and its other disturbingly mix. Nolde witnesses a trial held by the natives that mirrors the ones run by Europeans. Complete with prosecutors, defendants, and judges, the trial is disturbingly "almost like at home" (86). Like everything else in New Guinea, the *Urwald*, too, is "discovered and Europeanized." "They" act exactly like "us," right down to sporting European "haircuts" and "dressing as we do" (88, 91).

It is not suprising that the New Guineans resemble "us," given that, in Nolde's account, "we" are everywhere. Like Jacques' South American jungle, this one abounds with white men: "crazy officers, ruined businessmen, professional students." On one remote island, a leather-skinned European "runs around naked like a native," and, in a far-flung inland region, another European tortures the inhabitants "most inhumanely" (*Welt und Heimat*, 102, 91, 105). These experiences help to explain why Nolde turns down a final opportunity to travel farther up the river, to a "wild, absolutely primal region" that promises a "young girl in her transition years." Nolde cites his bad health, but he also, like Jacques, senses the futility of yet another heterotopic thrust. The jungle's hymen is everywhere already broken; no "enclave" has resisted penetration (105–6). The rain forest teems with European men.

Nolde's hated gatecrashers are generally German, but he points out that the original culprits were British, and he repeatedly complains about them: their omnipresence; their language ("stores," "globetrotters"); and their military atrocities (these "brutal" "absolute rulers" have "exterminated" a way of life) (*Welt und Heimat*, 57, 119, 89). Nolde's anti-British invective is typical of nationalist prewar German exoticism, which often claimed that Germans were more humane colonialists.[28] But hidden behind this self-righteous anger is resentment toward the British for arriving first and creating the conditions for the Germans' psychological disappointment. German travelers cannot be heroic and unique, only repetitive and uncanny. Like Jacques' protagonist (and, as we shall see in chapter 2, Hermann Hesse), Nolde suffers not just from arriving too late but also from being a second-level repeat. He follows the "crazy" German colonists, but even these had already followed the primary European adventurers. For Nolde and Wegener, this meant the British; for Jacques, the Portuguese; for Dauthendey, the Spanish; for Hesse, the Dutch; for Jünger, the French.

Cropping Europe: Zweig, Bonsels, Pechstein

Complementing this national travel neurosis was a flip-side psychosis: German travelers' claims that they had actually penetrated the world's last untouched spaces. Such delusional narratives generally begin, as did Jacques' and Nolde's, near the port cities, where the traveler sees European contamination everywhere. He then pushes deeper into the "virgin forests" in ever-smaller concentric circles until he—unlike Jacques and Nolde—apparently does find the unadulterated back space. Stefan Zweig, for example, begins his 1909 journey toward the holy Indian city of Gwalior with uncanny irritations: Bombay and Calcutta are "antipathetic mixed cities [*Mischstädte*]"; even Gwalior itself has European "broad squares," "streetcars," and "unit constructions of smooth brick"; and Gwalior's Maharaja is tragically "open to foreign influences" (*fremdenfreundlich*), leading to the imminent mixing of "orient and occident" ("Gwalior," 105). But these frustrations give way to exoticist relief. Zweig wanders into the Goldsmith's Lane and sees the saffron and turquoise turbans of the goldsmiths, the women's colorful muslins, and a half-naked bronzed man swinging his club into a pile of wet wash (106). Zweig then climbs the steep rocks to the ancient Gwalior fortress, which travelers can only reach by foot or on the back of an elephant. On high ground, he pauses before the "last gate" and experiences the outlandish thrill of one who is about to enter an auratic back space: the ultimate home of "unknown" Indian "secrets" (108, 109).[29]

Waldemar Bonsels likewise runs into uncanny "half-European mixed-breeds" at the beginning of his 1903–4 voyage to India, but eventually claims to experience liberation in exotic inner circles (*Indienfahrt* [*Indian Journey*], 58). At the gates of the *Urwald*, he finds the virgins that Jacques' narrator never could: fourteen- or fifteen-year-old girls at a water mill, "almost completely naked." Further in, he sees a twelve- or thirteen-year-old maiden, bitten by a snake and then another girl, "almost still the age of a child," lying naked on the ground with her small breasts exposed (60, 72, 93). Although this last vision is momentarily troubled by Bonsels's memory of an uncanny figure—a "virgin" prostitute from a Europeanized port city—he quickly reconfigures her only as "innocent" and "chaste" (97, 98). Similarly, the Expressionist painter Max Pechstein's April 1914 journey toward the "Elysian Fields" of the South Seas archipelago of Palau begins with corruptions: omipresent European goods in the major Asian harbors; the colonial architecture of Manila; and the European employees in Palau's southern port.[30] But Pechstein, like Zweig and Bonsels, eventually breaks through these front spaces to what seems to be an authentic back space: the real "paradise" in the interior, where he discovers "absolute foreignness" (*Erinnerungen*, 67, 84).[31]

Remarkable in Zweig's, Bonsels's, and Pechstein's accounts is the near absence of the Europeans who were omnipresent for Jacques, Ewers, Dauthendey, Nolde, and Wegener.[32] Although it is possible that the former indeed had some non-European encounters, it is more likely that they deliberately cropped their accounts: cutting away, as did nineteenth-century colonial postcard-makers, the ubiquitous Europeans.[33] How else could we explain Ewers's thoroughly inauthentic Gwalior, only one year after Zweig finds it auratic? Even though both Zweig and Ewers complain about the Europeanized maharaja, only Ewers sees here a hopeless tourist trap, replete with English architecture, Christian missions, and German goods. Ewers wanted to escape Germany to "search for India" but instead finds only objects marked "Made in Germany." Even the paint comprising the red dot of Shiva issues from tins labeled—beneath their Hindi, Tamil, or Urdu lettering—"Höchster Farbwerke." Ewers surmises that there is nothing "authentic" left anywhere in Gwalior (*Indien und Ich*, 162, 168, 163–64).

Similar doubts creep in when we compare Bonsels's actual travels with his literary claims that—in disagreement with Ewers—India still consists only of "eternal truth," "paradisiacal beauty," and "absorbed silence" (*Indienfahrt*, 39, 162). Although British soldiers were widely present in 1903–4 India, for example, they appear only once in Bonsels's 259-page book. Except for Bonsels's Indian friend, Panja, we see no guides and translators. But Bonsels actually spoke limited English and no Indian languages (even though his literary recounting has him speaking both fluently), so translators must have been present.[34] He moreover mentions German missionaries only at the fringes of his book, even though the Basel Mission financed his entire journey.[35] Bonsels diminishes these European elements along with those on the spatial edge of his voyage: the frustratingly Westernized points of entry (ship docks, Indian port cities, European hotels). These contaminated sites either vanish completely or appear only fleetingly, passed through quickly on Bonsels's way to the *Urwald*. And just as the points of entry shrink, so too does the *Urwald* expand. Bonsels's entire actual journey lasted only a few months, but he claims to have spent six months in the jungle alone (*Indienfahrt*, 103). Although Bonsels could assert poetic license (he does not label *Indienfahrt* as autobiography), it is noteworthy that each of his fictionalizations serves the same purpose: cropping Europe from India.

This metaphor of cropping is especially fitting for the painter Pechstein, who arrives in the South Seas just months after Nolde, in the archipelago of Palau, which had been a German colony since 1899. By 1914 Palau is already a modern, established European colony, as Pechstein notes disapprovingly when landing in Angaur, the southernmost island of the Palau group. Everywhere are "European employees," "European fuss," and "avaricious European commerce" (*Erinnerungen*, 64). But as soon as he hits the main Palau island of Babeldaob, at the German administrative seat of Melekeok, Pechstein exchanges this critical mode for a quixotic one, which he maintains for the rest of his memoir. His boat is greeted by the German station chief, Winkler, but, after this, Pechstein rigorously brackets Germans and Europeans from his account, replacing them with the realization of his long-standing dream: the same "Elysian" "paradise" that he had imagined before his departure (59, 71).[36]

Pechstein's paintings, too, uphold this nostalgic image of Palau, which was actually almost extinct by 1914. In typically belated German style, Pechstein borrows even his false exoticism from his predecessors: Bougainville, Loti, and Gauguin. If Pechstein can't find his own paradise in modern Palau, he will purloin one from the French: especially Gauguin's 1890s Tahiti. Instead of acknowledging that idol carving had almost vanished from Palau by 1914, for example, Pechstein reconfigures Gauguin's 1892 carvers, who themselves were likely already vanished in Gauguin's day. What is more, Pechstein borrows aspects from Gauguin's Tahitian *D'où venons-nous?* and from one of Gauguin's paintings of his young native mistress.[37] And he repeatedly paints the traditional Palauan "bachelor clubhouses"—where girls were offered to unattached men—even though these, together with their carved and painted beams, were already exceedingly rare by 1914. They had been replaced by European-style family homes, which never appear in Pechstein's work. Finally, Pechstein rigorously depicts only traditional Palauan art, scrupulously ignoring modern Palauan paintings, which depicted either Europeans (shooting at natives, evangelizing, taking photographs) or Palauans using Western equipment such as surveying tools.[38] Serving as Expressionism's self-appointed colonial postcard-maker, Pechstein gives the home front what it wants: exotic—non-uncanny—images stripped of European influence. In these snapshots, the artist, too, must remain invisible, as must his wife, whom

Pechstein masterfully effaces from his paintings and memoirs, reinserting her only at the very end of his journey. She appears as if out of nowhere when the Japanese arrest him and other German nationals in Palau in October 1914 (*Erinnerungen*, 99).

Repression, Uncanny Returns, and Violence

Throughout this chapter, I have referred to the shock of seeing the unexpectedly familiar as an upsetting, uncanny experience, which travelers either register as unsettling or, as with Pechstein, Zweig, and Bonsels, strategically suppress through cropping. But what about the Germans who stumbled across faraway little Germanys and welcomed them? These apparently non-uncanny encounters occur often in German colonial literature, for example the best-selling German-language novel of 1906: Gustav Frenssen's *Peter Moor's Journey to German Southwest Africa*. Here, Peter Moor and his compatriots travel deep in German South-West Africa to battle the Herero when they suddenly see a German farm, complete with a German mother who rises before them like a vision: "There, in the shadows of the veranda, stood a German woman; she had a small child on her arm. How we looked! How we rejoiced over the light, clean dress and the pure friendly face and the small white child!"[39] Non-colonial travelers, too, sometimes report joy when seeing bits of Germany in foreign lands. Hesse, for example, claims to have a comforting feeling when noticing—only after returning to Germany—"home" in Indonesia: he sees many of "our native wildflowers" atop the Pedrotallagalla and imagines, along a Sumatran river, German "fishermen and maidens" singing as if "on the Neckar and Rhein."[40] A similar scene graces the last lines of Bonsels's *Indian Journey*, where Bonsels exceptionally chooses not to crop. In the middle of rural India, he closes his eyes, sees an intact, peaceful village "from my German *Heimat*," and rejoices.[41] Like Peter Moor and Hesse, Bonsels sees here Germany and feels succor, not anxiety.

As I have been arguing, this discovery of the familiar in the foreign world ought to have given the traveler an uneasy sense of having "been here before": of either returning to the womb or of seeing the doubled phalluses that remind him of his replaceability and the inevitability of his death.[42] But these travelers welcome this return without anxiety. Why? Because their desire to overcome melancholia causes them to repress the uncanny nature of their return.[43] Moor imagines curing himself of alienation by returning to his mother, but he can only do so if this mother is, first, displaced onto another woman and, second, desexualized—so that this return is to a pre-Oedipal "virginal" mother.[44] Hesse's and Bonsels's location of a proto-German cultural paradise in India allows them, similarly, to retrieve their lost idealized pre-industrial German home of "fishermen and maidens." And it also helps them to erase entirely their memories of alienation both before and during their journeys. Hesse's new *Ur-Heimat* (India), for instance, has persisted throughout Europe's entire period of modern melancholy: "Our essence and our northern culture" were never really lost but were simply hidden from us in the present-day South and East.[45] "We" were just looking in the wrong places. This denial of loss is a defense against *Unheimlichkeit*—including the *Unheimlichkeit* Hesse felt during his own 1911 journey to southeast Asia (see my chapter 2). The traveler, or in Hesse's case, his Germanic people, has been present in India the entire time, making this not a return at all, but a rediscovery. Through this delusion, the traveler can claim he was always already in the feminized exotic realm, rendering it neither *unheimlich* nor *heimlich* but rather *heimisch* ("homely"). As in Freud's description of religion's anthropomorphizing of nature, this illusion allows the traveler magically, for once, to "feel at home in the uncanny" (*heimisch im Unheimlichen*).[46]

These attempts to deny uncanniness through cropping or repression are seldom successful. The repression fails, robbing the traveler of his hopes of deliverance and inciting him, now vengeful, to reactive violence. Consider, for example, a late scene from Bonsels's *Indian Journey*, when he uncharacteristically sees some otherwise-cropped Englishmen in the district collector's office. While there, Bonsels comes upon a part-Indian, part-British "half breed" (*Mischling*), whom he proceeds to slap across the face for no apparent reason: he can not even "explain to himself the brutality of this act." Why does he become violent? Is it perhaps a racist fear of mixed blood? According to Bonsels, such contamination through difference is not the problem. Rather, as in *Hot Land*, his fear issues from the other's uncanny similarity. This "slave" is skilled in mimicking Europeans. His "conceit" in pretending to know a culture that he could "not understand" "made me furious" (*Indienfahrt*, 163).

If, as Homi Bhabha claims, the colonial mimic indeed upsets the culture he mimics, then why should a *Mischling* mimicking British culture so offend a German?[47] The answer lies in *Indian Journey*'s previous chapter, when Bonsels, upon meeting an Indian king, pretends to be English (*Indienfahrt*, 150). By acting British, then, the *Mischling* "slave" reminds the German of Germany's own cultural insecurity within Europe. Both men are masquerading underlings who "arrogantly" and transparently attempt to demonstrate a political-cultural potency that they do not possess (154). This *Mischling* is of course uncanny to the British—"almost the same but not quite"—but he is even more uncanny to the Germans: his mimicking mimics the German's mimicking.

This German's sense of himself as an uncanny mimic helps to explain his spontaneous violence, especially if we consider the underlying family romance in which the British take on the role of the German's grandparents. The British preceded German travelers by at least two generations, and their Queen Victoria—the Empress of India—was in fact Kaiser Wilhelm's grandmother. Through this lens, Bonsels slaps the *Mischling* because he is a rival for his grandparents' affection. The German—like the Kaiser—claims to be the Englishman's legitimate grandson, whereas the *Mischling* is the illegitimate late-life stepson; the German grandchild lashes out at this other offspring, this bastard Indian-British uncle, in order to differentiate himself. Both are uncanny imitators, but only one, the German insists, is lawful. The German's underlying sense that he might not be truly British but rather a *Mischling* explains the otherwise baffling brutality. He experiences uncanniness more profoundly even than Jacques' narrator: he sees the British in India, meets the mimicking *Mischling*, and then views himself as a likewise mimicking *Mischling*. This identity crisis leads him to greater violence than Jacques' narrator and to personal confusion. Even long after Bonsels has calmed down, he still cannot explain this outbreak of "tropical rage."[48]

As in *Hot Land*, this uncanny encounter is followed immediately by Bonsels's naive assertion that a truly exotic India—free of *Mischlinge*—still exists.[49] This culminates in the final chapter when we discover again India's primitive "naked, brown figures" and the above-mentioned peaceful village that calmingly reminds Bonsels of "my German *Heimat*" (*Indienfahrt*, 217). Bonsels represses all uncanniness here in order to overcome his melancholia. For this, he employs both India and pre-industrial Germany as counterpoints to British modernization. If the technocratic British grandparents are responsible for the impure, *Mischling*-filled 1903–4 India (Bonsels's travel time) *and* for the hyper-modern, arms-racing 1916 Germany (*Indian Journey*'s publication year), then the psychotic grandchild needs to deny the existence of these grandparents and of these modernizations.[50] His psychosis reveals itself in this denial of reality, freeing him to believe in the truth of his romantic images of both India and Germany.

Sensing, however, that these images inhere only in his fantasies, Bonsels hedges his bets. He supports the technological German war machine—hoping that, through this modernization, Germany (and India) might eventually come full circle.[51] The Germans—the "better colonizers"—might finally defeat the British Empire and create their own prelapsarian "paradise" on earth: an ancient German village that would appear simultaneously on the Rhine and on the Ganges.[52] This fantasy at once criticizes British technologization and tries to outdo it in order to destroy technology once and for all. It calls to mind the number one German himself, the so-called traveling Kaiser, Wilhelm II, who used his modern naval prowess to fight his grandparents and so gain what his foreign minister Bülow called Germany's colonial "place in the sun."[53]

Heimlich/Unheimlich, and the *Verrücktes* Ending of *Hot Land*

Compounding these national-psychological reasons for German reactions to their belatedness is a psycho-linguistic one, leading us back to *Hot Land* and also forward toward the upcoming chapters. As mentioned in my introduction, Freud and, later, Heidegger point out that German is the only language where the disturbing conflation of "home" (*Heim*) and "away from home" occurs in a single word: *heimlich*. *Heimlich* developed over centuries into its opposite, until, as Freud notes, it seemed to contain "*unheimlich*" within it (Freud, *SE* 17:224–26). By transforming into its own converse, *heimlich* became a "dreadful" (*unheimliches*) lexeme. With this quotidian linguistic background, German speakers were more aware, if only unconsciously, of the troubling familiarity of fin de siècle travel. This peculiarity in German diction even helps to explain the ending of *Hot Land*, where the narrator looks up from his predecessor's book to stare at the Range of Wonder, which—cloaked in a haze of "*heimliches* blood"—shelters the genuine natives from him (*Heißes Land*, 225). Why does he not cross this range, tempted as he is? Perhaps he fears that the "*heimliches* blood" on the other side is not only "hidden" and "strange" but also "homey" and "familiar"? As he (like Bonsels) has learned over and over again in his concentric journeys, Brazil's blood is always uncannily tinctured with home; it is more familiar than you think. The narrator never attempts the passage. The book ends here.

This finale teaches us how to read *Hot Land*: as both a modernist and a pop-culture meditation on authenticity. When the narrator picks up his "*verschollen*" ("lost-without-a-trace") predecessor's book, we realize that he is not the only one with a book in his hands. We, too, are reading a volume left behind by an adventurer to Brazil's jungles, and we, too, are tempted to move into that one last concentric circle, the one the narrator never enters. Instead of an unflinching postmodern dismissal of authenticity, *Hot Land* constructs a seductive labyrinth, drawing the reader in. Jacques dangles a series of "real" natives before us while at the same time effacing these figures like mirages. Just as Kafka, also in 1911, sends his "*verschollen*" alter ego toward the exotic Nature Theater of "Oklahoma" [*sic*] but does not let him arrive (in *Der Verschollene*), Jacques promises utopian truths only continually to suspend them. *Hot Land* reveals how this ruse flows back and forth between modernism and popular culture. Like Kafka—but also like pulp fiction and travel guides—*Hot Land* pledges an exotic salvation that it can never deliver.[54] The first extra-European Baedeker guides were, after all, to the Promised Land. But Baedeker could not keep this promise from collapsing under its own weight. Baedeker giveth and Baedeker taketh away. If the average man can now surpass Moses by reaching Canaan—or Brazil or "Oklahoma"—he can do so only together with hundreds of others; modernity undermines modernism's hope.

This subversion of authenticity also appears in *Hot Land*'s form. Just as Europe bleeds into Brazil and the reader-narrator becomes the writer-narrator, so too does the popular travelogue commingle with the avant-garde novel. Although *Hot Land* begins as a straightforward first-person travelogue, it transforms without explanation into a hallucinatory third-person short story, complete with new characters and new landscapes—thereby resembling an experimental, Expressionist text.[55] Although the first-person perspective and the original plot eventually return, Jacques significantly undermines them in this third-person chapter, and he continues to do so throughout, especially when the narrator begins to read the book within the book—*Abu Telfan*—at the end. Like *Hot Land* itself, this book questions whether we can ever "say with certainty" if we are living in "reality" or fantasy (*Heißes Land*, 224). And Jacques' last concentric circle of readers and writers intensifies this question. The 1911 German reader reads a book left by a German traveler who himself is reading a book left by a German traveler. At the center of all of this is a German who is *verrückt*, *ver-rückt*, and *verschollen*. If *Hot Land*'s final perspective is mad, then is the whole narrative, too? We find here a story that is both "out of its mind" (*verrückt*) and "out of place" (*ver-rückt*).

At this *ver-rückt* center, Jacques asks what motivates us to try to penetrate the core of the jungle in the first place. We know from reading *Hot Land* that this heart of darkness is always displaced and violated, the hymen both disarranged and breached. As Jacques points out, however, such displacements only entrench the stubborn fantasy. The reader still dreams with the narrator of a dark, mysterious "Range of Wonder" even though he knows that behind it is not the exotically feminine "naked, brown figures" he longs for but rather the "uncanny white man" (*der unheimliche Weiße*). He is always there ahead of us, reading a book left by another *unheimlichen Weißen*.

The Politics of the Uncanny Encounter

Because the term "*unheimlicher Weiße*" stems from another 1911 travelogue that describes Germans committing a colonial massacre, it begs a question already suggested by Jacques: If the European in the jungle is unhomely to other Germans, isn't he doubly *unheimlich*—in the more conventional sense of "ghastly"—to the natives?[56] How does Jacques' book engage with this violent *Unheimlichkeit*? As I have argued, Jacques debunks his own erotopic male fantasies even as he continually reconstructs them. Because the exotic world is always already deflowered, there is no reason to penetrate it, as much as his characters still long to do so. Jacques exposes this desire by deliberately writing a book about disenchantment. Reading fuels narcissistic dreams of conquest,[57] as in the contemporaneous African journey described by Jünger, but it ends here only in a *mise en abyme* of disillusion. But this self-conscious formal structure leaves us with a conundrum in Jacques' biography: why does he become a supporter of German military expansion, authoring pamphlets favoring German re-colonization all the way into the 1920s and finally writing Nazi propaganda in the 1940s in his native Luxembourg? Although the attempt to convict Jacques of treason in postwar Luxembourg failed, he was banned for life from his home country and remains persona non

Figure 12. Max Pechstein in his studio (1926)

grata there to this day.[58] How do we reconcile Jacques' pro-colonial and collaborationist politics with his avant-garde Expressionist aesthetics? Why this apparent disjuncture between Jacques' art and life, between *Heißes Land* and the propaganda pamphlets—beyond the banal observation that the two have nothing to do with one another?

Critics have long debunked the cliché—based on Hitler's condemnation of "degenerate" art—that avant-garde aesthetics are politically progressive. Georg Lukács made this point already in 1934 and again in 1957, going so far as to coin an opposing cliché: that German Expressionism had a natural tendency toward fascism. Expressionism, like modernism in general, used formal techniques to create a "primitive awe"; this awe produced what Lukács called the "unity of decadence and regression" that constitutes "fascist demagogy."[59] L. D. Ettlinger wrote similarly in 1968 about the Expressionist primitivism of Emil Nolde, who embraced the Nazis even as his stark palette, savage bodies, and grimacing faces scandalized them. Ettlinger claimed that Nolde's "fervent advocacy of racial purity" created his aesthetic primitivism: primitive art became salutary for Nolde precisely because it was the "direct product of blood and soil." Ettlinger furthermore asserted that Nolde sided with the New Guinean natives against colonialism because he longed to preserve their "pure race," thereby connecting him to fascism.[60]

But how far can we take this line of argument? Does Expressionist primitivism uphold racial difference? If so, is it also racist and proto-fascist? As Jill Lloyd points out, Nolde was actually much less guilty of celebrating and

Figure 13. Pechstein and his wife at a costume party (1927)

creating "racial difference" than was his left-leaning Expressionist contemporary, Pechstein, who, now a respectable art professor, decorated his atelier in faux-exotic style and dressed up like a "savage" for costume parties—for decades after his return from the South Seas (figure 12; figure 13).[61] While in the South Seas, Pechstein falsified Palau by conjuring vanished images (idol carvers, traditional bachelor clubhouses, old-fashioned Palauan beams) and cropping foreign influences (European-style family homes, Europeanized Palauan art, his own wife). Nolde conversely emphasized a more accurate, less idyllic picture of his longed-for South Seas—including moments of European contamination, as in his famous pre-journey still life, *The Missionary* (figure 14).[62] As Lloyd writes, Nolde's coalescing of the primitive and the modern resulted in better art, but it also likely gave Nolde the "fright" that eventually led to his later fears of mixed categories and peoples.[63] The same could be said of Jacques. By noticing the modern and the European within the primitive, Jacques wrote a complex book. But this discovery of uncanny mixing may also have given Jacques the dread that led to his political conservatism and his support of German military expansion—even if he, unlike Nolde, never became a Nazi.

Jacques and Nolde give the lie to Lukács's theory: these two less exoticist Expressionists got closer to the fascists than did the thoroughly primitivist one (Pechstein). By attempting to suppress European contamination, however unsuccessfully, Pechstein never experienced an uncanny fright. Simultaneously with Victor Segalen, he continued to idealize alterity and encourage an

Figure 14. Emil Nolde, *The Missionary* (*Der Missionar*) (1912)

early form of what we now call multiculturalism.[64] Jacques and Nolde conversely faced modernism's uncanniness head on, but this confrontation led to their political defensiveness and conservatism. Their work and lives thus challenge the widespread claim that modernist formal complexity, which brushes history against the grain, runs counter to nationalism and fascism.[65] Such theories underestimate the psychological cost of attempting to represent the other during this apparent end of alterity—when the horror of similarity sent uncanny shockwaves through Europe.

Chapter 2

Europe in India

Hermann Hesse and the East

Just after Norbert Jacques published *Hot Land* in 1911, his old Lake Constance friend, Hermann Hesse, set sail for what he called India: today's Sri Lanka, Malaysia, Singapore, and Indonesia.[1] Hesse had long been frustrated with European consumerism and industrialization, leading him, in 1904, to move to a humble and remote Lake Constance farmhouse without gas, electricity, or running water.[2] But now—in a state of "sheer inner necessity"—Hesse took a more decisive step.[3] Accompanied by his friend, the painter Hans Sturzenegger, he fled Europe entirely, searching for the same India that his grandfather had traveled by ox-cart in the previous century: "My trip was a flight. I fled [Europe] and virtually hated it for its gaudy tastelessness, its noisy fairground bustle, its frantic restlessness, its raw, foolish pursuit of pleasure" (Hesse, *SW* 13:422–23).

Indian Disappointments

But Hesse's flight failed. He experienced a series of "Indian disappointments" repeatedly caused by the same thing: Europe was everywhere, and the savages had become dismayingly like "us" ("Pedrotallagalla," *SW* 13:277). Hesse's examples of the Europeanization of Southeast Asia from his autumn 1911 diaries are considerable, beginning already when, after three seasick weeks aboard ship, he sees Asian territory for the first time in his life ("Hot. Ceylon [Sri Lanka] visible about 10 o'clock"), only immediately to be disenchanted: "Arrival in Colombo after 11. . . . The new city lively and pretty, but brutally Europeanized" ("Tagebuch der Indonesienreise," *SW* 11:336).[4] Instead of finding Europe's opposite, Hesse, like Zweig, finds immediately "Europe in India."[5] This unnerving similarity haunts Hesse throughout the first leg of his journey, in the British-ruled cities of Penang, Ipoh, Kuala Lumpur, and Singapore. On his first night in Penang, for example, Hesse visits two different "Europeanized" theaters, one of which is dominated by a "ridiculously grotesque" Western stage design. The natives "lack their own culture," adopting instead the "height of European-cultured bad taste." Fittingly, this first Penang evening ends with a gramophone wafting upper Bavarian yodel music into his hotel (*SW* 11:338, see also 13:218). The following day, Hesse protests that Europe—its clothing, whiskey, playing cards—is "ruining the East." This leads him, like Jacques, to head off into the backwoods, only to find more of Europe: a streetcar emerges uncannily out of the "middle of the green tropical wilderness" (*SW* 11:339, 340). Cinemas and theatres in Ipoh and Singapore furthermore play "horrible European films" and "bad European music," and colonial lumber companies desolate the hinterlands of Kuala Lumpur through clear-cutting (11:341, 343, 341).

Frustrated by this Westernization, Hesse, like Jacques, heads further into the "primeval jungle" (*Urwald*)—boarding a steamer to the less modernized, Dutch-ruled island of Sumatra. Hesse and his traveling companions immediately head upstream, past a series of native villages, into the "never-ending *Urwald*." Hesse sees gigantic trees, "tangled swarms of ferns and aromatic plants," and Sumatrans on small boats. In the dusky evening, his boat stops, and a figure emerges from the jungle. It is not, however, the mysterious native for which Hesse had hoped but rather a man with almost the same name as Hesse—Hiese—who hails from Ulm, not far from Hesse's own birthplace. When Hiese opens his mouth, Hesse notices eerie remnants of his own Swabian accent ("Tagebuch der Indonesienreise," *SW* 11:345). Together with this almost-the-same Swabian doppelgänger, Hesse travels further upstream to the last town along the river, Jambi, where he sees small fishermen's huts floating on rafts. He enters one of them, only to discover that, even here, Europe is present: the hut is outfitted with modern European furniture, including a "Renaissance buffet" and a "Regulator clock." Jambi itself features stores filled with "horrible European things," and Hesse meets here yet another of the many Germans he will encounter in the jungle: Hasenfratz (11:346).

Not ready to give up, Hesse and his traveling companions push further upriver, to the tiny village of Pelayang, which initially strikes Hesse with its powerful alterity. He senses that he has finally found what he has sought: "First hours alone in the primeval jungle, I saw unattainable large butterflies and toward evening a whole swarm of monkeys, wandering pandemoniously with great leaps through the branches" (*SW* 11:348, 349). He sees a massive jelutong tree that is thirty-five meters high, experiences a sublime downpour, and enjoys wandering alone through the jungle searching for butterflies. "Pelayang," he writes, "is the first place on this journey that pleased me." A "pretty, dark, curly girl" boards a second, smaller boat with him, and he feels that he might literally have discovered "virgin" territory (11:350–51, 13:238).

But even Pelayang, it turns out, has been penetrated by colonializing European men, including Hasenfratz, who manages the Dutch Jambi Trading

Company and takes Hesse on a walk into the wilderness. Hesse watches as the company's powerful winches emerge among jelutongs to hoist primeval ironwoods out of gorges. This corruption of Pelayang brings on the melancholia that will haunt Hesse for the rest of his trip. After returning downstream to Jambi, Hesse writes without punctuation, "Jambi mute sad." And the following day is also upsetting, not least because of the "strange" feeling he gets standing with his traveling partners: this "little troop of Europeans" that gathers among natives' huts under the "jungle's night sky." This uncanny, disturbing mixture of Europe and Asia causes Hesse to entertain his first thoughts of returning home prematurely: "Bad day. Decision to turn back" (SW 11:352).

This bad day is followed by many more. Hesse takes sleeping pills to no avail—"deep sleep with Veronal, not refreshed"—and, four days later, registers his first intestinal "qualmishness," the onset of dysentery. Having given up on his plan to visit the Indian subcontinent and see the birthplace of his mother, Hesse makes a short journey to the floating city of Palembang. He feels increasingly unwell here, due to the beginnings of his dysentery but also because Palembang is so Europeanized (SW 11:352, 353). The bookshops are filled with Dutch detective stories and Karl May novels. The streets are modeled on kitschy German small towns, and the stores sell "tasteless and backward" provincial European goods: cheap sarong fabric from England and Switzerland; beer from Munich and Bremen; sterilized milk from Mecklenburg and Holland; and preserved fruit from Lenzburg (figure 15). The natives wear only "bad imported junk" and strut, smoking cigarettes, into billiard halls (11:354; see also 13:229, 253–54).

These disappointments from Palembang prompt Hesse to make two last excursions into the jungle, day trips up the Musi and Ogan rivers—hoping still, like Jacques' and Bonsels's heroes, to find somewhere an uncontacted native. As in Pelayang, he begins by sensing that he has entered a prehistoric idyll: "We sailed silently into a fairy-tale wilderness, the stream woven over with fantastic, multi-armed, grown-together trees above thousands of intricate, high-stilted roots" (SW 11:355). As in Pelayang, Hesse associates this apparently virgin territory with Sumatran girls. He stares through binoculars at "masses of naked children, the girls pixyishly ashamed, paradisiacal idyll" and then deboards to search for the "young, pretty girl who had waved at us." Although she eludes Hesse, he does nonetheless seem to get to enter a privileged back space—the chieftain's quarters—where he watches a shy, virginal Malaysian girl dance for him (11:357, 358).

But Hesse's glimpse at this virgin territory proves as fleeting as did the glimpses in the Pelayang jungle and in Jacques' Brazil. Hesse is again quickly surrounded by German men: Nägeli and also Kiefer, who is married to a half-caste woman and vows never to return to Europe. From Nägeli, Hesse hears of a Swiss named Brunner who likewise lives deep in the jungle. Like Hiese, these "representatives of a half-romantic adventuresome Europe in

Figure 15. Hermann Hesse and Hans Sturzenegger at the bazaar in Palembang in 1911 (at right, in tropical suits)

the East" have long taken Sumatra's virginity for themselves (*SW* 11:359, 360). Like most Europeans traveling to Sumatra, Hesse too had hoped to discover a "primitive paradisiacal innocence," an "exquisite original state," but he never gets to experience the pleasure of this "self-deception" (13:238). As much as he would like to, Hesse cannot deny what he sees. Europe has rendered the *Urwald* not only disappointing, but also uncanny (*"unheimlich"*), in Freud's sense of something "long familiar"—Europe itself—unexpectedly returning (Freud, *SE* 17:220). What is worse, Hesse knows that he, as yet another European male in the jungle, is partly responsible—also for the devastation of Indonesian culture: "More than the fever and the filth," this realization makes his stay "painful." He feels "half-dead" and now, after eighteen days in Sumatra, sinks into an "unbearable depression" (*SW* 13:229; 11:361).

Souvenirs, Intestinal Explosions, and Sinhalese Girls

Unfortunately for Hesse, his trip is still only half over. He turns back toward British Singapore, where he attempts to stem his melancholia through touristic fetish objects: postage stamps, postmarks, pictures, flutes, sacred sticks, indulgences, a gold brooch, brass dice, a comb. Hesse's Singapore diary reads like a manic shopper's day planner: "Friday, October 27th . . . purchasing photographs"; "Sunday, October 29th . . . we bought local stamps and had them postmarked"; "Tuesday, October 31st . . . Brandt came with me and helped me to shop for pictures, flutes, etc. . . . after 5 shopping with Hasenfratz"; "Thursday, November 2nd . . . I bought all sorts of things"; "Saturday, November 4th . . . through the Chinese quarter, small purchases in stalls."[6] Always the Swabian, Hesse complains about the high prices but cannot stop himself. He finally goes broke on November 5th, longing for that last souvenir that he cannot afford: a necklace hung with a golden fish. But even this final unattainable object—psychoanalysis's "*objet petit a*"—would not have lifted Hesse's spirits. Like the objects that he purchased on the previous days' sprees, this one too would have left him alone, tired, and "irritated"—feeling an emptiness that more shopping only deepens: "Friday, November 3rd . . . shopping; lonely cocktail in the Club" ("Tagebuch der Indonesienreise," *SW* 11:365, 367, 368, 370, 371).

Hesse understands the melancholic nature of buying things, even though this does not stop him. He realizes that no matter how many pieces of this "great colorful Asian bazaar splendor" he purchases, he will never be satisfied. Bringing home one crate or ten is equivalent to bringing home one or ten bottles of seawater: "Even if I were to bring home one hundred tons, it still would not be the sea." What is worse, even if he *were* to bring home the sea, he would never know whether it, like everything else in Asia, were fake. Most things that he purchases are "dubious" because the shop owners have "too many connections with Europe." They work with English and French designs and purchase from German small towns: Idar-Oberstein and Pforzheim (*SW* 13:226, 225, 222).[7] Hesse sees the irony: he can only soothe his fear of losing India by buying junk made in Pforzheim, a Swabian town just eighteen kilometers from his birthplace. Asia is lost to him; Europe, even Pforzheim, is everywhere. Hesse now takes even more sedatives—"sleep with Veronal"—but even this cannot still his pain. He remains "unhappy and tired" (11:364, 372).

This surfeit of familiarity in a foreign world becomes the psychological pendant to Hesse's dysentery. At the same time that Europe's omnipresence becomes more painful, Hesse gets bloated and, now back in Europeanized Sri Lanka, develops stomach pains that even his strong tranquilizers cannot suppress. He awakens in the middle of the night shivering, with nausea and violent diarrhea. The next day, he sees more Westernized natives: dandies in straw hats and sport-ties who speak better English than he does; at night, his intestines revolt again (*SW* 11:375–77). From this point on, Hesse writes at least once a day about his innards, as a random sampling reveals: "attacked again and again by diarrhea," "the diarrhea started up again," "the diarrhea returned with new force," "diarrhea again in the morning," "new intestinal explosion at 5 AM," "bad, new intestinal eruption," "intestine again in the afternoon," "the long-lasting diarrhea brought on an irritating bladder catarrh."[8] Hesse is ill, but this illness is also a metaphor. His body seems to want to shit itself clean, to purify itself of this entire uncanny world: this Pforzheim—or almost homophonically, "Furzheim" (fart home)—in Sri Lanka. He swallows bismuth and a "mysterious reddish brown drug" until finding a regular supplier of opium; for the next week, he ingests only "opiates, red wine, and bismuth," all "without any effect." Hesse looks everywhere for doctors and drugs. He finds himself steadily weakened from fasting, and increasingly "sad," "lonely," and "inconsolable." "A horrible state." Within this continual reiteration of dysentery, opium, and depression, Hesse makes a resolution to depart, forgetting that this decision is itself a repetition: he had already resolved to do this after his disappointments in Sumatra (*SW* 11:376, 380, 378, 379).

Like Jacques' protagonist in *Hot Land*, however, Hesse refuses to surrender his dream of an Indian paradise, leading him to turn away from his ravaged European anus toward fresh exotic vaginas. But these, too, now appear used up. Far from the virgin *Urwald*, Hesse stares at girls on the streets of Singapore, Colombo, and Kandy: "an eleven-year-old Chinese girl with black pants," "pretty young Chinese girls in a rickshaw," and "pretty girl faces" (*SW* 11:363, 365, 376). Before long, he is in the whorehouses: first in Chinese brothels, which are "apparently only for yellow-skins," and then in the brothels "for whites," which are filled with Japanese girls. He "knocks around till 3 AM in the whore district." But just as Hesse could not locate the authentic Asian girl in the jungle, he cannot do so in a brothel. Like the souvenirs he manically collected, the whores, too, are dubious: everywhere are "Russian harlots," not Asian ones. And the brothels themselves are filled with Europeans including a "brutal Englishman" who starts a brawl (11:368–69, 370). Knowing that his time is running short, Hesse goes with his friends in Colombo to find real "Sinhalese girls," whom he initially seems to locate in a "primitive, genuine" (*primitives echtes*) brothel. But even this disappoints him: the girls do not know how to perform authentic Sinhalese dances, and they, like all the others, speak with their johns in English (11:373).

Men in Whorehouses

Despite these dissatisfactions, Hesse remains stubbornly hopeful of having an *echtes* exotic experience—even on the trip back home. His ship stops one last time before Europe, in Port Said, where Hesse goes to one more brothel. It is his "last Oriental night"—for the rest of his life, it turns out—and he is especially melancholic. He again attempts to staunch this sadness with souvenirs: this time, with "brass objects" from Damascus. When this does not work, he again makes straight for the whorehouse:

I ran into Freudenberg, Weisflog and other passengers and joined
them. An oldish swindler led us through the city, i.e., to the brothels,
which the three of us went into, it was like everywhere else [*es war
wie überall*], and I will never try again to find something interesting
in such places. It was only strange [*merkwürdig*] to observe the Don
Juans [*Lebemänner*] in my entourage. Around 3 AM I'd had enough
and ran away alone through the grotesque city and to the port, after
3 I was in bed. ("Tagebuch der Indonesienreise," *SW* 11:385–86)

Hesse experiences here, again, the Orient's unsettling homogeneity most
pointedly in its brothels. Every Oriental bordello is like every other one (*es
war wie überall*). And all of them are filled with European men who remind
Hesse uncannily of himself: a *merkwürdig* parade of Don Juans.

Hesse's description shows that Freud did not know how right he was when,
just eight years after Hesse's report, he chose a red-light district to illustrate
how uncanny feelings result from returning to "the same place." At the fin
de siècle, this same place often was the foreign whorehouse, not just the one
Hesse visits in Port Said but also the one Ernst Jünger's Berger visits in 1913
Bel-Abbès (Algeria), which Berger explicitly describes as "*unheimlich.*"[9] During this heyday of brothel tourism, every house seemed like every other one:
populated by the same Western characters. In addition to Hesse in Singapore,
Colombo, and Port Said, and Berger in Bel-Abbès, we find Keyserling in 1912
Kyoto; Kellermann in 1907 Tokyo; Bonsels in 1903 Bombay; Ewers in 1910
Igatpuri; and, closer to home, Kafka and Max Brod in 1911 Milan and Paris.
In most of these accounts, the protagonist is together with other men, often
crowds of them, and he shows more interest in these men than in the prostitutes. Kellermann sees many buggies overflowing with "satiated, satisfied
men"; Keyserling observes European men in a Tokyo brothel; Brod watches
"men in hats, waiting seriously, as at the railway station or in a doctor's
office"; Jünger's Berger sees "many soldiers sauntering idly back and forth";
and Kafka sees an "intense traffic" of "single" men (*Einzelne*), who, in their
similarity, are more aptly "doubles."[10] Given these brothel visits' chronological concentration between 1903 and 1913, they start to resemble one another
and seem paradigmatic. It is as if there is one gigantic modernist whorehouse
containing copies of the same replaceable john—the "*Lebemann*"—whose
name shifts from "Hesse," to "Kellermann," to "Keyserling," to "Ewers," to
"Freud," to "Kafka."

When Hesse leaves the bordello claiming that the only remarkable things
were these European *Lebemänner*—not the Oriental women—we need to
take him at his word. European men are omnipresent in Hesse's East, as
they were in Jacques' Brazil. Hans Sturzenegger accompanies Hesse everywhere, and countless other European men cross his path: Sturzenegger's
brother Robert, Hiese, Hasenfratz, Nägeli, Kiefer, and Brunner, as well as
the anonymous "completely inebriated Englishman," "snoring Dutchman,"

"Bavarian," "Swiss chemist from East Africa," and German "hotel man-
ager."[11] And then there are the nearly uncountable named European extras on
the fringes of Hesse's trip: Falkwitz, Gehrmann, Kulsens, Delbrück, Tschudi,
Suhl, Klung, Beckmann, Brandt, Bébier, Tiffin, Pertile, Malchow, Müller,
Ellon, Rosenbaum.[12] Precisely because Hesse sees many of these men in
brothels, the brothel becomes uncanny in a way that Freud did not at first see.
Like Jacques' all-male jungle in *Hot Land*, this exotic whorehouse reverses
Freud's traditionally feminine ero-topography. Whereas Freud claims that the
vagina is *unheimlich* because it reminds men of whence they came, Hesse,
like Jacques, discovers during the first globalization that the uncanniest genitalia are the men's—thereby recalling Freud's lesser known claim that the
penis becomes "uncanny" in the moments when it seems to "doubl[e]" or
"multipl[y]" (Freud, *The Uncanny, SE* 17:235).

Merkwürdig ("strange") and grotesque, this unveiled multiplying phallus
causes Hesse to "run away," a flight which magnifies—intertextually—Hesse's
own uncanny doubling. Berger, too, "rushes" to the door and out of the
brothel; Freud "hurries" away from his Italian red-light district; Bonsels
"reels" out the Indian bordello's door, almost losing consciousness as he
gropes his way along the houses.[13] After watching another Don Juan—Max
Brod—head off to do "the thing" on a divan, Kafka "feels himself pulled
toward the exit"; like Bonsels, Kafka seems to lose consciousness: "impossible to imagine how I got into the street, it was so fast." Just as Hesse ran away
"alone" through a "grotesque" city, Kafka heads off—likewise in autumn
1911—for a "lonely," "absurd" walk home.[14] There is indeed something
merkwürdig going on here: men see brothels filled with other men and reel
in uncanny fright. They are afraid not of "the lack"—the female genitalia—
but rather of the "lack of the lack": the overproduction of penises.[15] And this
missing lack now takes on a racial quality. The dark—for Hesse, Indian—
vagina is missing, replaced by the overexposed, white phallus. This phallus
unsettles Hesse for the same reason that the general Europeanization of Asia
upset him throughout his trip. The uncanny presence of the familiar where it
ought not to be—the *horror plenitudinis* of European men—unnerves him.
Hesse describes how all such Western images "wander around like ghosts"
(*vorübergeistern*) throughout Asia, becoming "doubly spooky" because they
appear where they do not belong: "amongst Chinese and Malaysians." The
result is not a new reality, but what Hesse calls, just before returning home, a
too-familiar "unreality" (*Unwirklichkeit*) (*SW* 13:230–31).

Robert Aghion

This "unreality" appears strikingly throughout Hesse's *Aus Indien* (*Out of
India*), the collection of essays, diary entries, poems, and dream descriptions
that he published shortly after his journey. Most notably, we see this in *Out

of India's culminating hybrid masterpiece, *Robert Aghion*, which features the uncanny cross-fertilization of theoretical and popular narrative forms already prominent in Jacques' *Hot Land*.[16] Opening in essayistic style, *Aghion* recites a brief critical history of colonialism and missionarism and then transforms abruptly, in mid-paragraph, into a novella. Here, we learn the story of Robert Aghion: a young pastor who voyages eagerly to India as a missionary and exoticist, only eventually to become disillusioned with Asia and to give up his calling.

The few critics to pay attention to *Aghion* have disregarded its colonial Indian setting. Eugene Stelzig, for example, includes *Aghion* among Hesse's prewar "domestic" fictions, as if India were part of the fictional Swabian town (Gerbersau) that was the setting for many of Hesse's contemporaneous stories. According to Stelzig, *Aghion* echoes the Gerbersau stories' universal themes of developing self-will and reconciling "conscious and unconscious desires."[17] Joseph Mileck exceptionally discusses *Aghion*'s Indian backdrop but does not consider the colonial realities so central to *Aghion*. For Mileck, India is important as the catalyst for Hesse's/Aghion's discovery of religious pluralism, a theme that, Mileck claims, is wrongly overshadowed by *Aghion*'s focus on "imperialistic colonialism."[18] But if *Aghion* explicitly foregrounds imperialism, as Mileck admits, then why should the reader disregard this? This peculiar silence around *Aghion*'s colonial politics was broken only by an East German critic, Fritz Böttger, who argued in Marxist-Leninist terms that *Aghion* depicts the "exploitation and oppression of colonial peoples" through a "typical representative of the colonial exploiter-class": Aghion's brutish host, Mister Bradley.[19]

Although I agree with Böttger that *Aghion* criticizes colonialism, it is not because of *Aghion*'s negative depiction of Bradley, which comes, Böttger forgets, from a fictional character (Aghion)—not from Hesse. *Aghion* is not a straightforward exploitation narrative but rather a systemic critique of colonialism in which no one is innocent, not even the anti-colonial hero. Hesse's critique of Aghion begins with the latter's reasons for abhorring British colonialism, as embodied by Bradley. Aghion despises Bradley because he Europeanizes India, which Aghion, like Hesse, originally reveres as "authentic" and pure ("Besuch aus Indien," *SW* 13:422). Like Hesse, Aghion dreams of India's exotic flora, fauna, and "foreign nature-folk" (*fremdes Naturvolk*) (*Robert Aghion*, *SW* 8:34). And, like Hesse, he quickly becomes disenchanted with India's "brutal Europeanization." Through his self-fictionalization, Hesse casts a critical light on his own anti-colonial exoticism. Aghion, like the young Hesse, hates colonialism for disturbing India's purity and for creating what Aghion experiences as a frighteningly "uncanny" (*unheimlich*) mixture of India and Europe (8:58).

By referring to India as "*unheimlich*," Hesse's *Aghion* takes its place within a burgeoning early twentieth-century psychoanalytical discussion,[20] which, as I argue in my introduction, is more apt for understanding fin de siècle

exotic writings than is postcolonial theory. *Aghion*'s India even prefigures
Freud's 1919 essay about the unexpected return of the uncannily "long familiar" with astonishing exactness: this India is haunted by doubles, especially
during sexual adventures and particularly in mirrors; these doubles appear
as both image and reality, such that Aghion cannot distinguish between the
two; repressed infantile material recurs, specifically as homosexual desire
and the fear of castration; and, in the narratological pendant to these sexual crises, genres and voices collapse, until even the safe "ironic" distance
between narrator and character disappears (Freud, *SE* 17:252 ["ironic"]).
These sexual mirrorings, returns of the repressed, and narrative breakdowns
do more than simply illustrate *Aghion*'s thoroughgoing uncanniness. They
also present a vital historical psycho-narratological underpinning to what
today's postcolonial theorists still call "hybridity." In this way, Hesse—often
misunderstood as a romanticizer of the East—intervenes in the postcolonial
debate *avant la lettre*. He understands colonial contradictions in ways that
Kipling and Conrad did not and, in so doing, presents today's still British-
focused postcolonial theory with an essential term—uncanniness—that helps
us to comprehend colonialism especially during its pre–World War I zenith,
when the foreign world was becoming more frighteningly familiar every day.

Because *Aghion* begins in the same style as do some of the preceding essays
in *Out of India*, the first-time reader has no reason to expect anything other
than another piece of nonfiction. In this case, the topic is colonialism and
missionarism—presented from a critical, historical perspective. In the Age
of Discovery, we learn, Europeans pursued their commercial goals "narrow-
mindedly and violently"; "enlightened Christian Europeans behaved like
foxes in chicken coops throughout America, Africa, and India"; and they
"hunted and shot dead terrified natives as if they were vermin," acting
"abominably"—"crudely and swinishly thieving" wherever they could. This
critical tone diminishes by the end of *Aghion*'s first page, where we learn that
Europeans felt "shame and indignation" at their crimes during the eighteenth
century, leading them to establish an "orderly and respectable colonialism."
Missionarism, despite its many flaws, was part of this Enlightened attempt to
create a kinder, gentler colonialism; it, too, aimed to bring something "better
and nobler" to the lives of the natives (*Robert Aghion*, *SW* 8:26).[21]

As tempting as it is to view this apologia as Hesse's own—proving that
he was trapped in "the liberal ideas of his day"[22]—to do so would be to
ignore *Aghion*'s most striking formal point: that its genre shifts abruptly at
the end of the second page. The exclamation "That's enough of introduc-
tions!"[23] is followed by a turn from essay to what appears to be fiction: the
story of Aghion, told from the perspective of what we assume is a fictional
narrator, not Hesse. What is the purpose of this awkward change from essay
to novella? If Hesse was primarily interested in pointing out colonialism's
crimes and their partial reduction during the Enlightenment, then why did he
not continue with the essay format otherwise common in *Out of India*? Why

did he instead interrupt this and begin telling a story? Perhaps Hesse realized, as did Conrad a decade earlier, that colonialism's murky, unconscious contradictions surfaced more powerfully in imaginative writing than in nonfiction. But if this were so, why did he not simply delete the essayistic introduction? Or at least attribute these opening declamations, as Conrad does in *Heart of Darkness*, to a garrulous narrator—not to what seems to be Hesse himself? The fact that Hesse left this introduction intact even in a later revised version suggests that he found this genre-blurring essential to *Aghion*. It is as if Hesse realizes that his topic—colonialism's uncanny homogenization of the world—demands an equally uncanny form. Just as *Robert Aghion* tells a story about Europe and Asia becoming uncannily similar, it also shows us that a theoretical essay on this topic cannot maintain its form.

Before investigating more thoroughly how this formal blurring relates to *Aghion*'s content, let us turn to that content, which, inspired by Kipling, is straightforward: young Aghion falls in love with a native woman, only to decide in the end, for mysterious reasons, that he neither wants to marry her nor proselytize anymore, choosing instead to become a coffee plantation manager. Like Hesse before his own trip to Asia, Aghion begins with dreams of an exotic India filled with tigers, monkeys, enormous snakes, and fabulous butterflies. But he discovers upon arrival that India has already been thoroughly Europeanized, primarily by Englishmen such as the domineering businessman Bradley, who is intent on re-creating English customs in India.

Because such contact with "European sailors and businessmen" has "corrupt[ed]" the Indians, Aghion decides midway through the story to head for the hinterlands. He presses deeper into the wilderness, like the hero of *Hot Land*, in search of unspoiled "simple country people" (*Robert Aghion*, *SW* 8:43). Riding his horse far into the palm-treed hills, he finally arrives in a peaceful valley that contains a single-room clay hut. Inside is an Indian family with a beautiful teenaged daughter, Naissa. Aghion repeats here Hesse's own ogling of pubescent girls in 1911 Sumatra by staring at Naissa's "smooth bare shoulders," "young mouth," and naked breasts, then running his fingers through her "soft, sleek hair." Aghion gives Naissa a present of metal cosmetic scissors. In gratitude, she presses her "flowerlike lips" against his hand, causing him sexual excitement. When he asks her how old she is, she says, "I don't know" (*SW* 8:45–46). Uneducated, virtually mute, and living far from European traders, Naissa becomes the perfect combination of virgin girl and virgin territory that Hesse himself had been unable to find. Aghion seems to have discovered the paradisiacal "joy" and "true, natural, self-sufficient way of life" that had eluded his author (8:45).

But here Aghion's troubles begin. That same night, after returning to the home he shares with Bradley, Aghion senses that this "bachelors' house" has become "*unheimlich*" (*SW* 8:47). He has a strange dream about Bradley and about Naissa, where, in the end, Aghion kisses Naissa on the mouth. Confusing "all his emotions and urges [*Triebe*]," this dream creates in Aghion the "half-conscious impulse" and "instinctive need" (*triebhafte(s) Bedürfnis*) to get up and walk toward Bradley's bedroom. He creeps quietly across the veranda, pushes open Bradley's door, and tiptoes toward his bed. After opening the mosquito netting and preparing to whisper Bradley's name, Aghion realizes that Bradley, wearing only a thin silk nightdress, is not alone. Next to him lies a Hindu woman. Aghion flees the room, but, too "excited" to sleep, he stays up for the rest of the night reading his Bible. The following morning, Aghion confronts Bradley on moral-religious grounds. Bradley is enraged at this invasion of his privacy and orders Aghion out of his house. Aghion agrees to depart, claiming that he can no longer live in this house anyway, especially considering what he vaguely terms his "unsatisfied desires" (8:50–52).

The story continues later that day with Bradley and Aghion sitting down and reconciling, feeling "closer to one another" than ever before (*SW* 8:54). But Aghion nonetheless decides to leave Bradley, resign as a missionary, and propose marriage to Naissa. Bradley finds the idea of marrying Indians—who resemble "little animals"—absurd, but Aghion is unfazed (8:56). He returns resolutely to Naissa's hut to propose and, just outside the hut, sees a girl whom he recognizes as Naissa. But she does not acknowledge him, even tries to avoid him until he offers her another present: this time, an enamel tin, which he opens for her, revealing a mirror inside. As before, he begins stroking her hair and bare arm, and imagines what it will be like to kiss her on the mouth. Suddenly, however, Aghion becomes "terrified" by another, "spook-like" apparition emerging from the hut. It is "a second Naissa, a mirror image [*Spiegelbild*] of the first, and the mirror image [*Spiegelbild*] smiled at him." Twice identified by Aghion as a mirror image, this *Spiegelbild* gestures to Aghion by lifting his metal scissors high above her head. Instead of simply going to this second Naissa—who turns out to be the "real" one, the sister of the first—and proposing to her, Aghion stands still. Shocked, he watches as his "love" for Naissa eerily breaks apart and disintegrates "into two halves just like the image of the girl [*Mädchenbild*], which had doubled so unexpectedly and uncannily [*unheimlich*] before his eyes" (8:58). Aghion now leaves Naissa behind, never to return. This hallucinatory scene in the story's penultimate paragraph leaves us with *Aghion*'s main question: why is this image—*Spiegelbild* and *Mädchenbild*—so terrifyingly *unheimlich* that it causes Aghion to run away from the woman he claims to love?

On the surface, Naissa and her sister appear to be absolutely exotic and therefore lacking the whiff of familiarity (*Heim*) necessary for *Unheimlichkeit* in the Freudian sense. But it is ultimately this absolute exoticism that renders them uncannily familiar. Dark, young, deerlike, and barely able to speak English, they embody what Aghion calls a Western "prejudice"—a cliché—about Indian girls: "they" all look alike; their "pretty" faces are impossible to tell apart. Always the moral counterpoint to Bradley, who has "a good deal of respect for prejudices," Aghion originally spoke out against these, claiming that Naissa was unique. But it turns out that Bradley's racial discourse has had a greater effect on Aghion than he knows. After the frightening moment of mistaken identity, Aghion could have sorted out the differences between the girls and still proposed to Naissa (he "gradually recognizes" the "real Naissa"). But it is already too late. The shock of the *Spiegelbild* awakened in him a belief that he did not know he held: that Indian girls are, he claims, indeed "barely distinguishable from one another." He goes so far as to repeat unwittingly Bradley's metaphor for the girls, against which he had rebelled just one day earlier. Bradley had claimed that the girls looked like "pretty deer [*Rehe*]"; Aghion now says that "two deer [*Rehe*] could not look more alike" (*SW* 8:56, 58).

By having Aghion repeat these stereotypes, Hesse presents us with a "belated," typically German, form of colonial stereotyping. It occurs after the encounter described by Homi Bhabha, in which the colonialist arrived in time still to see the native's difference (both from other natives and from the colonialist) and then to "disavow" this difference through the "fetish" of stereotype.[24] Aghion, conversely, arrives in a colonial world already so fully stereotyped that the subtle distinctions within the other culture have long been effaced. This produces an anxiety beyond the fear of difference and so demands a conceptual tool other than fetishism. Whereas Bhabha's (Freudian) fetishist ambivalently disavows a difference that he knows to be true (the mother's genitalia, the colonized person's culture), the belated traveler to the world of established stereotypes sees no original truth, just an endless series of confusingly similar images. He arrives in an *unheimlich* world that can be best comprehended through this analytic lens.

Instead of fearing difference-within-sameness, as Bhabha would have it, Aghion fears the *unheimlich* confusion created by too-similar images and, with this, a confusion of representation with reality. The "image of the girl" (*Mädchenbild*) is uncanny not because it splits in two but because this splitting renders it at once actual and spectral: it blurs the line, as in Ernst Jentsch's theory, between the animate and the inanimate. The "spook-like" second Naissa (who is actually the first) has the same effect as the doll Freud describes in E. T. A. Hoffmann's "The Sandman": it makes the hero wonder whether he is in love with a woman or a puppet, a human or an image of a human. Far from creating a stereotype to disavow the truth and stabilize his world, Aghion enters a world already so satiated with stereotyped images that he cannot, even if he wanted to, discover a truth to disavow. He cannot even distinguish an original from a copy. First, he calls Naissa, not her sister, the *Spiegelbild*. Then, after apparently distinguishing the one from the other, he insists that there is no "first": not the *Mädchen* (Naissa) splits in two but rather the *Mädchenbild* does, suggesting that the starting point all along was the image (*Bild*), not the person. Aghion's colonial/sexual crisis is a crisis of representation. The image preempts reality—questioning, as in Jentsch's and Freud's theories, the primacy of the real over the imaginary. On a conceptual level, this muddying emphasizes the *unheimlich* nature of "stereotypes" in general: they are images that appear, like ghosts, to become frighteningly "solid" (*stereós*) in space.

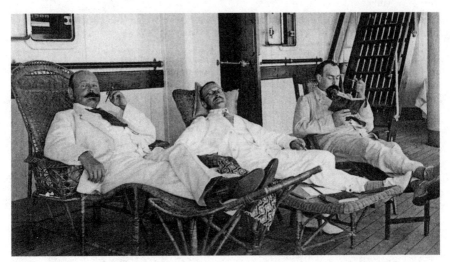

Figure 16. Hesse (*middle*) and Hans Sturzenegger (*right*) aboard the *Prinz Eitel Friedrich*, bound for Colombo in 1911

This stereotyping proves contagious when it catalyzes a second uncanny doubling: this time, of Aghion's own male image. When the Indian girl becomes the same within her difference, producing a solidified image that seems to come to life, her suitor likewise congeals into a stereotypical *Bild*. "They" all look alike, but so do "we." When Aghion shows the "wrong" Naissa how to open the enamel tin, he inevitably sees in its mirror more than just her (already a *Spiegelbild* of her sister). He also sees himself, a white-suited European in the tropics (figure 16). As in Freud's experience with the mirrored door in his wagon-lit from *The Uncanny*, Aghion sees here his doppelgänger. This sight returns Aghion, like Freud, to the memory of the "archaic" superstition that civilized Europeans claim to have surmounted: that every double is an "uncanny harbinger of death" (*SE* 17:248n1, 235).[25]

Aghion's mirror image is uncanny not only within the story but also within its historical context. When Aghion looks in the mirror, he sees more than just a man in a tropical suit. He also sees this man touching a destitute Indian girl who is willing to do nearly anything for gifts. As such, Aghion sees himself here as Bradley, the stereotypical phallic European in the colonies: the "domineering-looking" man with "tan dark-haired hands" and "white tropical clothing" who has his way with Indian concubines (*SW* 8:32–33). Aghion even adopts Bradley's diction for these "pretty" Indian girls; for Aghion too, they now resemble deer (8:58). By discovering his own uncanny resemblance to the phallic European on tour, Aghion again echoes Hesse, who realized he was a comic "Don Juan" among comic Don Juans in an Oriental brothel. Hesse's observation of his own doubling in an exotic brothel reveals another prefiguring of Freud: of the above-mentioned foreign red-light district that

Freud chose to illustrate the production of "uncanny" feelings. For both Hesse and Freud, the foreign brothel was *the* example of that "same place" to which "we," in delight and horror, always return: to "our" own male genitalia. This horrific return helps to explain, together with the spook-like doubling of the *Mädchenbild*, Aghion's *unheimlich* crisis.

A third doubling further elucidates why Aghion flees the final scene with Naissa: the doubling of his "love" (*Liebe*), which "disintegrated into two halves just like the image of the girl [*Mädchenbild*]" and in so doing recalls the split in Aghion's desire between heterosexuality and homosexuality. When Aghion crept into Bradley's bedroom and discovered him sleeping half-naked with the Hindu woman, Aghion claimed to be "excited" by the woman and "disgusted" by Bradley. But beneath this professed heterophilia lurks a strong homo-longing: a desire to "make a friend" of Bradley, as Aghion said to himself a few minutes earlier (*SW* 8:51, 50). This desire repeatedly creates in Aghion the "instinctive need" to be close to Bradley, explaining why he always has "unsatisfied desires" in Bradley's home (8:50, 52). Because this desire doubles his "love"—as "homo" and "hetero"—it is no surprise that Aghion uses the same word to describe his "bachelors' household" with Bradley as he did to describe his divided love at the end: both are "*unheimlich*" (8:47). Aghion's homosexuality becomes the distorted double of his heterosexuality, eerily almost the same but not quite.

This bachelor's desire is uncanny also for cultural-political reasons: Aghion's longing for the "same"—"*homós*"—threatens his dreamed-of Indian heterotopia in the same way that Bradley's colonial homogenizing had. Aghion professes desire for a dark *heimlich* (mysterious) feminized Indian subcontinent but harbors a longing for a *heimisch* (homey) European man. To penetrate the former, he must suppress the latter, and this is what leads to the "painful confusion" of his urges and the "confusion of all his affairs" (*SW* 8:50, 53). It also explains why, immediately after feeling "closer" to Bradley than ever before, he inexplicably and abruptly decides to marry Naissa at all costs. Aghion hopes that marrying Naissa will protect his heterophilia against his secret desire for what Bradley calls "*meinesgleichen*" (the "likes of me"; literally, "my same ones") (8:56). But Aghion undermines this hope when he returns, after each of his meetings with Naissa, to Bradley's "leathery English mug" (8:58).

Aghion's doublings (Naissa/sister; Aghion/Bradley; hetero/homo) illustrate the two fears of sameness—homosexuality and race-mixing—at the heart of fin de siècle exoticism. At first glance, Aghion's desires for Bradley and for Naissa seem opposed. With Bradley, Aghion longs for his European brother; with Naissa, his Indian other. But because intermarriage with Naissa could end up producing a homo-racial—mulatto—universe, it, like homosexuality, threatens Aghion's proclaimed heterophilia. Aghion's vague reference to "unpermitted contact" (*unerlaubter Umgang*) calls to mind the imperial German parliament's much-publicized 1912 debate about prohibiting interracial marriages in the colonies, and it reveals the ultimate paradox in Aghion's anti-colonial exoticism (*SW* 8:52).[26] Aghion hates colonialism because it homogenizes the world, undermining his capacity to "conceive otherwise."[27] But *Aghion*'s final scene demonstrates how this capacity is uncomfortably bound up with the colonial ideology it claims to resist. Sexual mixing with Naissa would confound Aghion's wishes because he, like the anti-"hybridity" racists of his day, needs to maintain a pure other (a "foreign nature-folk") to satisfy his desire for difference.[28]

Within this sexual crucible, we see the political ambivalence in the wider discourse of fin de siècle exoticism: the exoticist's hatred of colonialism sometimes coincides with his vision of racial purity. The exoticist needs to stay away from his European brother *and* his Indian other. And although this heterophilic non-engagement policy might sound peaceful, it covers a deeper desire to thrust away violently all forms of similarity: first the Indian girl, whose eroticism threatens Aghion with the end of difference, and then the Englishman, who has beaten him to India and taken from him his virginal "place in the sun." Psychoanalytically, we have here the bridge between Freud's "uncanny" and Lacan's "mirror stage," a connection that Lacan never mentioned: the *uncanniness* of the distorted image in the mirror—its foreign-familiarity—spawns the subject's aggression.[29]

Returning now to my earlier formal question: how do these exoticist sexual and political contradictions connect to *Aghion*'s structure, especially to the slips in narrative perspective that start with the opening's shift in genres? If Hesse indeed realizes in the big picture that a text about the uncanny homogenization of the world cannot maintain a discrete genre, how does he understand the smaller formal blurrings that occur throughout *Aghion*? Just as *Aghion*'s beginning moves uneasily from what seemed to be Hesse's authorial voice to his fictional narratorial one, this new narratorial third-person perspective becomes remarkably labile throughout *Aghion*, slipping back and forth between omniscience and focalization—including free indirect style. Omniscience dominates the story's first half, when the narrator uses epithets to remind us of his ironic detachment from his protagonist (Aghion is the "young theologian," the "Indian candidate," the "drowsy apostle," etc.), but, during Aghion's erotically charged meeting with Naissa, the perspective shifts, for the first significant time, to focalization (*SW* 8:28, 30). This occurs strikingly in mid-sentence when Aghion first sees Naissa:

> The Englishman set his hand gently and embarrassedly on her and pronounced a greeting, and, while he felt the soft sleek hair alive in his fingers, she lifted her face to him and smiled friendly at him out of her lovely eyes. (*Der Engländer legte freundlich und befangen seine Hand darauf und sprach einen Gruß, und während er das weiche geschmeidige Haar lebendig in seinen Fingern fühlte, hob sie das Gesicht zu ihm auf und lächelte freundlich aus wunderschönen Augen.*) (8:46)

The narrator's initial detachment from Aghion ("the Englishman") disappears by the sentence's midpoint, when he describes from Aghion's perspective how Naissa's soft hair feels in his hand: "alive in his fingers." The narrator then loses all distance by reporting Aghion's sentimental judgment of Naissa's "lovely" (*wunderschönen*) eyes smiling on him—without any irony or attribution.

As abruptly as this focalization appears, it now disappears. Just two sentences later, the narrator detaches himself again from Aghion, and, as in *Aghion*'s first half, epithetically: "Thus she stood in her simple beauty before the astonished stranger." But by the next sentence, narrative proximity returns again: "The moist fragrance of her hair and the sight of her bare shoulders and breasts confused him such that he soon cast his eyes down from her innocent gaze [*vor ihrem unschuldigem Blick*]" (*SW* 8:46). By un-ironically relating Aghion's judgment of "innocence," the narrator loses critical distance from Aghion; the narrative and figural perspectives collapse.

It is tempting to attribute these slips to Hesse's lack of perspectival control, until we notice that they occur primarily when, as in this first meeting with Naissa, Aghion is erotically excited; that is, when his "half-conscious impulses," "instinctive needs," and "unsatisfied desires" come to the fore. Later in the story, for example, when Aghion visits Bradley's bedroom and falls into confusion, the narrator again abruptly drops all epithets and zooms in, once more inhabiting Aghion's viewpoint: "He almost wanted to curse all of India or at least his curiosity and wanderlust, which had led him to this impasse." The same perspectival collapse occurs when Aghion mistakes Naissa's sister for his beloved: "the gulf between him and her suddenly seemed monstrous." As further evidence of Hesse's deliberateness, these sexually catalyzed focalizations are followed immediately, as in the scene when Aghion first met Naissa, by returns to omniscience and irony: the narrator describes Aghion as "the missionary" and "the smitten Aghion" (*SW* 8:51, 58). That all these scenes follow the same narrative pattern suggests a literary strategy: stable narrative omniscience gives way in libidinally charged scenes to focalization, which is followed by a return to omniscience, and so on.

Returning to *Aghion*'s large-scale formal movement (from stable omniscient narration in the first half to focalization and lability in the second), we likewise see a mirroring of psychological states: both Aghion's and the narrator's, whom we must now consider as a character in the story.[30] Aghion begins the tale as an observing anthropologist or, in literary terms, a distanced narrator: noting, from a safe remove, the natives' religious rituals, their language, and the beauty of their flora and fauna. During this section, the narrator, likewise, plays the role of a detached literary anthropologist, whose object of study is not India but Aghion himself. When Aghion meets Naissa and becomes an actor, not an observer, the narrator also loses his distance from his object (Aghion). By leaping onto the erotic stage, Aghion becomes uncannily "theatrical": a subject and an object at once.[31] And he takes his narrator with him. From Aghion's first meeting with Naissa, when he ostentatiously caresses her in front of her observing family, the narrator, too, moves from being an observer of Aghion to an object whose shared touching of Naissa we watch. This loss of the narrator's implied "I" (*Ich*) within the perspective of Aghion's "he" (*Er*) is strongest in the story's final half, but it continues a trajectory of ego loss that is already suggested in *Aghion*'s opening pages. What at first seemed to be the "I" of the author, Hesse, dissolved into the implied, fictional "I" of a narrator, which eventually lost itself within the "he" of the character.

Samuel Weber correctly views such narratological confoundings of the first and third person as "uncannily" illustrative of psychoanalysis's first-person ego's (*Ich* or "I") entanglement within the third-person id (*Es* or "it").[32] But Weber's point must be expanded from psychoanalysis to ethnography—to writing about (other) people—in the broadest sense. The narrator's/anthropologist's/analyst's "I" needs to get close to "him" to understand him, but this very closeness destabilizes the "I." Because this uncanny confusion of observer and object is a problem of *perspective*, it is no coincidence that Freud—as if learning from Hesse—describes this in literary terms: "ironical" stories, regardless of their content, never strike us as uncanny because we, as readers, are safely ensconced in the "superior" position of the narrator. Like the narrator's ironic "I," we, too, know more than the third-person character; we "do not share his error." Uncanniness occurs only when, as in *Aghion*, the narrator/anthropologist drops this ironic distance and, in Freud's words, puts himself in the "place" of the character (or the native or the patient, in anthropology and psychoanalysis) (Freud, *SE* 17:252). As we have seen in *Aghion* and will see again in my following chapter, the stakes of this uncanny removal of distance are high: the narrator's "I" destabilizes such that the whole process of observation seems impossible.

If uncanniness also implies a fear of castration—and Freud insists that it does—then we must understand this, too, in narrative terms: as a story told by the male subject (by "little Hans," by Freud himself, by Aghion) to protect himself from dissolution.[33] Like Freud's little Hans, Aghion generates his castration horror—Naissa "triumphantly" raising the scissors over her head—out of a fear of becoming the same as her, both sexually and culturally. But Hesse supplies a twist to Freud's narrative. Whereas little Hans began with an assumption of sameness (his sister once had a penis too), Aghion, the true exoticist, begins with a presupposition of difference: Naissa has always been absolutely different from him, and he needs desperately to preserve this (distinguishing Aghion again from Bhabha's difference-fearing colonialist). When Naissa shows the scissors triumphantly, wanting to identify herself as the "real" Naissa whom Aghion plans to marry, Aghion becomes afraid. It is precisely this claim to conjugal rights that causes his crisis: she becomes a "spook" who "frightens" him (*SW* 8:58). He now sees in her not only the hallucinatory double of her sister but also the future bearer, through "unpermitted contact," of an uncanny race;[34] not surprisingly, he views her brother with "displeasure" at the thought of becoming his "brother-in-law" (8:57). Unlike the usual *vagina dentata*, Naissa's threatening femininity is here racialized as the *vagina nigra*. Its darkness threatens the whiteness of Aghion's penis. More important, through its promise of mixed offspring, it endangers the darkness of India itself, which Aghion, the unrepentant exoticist, wants to preserve at all costs.

This looming slice through Aghion's identity corresponds to the final cut in the text, when, after Aghion's *unheimlich* hallucination with Naissa and her sister, the text, too, suffers a blackout. During a paragraph break, Aghion is somehow transferred back to Bradley's home. When the story resumes, Aghion's already fractured perspective is completely gone. We discover nothing of his emotions after his fateful encounter because the narrator has again distanced himself from Aghion ("the departing one"). Aghion prepares quietly to leave for the coffee plantation he will manage. For the first time in the text, the narrator is perspectivally now slightly closer to Bradley, whose own perspective opens this paragraph: "Bradley learned nothing of this incident [Aghion's second meeting with Naissa], and he asked no questions." By the end of this final paragraph, the narrator's own increasingly unstable perspective vanishes, too, and he hands over the final word to Bradley. As if to emphasize Bradley's complete narrative usurpation, the narrator grants him the immediacy of direct speech. Bradley seems to be talking not only with Aghion but also directly with us: "'Bon voyage, my boy! A time will come later when you will be dying with longing to see an honest leathery English mug [*Engländerkopf*] again instead of those sweet Hindu snouts! Then you will come to me, and we will agree [*werden . . . einig sein*] about all the things we still see so differently today'" (*SW* 8:58).

This final sentence may seem to reassure Aghion of the absolute exotic difference between "us" and "them," but, beneath the surface, this image of the *Engländerkopf* likely troubles Aghion with further uncanniness. If Aghion is indeed a thinly disguised version of Hesse, as most critics agree,[35] then the English Bradley disturbs Aghion not only because he ruins his fantasy of a pure India. As an Englishman, Bradley is also Hesse's/Aghion's "relative": uncannily almost the same but not quite. Emil Nolde called the British he met in Southeast Asia "our cousins."[36] But it would be more accurate to consider them as "our grandparents." As discussed in chapter 1, British travelers to Southeast Asia preceded the fin de siècle Germans by at least two generations, and, more literally, their Hanoverian Queen Victoria—the Empress of India—was Kaiser Wilhelm's grandmother. This family romance adds a national-psychological twist to Aghion's final hallucinations. When an early twentieth-century German traveler feels his longing for an Englishman, he remembers not only his homosexual but also his incestuous desires. If, as Gilles Deleuze and Félix Guattari claim, our relation to our grandparents tends toward "psycho[sis]" (and toward neurosis with our parents), then we can begin to explain Aghion's erotic sleepwalking in Bradley's bedroom, his blackout when seeing himself as Bradley in the mirror, and his repeated returns to Bradley after each visit to Naissa.[37] The Englishman is what the German traveler vehemently wants and does not want. The German longs to be near to these grandparents yet resists them, not least because he still harbors a more correct, "straighter" fantasy: of an undeveloped, utterly exotic "virgin territory" that he still might be the first to penetrate.

As Freud writes thirteen years later, the "dark continent" should be the site of *female* sexuality. But, as in *Hot Land*, this fantasy is long impossible. The British phallus is always already in the tropics, preceding the Germans and so despoiling their dreamed-of feminized "place in the sun." The historical result was the Germans' erratic game of attraction and repulsion with the British. This game's most public player, the number one German himself—the "traveling Kaiser," Wilhelm II—alternatively fawned before and bombastically challenged his Hanoverian-British ancestors throughout the colonies in the decades preceding World War I.[38]

Because *Robert Aghion*'s colonial master gets the final word, Hesse's story might be seen as a cynical defense of colonialism, reminding us of the apologia from the narrator's opening peroration; the lesson here would be that even sensitive travelers like Aghion, who initially love the natives, inevitably learn to despise them and long for good old Europeans. But, as in Conrad's *Heart of Darkness*, where the megalomaniac Kurtz's words—"Exterminate the brutes!"—ring in our ears after we finish reading, a closer examination of *Aghion* suggests a more complex message. For *Aghion* is not only about the relation between Europeans and non-Europeans but also about an uncanniness that extends to intra-European relations and, what is more, an intertextual realm. Hesse's Aghion goes into the hinterlands only to find there a version of the same brutal European we already know from other adventure books, both "high" and "low." A relative of Conrad's Kurtz, Jacques' "crazy" German, and Kafka's contemporaneous officer from "In the Penal Colony," Bradley knows the best way to deal with "Hindu snouts": with a gun. This violent European in the tropics is uncanny in the senses both of terrifying and of hauntingly familiar. Like Kafka's officer, whose uniform reminds us of "home" (*Heimat*), this historical figure is "uniform": disturbingly like "us."[39] Such "uncanny white men" run through modernist and popular culture in the pre–World War I era;[40] like the replicating sex tourists that Aghion sees in the mirror, they are everywhere. My point is not that Aghion becomes one of them, although he does (ultimately deciding to "conquer this land for himself"),[41] but that this becoming "uniform" haunts him and the entire colonial project, leading to the text's hallucinatory breakdown in its final pages (*SW* 8:53).

By creating yet another uncanny white man, Hesse asks: If "we" go to the exotic world looking for savages but instead find this doubled, "uniform" European who reminds us of ourselves, are we even going to the right place? If yes, are we going there to conquer ourselves? Our cousins? Our grandparents? Aghion's experience suggests as much. At the far end of the world, next to the hut of a beautiful half-naked Indian girl, he looks in a mirror and sees a European in a white tropical suit: himself, but also Germany's British grandparents, who attract and repel him—just as they did Nolde, Bonsels, and Wegener. And Germany will of course fight these grandparents only one year later for control of Europe and of the colonial world.

This turning inward of colonialism's crisis reveals the conceptual value of uncanniness for understanding both *Aghion* and the colonial theater around 1900. Like Bhabha's "hybridity," "uncanniness" describes a world that is frightening in its almost-sameness. But the horror of uncanniness, unlike that of hybridity, results primarily from a surfeit of the "long familiar" (not of "difference"). This surplus of familiar-foreignness allows us better to comprehend why *Aghion*'s "European sailors and businessmen," including Bradley, haunt Aghion. Bradley represents a series of "uniform" doppelgänger appearing in the colonial world (and in books about it), and Aghion, too, begins to see himself as one of these men. When such uncanny white men meet, they experience not only the horror of doubling but also, as in *Aghion* and Freud's *The Uncanny*, existential unmooring. Images (their own and others') blur with reality; repressed infantile desires and fears return; and perspectival differences collapse until there is no safe "ironic" position.

By matching thematic uncanniness with perspectival instability—an authorial essay-voice gives way to a fictional narratorial *Ich* that gives way to a figural *Er*—Hesse hints at an ethnographic uncanniness that, as we will see in the next chapter, Freud eventually discovers in *The Uncanny*: every subject is in danger of becoming the object of someone else's gaze.[42] Uncanniness is thus the predicament of culture itself, with the crises of colonialism simply rendering this predicament most visible.[43] Aghion, the sovereign European observer of the Indian girls, is also the narrator's ironic plaything ("the sleepy apostle," "the new arrival") (*SW* 8:30, 33). But this narrator, too, exposes himself to his readers by losing himself, with Aghion, on the sexual stage. By the story's end, the narrator suffers a castration anxiety equivalent to Aghion's: just as Aghion upsettingly becomes almost the same as Bradley and every other colonist, the narrator becomes almost the same as the doubled character whom he has been observing. Having lost his distance from Aghion, the narrator, too, becomes a phallic repetition, a mirror image, a "spook."

Aghion's complex ethnography shows us how any observing *Ich* is never far from becoming the observed *Er*. This threatens the reader, too, especially if we consider him to be a male German who, like Jünger's 1913 hero, reads books about "adventurers" to inspire his own travels (Jünger, *Afrikanische Spiele*, 9). When reading *Aghion*, this future adventurer senses the risk of becoming someone else's object and even a victim of that person's violence—like the male subordinates of Jacques' "Wolf." By depicting such an uncanny colonial world, Hesse, like Jacques, unsettles mainstream exotic fantasies. If all virgin territories are breached and all travelers are threatened by homo-genization, then the traditional penetration narrative could reverse itself. It could turn against the European, in the forms of war and sexual violence, as hinted by Bradley's "powerful" handshake at the end, which guarantees that Aghion will someday "die with longing" in relation to this "*Engländerkopf.*" When Hesse ends his story about India with this compelling attraction and repulsion between an Englishman and a German just one year before war begins, he is telling us about more than just colonialism. He is describing the fate of exotic desire during the swan song of the first globalization, when the concentric circles of homogenization fears grew ever tighter—leading Europeans to thrust away all forms of similarity in the desperate chase for difference. This *unheimlich* dread of similarity, which Hesse presents as the key to understanding his own global world, adds an even greater threat to Bradley's apparently peaceful final promise to Aghion: You will one day "come to me," Bradley assures him, and we will then be "united" (*einig*) about all the things over which we now "differ" (*SW* 8:58).

Hesse's Indian Fairy Tale

Given this sophisticated aesthetics in *Robert Aghion*, it initially seems surprising that Hesse's vision of India eventually takes its well-known idealizing turn. This idealization begins after Hesse comes back from the Far East in December 1911. Although many of the Indian pieces that Hesse wrote for magazines after returning to Europe remained true to the uncanny events recorded in his diaries, several of these works feature deliberate distortions. A December 1913 essay, for example, transforms what Hesse originally called "brutally Europeanized" Ceylon (Sri Lanka) into "colorful Ceylon, unreal, like a fairy tale": a "beautiful improbable dream" painted in "loud abundant colors" ("Tagebuch der Indonesienreise," *SW* 11:336; "Nikobaren," 13:210). Hesse similarly converts Penang's "Europeanized Chinese theater" with its annoyingly familiar elements (a "backdrop, painted in perspective," European seats, "electric lights") into a purely Chinese stage with "nothing European" at all (*SW* 11:338; "Abend in Asien," 13:218). And a poem, "Fluß im Urwald," likewise transforms a jungle filled with creepy German expatriates and Dutch loggers into a prehistoric paradise, unchanged for "a hundred thousand years" and filled with tigers, elephants, and jaguars—all animals that never appear in Hesse's diary and one (the jaguar) that does not even exist in Asia (*SW* 11:348–51; "Fluß im Urwald," 10:176).

When not idealizing India, Hesse often simply crops Europeans and Europeanized natives from it, as Pechstein would do two years later in Palau: the "bad European" music disappears as do the Sturzenegger brothers, leaving Hesse alone among Sumatrans pulling "sarongs over their hips," untying turbans, and staring "dumb and sober into the damp morning" ("Tagebuch der Indonesienreise," *SW* 11:343, 351; "Hanswurst," "Nacht auf Deck," 13:226,

247). Hesse similarly retouches the Sri Lankan city of Kandy, which, in his diaries, was a "corrupted" "tourist town" awash with beggars, salesmen, and Westernized dandies; in 1913 he sees here only the "primitive natural humanity" of "half-naked Sinhalese youth" (*SW* 11:375–76; "Spaziergang in Kandy," 13:269). Hesse even reconfigures his final experience in Asia. A banal hike up a mountain interrupted by thoughts of whether his diarrhea was improving ("intestines feeling better") becomes an exotic event par excellence: he discovers a landscape free of Europeans and has a vision of the "plain, simple, childlike inhabitants of paradise" (*SW* 11:380; "Pedrotalla-galla," 13:278).

These idealizations become more pronounced as the years pass, most notably in the 1917 essay he wrote for an exhibition of Hans Sturzenegger's paintings: "Memory of India." Here, Hesse reduces his "Indian disappoint-ments" to two small details: the "slightly" Europeanized Indian port cities and one Europeanized theater. The rest of this essay creates the exotic India that Hesse never actually saw. He begins by transforming Penang from a town "ruined" by "terrible" European goods and streetcars that cut through wilderness into an exotic postcard: "savage, colorful swarming masses," "shy naked children," and "dark, rowing fishermen in primeval boats!" ("Tage-buch der Indonesienreise," *SW* 11:339; "Erinnerung an Indien," 13:379). The Sumatran jungle likewise loses its surfeit of European furniture and men, fea-turing instead only "reed roofs on huts," "black naked youths," and "a pair of peering black eyes shining from behind a palm trunk." And Palembang metamorphoses from a stinking tourist trap filled with cheap Dutch detec-tive novels, tasteless European shops, and Malaysians in European clothing into a thrilling, Sumatran Venice: a city on stilts above a powerful river, trav-eled by thousands of native "floating merchants" who offer carpets, fruit, and Mohammedan prayer books ("Erinnerung an Indien," 13:380). Even the Malaysians and Sinhalese metamorphose from uncannily adept mimics of European manners and languages to tantalizing fetish objects: "soft," "sad," "beautiful," "doe-eyed," and "obliging." Together with the Chinese, whom Hesse had always found more "authentic," these figures now embody South-east Asia's enticing strangeness.[44] Wide metal combs pin back their hair, as it rises up outlandishly above "magnificent serious faces" (13:381).

This 1917 "Memory" hardens into the stereotypical India that accompanies Hesse for the rest of his life: "quiet, pathless primeval jungles," "fairy-tale-like childhood conditions of humanity," and the mysterious "stuttering of a beggar in a murmured, foreign tongue" ("Erinnerung an Indien," *SW* 13:378, 381). Hesse's whitewashing of his 1911 experiences is so effective that it fools most of his readers: the fin de siècle German exoticists, the 1970s American hippies, and today's literary critics—even though these critics had access to his 1911 diaries. Ralph Freedman seems deliberately to misread the diaries, claiming that they do not ring "true" because they focus on "the noise, the beggars, the dirt" and that Hesse was only able to describe accurately his experiences later, in "Memory."[45] But the opposite is the case. Hesse transformed the globalized, uncanny India that he experienced into the nostalgic one that Freedman now reads as true.[46] Joseph Mileck similarly claims that Hesse's journey to India resulted in "little more than a purely physical experience" and that Hesse had his first "meaningful spiritual encounter with the Orient" in *Siddartha*.[47] But precisely because Hesse's diaries, like *Robert Aghion*, focus on "physical experience," they speak a truth that *Siddartha*'s spiritual abstractions—which repress this knowledge—do not. Albert Ehrenstein wrote insightfully already in 1914 that Hesse's "unadorned" early writings about Asia, including *Robert Aghion*, admirably discovered the "unreality" of Western affairs among Indians and Malaysians; as if predicting the future, Ehrenstein claimed that these early writings surpassed many of Hesse's other works, which tended to drift into idealization and "unrestrained lyricism."[48]

What brings Hesse to the overly lyricist, exoticized image of India that is so familiar to us from *Siddartha* (1922), *Die Morgenlandfahrt* (*The Journey to the East*; 1932), and parts of *Das Glasperlenspiel* (*The Glass Bead Game*; 1943)? The answer lies, as with Jacques, in the uncanny encounter. Like Jacques, Hesse traveled to the ends of the earth expecting utter foreignness—the ox-cart idyll of his parents and grandparents—only to discover modernity. Indonesia was "brutally" Europeanized: "More than the fever," this violent homogenization of Southeast Asia shocked and depressed him ("Architektur," *SW* 13:229). Indeed, the irritating effects of India's Westernization preceded Hesse's dysentery, causing him, even before his diarrhea sets in, to give up his goal of visiting his mother's birthplace on the Indian mainland. With the political uncanny too much for him to take, Hesse was not about to tempt the psychological one.[49] This uncanniness led Hesse to write a disturbing work—*Robert Aghion*—which, like Jacques' *Hot Land*, uncompromisingly depicted the trauma of globalization's foreign-familiarity in terms of both content and form. But Hesse, like Jacques, eventually turns away from this insight, as if it were too much for him to take. Like Hesse with *Siddartha*, Jacques followed his uncanny *Hot Land* with a best-selling description of an unadulterated exotic paradise: *Pirath's Island* (1917). The same goes for Bonsels, who overwrote the uncannily foreign-familiar India he saw in 1903–4 with an exoticized 1916 account, *Indian Journey*: he creates there a girl "almost still the age of a child" lying naked in the *Urwald* with her small breasts exposed, a wild tiger, and an endless stream of "brown, naked figures" (*Indienfahrt*, 92–93, 132, 217).

Hesse differs from Jacques and Bonsels (and Nolde) in that this trauma does not lead him toward the political right: he does not imagine that nationalism or fascism will protect him from the uncanny mixture of categories and people. While Jacques and Bonsels began propagandizing for the imperial German war machine during World War I,[50] Hesse spoke out against nationalism, claiming that his Indian experience had taught him to accept all cultures and all peoples.[51] In the decades following his Indian journey, then, Hesse's conservatism is primarily aesthetic. He develops a strategy of cropping reminiscent of Pechstein's paintings: he systematically purges modern Europe from his work about the East, creating an anachronistic oriental "paradise." Disavowing the truths of "physical experience" at the heart of *Robert Aghion*, Hesse uncovers the spiritual idealization that dominates his work from "Memory of India" and *Siddartha* onward.

Although Hesse did not adopt Jacques', Nolde's, or Bonsels's nationalism, we can see in him hints of the political effects of the fin de siècle uncanny encounter. Hesse, too, discovers the disturbing similarity of the exotic world in the age of the apparent end of alterity. And Hesse, too, is shocked by this encounter. It leads him to purge India of its uncanniness so rigorously that most readers do not even know of Hesse's 1911 diaries or of *Aghion*— assuming instead that he always described India as he did a decade later in *Siddartha*, or, after this, in the "Indischer Lebenslauf" section of *The Glass Bead Game*.

Before this, the political fright of this uncanny encounter produced, in *Robert Aghion*, aesthetic innovation. And this same blurring of identities led to a new mixing of aesthetic cultures, registers, and categories throughout Europe. I think not only of the Africanizing of European art through artists' visits to European ethnographic museums around 1900 and of Carl Einstein's 1915 *Negerplastik*[52] but also of the commingling of "high" and "low" in Dadaism. As *Robert Aghion* and *Hot Land* demonstrate, these encounters also catalyzed a hybridization in literary form. Popular and elite styles lost their borders, blending adventure stories, scientific essays, and avant-garde fiction. The uncanniness of this breakdown—of both "European" identity and "high" form—often led to unpredictable aesthetic and political turnabouts, as evidenced in Hesse, as well as in Jacques, Nolde, and Bonsels.

As we shall see in the next chapter, similar tensions pertained in the fin de siècle scientific discourse of ethnography, especially its intra-European sort: psychoanalysis. The colonial, ethnographic unearthing of a "primitive" world that was too much like "ours" contributed to Freud's understanding of this uncanny crisis as *intensive*; that is, as taking place within the psyche and within psychoanalysis itself. In the process of describing this predicament, psychoanalysis entered a formal crucible. Its scientific structure, like *Robert Aghion*'s essay style, could not hold. Over the course of years, Freud began to view this instability as essential to psychoanalysis. Psychoanalysis itself, it turned out, was "uncanny." It, too, ventured into strangely familiar regions where its form began eerily to resemble that of its "cousin": adventure fiction.

Chapter 3

Savage Freud

Primitives, Adventurers, and the Uncanny Method

Just as the discourse of uncanny travel formed slowly, from the Age of Discovery to the pre–World War I journeys of Jacques, Nolde, and Hesse, so too did the uncanny's theorization. Uncanny thinking only became possible after the Age of Reason, as discussed in my introduction, and the word "uncanny" only took on its modern quotidian meaning around 1800. Shortly thereafter, German thinkers began to theorize the term at the fringes of their work: from Schelling and the Romanticists through to Marx and Nietzsche. But these speculations were fragmentary, not conceptual. They only gained crucial momentum at the beginning of the twentieth century when, in 1906, Ernst Jentsch discovered the uncanny's importance for the fledgling science of psychoanalysis: uncanniness described a state of "psychic uncertainty," especially about whether an object was living or dead. Following Jentsch, Otto Rank (1914), Rudolf Otto (1917), Theodor Reik (1923), and Martin Heidegger (1927) all wrote about uncanniness. In the midst of this burst of theoretical activity, Freud conceptualized the term in *The Uncanny* (1919) as the unexpected return of "what is known of old and long familiar" (Freud, *SE* 17:220).[1]

Conceptual investigations into the uncanny had thus begun by the time fin de siècle travelers started writing about their foreign encounters, but the term was far from adequately formulated. As I stress in my introduction, we would be mistaken to claim that a discourse of the uncanny preordained these stories about belated adventurers. In fact, it is more likely that the converse was true: that the recurrent accounts of uncanny encounters during the first globalization stimulated (together with other influences) the new hypotheses by Jentsch, Rank, Otto, Freud, Reik, and Heidegger. *Unheimlichkeit* sprang from two intellectual watchwords that had been gaining prominence throughout the nineteenth century: estrangement (*Entfremdung*), generated by industrialization and mass relocation to cities, and unhomeliness (*Unheimlichkeit*), including the actual homelessness created by wars and an increasingly skewed distribution of wealth.[2] These changes affected not only the poor but also the burgeoning middle class, whose move from the countryside to the cities produced its own *Entfremdung*. As an antidote, the middle class traveled touristically into foreign worlds (the *Fremde*) in a paradoxical attempt to overcome their *Entfremdung*.[3] But this alienation only increased: the *Fremde* they discovered was not exotic but *unheimlich*, leading to even greater *Entfremdung*.

Such uncanny experiences gained momentum through the spread of European imperialism. The fear of strangely hybridized "natives" and of foreign-familiar things brought back from colonial adventures likely triggered increased conceptual interest around 1900.[4] Consider, for example, Freud's use of a popular colonial source to develop his own theory: a 1917 story from "the English *Strand Magazine*" produced in Freud an "uncanny feeling" that he found "quite remarkable" (*SE* 17:244–45). Entitled "Inexplicable" and virtually unnoticed in Freud scholarship, this story describes creatures from the far corners of the British Empire (the New Guinean swamps) invading a couple's suburban London home. Here, the foreign-familiar residue of travel comes home to roost, and Freud senses the importance of this for his theory.

This exotic tale is part of a larger context of travel culture that conditioned Freud's conceptualization of the *unheimlich* as an unexpected return. This conditioning starts already in Freud's 1899 dream about H. Rider Haggard's adventure novels, which led him to begin speculating that familiar-seeming foreign worlds catalyzed uncanny feelings. During Freud's 1910–11 research for *Totem and Taboo*, he read more popular travel writing as well as anthropology and folklore (*SE* 13:xi), leading him to begin theorizing uncanniness here—several years before *The Uncanny*. According to Freud, anthropological writings about "primitive" peoples incorrectly considered them to be absolutely different from us; instead, they "resemble" us uncannily, as Freud insists already in *Totem and Taboo*'s subtitle. What is more, before and during the First World War, Freud learned from *The Strand*'s adventure story and from his "Rat Man" patient about the uncanniness of travel during the war: soldiers rediscovered their all-too-familiar childhood homoeroticism in faraway colonial barracks. During and after the war, Freud read again about soldiers in distant lands—this time, about their shell shock on the French, Italian, and Russian fronts. These young men returned home like the uncanny fairy-tale figures that Freud would later describe in *The Uncanny*: their shaking bodies "danc[ing] by themselves," eerily "capable of independent activity" (*SE* 17:244).

Considering the importance of this travel culture for Freud's theorization of the uncanny, it is not surprising that he structures *The Uncanny* itself as a travel story—specifically, as an uncanny one.[5] Freud had already stylized himself in "The Aetiology of Hysteria" as exploring the "Source of the Nile," in *The Interpretation of Dreams* as an intellectual "adventurer" searching for the "dark" heart of dreams, and, in *Totem and Taboo*, as questing for the long-lost "savage" (Freud, *SE* 3:203; *FLF* 398; *SE* 5:525, trans. rev.). In

The Uncanny, Freud decides similarly to present himself as seeking, like a nineteenth-century Nile explorer, the "source" of the uncanny (*SE* 17:233). Although this source resembles the one in *Interpretation of Dreams* (repressed material), *The Uncanny* insists now on its eerie familiarity, not its apparent newness; it is not the excitingly unknown "secret of dreams" (*FLF* 417, trans. rev.). In this sense, *The Uncanny* mirrors the contemporaneous travel tales that Freud knew: a heroic ethnographic adventurer, "Freud," searches for an unmarked space only to discover there something hauntingly familiar (a familiarity that was repressed in *Interpretation of Dreams*). This *unheimlich* journey produces a crisis for "Freud," through which psychoanalysis eventually discovers its uniquely uncanny methodological strength.

Dreaming of Rider Haggard, Becoming an Adventurer

Freud knew explicitly the work of some of the German-language travelers I described in the preceding chapters—Zweig, Ewers, Hesse—and also of similar exotic tales by other Europeans and Americans. From the latter group, consider just those that Freud either kept in his professional library or referred to in his writings: "Red-Indian Poetry," especially James Fenimore Cooper's *Leatherstocking* cycle, Hermann Melville's *Typee: A Romance of the South Seas*, Helen Hunt Jackson's *Ramona*, Robert Louis Stevenson's *Treasure Island*, Rudyard Kipling's *Barrack-Room Ballads*, "Phantom Rickshaw," *The Light That Failed*, and *The Jungle Book* (which made Freud's 1906 list of "ten good books"), Johannes Jensen's *The Lost Land* (*Det tabte Land*), Villiers de L'Isle-Adam's *Claire Lenoir*, Mark Twain's *A Tramp Abroad*, Mungo Park's *Travels in the Interior of Africa*, the above-mentioned *Strand* story, and Haggard's *She* and *Heart of the World*.[6]

Critics have generally ignored the significance of these popular adventure writings for Freud's work, first, because the otherwise excellent *Freud's Library: A Comprehensive Catalogue* contains only the texts that Freud kept in his professional, working library—meaning that even books as important to him as *She* and *The Jungle Book*, likely kept in the familial living quarters, do not appear in this catalogue.[7] Second, a long-standing scholarly prejudice assumes that "light reading has no purpose or end except transient pleasure," thereby leaving "no observable trace" in Freud's scientific work.[8] The adventure stories that Freud read, however, made an undeniable mark on his writing: the travel tale from *The Strand* on *The Uncanny*; the Haggard novels on *Interpretation of Dreams* and *The Uncanny*; and the general trope of the undiscovered land—which Freud would have known from Hesse, Zweig, Stevenson, Villiers, and Haggard—on Freud's rhetorical construction of himself as "an adventurer." Especially important were the Haggard romances, which, in 1899, inspired Freud to dream of traveling to an exotic land that, as in the Haggard novels, seemed uncannily familiar.

The dream begins with Freud dissecting "the lower part of my own body," then taking a journey with a guide through boggy ground, which Freud masters well despite the surgery. But his legs eventually tire, and the guide must carry him, past an exotic population that includes "Red Indians or gypsies— among them a girl." The guide finally deposits Freud in an Alpine "wooden house," at the far end of which is a window. The guide lays two boards on the sill to bridge what now appears to be a "chasm" beyond the window. The thought of crossing this chasm makes Freud "frightened about my legs." Distracted by two adult men sleeping beside children on benches on either side of the house, Freud then imagines that these children—not the boards—will make the crossing possible. He wakes in "a mental fright" (*Gedankenschreck*) (*SE* 5:452–53; *GW* 2+3:456).

Freud reports that this dream was catalyzed by his recommendation to "Louise N." of Haggard's *She* (1887): a "strange book, but full of hidden meaning"—about "the eternal feminine, the immortality of our emotions." Louise N. says that she has already read *She* and so would prefer a book by Freud instead. When Freud tells her that his "own immortal works have not yet been written," she asks sarcastically when this will finally happen. Freud reflects silently on how hard he has worked yet not even completed one book (*Interpretation of Dreams*) and then worries that even this book will fail because it reveals too much of his private life (through self-analysis). Further thoughts stimulated by this conversation with Louise N. "went too deep to become conscious" and were therefore "diverted in the direction of the material that had been stirred up in me by the mention of Rider Haggard's *She*" (*SE* 5:453–54).

In Freud's interpretation of his own dream, his self-dissection is his self-analysis, and his Haggardesque "perilous journey" across swampy ground is his risk-filled discovery of psychoanalysis in *Interpretation of Dreams*. Freud's dream-voyage borrows several elements from *She*, he tells us, as well as from Haggard's later novel, *Heart of the World* (1895): "the Red Indians, the girl and the wooden house" are from *Heart of the World*, and the "boggy ground over which people had to be carried" as well as the "chasm which they had to cross by means of boards" come from *She*. The Alpine "wooden house" symbolizes "a coffin" or "the grave," further signaling the dangers of Freud's *She*-inspired intellectual adventure. But like all of Freud's dreams in *Interpretation of Dreams*, this one ends, Freud insists, in wish fulfillment. The bodies on the benches recall the ones Freud recently saw in an Etruscan tomb, meaning that, for him, the dream satisfied his desire to rest ultimately in such a tomb. Further to this fulfillment intepretation, Freud claims that the children signify "the successful emergence of the idea that children may perhaps achieve what their father has failed to—a fresh allusion to the strange novel [*She*] in which a person's identity is retained through a series of generations for over two thousand years" (*SE* 5:454–55). Freud senses here a happy ending, prefiguring his "A Disturbance of Memory on the Acropolis": either he or his disciples will complete a scientific adventure to the Haggardesque realms that Freud's less successful father could never have imagined.

As any reader of both *She* and *Interpretation of Dreams* knows, the influence of the former on Freud's dream is even more striking than he describes. Consider how clearly *She*'s chasm-crossing scene prefigures Freud's dream voyage: servants carry the European heroes and the African Queen Ayesha ("She") on litters across boggy ground. When the carriers reach the nest of concentric caverns lying beneath the lost city of Kôr, they set down the travelers, who, like Freud, hike inward to a "mighty chasm" that they then attempt to cross with a precariously thin "long board."[9] What is more, the novel's protagonist, L. Horace Holly, shares Freud's fear of this crossing. And Holly, like Freud, feels this fear primarily in his legs, which become so weak that he struggles even to get to his knees (*She*, 241). Although Holly (unlike Freud) eventually does make the crossing, he ends up having the same kind of nightmares about it that Freud does. Holly, too, wakes regularly in a "mental fright": "I often see it [the chasm] in my dreams, and wake up covered with cold perspiration" (239).

Noticing these and other correspondences, readers from the 1960s onward have studied the importance of Haggard's travel narratives for Freud. Early interpreters viewed these as ahistorical metaphors for the inward journey, thereby echoing Freud's own interpretation. Alexander Grinstein, for example, sees in Haggard's expeditions Freud's "lengthy voyage of discovery and exploration into a strange and inaccessible territory": into the "country of the unconscious and the repressed area of early childhood."[10] Didier Anzieu similarly claims that Haggard's "perilous journeys into unknown territory" signify Freud's risk-filled "exploration of the unconscious."[11] Norman Etherington reinforces these earlier readings by insisting that Holly's trek into Africa (and Freud's dream about it) is not about Africa at all: it is merely a metaphor for the "trek from the known into the unconscious unknown self."[12]

Influenced by postcolonial theory, critics began in the late 1980s to insist that Freud's interest in Haggard *was* about contemporaneous Africa and, what is more, about Freud's apparently Haggardesque pro-imperial, misogynist beliefs. For Sandra Gilbert and Susan Gubar, Freud borrows from Haggard a typically Victorian-gendered, imperial topography: Haggard's vaginal African caves and breast-like mountains eventually become Freud's "dark continent" of female sexuality.[13] Robert Young similarly claims that Freud, "like Holly," identifies himself as an "explorer of darkest Africa," which holds the enigma of "female sexuality."[14] And Rubén Gallo argues that Freud identifies with Haggard's "Orientalist" "conquistador" figure from *Heart of the World*, after whom Freud modeled his own scientific "adventure to an unknown land."[15]

At first glance, this Orientalist reading of Freud's interest in Haggard seems to make sense. Haggard's romances begin with the same imperial template used by the contemporaneous German adventure writings I described in chapter 1: a down-on-his-luck European survives a stormy sea passage (a shipwreck, for both Haggard heroes), contracts malaria, has a violent confrontation with the locals, and, finally, falls in love with a beautiful native woman. More important, Haggard's protagonists share the German travelers' driving desire to reach a feminized blank space, symbolized most obviously by a female topography as in *She*'s "virgin," "womb"-like caves (*She*, 245, 251, 252, 263). As Freud senses, this fantasy of reaching virgin territory was vital to his dream: like Haggard's heroes, the dreaming Freud travels along "an adventurous road that had scarcely ever been trodden before, leading to an undiscovered region" where he, too, finds "a girl" (*SE* 5:454).

Furthering this interpretation is Freud's assertion, just months after his Haggard dream, that he was an "adventurer" and "conquistador," with "the curiosity, boldness, and persistence typical of these men."[16] He even claims to have structured *The Interpretation of Dreams* as a journey, with himself the heroic expedition leader (thus the scientific "we") who brings his "hopelessly lost"[17] readers "through a narrow defile" onto bright, high ground: "We find ourselves in the full daylight" of "sudden discovery." From this elevated path, which divides in two, Freud sees the "finest prospects open up on every side," then pauses to consider "in which direction we shall first turn our steps" (*SE* 4:122). By *Interpretation of Dreams*'s final chapter, these steps have led Freud toward a Haggardesque heart of darkness: So far "all the paths [*Wege*] along which we have traveled have led us towards the light," but now that we are "penetrat[ing] more deeply," "every path will end in darkness" (*SE* 5:511; *GW* 2+3:515). This end is the "dream's navel," a jungle-like "tangle" that can never be fully "unraveled"; it is "unknown" and "dark" (*im Dunkel*). Like the lightless vaginal caves beneath *She*'s "Temple of Truth" and *Heart of the World*'s "City of the Heart," this obscure "spot" (*Stelle*) lures Freud with the hidden, virginal secret both "of dreams" and of female sexuality (*SE* 5:525, trans. rev.; *GW* 2+3:530).

Thinking about Rider Haggard, Discovering the Uncanny

But this "imperial" reading misrepresents both Haggard and Freud. Like the fin de siècle German-language stories discussed above, Haggard's novels in fact overturn their own heroic template—even though critics have generally not noticed this.[18] At the heart of Haggard's darkness is not the longed-for virgin territory but rather a shockingly well-trod region filled with white men. The English hero of *Heart of the World*—Strickland—for example, imagines that he will be the "first white man" to reach the mighty lost Aztec city. But he arrives there only to discover that the city's ancient founder was a "white god" who spawned a race of light-skinned Indians that now surrounds Strickland (*Heart*, 157, 254–55, 196). In *She*, Holly and his young

English ward, Leo, are similarly certain that they are the "first white men ever" to sail up a wild east African river (*She*, 65). But they, too, find eerily recognizable natives: "light in colour," with "aquiline" features, "snowy" white beards, and beautiful "curling hair—not crisped like a negro's" (74, 75, 76, 78). This combination of familiar European visages with otherwise "evil" qualities (which Holly associates with savages) strikes fear into him. At a loss for words to describe this mixture of foreignness and familiarity, he finally defines it exactly as Freud will two decades later: it is "almost uncanny" (*She*, 75).

At the center of this *unheimlich* world in both Haggard novels is a queen/princess who, like her subjects, is oddly white—giving the lie to Young's claims that the doomed Ayesha and Maya are both "exotic" and that all "black" women must die in Haggard novels.[19] It is precisely the whiteness of *Heart of the World*'s Aztec princess, Maya, that shocks the travelers: "She was an Indian, but such an Indian as I had never seen before, for in colour she was almost white . . . . Her was face was oval and small-featured, and in it shone a pair of wonderful dark-blue eyes" (*Heart*, 125). Maya's beauty is "strange" because she seems too European—"more like a white woman than one of Indian blood"—and, because of this, eerily artificial: her "deep-blue" eyes, like E. T. A. Hoffmann's Olympia's, do not even seem "human" (294). In *She*, Holly and Leo similarly wait excitedly for the "naked savage queen," Ayesha, to reveal herself. But instead of the spectacularly wild African they expect, they see a European lady with a "beautiful white hand," "the pinkest nails," and "pink flesh" (*She*, 131, 132). Images of this white "savage" published in *Heart of the World* and *She* drive home the point of the uncanny woman (figure 17; figure 18). Like Maya, Ayesha is caught between Europeanness and primitiveness (a "white sorceress") and between animation and death (a "ghost-like apparition"). For this reason, she frightens Holly beyond words. He can't put his finger on what he feels but senses that he is "in the presence of something that was not canny" (*She*, 147, 132).

Ayesha's uncanny in-betweenness extends to her gender, which is not Ur-female and maternal (as critics generally claim)[20] but hermaphroditic. When Ayesha unveils herself to Holly, she warns him that her waist will seem to bulge: "Perchance thou thinkest [my waist] too large, but of a truth it is not so; it is this golden snake that is too large, and doth not bind as it should." Ayesha now asks Holly to touch this protruding lap "snake" that does not bind properly: "give me thy hands—so—now press them round me, there, with but a little force, thy fingers touch, oh Holly." Ayesha's pleasure produces initial mortification in Holly: "I am but a man, and she was more than a woman. Heaven knows what she was—I do not!" But Holly's shock quickly transforms into lust, of an order he has never known. Touching Ayesha's "snake" generates in him a desire that he has never felt for a mere "woman." He craves Ayesha as something beyond femininity—"as never woman was worshipped"—falling to his knees and proposing marriage to "her" (*She*, 172).

Figure 17. Image of Maya from H. Rider Haggard's *Heart of the World* (1895)

Figure 18. Image of Ayesha ("She-who-must-be-obeyed") from the first, serial publication of Haggard's *She* (1886–87)

Just as this phallic Ayesha is not as womanly and exotic as the reader had presumed, so too are Haggard's "exotic" landscapes surprisingly empty of women. Everywhere we look, we find men—more specifically, European men. In addition to the ancient race-founding white man from *Heart of the World*, we have Strickland himself, the new god of the city, as well as a "certain English gentleman," Mr. Jones, who travels all the way from England only to stumble upon the stories of both Strickland and the white god (*Heart*, 1). *King Solomon's Mines* (1885), the lost-world novel that provides the template for both *She* and *Heart of the World*, likewise presents a foreign world peppered with European-seeming men. The novel's traveling Englishmen find in the heart of Africa the uncannily familiar frozen corpse of a Portuguese predecessor, then a peculiarly light-skinned people spawned by vanished whites, and finally the lost brother of a member of their expedition: George Curtis.

Most striking among these intra-European encounters is the one that inspired Freud to remark that, in *She*, "a person's identity is retained through a series of generations for over two thousand years." Although Freud initially interpreted *She*'s retention of identity positively, he later changed his mind—perhaps remembering how Haggard actually describes it (Freud, *SE* 5:455, 478). In arguably *She*'s most memorable scene, Holly and Leo follow Queen Ayesha into a mysterious tomb beneath her bedroom, which holds an ancient secret that Ayesha visits every night. Expecting a spectacularly exotic vision, Holly and Leo instead find the ultimately uncanny one: a mummified version of Leo's still-young self, an alter ego that looks alive but has apparently been dead for millennia. The two Leos—living and dead—are perfect replicas, right down to their youthful skin and wavy blonde hair. Holly is shocked: "I stared from Leo, standing *there* alive, to Leo lying *there* dead, and could see no difference . . . . Feature for feature they were the same, even down to the crop of little golden curls" (emphasis in original). He continues: "I never saw twins so exactly similar as that dead and living pair." Having traveled to the jungle only to find a mirror image of his ward, Leo (whose May 1856 birthdate Freud must have noticed),[21] Holly is initially speechless. But then he—who shares Freud's uneasy dreams and whose ward shares Freud's birth month—finds a term that again anticipates Freud: "the sight was an uncanny one" (*She*, 211).

Holly describes his African world at least five times as "uncanny" or "not canny," which Freud would likely have noticed and could well have spurred him toward his earliest conceptualizations of the uncanny (*She*, 24, 75, 89, 132, 211). In the sentence immediately following his second analysis of his Haggard dream, for example, Freud first poses the question that will become central to this conceptualization: what does it mean when someone, in the midst of dreaming, says, "I've dreamt of that before" (*SE* 5:478)? This problem so obsessed Freud that he once even dreamt of solving it and, when the dream did not provide the proper answer, continued working on this question for years (5:446-47). In the midst of this work, Freud noticed that his patients—perhaps inspired by adventure books, like Louise N. and

Figure 19. Freud hiking in the mountains with Sándor Ferenczi and Victor Gonda (1917)

himself—were not actually dreaming the same dream twice. They were dreaming of the same *place* twice. As Freud added ten years later to *Interpretation of Dreams*, the dreamers kept seeing "landscapes or other localities" that were, like Haggard's Mexico and Africa, eerily familiar: they sensed having "been there once before" (5:399). Based on this evidence, Freud revises his question. He no longer asks why dreamers, while still dreaming, say "I've dreamt this dream before," but rather "I've been to this place before." This question's geographic turn allows Freud to begin to develop an answer based on a fear of unexpectedly familiar places.

Freud famously concluded that this place was "the genitals of the dreamer's mother" and that returning to them was the paradigmatic *unheimlich* experience (*SE* 5:399; see also *The Uncanny, SE* 17:245). This interpretation initially seems appropriate, not only for Freud's patients' dreams but also for his own. Like his patients and Haggard's characters, the dreaming Freud journeys into what seems to be virgin territory—"an undiscovered region"—only to discover there something strikingly familiar. Traveling past outlandish Red Indians and gypsies, he ends up in a well-known space: an "Alpine" "wooden house," reminiscent of the cabins Freud would have seen on his "tramps in the mountains" during his annual vacations (figure 19).[22] This recognizable building cropping up in an otherwise exotic landscape illustrates Freud's theory of how all-too-familiar repressed desires return when not expected— thereby causing uncanny fear. And what could be more familiar, Freud insists, than the mother's genitalia: the only place where, for certain, every one of us has been before? The wooden house, then, would be the mother's genitalia; this is what creates the dreaming Freud's "mental fright." This reading would reconnect to the older interpretations by Grinstein and Anzieu, who concluded (albeit not in connection with the wooden house) that Freud's dream represented his own repressed desire for and fear of his mother's body.[23]

But a closer look at this dream reveals that Freud's *unheimlich* fright resulted more likely from the unexpected return of *masculine* bodies. Freud catalogues the "numerous elements" from his dream that derived from Haggard's novels: the bogs, board, and chasm from *She*; the Red Indians, girl, and wooden house from *Heart of the World*; and his dream's "guide" from both Haggard novels, in which, as Freud correctly points out, "the guide is a woman." But, as Freud has just told us, the guide in his own dream was a man (a "*Führer*") (*SE* 5:453; *GW* 2+3:455). Why does Freud not mention this obvious contradiction in his interpretation, but rather include the guide as a similarity between his dream and the Haggard books? In a comparable vein, Freud connects Haggard's apparently "eternal feminine" to his dream, suggesting that his dream, too, leads him to the Ur-female. But Freud's male guide takes him past the dream's only female person (a "girl") to, in the last scene, a wooden house conspicuously devoid of women: "I saw two grown-up men lying on wooden benches" (*SE* 5:453). Freud's dream interpretation (a female guide leading him to the eternal feminine) turns out to be quite different from his actual dream, in which a male guide leads him to a hut filled with men. In this masculine center, we see what Freud repressed, both from his interpretation and from his knowledge of Haggard's novels: the most upsetting place to which the male dreamer returns is not the eternal feminine but the everlasting masculine.

What terrifies Freud is neither the "perilous journey" to an "undiscovered region" (his original interpretation) nor to the "uncanny" mother (his later implied one). Rather, Freud, like Haggard's heroes, fears the abrupt transformation of a mythical feminine unknown world into an uncannily familiar, masculine one. Freud's dream begins exactly as do Haggard's stories: with a servant carrying him into an exotic, feminized landscape (complete with Red Indians and a girl). But his dream ends also like a Haggard novel, and frighteningly so: Freud travels past the Red Indians and the girl to an Alpine cabin filled with European men. To take the larger social view suggested by Haggard and other contemporaneous adventure writers, Freud fears a newly globalized world that robs him of the fantasy of being a "conquistador" who penetrates "virgin" landscapes.[24] The temptingly dark female is replaced everywhere by the too-bright European phallus. Like Holly (with Leo) and Stickland (with Ignatio), the intellectual adventurer Freud (with his co-adventurer, Wilhelm Fliess) journeys to the Dark Continent to find not female sexuality but rather an *unheimlich* male love that, as Ignatio points out, "pass[es] the love for a woman" (*Heart of the World*, 6).[25]

Much has been made of the fact that—contra Freud—there is no wooden house in *Heart of the World*. Gallo concludes that Freud's dream-house is a displacement from what Freud, the "conquistador," really fears in *Heart of the World*: the Aztec stone pyramid, which, Gallo claims, is a site of the "living dead" and of the sacrifice of European conquistadors. More important than this statement's factual inaccuracy (there is no mention of the living dead in this pyramid)[26] is its psychological inconsistency: if Freud feared Gallo's exotic storyline—a conquistador risks his life among savage Aztecs—then why would he offer a version of this same interpretation right after his dream? More likely, Freud's wooden house is a displacement from what Freud did not want to know and what he repressed from his dream: the *unheimlich* European men that continually appear in the Haggard novels. Helpful here is a correction of Gallo's claim that "there are no wooden structures in *Heart of the World*,"[27] for there is one: an old European-style timber mineshaft that anticipates both Robert Musil's *Grigia* (1921) and Freud's Haggard dream. Just as Freud had sensed that his dream wooden house was actually a "grave," this crumbling timber mine almost becomes Strickland's and Ignatio's tomb. Burrowing their way inside, they find the skeleton of an unlucky predecessor and then watch as a rock falls on Ignatio, trapping him. With the mine now collapsing, they fear burial alive, but manage to escape at the last second: Strickland carries Ignatio out just as the roof falls, leaving the mine's entrance "piled high with rocks" behind them (*Heart*, 61).

Carted out of the mine on a litter (like the dreaming Freud) and then falling ill (speaking to no one for days), Ignatio confirms Freud's claim that the fear "of being buried alive" is "the most uncanny thing of all" (Freud, *SE* 17:244; see *Heart of the World*, 61). But Ignatio subverts Freud's assertion that this fear springs from the "lascivious" fantasy of returning to the mother's womb; for Ignatio's fantasy has nothing to do with his mother, or with women. He has already admitted that he loves Strickland "with a love passing the love for a woman," and, in the chapter before they discover the mine, Ignatio ogles down Strickland's open-necked shirt at his skin, "white like milk," and then desires "to become friendly with this white man" (*Heart*, 6, 34, 35). For Ignatio, the fear of burial alive connects to his longing to be alone with Strickland's body, which, in Ignatio's fantasy, will "die with me" (*Heart*, 56). This timber mine holding the beautiful European male body reveals itself, here, as the hidden source of Freud's invented wooden house where, likewise, "two grown-up men" lie next to each other (Freud, *SE* 5:453). Because he needs to repress the all-too-familiar intimacy of Strickland/Ignatio (and of Freud/Fliess), Freud does not notice this displacement. Instead, he insists that his dream is about a journey to "the eternal feminine" (*SE* 5:453).

Because Freud represses this *unheimlich* closeness of Strickland/Ignatio and Holly/Leo from his interpretation, one could argue that it is unimportant for his theorizing of uncanniness. But Freud's revisting of his dream in the next section of *Interpretation of Dreams* suggests at least partial awareness.

Here, he reverses his interpretation of the dream's children in the same way that all people reverse, as he writes in *The Uncanny*, their youthful interpretation of "the 'double'": from an "insurance against the destruction of the ego" to an "uncanny harbinger of death."[28] In this same paragraph from *The Uncanny*, Freud says that the double recalls castration fears when, in dreams, we witness the "doubling or multiplication" of the phallus (*SE* 17:235). By opposing Freud's more famous claim that the *lack* of penises—the vagina— causes castration anxieties and uncanny fears, this image reminds us of Freud's insistence on the symbolic nature of these anxieties: they need not always include the fear of literally losing one's penis. As Lacan elaborates, it is not the "lack" of penises (the female genitalia) that causes uncanny castration anxieties but rather the "lack of the lack."[29] This insight explains Ignatio's castration fear when in the mine with the strong, handsome Strickland (a giant rock will strike directly "between my thighs") (*Heart of the World*, 60). Haggard and other adventure writers had indeed discovered this castrating phallic *horror plenitudinis* in the exotic world before Freud did. Their insight made its way into Freud's nightmare about traveling past "a girl" to an uncanny hut filled with men. And this vision caused a "mental fright" in Freud that forced him to keep revisiting it until he discovered, however fleetingly, that—contrary to his theory about vaginas—the multiplication of *phalluses* caused uncanny fear.

In this sense, Freud's Haggard dream does end up fulfilling Freud's wish, although not the wish he had originally surmised (burial in an Etruscan tomb). Rather, the dream fulfills another wish of which he had dreamt: of answering the plaguing question of why dreamers—readers of adventure stories, like Freud—kept dreaming of faraway places that seem *unheimlich* familiar. Freud's initial answer comes from a typically superficial reading of Haggard and of fin de siècle adventure fiction in general: these stories' Dark Continent is the "eternal feminine," which reminds readers of their uncanny desire to return to their mothers' all-too-familiar bodies. But the not-so-hidden phalluses in both Freud's dream and Haggard's books reveal something more terrifying: that this recognizable "place" is the male European body. It is the father, the brother, and the "friend" whom the traveler simultaneously fears and desires.

Despite the many psychoanalytical readings of adventure literature, including of Haggard, it makes sense now to reverse the hierarchy: to read psychoanalysis through adventure literature. The question is: Why do Freud's patients keep having *geographic* dreams about repetition? Why do these dreams seem to emerge directly out of *She* and *Heart of the World*, as well as Norbert Jacques' *Hot Land*? And why does Freud choose these dreams to exemplify his theory of the uncanny, when other dreams could have served equally well as illustrations of the displacement of Oedipal desire? Did Freud notice that his patients, like Jünger's Herbert Berger and Freud himself, were reading too many "bad books" about "adventurers" (Jünger, *Afrikanische*

Spiele, 9)? And that these books were infiltrating their dreams? And, moreover, not with the promise of blank spaces but, as in the Haggard novels, with the withdrawal of that promise? Does the unconscious psychological fear of returning "home" originate in adventure stories and then make its way into psychoanalysis—not the other way around?

What is more, does Freud's later claim that the multiplying male genitalia are uncanny also stem from these adventure books? Specifically, from these tales' depiction of an extra-European world that, for the first time ever, did not offer a space for male self-realization and uniqueness but rather for the traveler to discover that he was replaceable, not the "first white man ever"? Freud would have learned from Haggard and other popular writers that the Dark Continent was no longer as feminine and exotic as it was supposed to be: that the multiplying white phallus was everywhere, reminding each traveler of his uncanny fear of and desire for it. Freud's Haggardesque dream about men in an Alpine "wooden house" allowed him to imagine this and, years later, to begin to conceptualize it on the fringes of *The Uncanny*.

The Uncanny as a Travel Narrative

Just as popular adventure literature influenced Freud's theorization of the uncanny, this literature affected how he wrote *The Uncanny*. As we saw in *Interpretation of Dreams*, Freud had already stylized himself as an "adventurer": a heroic explorer leading an expedition toward the world's last blank space. *The Uncanny* starts similarly with Freud telling us, at the end of the first paragraph, that he will travel to a "remote" (*abseits*) "province" (*SE* 17:219; *GW* 12:229). Freud's language mirrors *Interpretation of Dreams* exactly when he tells us that he will pursue an epistemological heart of darkness (the uncanny's "unknown nature") after first pausing on figurative high ground to choose between two different paths (*Wege*). In order to penetrate a foreign world about which he claims to know nothing (the realm of "uncanny feeling"), Freud will need to "go native." He must live among his subjects and transport himself wholly into their primitive states: "he [the psychoanalyst] must start by translating himself into that state of feeling [*sich erst in das Gefühl hineinversetzen*], by awakening in himself the possibility of experiencing it" (*SE* 17:220; *GW* 12:230).

Freud's reference to himself in the third person here emphasizes the self-alienating dangers of this journey. As stated in the essay's first words, "*Der Psychoanalytiker*"—not "I" (*Ich*)—will undertake this voyage. Freud continues to speak of himself in this third person (as "he" or "one" [*man*]) throughout the opening two paragraphs: "He" will journey to this out-of-the-way region, and "one" will try to get to the core or essence (*Kern*) of "it" (*es*) (*SE* 17:219; *GW* 12:229). These dislocations evoke the dangers of heroic travel, which mirror the grammar of psychoanalytic treatment: in order to experience the great unknown *Es* that contains the source of "uncanny feeling," the analyst must, together with the analysand's ego (*Ich*), go on a journey and become other to himself.

But already by *The Uncanny*'s second page, we get a sense that this travel narrative will have a different outcome than does *Interpretation of Dreams*. Even though both works ultimately return us to the same familiar ground—repressed childhood material and, in *The Uncanny*, surmounted primitive beliefs—*Interpretation of Dreams* persistently stylizes this return as a revelation: the "sudden discovery" of the "secret of dreams" in the "dream's navel." In *The Uncanny*, conversely, Freud suggests that the voyage will be disturbingly and disappointingly uncanny. It will, like *Interpretation of Dreams*, provide us with two different "*Wege*" (paths) but both, Freud reports apologetically, will lead back "to the same result": to that single same spot that itself expresses only "what is known of old and long familiar" (*SE* 17:220; *GW* 12:230). What kind of journey is this that will return us only to what we already know? Everything in Freud's strange travel story will begin to resemble everything else, he hints already here, until even "psychoanalysis . . . itself" becomes not a heroic voyage but an uncanny repetition (*SE* 17:243).

Searching for the Source: *Ersatzbeziehung,* Infantile Belief, and Primitive Man

Although Freud has already here "given away" (*verraten*) his quest's ending—uncanniness results from returning to what is "long familiar"—*The Uncanny* nonetheless proceeds to tell this story (*SE* 17:220, trans. rev.; *GW* 12:230). "Freud" resembles the "spirit" from Hegel's *The Phenomenology of Spirit*, which serves simultaneously as the narrator (who knows the outcome) and the character (who does not).[30] Freud, as narrator, sends his picaresque hero, "Freud," off into the world. A modern Don Quixote or Tom Jones, "Freud" will review all of the "things, persons, impressions, events, and situations" that bring about in him uncanny feelings (*SE* 17:226). Freud adds to this image of the picaresque traveler the flair of the Nile explorer: he is searching for the uncanny's "source" (*Quelle*), a metaphor that will run through the entire essay (*SE* 17:233; *GW* 12:246).[31] Freud's quest takes him famously first to Hoffmann's "The Sandman," where this source seems to present itself straightforwardly: in the fear of losing one's eyes. But this horror of enucleation turns out to have a substitutive relation (*Ersatzbeziehung*) with the infantile fear of castration, leading Freud to insist that castration is the more original (*ursprünglich*) source of uncanny feeling (*SE* 17:231, 232n1; *GW* 12:243, 244n1).

But once this *Ersatzbeziehung* is invoked, it haunts the hero's journey, substituting for castration, first, the "living doll" then the "double." With castration temporarily displaced, Freud now reverts to "infantile belief" as the overarching source that will encompass castration *and* all of its substitutes (*SE* 17:233).[32] Whether this infantile belief was originally a fear (as in castration) or a wish (as in the child's doll coming to life) does not matter. What counts is this belief's unexpected return, long after we thought we had surmounted it. Emerging *out of context*, any "early mental stage" can be felt as uncanny, regardless of its content. Infantile recurrence is a structure that can include anything. As such, it gives Freud an apparently iron-cast origin that will contain all elements of his otherwise already uncontainable substitutive series (*SE* 17:236).

But the *Ersatzbeziehung* haunts even this structure, when Freud discovers that his new meta-source—"infantile belief"—likewise has an apparent substitute: "primitive man's" superstitions. Throughout this second section of *The Uncanny*, Freud presents "infantile" and "primitive" beliefs as relatively interchangeable origins for uncanniness. Uncanniness results when we unexpectedly leap backwards to stages that are interchangeably ontogenetic and phylogenetic: toward that "primary narcissism which dominates the mind of the child and of primitive man"; toward that "old surmounted narcissism of earliest [primeval] times [*Urzeiten*]"; and toward that fantasy of the "double" from "a very early [primeval] mental stage [*seelische Urzeiten*]" (*SE* 17:235, 236; *GW* 12:237, 248).

Freud eventually takes this new prominence of primitive man one step further. Although he insists that the minds of the child and the primitive are at similar developmental stages, he now claims, logically, that the latter precedes the former chronologically: the primitives are "our" "forefathers" (*Urahnen*) and so necessarily also the precursors of our children (*SE* 17:247; *GW* 12:262). When we, as adults, experience our present-day superstitions and animistic beliefs as repetitions, we are actually experiencing a double repetition: of a childhood feeling and of this same feeling present millennia ago in our *Urahnen*, as demonstrated in *She*, through what Freud calls the retention of identity "through a series of generations for over two thousand years" (*SE* 5:455). From this phylogenetic perspective, "infantile beliefs" are themselves already recurrences, and childhood is necessarily uncanny. Primitive man is both the child's double *and* his antecedent, a temporally uncanny figure toward which "Freud"—the long-time reader of adventure fiction, folklore, and anthropology—knows he must journey.

Primitive Man (Excursus I): Anthropology, *Völkerschauen*, and the Uncanny Jew

Who is this "primitive man" who takes on such importance in *The Uncanny*? He is not Freud's invention but an amalgamation of his extensive readings in fin de siècle adventure writing, folklore, naturalism, and post-Darwinian cultural anthropology, where aboriginals appeared uncannily as both our ancestors and our contemporaries.[33] This claim depended on anthropology's use of the "comparative method": today's savages (in Africa, Australia, the South Seas, etc.) were on a chronological journey, working their way forward along the evolutionary track toward European civilization. According to this model, "primitives" were uncannily past and present: Europe's long-dead evolutionary forefathers but also the contemporary aborigines living in Australia. The savage's temporal status was further complicated by the fact that he was most present in his pastness and most past in his presence. His forefather-status (his pastness) rendered him hauntingly current in evolution-minded Europe, while his contemporary instantiation in Australia, Africa, or America (his presence) appeared hopelessly past. Primitive man became most present in his temporal absence: as an evolutionary spook stubbornly and uncannily inhabiting Europeans' phylogenetic constitutions.[34]

This uncanny primitive existed not only in scientific books. Scores of exhibitions of primitive peoples—*Völkerschauen*—traveled through Europe from the 1870s onward. In Freud's youth and middle age (1870–1910), for example, there were at least fifty such exhibits in Vienna.[35] When in town, *Völkerschauen* dominated the front pages of the Viennese newspapers, including the *Neue Freie Presse*, which Freud read regularly.[36] Most notable was the famous Ashanti exhibit in the Prater in 1896, while the forty-year-old Freud was seeing patients in the nearby Berggasse. Brought to Vienna from the west coast of Africa (today's Ghana), seventy Ashanti men, women, and children drew record numbers of visitors for three straight months. The newspapers proclaimed "Ashanti-Fever!"[37] But observers noted that these "savages" were not so wild after all. The poet Peter Altenberg, who spent days in the Ashanti village, reported on an Ashanti woman who remarked ironically in her combination of German and English: "Wilde müssen wir vorstellen, Herr, Afrikaner. Ganz närrisch ist es. In Afrika könnten wir so nicht sein. Alle würden lachen. Wie 'men of the bush,' ja diese. In solchen Hütten wohnt niemand. . . . Quite foolish. Man wünscht, dass wir Thiere vorstellen."[38] She and her compatriots, many of whom had spent time in Europe before, became actors: "playing" (*vorstellen*) savages.

Freud's "doppelgänger,"[39] Arthur Schnitzler, puts a fine point on this when his protagonist, Andreas Thameyer, refers to the Ashantis in the Prater as "uncanny blacks" (*unheimliche Schwarzen*)—who have, at Thameyer's expense, also created a new uncanny race. Thameyer's wife has given birth to a child with a "peculiar skin color" exactly nine months after visiting these "giant people with their glowing eyes and great black beards."[40] Although Thameyer tries to deny it, he senses that this baby is one of the "Ashanti-Children" (*Aschanti-Kinder*) who featured prominently in the Viennese press in the spring of 1897. It is not clear how many *Aschanti-Kinder* existed and whether they were primarily the product of fantasies about African virility, but this image of the Ashanti-Child was a mainstay in the popular Viennese imagination for years. One sees him repeatedly caricatured in satirical journals such as *Kikeriki* and the *Humoristische Blätter*.[41] And behind these *unheimlich* "black-white" babies lurked the threatening image of the "Negro dandy" (*Negerdandy*), the "Ashanti Don Juan," who, like the white-suited Malaysians described by Hesse in 1911, uncannily combined a dark-skinned body with European style and manners.[42]

Visitors to Berlin's "German Colonial Exhibition" from that same 1896 summer similarly discovered "primitives"—ninety-five Africans and eight New Guineans—who disturbingly resembled Europeans. This exhibition achieved its goal of "bringing them closer to us" too well, revealing how most of "them" were already too close.[43] Over half of the inhabitants of Treptow Park's Negro Village were Christians, some of whom had already lived in Germany and spoke excellent German, including one, Samuel Garber, who perfected Berliner slang. One Christian Herero, Josephat Kamatoto, inquired with the authorities about how to perform authentic "heathen" customs.[44] Another inhabitant of the exhibit's "Spree-Africa," the Camerooner Bismarck Bell, used his earnings to purchase binoculars, through which he observed the Berliners while they were observing him.[45] In their free time, many of the Africans sang German folk songs, including the chauvinistic "Wacht am Rhein," and mimicked members of the audience by pretending to wear monocles and strut around with walking sticks.[46] Some of the Africans who didn't already live in Berlin ended up staying there, working as tailors, butchers, and salesmen in "colonial stores." Martin Dibobe even became one of the first conductors on the new Berlin subway, only to be cursed, like other "too-civilized" Africans, as a "pants-wearing nigger" (*Hosennigger*).[47]

This same irritation from "primitives" seeming too European subverted Germany's American Indian exhibits, starting from the time Karl May first saw one in Dresden in the 1870s.[48] This problem increased steadily, such that after the turn of the century, the Indians—who had been living in Western metropolises and spoke English with ease—had to be taught "Indian behavior." The men were instructed in the use of the bow and arrow, the women in embroidering, and the children in "primitive family-living." Like Jacques' and Hesse's protagonists, visitors were upset by this spuriousness, especially when, because of the lack of real Indians, "costumed Germans" started playing their roles.[49] Professional anthropologists shared this authenticity anxiety: they often spent their post-exhibition conferences confusedly trying to determine "the true ethnic and racial typology of the people on display."[50]

Within this framework of the eerily similar savage, Freud developed his concept of the uncanny "primitive." At once long forgotten (our dead "forefathers") and surprisingly present (in Vienna's Prater *and* our own psyches), primitive man became, for Freud, more than just one uncanny example among many: he became the uncanny figure par excellence. Most Europeans, Freud claimed, still carry savagery within them, proven precisely by their daily neurotic encounters with the uncanny: they cannot surmount the magical thinking of "primitives."[51] Ernst Haeckel's use of the comparative method for his recapitulation theory—"ontogeny recapitulates phylogeny"—increased Freud's conviction of the uncanny presence of the savage. Because the individual's personal development from infancy to adulthood re-created the evolutionary development of humanity (from fish to ape to *Homo erectus* to modern man), the attentive psychoanalyst could see the ghost of prehistoric man still lurking in the eyes of today's children.[52]

Freud insisted that this savage was present not just in children and neurotics but in everyone, through our unconscious: the "aboriginal population of the mind" (*SE* 14:195). This assertion placed him in the camp of the evolutionary universalists, who saw "savages" as possessing mental activities comparable to "our" own and primitiveness as part of Europe's psychic makeup. For this reason, Freud stated in *Totem and Taboo*—where he first began to theorize the uncanny—that he expected criticism for "endowing today's savages with a subtlety of psychic activity that exceeds all probability" (*SE* 13:99). Through Freud's preemptive defense, we see the incipient political impact of his position. More than just a metaphor for the return of the repressed, the uncannily similar savage unsettled turn-of-the-century Europe's carefully constructed relation to its other; he got close enough to "civilization" to give it a fright.

Although Freud claims in *The Uncanny* to have rid himself of "animistic beliefs" (and not to fear his primitive double), he would likely have gotten a fright of his own (*SE* 17:247). Late nineteenth-century anthropological, colonial, and anti-Semitic rhetoric converged to describe Jews as black—"African," "mulatto," "Jewish-Negroid"—and as members of a "dark-skinned race": the "Negroes of Europe" (figure 20).[53] To name just one of many examples, a nineteenth-century Polish nobleman visiting the United States claimed that European Jews bore a great resemblance to light-skinned African-Americans: "Sallow carnation complexion, thick lips, crisped black hair. Of all the Jewish population scattered over the globe, one-fourth dwells in Poland. I am therefore well acquainted with their features. On my arrival [in America] I took every light-colored mulatto for a Jew."[54] And Jews themselves, from Karl Marx to fin de siècle novelists and poets such as Ludwig Jacobowski, Joseph Roth, and Franz Kafka, internalized this stereotype—speaking of the "Jew" as a "nigger" (Marx), as "black" (Roth), and as having a "Negro face" (Kafka). Jacobowski remarked on Jews' "protruding thick lips," and in a poem ("Self-Portrait"), assessed his own facial features as black: "From the Negro I have my hair and forehead" (*Vom Neger hab' ich Stirn und Haare*).[55]

Freud would have known this image of Jews as black—and sometimes as mulatto, "Oriental," or even American Indian—from such popular and literary depictions as well as from his own anthropological readings. These included Carl Heinrich Stratz's *What Are Jews? An Ethnographic-Anthropological Study* (1903), which featured photographs of "exotic" (*fremdländisch*)-looking Jews alongside "Jewish"-seeming Africans (Berbers), Turks, and South American Indians (figure 21; figure 22).[56] Popular discourse had in fact

Figure 20. Late nineteenth-century medical anthropology's depiction of the Eastern Jew as exemplary of the "dark-skinned" races (part of the frontispiece from Carl Ernst Bock's *Das Buch vom gesunden und kranken Menschen* [1893])

long made this same point, especially about the *Ostjuden* from the eastern parts of the Austro-Hungarian Empire. *Kikeriki*, for example, noted in 1896 the "easily provable" comparison between the "fetish dances of the Ashanti savages" and the orthodox rituals of the *Ostjuden* in Vienna's Leopoldstadt ghetto, where Freud had spent most of his childhood and early adulthood.[57] This apparent proximity between Jew and savage unsettled many assimilated Jews in increasingly anti-Semitic Vienna, causing them to distance themselves from the *Ostjuden* even though most, like Freud, had been born one.[58]

This perceived resemblance between Jews and "savages" was heightened by the contemporary stereotype that both were "ghosts." Just as primitive man was simultaneously alive (in the Prater and in our children's minds) and dead (a long-deceased ancestor from "dead" lands), so too was the contemporary Jew.[59] He walked the streets of Vienna and so seemed to be alive, but only as part of a moribund people: "mummified" since biblical times. From the middle of the nineteenth into the early twentieth century, this image of

Figure 21. An "old Jewish woman" from Tunis with an "exotic" physiognomy (from Carl Heinrich Stratz, *Was sind Juden?* [1903])

the "uncanny Jew" ran through Gentile- and Jewish-German writing: the Jew was a "living corpse, a dead man who has not yet died" (Gutzkow); a "ghost" (Schopenhauer); and a "specter" from a "mummy-nation" (Heine). As the Zionist Moses Hess wrote in 1862, the Jew wandered "like a ghost through the centuries," a "lifeless mummy." A later Zionist, Leo Pinsker, referred in 1882 to the Jews as uncanny: "The world saw in this people [the Jews] the uncanny [*unheimliche*] form of . . . the dead walking among the living." Pinsker continued by claiming that Jews appeared to be the "ghostlike apparition of a living corpse." Mankind's inborn anxiety toward anything "dead but still living" explained the ancient hatred of the Jews: this "fear of ghosts" was the "mother of Judeophobia." Ahad Ha'Am echoed Pinsker in 1902, claiming that Jews inspired a "ghost-fear."[60] Just as the savage appeared to live long after evolution had left him for dead, the Jew persisted like a specter—centuries after his people's apparent demise.[61]

This uncanny correlation of the Jew and the savage would have intensified, for Freud, the fright that he otherwise diagnosed in his contemporaries.

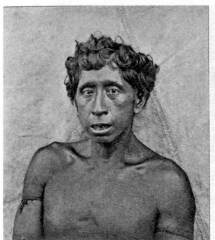

Figure 22. A Bakairi Indian "with Jewish features" (from Stratz, *Was sind Juden?*)

"Primitive man" eerily resembled all Europeans but looked especially like this "black" Jew. What is more, the savage and the Jew were *unheimlich* in exactly the same way: they were half-dead and half-living, at once present and past. This resemblance haunts Freud's description of primitive man in *The Uncanny* and provides a new twist to his sense of himself—in *Interpretation of Dreams* and also at the beginning of *The Uncanny*—as an "adventurer" searching for an "unknown" essence. When Freud gets to this *Kern* in *The Uncanny*, he finds not something unknown but rather a "savage" who is familiar in more ways than one: he is every European's ghostly "forefather" and is particularly similar to the "Moorish" psychoanalyst who came to examine him.[62]

A Voyage of Discovery: The Repetition of the Same Thing and the Uncanny Brothel

The Uncanny's traveling protagonist, "Freud," emerges from this first encounter with "primitive man" disoriented. What he had once pronounced as the uncanny's undisputed source—the return of "infantile beliefs"—now finds both its antecedent *and* its double in primitive man. The sought-after single origin has become distractingly plural. Faced with this multiplying source, Freud does not resist, admitting that even these multiple sources are only part of the answer: "I believe that these factors are *partly* responsible for the impression of uncanniness" (*SE* 17:236, my emphasis). Because the uncanny's origin is now multiple and fractional, Freud's earlier goal of "differentiating" its singularity seems unlikely.[63] He fittingly ends this same sentence by emphasizing this improbability: "it is not easy to isolate and determine exactly [these factors'] share" in creating uncanny feeling (17:236).

But immediately after this, Freud again refuses to accept this proliferation, resorting to another single organizational "source" (*Quelle*)—the "repetition of the same thing"—which should encompass childhood and primitive beliefs, as well as any other of the multiple factors that might come along. Anything that reappears to us unexpectedly, whether from childhood, primeval times, or elsewhere—Freud insists—is "uncanny" (*SE* 17:236; *GW* 12:249). To prove this hypothesis, he again dons his figurative tropical helmet and heads off on a "voyage of discovery," as he did two decades earlier in *The Interpretation of Dreams*. He travels to a town in exotic, yet nearby, Italy: "As I [*ich*] was once [*einst*] walking, one hot summer afternoon, through the deserted streets of a provincial town in Italy which was unknown [*unbekannt*] to me, I found myself in a quarter of whose character I could not long remain in doubt." In this quarter, "Freud" wanders through "narrow" passages in an "unknown" region—repeating these words from *Interpretation of Dreams*—and searches for secrets (*SE* 17:237; *GW* 12:249). Like his readers in *Interpretation of Dreams*, Freud now loses his way. By getting lost in Italy's obscurity, he reenters the heroic mode from *Interpretation of Dreams* and the opening paragraphs from *The Uncanny*.

"Freud's" lostness, however, does not result in heroic self-relocation—the discovery of the "secret of dreams"—because he never gets really lost. Rather, he keeps returning to the same spot, involuntarily: "I [*Ich*] found myself in a quarter"; "I suddenly found myself back in the same street"; "I hurried away once more, only to arrive by another *détour*" (*SE* 17:237; *GW* 12:249). Freud dislocates himself but cannot recall himself in the end. He cannot emerge from the town's labyrinth onto "high ground" and then choose the proper split in the path because his dislocation is circular. This physical dislodging corresponds to the ego's—*Ich*'s—psychological unmooring. This *Ich* metamorphoses from subject to object: "A feeling seized me [*mich*]." Now the *object* of a foreign feeling, "Freud's" *Ich* gets seized; it inheres only in a foreign yet uncannily similar "me" (*SE* 17:237, trans. rev.; *GW* 12:249).

Intertextually uncanny also is the anecdote's setting: the foreign brothel is the "same place" to which the European traveler, "Freud," returns over and over. As discussed in my previous chapter, this "same place" was often explicitly a foreign whorehouse: not just Freud's in Italy but Hesse's in Port Said, Bonsels's in Bombay, Keyserling's in Kyoto, Kellermann's in Tokyo, Ewers's in Igatpuri, and so on. "Freud" insists that the streets near his Italian brothel were "deserted," but how could this be, given that, as his contemporaries insisted, foreign brothels were crowded with other traveling men? When Freud claims that this district is uncanny because of the recurrence of the "same thing," could he not also mean the mirror images expunged from his story: the same "strange" Freudenbergs, Weisflogs, and Sturzeneggers observed by Hesse in the Egyptian whorehouse? "Freud" claims that his returns begin to "excite attention," but from whom? Why would a john, the most normal visitor possible, provoke attention among prostitutes? Is it not perhaps the other male customers whom Freud "excites," and vice versa? Does this uncanny "homo" experience cause him retroactively to erase all of them—just as he erased the male guide from his Haggard dream—leaving the streets deserted except for himself and the women? Such an effacement would allow him to avoid the real horror, which Hesse encountered in Port Said: an uncanny parade of "Don Juans" that led him to "run away alone through the grotesque city."

Franz Kafka and Max Brod's visit to an Italian brothel in the same years as Freud's—perhaps to the same house?—likewise doubles Freud's experience and lets us know what Freud would more likely have seen: streets filled with "single" men who don't know that they are actually doubles, all crammed together in brothel antechambers like patients in a "doctor's office."[64] Anonymous sex tourists look at anonymous sex tourists. "Freud" looks at "Kafka." What becomes uncanny here, as in Freud's Haggard dream, is not the female genitalia but the "doubling or multipl[ying]" phallus, which Freud cites as uncanny just one page earlier in *The Uncanny* (*SE* 17:235).

How this fright affects "Freud," the adventurer, becomes clear when he renounces, however ironically, additional "voyages of discovery." He instead now undertakes only mundane trips that further demonstrate "the repetition of the same thing," at the cost of his heroic *Ich*. Freud becomes the anonymous "one" (*man*): "when, caught in a mist perhaps, one has lost one's way in a mountain forest." Freud's "*man*," like the *Ich* before it, is disoriented in "dark" "unknown" regions but, unlike the narrator-hero of *Interpretation of Dreams*, never emerges onto high ground. Instead, "*man*" circles within the forest back to more "same" places: "one" returns "again and again to one and the same spot." Or, in another of Freud's examples from this paragraph, "one" wanders about in an "unknown, dark" (*unbekannten, dunkeln*) room only to collide "time after time with the same piece of furniture" (*SE* 17:237; *GW* 12:249–50).

These returns prove the truth of Freud's theory—the uncanny is "the repetition of the same thing"—but only by further disintegrating "Freud," the explorer. He has performed too well his job of "translating himself" into the minds of primitives and neurotics, whose feelings he at first could not understand. Now he, like them, sees uncanny significance everywhere: when "one comes across the number 62" several times in one day (as one's coat-check ticket, as the number of one's ship cabin), "one begins to notice that everything which has a number—addresses, hotel rooms, compartments in railway trains—invariably has the same one." As Freud concludes, "One [*man*] finds this uncanny." And unless utterly immune to "superstition," "one" starts to take this number, sixty-two, as an indication of one's allotted life span especially when "*man*," like Freud, is sixty-two years old when all of this is happening (*SE* 17:237–38, trans. rev.; *GW* 12:250).

Freud's slippage from the *Ich* to the *man* corresponds to the traveler's descent into the unconscious realm of the "it" (*Es*), which turns out to be surprisingly nearby. In this nether region, where primitive beliefs reign and "chance" or "coincidence" (*Zufall*) gives way to "superstition," the scientific *Ich*, now called "*man*," finds himself strangely at home. He turns out not to be as firmly hardened against superstition as he had thought at the essay's beginning. In the form of "*man*," "Freud" starts to see how he resembles his own "neurotic" patients (*SE* 17:237, 238; *GW* 12:250, 251). Like them, he begins to report on "'uncanny' experience[s]," and, like them, he is "never surprised" by "coincidences," seeing instead only "'presentiments' which 'usually' come true" (*SE* 17:239–40).

The Source of Everything: Animism and the Omnipotence of Thoughts

Freud's use here of "neurotic patients"—especially his "Rat Man"—to understand the "source" (*Quelle*) of uncanny superstitions (such as the "evil eye") brings him back to familiar ground. "Freud" claims to have found this source, now, in the "omnipotence of thoughts," which returns him to the uncanny's ancient source in "the old, animistic conception of the universe." Freud claims that all of us occasionally return to this belief system, which troubles us because this reminds us of how we—like primitives, children, and "*man*"—still sometimes attribute superstitious meaning to coincidences. Nothing just happens because it happens; it must involve us. Despite the fact that we know better, we still believe this. Following Haeckel, Freud states that this "savage" superstition is familiar to us because we believed in it as children: "each of us has been through a phase of individual development corresponding to this animistic stage in primitive men." We still carry "traces" of this within us (*SE* 17:240; *GW* 12:252). Directing his reader frankly to "my book, *Totem and Taboo*," Freud defines uncanniness in the clearest possible terms: "everything which now strikes us as 'uncanny' fulfills the condition of touching those residues of animistic mental activity within us and bringing them to expression" (*SE* 17:241n1, 240–41).

Occurring two-thirds of the way through Freud's essay—and before he even mentions the word "repression"—this claim that "everything" uncanny touches on primitive animism seems to provide "Freud," the adventurer, with this essay's equivalent of the "secret of dreams." Freud now knows the secret of the uncanny, such that he can temporarily interrupt the string of source-substitutions and -excavations: from enucleation to castration to doubling to "infantile belief," to the latter's simultaneous doubling and antecedence in "primitiveness," to the umbrella concept of "the repetition of the same thing." Freud claims to put a stop to this proliferation by citing a specific version of primitiveness and repetition that explains "everything." At the heart of all uncanny feeling, he insists, is the return of "animistic mental activity." He even footnotes later, for a second time, his book about savages, *Totem and Taboo: Some Resemblances between the Mental Lives of Savages and Neurotics*, to prove his point. We find the dead uncanny because we still "think like savages" (i.e., animistically) about death: we retain our "primitive" fear that ghosts will carry us off to the netherworld (*SE* 17:243n1, 242, 241). Freud's new certainty temporarily stabilizes his theory and, correspondingly, his literary perspective. The *Ich*, *Er*, and *Man* have given way to the scientific first-person plural, reminiscent of *Interpretation of Dreams*: "We can no longer be in any doubt about the ground on which we now find ourselves" (*SE* 17:240, trans. rev.; *GW* 12:253).

This certainty rests on "my book," *Totem and Taboo*, the only one of Freud's works that he footnotes twice in *The Uncanny* and where, as is often forgotten, Freud first began theorizing the uncanny. This theorizing begins precisely in the footnote that Freud now repeats verbatim in *The Uncanny*:

> Cf. my book *Totem and Taboo* (1912–13), Essay III, "Animism, Magic and the Omnipotence of Thoughts," where the following footnote will be found: "We appear to attribute an 'uncanny' quality to impressions that seek to confirm the omnipotence of thoughts and the animistic mode of thinking in general, after we have reached a stage at which, in our judgment, we have abandoned such beliefs." (*SE* 17:241n)

This quotation from *Totem and Taboo* (*SE* 13:86n2) encapsulates exactly what Freud has just claimed to be *the* secret of uncanniness in the main text of *The Uncanny*, seven years later. Freud's 1919 "discovery" of this secret is thus an uncanny rediscovery. He finds here what he had already found while writing *Totem and Taboo* in 1911–12. How exactly did Freud make this first discovery, which he rediscovers in *The Uncanny*? And what can we, by returning to this "same" spot in *Totem and Taboo*, learn about Freud's new explanation for "everything"?

Primitive Man (Excursus II): *Totem and Taboo*'s Uncanny Footnotes

If, as Hélène Cixous claims, the footnote is the typographical marker of repression, then what is repressed when Freud directs us from a footnote in *The Uncanny* back to another footnote in *Totem and Taboo*?[65] What is hidden in a sentence that travels from text to text but remains *beneath* both? What is *under* the assertion: "we appear to attribute an 'uncanny' quality to . . ."? Is something perhaps repressed already in the first word, "we"? Something beneath the traditional scientific nominative plural? *Totem and Taboo*'s main text tells us that this "we" also refers to something else, something even opposed to the scientific plural: to an uncanny collaboration between the doctor and a "neurotic patient." That same patient whom Freud had just mentioned in *The Uncanny*, the Rat Man, turns out to have already discovered a central aspect of the very theory that Freud is now expounding: "I [Freud] have adopted the term 'omnipotence of thoughts' from a highly intelligent man who suffered from obsessional ideas and who, having been set right by psycho-analytic treatment, was able to give evidence of his efficiency and good sense." The neurotic has become the theoretician, blurring the border between science and madness, reason and irrationality, and so revealing cracks in science's "we." As in the collapse of narration in Hesse's *Robert Aghion*, this Rat Man's third-person "he" (*Er*) resembles the "id" (*Es*) that comes dangerously close to the scientific "ego" (*Ich*): "I" have adopted the term from "him," Freud states. "*He* had coined the phrase as an explanation of all the strange and uncanny [*unheimlichen*] events by which *he*, like the others afflicted with the same illness, seemed to be pursued" (*SE* 13:85–86; *GW* 9:106, my emphasis). The "I" and the "he" mix here to create a theory for "everything" uncanny.

It is no coincidence that Freud defines uncanniness for the first time at this moment when the "he" intrudes into his "I." The scientific ego cannot discover the uncanny alone; the ego requires this illicit, primitive collaboration. The "rat" is, "in legends," a paradigmatically "uncanny" creature, meaning that the Rat Man is much closer to uncanniness than the doctor ever could be.[66] When the Rat Man tells Freud of the "uncanny events" and "uncanny feeling[s]" in his life, Freud takes careful note (*SE* 13:86, 10:162). The doctor can discover the "uncanny" only together with this neurotic, and only in a footnote, which corresponds to the underground world of "sewers" and "grave[s]" where rats are at home.[67] In this netherworld, the doctor can keep his collaboration out of sight. The only trace of it remains in the footnoted cracks in the scientific "we."

If science borrows a concept from a "primitive" still in the process of being "set right," is it still science? We receive an answer two pages later in *Totem and Taboo*, when the concept the Rat Man uses to describe his "uncanny" feelings—"omnipotence of thoughts"—threatens science's foundations. Humanity progresses from animism to religion to science, Freud argues, and each phase corresponds to different historical fantasies about omnipotence: in animism, men think themselves omnipotent; in religion, they ascribe omnipotence to god; and in science, they no longer believe in omnipotence, except for their "primitive belief" in their own mental supremacy (*SE* 13:88). The term smuggled into Freud's text by a neurotic now proves that science itself is wild, especially in the moment when it most vehemently denies this. Here we see Freud's ability to reflect critically on "science," if not yet on psychoanalysis. He adopts the terminology of one of Europe's internal primitives and then lets it run amok in his book, undermining the self-justifications of science itself. This rat-voice allows Freud to reveal what he has been implying in *Totem and Taboo* all along: that rationality is not free from savagery.

Because this uncanny blurring of science and primitiveness begins in a footnote, it leads us to *Totem and Taboo*'s other remarkable footnotes, which likewise represent a truth repressed from the "science" preached above. These notes, too, overturn general assumptions about what belongs down below, with the rats, and what belongs up above, with the scientists. Consider, first, how Freud undermines his main-text assertions about the history of totems—borrowed from nineteenth-century British anthropology and folklore—already on the third page of *Totem and Taboo*. A three-paragraph, two-page footnote warns Freud's reader that the ethnological "facts" that he has just cited in "the text above" are actually "scarcely capable of being expressed."[68] His main text, Freud whispers, will issue "scarcely a statement" that will not "call for exceptions or contradictions." The authenticity of the totem rituals upon which Freud bases his case must be doubted because "even the most primitive and conservative races are in some sense *ancient races*" (emphasis in original). They have "a long past history" during which "their original conditions of life have been subject to much development and distortion."

Freud's footnote continues by claiming that totemic traditions cannot even be defined because they are fundamentally in flux: in "various stages of decay and disintegration"; in processes of "transition to other social and religious institutions"; or, if in "a stationary condition," then one differing "greatly from the original one." For this reason, scientists can never know whether to consider "the present state of things as a true picture of the significant features of the past or as a secondary distortion" (*SE* 13:3n2–4n2). What Freud criticizes here is the methodology of the fin de siècle anthropologists—primarily James Frazer and Andrew Lang—upon whom he otherwise bases his argument. How, he asks, can we attach an original status to societies that, like our own, are constantly changing? How can we ignore these societies' developments, including those caused by our own missionaries, colonists, and anthropologists? Are these cultures not necessarily, like Europe's own, always in a process of transition? Is it thus not impossible to use the term "primitive" in any reliable way?

Freud anticipates here his own careful reader, Bronislaw Malinowski, who ten years later described ethnology's poignant essence: "Ethnology is in the sadly ludicrous, not to say tragic, position, that at the very moment when it begins to put its workshop in order, to forge its proper tools, to start ready for work on its appointed task, the material of its study melts away with hopeless rapidity." The natives die away "under our very eyes" because of our weapons and our illnesses.[69] And those who survive do not remain as they were. They are transformed, not least by the presence of anthropologists such as Malinowski himself. Like the Ashanti in Vienna, Malinowski's aborigines in New Guinea, Freud insists, are already distorted from their "original" state. "We" can never find the real savage because we are out there looking for him. All that remains is a mélange of instability: "development," "distortion," "decay," "disintegration," and "transition." The savage slips through our fingers in the moment that we attempt to lay hold of him.

But this insight does not keep Freud from continuing for the next two "shadow-boxing" chapters to pronounce on savages in the text "above"—regurgitating Frazer's and Lang's theories of totemism, incest-fear, and animism—until he reaches the book's final momentous chapter, which he again interrupts with a long footnote.[70] Likewise extending over two pages, this note again "warn[s]" Freud's readers not to believe what he says in the main text about the "savage." This figure is necessarily "distort[ed]," Freud insists, by anthropology's methodological flaws, which he now categorizes into roughly four parts: (1) "observation"; (2) "communication"; (3) temporality ("present-day conditions" versus the "primeval past"); and (4) empathy (understanding "primitive modes of thinking").

First, the armchair anthropologists that Freud regularly cites—Frazer, Lang, John McLennan, E. B. Tylor, William Robertson Smith—rarely traveled to the contact zones (never setting "eyes on the objects of their researches"); instead, they borrowed their observations from travelers and missionaries. Second, these travelers and missionaries could not communicate in the target language, and, even if they could, they often encountered natives who gave "false or misleading information for a great variety of motives." Third, "primitive" societies have developed for millennia, as Freud mentioned in his earlier note; they are not petrified in some primeval yesteryear. Finally, European observers have trouble comprehending indigenous peoples' ways of thinking: "We misunderstand primitive men just as easily as we do children, and we are always apt to interpret their actions and feelings according to our own mental constellations." Due to these methodological shortcomings, we cannot gain access to the savage in his "original" form. He always remains a "matter of construction," a bricolage of anthropology's secondhand observations, miscommunications, temporal rifts, and unsuccessful empathies (*SE* 13:102n1–103n1).

As if deaf to his own warnings, however, Freud immediately re-hitches his main-text argument onto anthropology's (especially Frazer's), speaking again uncritically of "the savage" as if he really existed—until Freud's disapproving voice interferes again, just before he reaches his famous, audacious conclusion. This time, Freud's criticism creeps into the main text, where he tells us that primitive cultures have not retained their original form, meaning that "we have nothing whatever but hypotheses to fall back upon." This most radical objection yet—"we have nothing whatever"—continues in the corresponding note, where Freud insists, with Lang (who collaborated regularly with Haggard), that all of our conclusions about aboriginal cultures are mere "conjecture." The savage remains forever beyond our grasp: "Nowhere do we see absolutely *primitive* man" (*SE* 13:109, 109n1, emphasis in original). A few pages later, Freud's footnoted objections infiltrate the main text again, this time to attack his otherwise beloved Frazer. According to Freud, Frazer projects his own "wishful fantasies" of the Golden Age onto the Australian Arunta tribe, which was in fact "highly developed" (*SE* 13:116).

But Freud's questioning voice quickly gives way again to his own wishful fantasies, emerging this time even more pronouncedly than before. He begins by accepting Charles Darwin's and James Atkinson's claims that prehistoric man lived in primal hordes dominated by one male who expelled all of his sons until he had exclusive sexual rights over his wives and daughters. Freud then adds his own famous psychoanalytic twist. Barring "anything more than a misleading trick of chance [*Zufall*]," Darwin's banished sons must have had the same unconscious desires as Oedipus: to murder their father and marry their mother. The entire totemic system, Freud continues triumphantly, "was a product of the conditions involved in the Oedipus complex" (*SE* 13:132; *GW* 9:160). Telling here is Freud's conviction that he—unlike Frazer—is not being misled by wishful thinking. In this certainty, Freud resembles the "primitive" neurotics he diagnosed earlier in *Totem and Taboo* and again six years later in *The Uncanny*. These patients, Freud maintains, always deny "chance" or "coincidence" (*Zufall*), speaking instead of "uncanny" correlations that prove the truth of their own "presentiments" (*The Uncanny*, *SE* 17:237, 239–40; *GW* 12:250; see also *Totem and Taboo*, *SE* 13:86).

Freud's main text of *Totem and Taboo* now continues its flight undaunted, following its own presentiments toward its legendarily bold conclusion. According to Freud, the originally exiled sons formed a "band of males" that returned to kill the father and devour him. With the father eaten, the sons were ready to turn on each other and determine the next patriarch. But they feared each other's aggression, and so decided instead to form humanity's first social contract: each voluntarily renounced his desire for the horde's women (who became "taboo") in order to live peacefully with the other brothers (*SE* 13:141–43). Afterward, out of guilt for killing their father, these sons created a father-substitute—a sacred totem animal—who became their first god. The sons were not allowed to kill this totem, except when they had to, in preparation for their sacramental meal. This culminated in Christianity, in whose name bands of mortified brothers assembled regularly to atone for their great "crime" by repeating it: they ritually killed and ate their father. This social contract based on original guilt, Freud claims, explains why modern man today willingly forbids himself the very things for which he once fought: sexual intercourse with his mother, sisters, and daughters, as well as the right to murder his father (*SE* 13:154).

Beyond the sheer audacity of Freud's conjectures—on a par with the genesis stories of Vico and Nietzsche—we are astounded by Freud's style, which discards all scientific trappings for the bravura of the raconteur. Consider the explosive opening sentence: "One day [*Eines Tages*] the brothers who had been driven out came together, killed and devoured their father and so made an end of the patriarchal horde." Freud continues deftly and economically, condensing the entire myth and its subsequent explication into one paragraph, only whispering—in back-to-back footnotes beginning directly at "One day"—his apologies for his "lack of precision," especially his literary "abbreviation of the time factor" and "compression of the whole subject-matter." But Freud nonetheless continues in this confident mode of "One day," redolent of the fairy tale's "Once upon a time" and anticipating already the "once" (*einst*) from *The Uncanny*'s "voyage of discovery." Within this concentrated temporality, Freud forges his fabulous eruption. The sons killed their father, and "cannibal savages as they were, it goes without saying" that they ate him, who was "doubtless" their envied model (*SE* 13:141–42, 141n, 142n; *GW* 9:171–72, 171n, 172n). Here, Freud's speculation transforms into magical certitude. *Totem and Taboo*'s scientific rationality loses itself in the unconscious time of "One day," where anything is possible. Without explanation, time condenses, a dramatic past becomes present, and a swashbuckling adventure story comes true.

With this finale in mind, we see how *Totem and Taboo*, too, is an adventure story—as suggested by Freud's amused reaction to a critic's claim that *Totem and Taboo* was, like Kipling's exotic origin stories about elephants, leopards, and cavemen, a "*Just So Story*" (*SE* 18:122). Specifically, *Totem and Taboo* bridges *The Interpretation of Dreams* and *The Uncanny* by moving from a heroic tale to the kind of uncanny travel narrative so prominent in Freud's day. Freud begins again as the "conquistador" from *The Interpretation of Dreams*, setting off in search of "savages" at the moment when the last cartographic blank spaces were filled. But like Jacques, Hesse, and Haggard, Freud experiences an uncanny shock when he discovers that these savages are familiar, bearing many "resemblances" with all Europeans and especially with the "dark-skinned" doctor who came to examine him. And Freud, like his predecessors, partially suppresses this knowledge by retaining the dream of a true aborigine beyond these uncanny resemblances: Haggard's imagined "last pure race of Indians" (*Heart of the World*, 339). Freud, too, constructs a fantasy of absolute savages, still living on the other side of the "Range of Wonder": a murderous band of cannibals, devouring over and over again, in magical fairy-tale time, their incestuous father.

Freud clings to this fantasy despite all indications to the contrary. Even if this band of brothers harbored patricidal and incestuous desires, how could Freud know that they actually carried out the murder? If they resembled modern neurotics as much as Freud claims they do, how did they dare to kill their father? Freud mentions this possible criticism on the last page of *Totem and Taboo* but then immediately dismisses it. Despite his earlier insistence, from his subtitle onward, on "resemblances" (*Übereinstimmungen*) between savages and modern men, he now claims that the two were not similar at all. Whereas modern men are like Hamlet, afraid to act, primitive men were "uninhibited": their "thought passe[d] directly into action." They "actually *did* what all the evidence shows that they intended to do" (*SE* 13:161, emphasis in original). To what evidence is Freud referring? He can only mean the anthropological "facts" of Frazer, Atkinson, Darwin, and Robertson Smith, which Freud has been debunking all along in his notes. By confidently creating this story in which his own "presentiments" come true, Freud engages in the same wishful thinking of which he accuses savages, neurotics, and anthropologists earlier in *Totem and Taboo*. The doctor has located "absolutely *primitive* man" but, in so doing, has become primitive himself—undeterred by his own awareness of this. Freud inadvertently cements what he had already revealed through his theorizing Rat Man: rationality and savagery are always intertwined, a maxim that applies also to psychoanalysis, even if Freud does not yet see this.

Returning to *The Uncanny*, we now see that "my book, *Totem and Taboo*" cannot define the uncanny as Freud has wished. It cannot prove that "everything" uncanny touches on primitive beliefs, most obviously because *Totem and Taboo* cannot even tell us what primitiveness is. This term emerges only within a series of contradictions: the savage is knowable and unknowable; the savage is like us and not like us; and modern science is at once rational and savage. If *Totem and Taboo* is psychoanalysis's "foundational text"—not an insignificant dalliance of the master—then this is not, contrary to Celia Brickman, because it establishes psychoanalysis's authority over primitiveness.[71] Rather, *Totem and Taboo* inaugurates a dialectics of bold speculation and self-deconstruction that, however crudely at this point, characterizes much of Freud's later writing, especially *The Uncanny*. This is the service that "my book" ends up performing for the later work. Although Freud ultimately creates in *Totem and Taboo* a fiction about the absolute savage, he remains persistently ambivalent about this fiction, and so conditions the sophisticated reflections that eventually appear in *The Uncanny*. The savage may not exist at all, Freud repeatedly warns us in the footnotes, even as he continues to hold forth about him in the main text. What is more, the anthropological and psychoanalytic sciences occupied with savagery might not exist either, or, if they do, only as wild fictions that continually expose their own fantasies of omnipotence.

"Inexplicable": The War Neurotic, the Fallen Son, and the Analyst as *Man*

Because *Totem and Taboo* cannot confirm that everything uncanny touches on primitive beliefs, Freud turns back to his standby source: the "repetition of the same," which he now outfits with the psychoanalytic terminology of "repression." Freud's "new hypothesis" states that the uncanny is something familiar that "has become alienated from [the mind] through the process of repression" (*SE* 17:241). Today's critical shorthand often takes this to be Freud's final word on the matter,[72] forgetting that he only introduces repression two-thirds of the way through the essay and, even then, does not employ it consistently. Freud sometimes abandons the term for significant periods or, as he admits later, stretches it "beyond its legitimate meaning" (17:249). Already here, Freud uses "repression" to describe a dazzling series of things, such that it comes to mean everything and nothing: "animism, magic and sorcery, the omnipotence of thoughts, man's attitude to death, involuntary repetition, and the castration complex" (17:243). And the confusion mounts. Freud proceeds to drop "repression" from his argument for three pages, pointing instead to sources that seem to be outside of repression's conceptual framework. He lists again primitive animism as the "origin" (*Ursprung*) of many "uncanny effects," followed by a dizzying array of other causes: "psychoanalysis itself," "the castration complex," the fantasy of "intra-uterine existence," and uncertainty about whether things are real (*SE* 17:243–44; *GW* 12:257–58).

As evidence of the latter, he refers to the above-mentioned adventure story from an issue of *The Strand* that fell into his hands in "the middle of the isolation of wartime." Amidst other "somewhat redundant matter" in this magazine, Freud discovered that this story—although "naive"—produced in him an "uncanny feeling" of "remarkable" power (*SE* 17:244–45). What was it about this story that affected Freud so mightily? And, given that this story has been relatively ignored by scholars, what new insights can it offer about the tension between primitiveness and science in Freud's construction of the uncanny?[73]

Although Freud does not name this tale's title, he describes its plot such that we can easily locate it in wartime issues of *The Strand* (figure 23). Called "Inexplicable," by L. G. Moberly, the story appeared in 1917 and begins with an "ordinary" couple moving into a suburban London house whose previous owner had left behind a table inlaid with decorative alligators (figure 24). Soon, the couple notices a stench in the house, and the husband even trips over an object slithering around at his ankles (some loose carpet, he says). When the husband's old friend, Jack Wilding, joins the couple for dinner, he insists that this odor is the same one that he had smelled years ago in a crocodile swamp in New Guinea, where his own good friend had been killed. The husband dismisses Wilding's irrational "association of ideas," and Wilding eventually agrees, even if he remains haunted by flashbacks for the remainder of the evening.[74] After Wilding leaves the following day, the husband and wife begin to see alligators in the house. Panicked, they spend the night in the garden cottage. The following morning, the husband burns the carved table, and the alligators miraculously never appear again. The wife—also the story's narrator—says that this entire experience remains "inexplicable" to her even

Figure 23. Cover page of the December 1917 issue of *The Strand*, in which Freud found the story "Inexplicable"

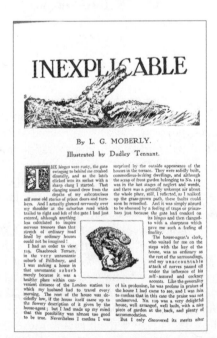

Figure 24. First page of "Inexplicable," about which Freud wrote, "It was a naive enough story, but the uncanny feeling it produced was remarkable."

Figure 25. Jack Wilding recalling how his friend was snatched to his death by "loathsome brutes" in the swamps of colonial New Guinea (from "Inexplicable")

today, after all these years. She closes with a challenge to the reader: "Does any explanation of it all occur to you?" ("Inexplicable," 581).

Freud does not respond explicitly to the wife's challenge, but we can see, if we follow the story's own "association of ideas," a subtext that would have intrigued him. The pre-story—the death of Wilding's friend—takes place in New Guinea, part of which Germany still ruled when the story was published, and which Freud would have read about when the Australians defeated the Germans there in the 1914 battle of Bita Paka. New Guinea's military-colonial background becomes explicit in a drawing accompanying the story. Outfitted in imperial garb—tropical helmet, swamp boots, rifle— Wilding walks across a bridge while his similarly dressed friend is snatched to his death by crocodiles: those "loathsome brutes" ("Inexplicable," 577; figure 25). Unlike the human man-eating "brutes" from Conrad's *Heart of Darkness* two decades earlier, Wilding's reptiles will not be "exterminated." Rather, they, like the cannibal in another adventure book owned by Freud (*Claire Lenoir*),[75] take revenge on the invaders: they steal the Englishman into "the darkness" and devour him. In this attack, we see the political unconscious in this 1917 English story. The colonies will strike back. England's sons will die in New Guinea. If they return at all, it will be as corpses, rankly "decaying" like the swamps themselves. Just after Wilding finishes telling his tale, he trips over an ominous "dark shape," and a "cloud of uncanny, shuddering sensations" creeps over the narrator ("Inexplicable," 576, 578).

This story would likely have affected Freud on a similarly historical register because two of his own sons were, at that moment, fighting in some of Austria's own colonies: Martin Freud in Galicia and Ernst Freud in the northern Italian territories.[76] Freud hints at his fears of his sons' death in "Thoughts for the Times on War and Death" (1915), around the same time that he would have been conceiving *The Uncanny*;[77] he repeats here the phrase *"an der Leiche der geliebten Person"* (at the dead body of the loved one) on consecutive pages (*SE* 14:294, 295, trans. rev.; *GW* 10:347, 348). Likewise in 1915, Freud dreamt repeatedly of his sons dying in the war: as he wrote to Sándor Ferenczi, he dreamt of "the deaths of my sons, Martin first of all."[78] And in 1918, after being "without news of our son on the front" for over a week, Freud had a famous dream about his son mounting a basket and "falling" (in Freud's post-dream association).[79] Freud added this dream to his 1919 republication of *The Interpretation of Dreams*, where he interpreted his son's "fall" in the figurative sense of having been killed at war (*SE* 5:559–60).

Despite Freud's emphasis in this dream on his son dying ("falling"), a close reading reveals that, disturbingly, this son is *not* dead but rather injured and alive. Like Wilding, Freud's dream-son has the telltale symptoms of that postwar figure who—ever present, unlike the dead son—did not allow Europe to forget the war: the war neurotic. The dream-son's bandaged forehead implies cranial damage; he is grey and unusually exhausted; and he is peculiarly unable to speak (he does not reply to his father's calls).[80] Freud even states that his dream-son's uncharacteristically silver hair reminds him of his real-life son-in-law, whose hair had turned prematurely gray after being "hit hard by the war." Like the war-damaged son-in-law, Freud's dream-son is now "hit hard," to the point that he cannot master the tasks of daily life: he seems to want to put something on a cupboard but apparently has nothing in his hands; he instead fidgets his fingers vaguely in his mouth. Although Freud claims that his dream-son's sports clothes recall a real-life skiing "fall," meaning that it is proper to interpret him as having "died in war," Freud is not completely convinced by his own logic. His dream-son is, Freud admits, "climbing," not "falling." What Freud does not discuss—but what would have been clear to any reader in 1919—are the dream-son's symptoms: the head injury, the premature gray hair, the muteness, and the nervous fingers all suggest war trauma, not death (*SE* 5:559).

Freud's traumatized dream-son returns us to *The Uncanny* where, just one paragraph before Freud mentions "Inexplicable," he lists a series of generally uncanny attributes in humans: "Dismembered limbs, a severed head, a hand

cut off at the wrist, as in a fairy tale of Hauff's, feet which dance by themselves . . . all these have something peculiarly uncanny about them, especially
when, as in the last instance, they prove capable of independent activity in
addition" (*SE* 17:244). No Central European reader in 1919 would have connected these dismembered, shaking bodies solely with fairy tales, or, as Freud
insists later, the castration complex. Freud had already admitted that "the
times in which we live" color *The Uncanny*, but here we see this influence
occurring in ways that Freud did not expect: his uncanny amputated, quiver-
ing bodies wavering between life and death recalled Europe's traumatized
postwar sons (17:220).

Dismembered and nerve-damaged, these "war-shakers" (*Kriegszitterer*)
peppered the streets of Freud's Vienna just as they did Wilding's London,
home of, among others, the shell-shocked World War I veteran from Virginia
Woolf's *Mrs. Dalloway*, Septimus Smith. When Freud mentions "epilep[tic],"
"danc[ing]" bodies in *The Uncanny*, then moves on to discuss the "world
war" (*Weltkrieg*) and an English story about colonial New Guinea, his readers would, like Wilding, indeed have had an "association of ideas" (*SE* 17:243,
244, trans. rev.; *GW* 12:257). But their ideas would have gone well beyond
a theory of the uncanny in fairy tales. They would have seen the *Kriegszitterer* and, figuratively inscribed on them, the *unheimlich* watchwords of the
postwar era: estrangement and unhomeliness.

In 1919 these *Kriegszitterer* were everywhere in *Mitteleuropa*: in private
homes, begging on the streets, and, more important for my purposes, in
bureaucratic documents—both the military-psychiatric reports read by Freud
and the benefits claims processed by Freud's fellow Austrian, the insurance
specialist Dr. Franz Kafka.[81] Charged with managing the treatment of war-
damaged soldiers in Prague, Kafka described these "shakers" and "leapers"
in 1916 in ways that resemble both Kafka's own fiction and Freud's account
of uncanny bodies: "shaken as if by a terrible shiver-attack, . . . poor, pale,
emaciated men carry out leaps, as if gripped in the back of the neck by a
merciless hand that drags them to and fro in agonizing motions."[82] Kafka's
Kriegszitterer recall here Freud's "dismembered" bodies whose feet "dance
by themselves" as well as Hoffmann's Olympia, who seems at once to be
"a human being" and "an automaton" (*SE* 17:227). Although Freud never
names these *Kriegszitterer* in *The Uncanny*, they appear silently through his
reference to "Inexplicable" and, a few pages earlier, to his just-finished book
inspired by war neuroses: *Beyond the Pleasure Principle* (17:238). In this
latter work, Freud observes that the "terrible war that has just ended" has
caused an unprecedented increase in trauma cases, which Freud attempts
to understand (*SE* 18:12). In this way, the "times in which we live" and the
"*Weltkrieg*" influence *The Uncanny* more than Freud explicitly states.

The war neurotic's ghostly presence in this section of *The Uncanny*
intensifies when we consider Wilding—the traumatized figure from
"Inexplicable"—in relation to Freud's pre- and postwar writings. "Wilding"

recalls the "*Wilde*" ("savage") from *Totem and Taboo* (1912–13) who, as Freud insisted in that work's subtitle, was uncannily similar to modern neurotics. And Wilding likewise embodies the modern primitive, whose main incarnation during and after the war was the "shell-shocked" war neurotic. Wilding has flashbacks that resemble a "waking nightmare," causing him to sweat and turn gray, to be suddenly unable to speak (talking is "impossible"), and to twitch his head in "a curious uneasy movement" ("Inexplicable," 577–78). Similarly disturbed returnees appear in four Freud texts bunched precisely around the publication of *The Uncanny*: the above-mentioned wartime dream published in the 1919 edition of *The Interpretation of Dreams*; *Beyond the Pleasure Principle* (1920); the introduction to *Psychoanalysis and the War Neuroses* (1919); and Freud's expert contribution to the postwar inquiry into Austrian doctors' brutal treatment of soldiers, "Memorandum on the Electrical Treatment of War Neurotics" (1920). In these four writings surrounding *The Uncanny*, Freud repeatedly returns to military men who, like Wilding and the dismembered dancers from *The Uncanny*, have "puzzling disorders." They experience nightmares, speechlessness, "tremors," and "paralyses," all pointing toward "severe disturbances in their mental life and in their nervous activities" (*SE* 17:207, 18:13, 17:212, 211).

Wilding's symptoms culminate in a "fall" that recalls his friend's fall to death in the swamps, the narrator's husband's stumble over "alligators," and the "fall" of Freud's own dream-son. We read that Wilding staggers, throwing out his hands and then landing heavily on the ground, "his eyes as dazed as his voice"—as if in a fit. At this precise moment—and for the only time in the entire "Inexplicable"—the wife-narrator uses the word "uncanny," claiming that Wilding's fall produces in her "uncanny, shuddering sensations" ("Inexplicable," 578). The source of the uncanny in "Inexplicable" is thus the same as it is in this section of *The Uncanny*: the war-traumatized body that the home front does not want to see. The fact that this body appears in neither "Inexplicable" nor *The Uncanny* cements the point of its repression. Just as Freud cannot mention the war neurotic by name, the narrator of "Inexplicable" is aware of him—as of everything else in her story—only in her "subconscious self" ("Inexplicable," 572).

Why can Freud not name this connection between the war neurotic and uncanniness that is so evident both in *The Uncanny* and in his own dream life? As is often the case with his own repressions, Freud hints at the answer himself: he might have repressed the war neurotic from his 1919 writings because of his guilt in relation to his sons. Like so many fathers, Freud had uncritically seen his sons off to war in 1914; and when he wrote about the dream of the injured son in the 1919 edition of *The Interpretation of Dreams*, he found within it "a hostile impulse aimed at the gallant soldier," one that derived from the "envy which is felt for the young by those who have grown old" (*SE* 5:560). In *The Uncanny*, this guilt registers subconsciously in Freud's grammar: through extraordinary shifts in the pronoun "one" (*man*) in the two sentences that conclude his comments on "Inexplicable." Describing the fears of the story's characters, Freud writes:

> They [*man*] stumble over something in the dark; they [*man*] seem to see a vague form gliding over the stairs—in short, we [*man*] are given to understand that the presence of the table causes ghostly crocodiles to haunt the place . . . . It was a naive enough story, but the uncanny feeling it produced was quite remarkable [*verspürte man als ganz hervorragend*]. (*SE* 17:244–45; *GW* 12:258)

"*Man*" moves here from twice meaning "they" (the frightened, stumbling characters from "Inexplicable") to "we" (the readers of "Inexplicable") to a subject-mishmash so confusing that James Strachey deletes it entirely from his translation ("the uncanny feeling it produced was quite remarkable"). But, contra Strachey, Freud does give us a subject in this final sentence— "*man*"—which denotes "one" but refers also to "I," in this case to Freud, the reporting reader: "*ihre unheimliche Wirkung verspürte man als ganz hervor-ragend*" (literally, "one ['I'] sensed its [the story's] uncanny effect as quite remarkable"). Through this shift in meaning from "they" to "we" to "I," the guilty Freud slips from the safe position of the outside observer into the shoes of the neurotic soldier, Wilding, who represents by association Freud's sons and his son-in-law: all "hit hard by the war."

By thus identifying with both the doctor-father and the neurotic-son, Freud recapitulates in his own body the entire primal crime from *Totem and Taboo*. But more than simply repeating this scene, Freud complicates it— in two ways. First, he points out the event's circularity: each of *Totem and Taboo*'s "sons" knows that, when he becomes a father, he will become the target of aggression from his own son—who represents both this (new) father when he was young and, more important, the original father (now the dead grandfather), returning in youthful form to take his revenge.[83] Second, Freud modernizes this primal crime, connecting it to the end of the First World War, specifically to the neurotically damaged sons who returned home to chal-lenge the fathers who had ambivalently given them up for dead. By linking the primal son from *Totem and Taboo* to the war-neurotic son from 1919, Freud creates here a pivot between *Totem and Taboo*, *The Uncanny*, and his 1920 text inspired by the war neurotics: *Beyond the Pleasure Principle*. Given this blurring of subjects (father/son) and of texts at this point in *The Uncanny*, it is not surprising that Freud, as the "*man*" who is both doctor/ father and neurotic/son, feels himself, too, to be falling: "One [*man*] stumbles over something in the dark." Reduced now to the third (or fourth) person, this falling doctor resembles the war neurotics, the primal sons, and *She*'s Holly, who feels himself "falling" into the chasm that caused Freud's night-mare (*She*, 242). He can no longer deny what he sees: "One [*man*] sensed" the "uncanny effect."

Traveling to a Country Familiar to Me:
Of Genitalia, Female and Male

Freud exits these swamps, like the bogs from his Haggard nightmare, shaken but still carrying on. Admitting that his essay's "collection of examples" remains "incomplete," he vows now to convince the skeptical reader through yet one more anecdote. "Unless it rests upon mere coincidence" (*einem zufälligen Zusammentreffen*), this new story should provide the most convincing confirmation yet of Freud's "theory of the uncanny" (as the "return of the same" or "repression"). But like his earlier accounts of wandering through forests and bumping into furniture, this new travel tale convinces only through a neurotic logic. "Freud" resembles again his own primitive patients, who refused to accept *Zufall* ("coincidence") as *Zufall*. Everything appears for a reason, including this new story, which, like the Rat Man's earlier one, is told to Freud by a neurotic. His neurotic male patients—as discussed above in relation to Freud's Haggard dream—always find "something uncanny" about the female genitalia, and they equate this discovery, in their dreams, with a journey to a faraway land: "whenever a man dreams of a place or a country and says to himself, while he is still dreaming: 'this place is familiar to me, I've been here once before,' this place may be interpreted as the mother's genitals or her womb" (*SE* 17:245, trans. rev.; *GW* 12:259).

Coming on the heels of Wilding's journey to the crocodile swamp, this "place" may recall the *vagina dentata*,[84] but a closer look reveals—as in Freud's Haggard-dream bogs—something at once more familiar and more disturbing: the *male* genitalia, appearing in the uncanny "multiplic[ity]" that Freud cited earlier in *The Uncanny* (*SE* 17:235). As with the brothel visits described above, a journey to a faraway country during the "world war" led not to the Ur-feminine "former *Heim* [home] of all human beings, . . . the place where each one of us lived once upon a time and in the beginning" but to the hyper-masculine world of the military barracks (*SE* 17:245). "Wilding" connects here to both Oscar Wilde (mentioned later in *The Uncanny* [17:252]) and to the "*Wilde*" from "Thoughts for the Times on War and Death" and *Totem and Taboo*: the prehistoric "savage" (*Wilde*) who lived in a militarized band of brothers founded upon "homosexual feelings and acts" (*SE* 14:295 [*GW* 10:349]; *SE* 13:144). Like these ancient bands, fin de siècle armies produced "contingent inverts"—as Freud learned from Sándor Ferenczi's powerful homosexual urges during his war service.[85] The homoerotic voyage to a country "familiar to me" further evokes the Rat Man, whom Freud mentioned just a couple of pages earlier in *The Uncanny* and who once told Freud of a journey to a barracks on Austro-Hungary's eastern fringe (today's Ukraine). The Rat Man had there a cruel captain who told of corporal punishment still practiced "in the East": insubordinate soldiers were bound prone, with a pot of rats turned upside down onto their buttocks (*SE* 10:166). At this exotic yet familiar spot—an outlandish Ukraine filled with

Austrian comrades (with penises like "rats")—the Rat Man has a paradigmatic uncanny experience.

This exotic journey to the *male* genitalia returns us to Wilding's military
voyage to New Guinea, where he once lived so closely with his "friend."
Wilding's homo-social soldierly desire resurfaces when he sits down alone
with the husband after dinner to smoke. At the precise moment when the
two men deepen their talk, the "indescribable odor to which I could give no
name" appears (leading to Wilding's hysteria). This "ordinary" English house
has become "queer": run through by a "queer smell," the "awfully queer
smell," and the husband's "queer little shiver" which ends with him taking
his friend up "into bed" ("Inexplicable," 573, 576, 574, 578).[86] The house's
queer smell coincides with this return of Wilding's homosexual desire, which
reminded the Rat Man of the odoriferous sewers that rats liked to penetrate.
This same metaphor runs through "Inexplicable" when the husband suspects
the sewage drains as the odor's source: "I would have every drain carefully inspected again"; "an expert declared the drains to be entirely above
reproach"; and, just before Wilding breaks down, *"Drains!"* (573, 574, 576,
emphasis in original). Like Hesse's Robert Aghion and Haggard's Holly and
Ignatio, Wilding is haunted by this desire—nurtured in the all-male Ocea-
nian swamps: not for an exotic feminine "bush" but for the all-too-familiar
European anus. When Wilding shouts *"Drains!,"* he remembers his longing
for "the same—same—," which now seems to traumatize him as much as did
the war itself. Diagnosing soldiers like Wilding in this same year (1917), Karl
Abraham argued (in a lecture praised by Freud) that homosexual desire and
"war neuroses" were connected: when repressed homosexuality surfaced in
all-male barracks, it weakened the constitution of "labile" men, rendering
them more susceptible to shell shock.[87]

These homo-soldierly journeys of Wilding, the militarized *"Wilde"* from
Totem and Taboo, and the Rat Man lurk within Freud's *The Uncanny*. What
they tell us about genitalia and uncanniness is opposed to what Freud states
overtly. Not the vagina is uncanny; rather, the proliferating phallus is, along
with the male anus. The "awfully queer smell" accompanying the neuroses
of the 1918–19 returnees comes from anal "sewers," not maternal swamps.
The Rat Man's travels to the "East" bring him to this familiar "place" on
the man's body, which he recalls just after reporting an "uncanny feeling"
("Notes upon a Case of Obsessional Neurosis," *SE* 10:162). This torture
story, along with the "Southern Slav" practice of "arse-fucking," transport
the Rat Man back "horrified" to childhood "homosexual games" in which
his brother's penis touched the Rat Man's anus (10:215, 311, 313). This early
anal eroticism takes the Rat Man back even further, to a yet earlier childhood fantasy: that babies issued from anuses and, consequently, that fathers
could give birth too (220). He has now returned to a "place" that precedes
the womb: to the father's anus, where the child imagines babies incubating—
before this child even understands the function of the womb. In this place,

the child is convinced that it, too, resided "once upon a time and in the beginning" (*The Uncanny*, 17:245).

Another Adventure: A Train Journey
and the Return of the Savage

"Freud" emerges from this adventure to a familiar land sapped, sensing that the sources of the uncanny are proliferating commensurately with the erogenous zones, and he worries that his readers are now filled with "doubt." He returns to his "new hypothesis"—that the return of the repressed causes uncanniness—but immediately questions this: "Not everything that recalls repressed desires" is uncanny, he admits (*SE* 17:245). What is more, renegade sources appear that seem to have no connection to repression: "silence, darkness, and solitude," "danger," and "intellectual uncertainty" (17:246–47). Freud first tries to exclude these outliers, claiming that they produce uncanny effects only in literature, not in real life, but then admits that this exclusion would open the door to even more doubts about the diagnostic value of his theory. Freud nonetheless initially goes forward with this exclusion, insisting that "nearly all" of the examples contradicting his repression thesis come from fiction. He then summarizes with a statement of belief that again omits all fictional depictions: the return of "something familiar that has been repressed" always causes uncanny experiences in real life, "I think" (17:247).

As if to dilute his theory further, Freud tells us that, even in "real life," uncanny experiences don't generally issue from the return of "repressed infantile complexes" but rather from the recurrence of "primitive" "animistic beliefs": from material that is "surmounted," not "repressed" (*SE* 17:248, 249). Our "primitive forefathers" once believed in the "omnipotence of thoughts," the "prompt fulfillment of wishes," "secret injurious powers," "the return of the dead," and the hauntings of one's "double." We now imagine that we have surmounted these beliefs while actually still holding them. One strange coincidence suffices to give us the uncanny feeling that these beliefs were correct all along. It is as if, Freud claims, we were making the judgement: "So, after all, it is *true* that one can kill a person by the mere wish!" (17:247–48).

As if to separate himself from the neurotics with which he identified in "Inexplicable," "Freud," the doctor, claims that he has "completely and finally" surmounted such primitive beliefs. To prove this to us, he reverts, strangely, to adventure fiction about his "double": "Freud" dons his traveling hat and relates a first-person "adventure" (*Abenteuer*) anecdote that, not surprisingly, appears in a footnote. "I was sitting alone in my *wagon-lit* compartment when a more than usually violent jolt of the train swung back the door of the adjoining washing-cabinet, and an elderly gentleman in a dressing-gown and a traveling cap came in." Assuming that this gentleman had taken a wrong turn, Freud jumped up "with the intention of putting him right," but "at once realized to my dismay that the intruder was nothing but my own image, projected from the mirror on the connecting door." Still insisting that he is impervious to uncanny feeling, Freud claims not to have been frightened by this doppelgänger, but rather, like his healthy fellow scientist Ernst Mach, to have felt only a mild "dislike" for it (*SE* 17:248n1; *GW* 12:262n1).

Considering Freud's earlier susceptibility to uncanny feelings while getting lost in the red-light district, when seeing "62" on hotel doors, and when reading "Inexplicable," this invulnerability is unconvincing, and Freud immediately acknowledges as much. In the self-reflectivity that we have learned to expect from *The Uncanny*, Freud asks, in the note's final sentence, whether his feeling of mild displeasure might actually be a "vestig[e]" of his primitive belief that his double is indeed uncanny. The same question could be asked of travelers and anthropologists who claim that stumbling upon other Europeans in the jungle is only annoying. Does their "dislike," too, camouflage vestigial uncanny fears?

If this residual fear reveals the recurrence of savage, neurotic beliefs in the apparently healthy Freud, then this recurrence would be exaggerated after a "violent jolt" in a train, which likely reminded Freud of his earlier, apparently surmounted train-phobia.[88] Might the recollection of this phobia not in turn harken Freud back to his earlier admitted "hysteria," which included strong "homosexual investments"?[89] What exactly does the doctor see when he looks in the mirror and sees a strange "gentleman"? A half-undressed comrade sharing his compartment? Or another swarthy "little Moor" who, unlike the non-Jewish Mach, looks too much like a savage?[90]

Freud suggests that this wild neurotic resides within all "enlightened" explorers, including himself, as a closer look at this anecdote's narrative perspective reveals. Freud gives a critical, anthropological turn to Heideggerian ontology when his "I" projects/drafts/throws (*entwerfen*) itself into the position of the primitive "him": "Jumping up with the intention of putting *him* right [*ihn aufzuklären*], I at once realized to my dismay that the intruder was nothing but my own image, projected [*entworfen*] from the mirror." This relation of the first-person "I" (*Ich*) to the third-person "he" (*Er*) echoes the grammar of psychoanalysis, in which the ego (for which Freud uses the idiomatic *Ich* or "I") must inhabit—and so defuse—the third-person id (*Es* or "it"). Unlike the educable Rat Man, who Freud claims was "set right by psycho-analytic treatment," this new "he" from *The Uncanny* ten years later stubbornly will not let himself be "put right" (*ihn aufzuklären*; literally, "to enlighten him"). He rebuffs the "I's" attempts to enlighten "him" and takes on instead a life of his own, refusing the "I's" urgent warnings that he is on the wrong path: "*I* assumed that . . . he had taken the wrong direction." Unable to straighten out this "he," the "I" gets drawn ever further into the depths of "his" footnote. Realizing his similarity to this third-person other, the doctor's "I" now becomes "helpless,"[91] until he must admit that he is not as civilized and secure as he thinks: "I," too, am ultimately defenseless against the return of "vestigial" neuroses.

The tension Freud lays out here between the doctor's "I" and the primitive double's "he" does more than unsettle the analyst's position: it exemplifies the uncanny perspective at the heart of psychoanalysis. In his train "adventure," Freud presents us most clearly with what Samuel Weber sees as the inimitable quality of psychoanalysis, as revealed by Hoffmann *avant la lettre* in "The Sandman": the "inextricable confounding of the perspectives of first and third person, ego and id."[92] The primitive id lies both outside of the ego and within it, just as this third-person (*Er* or *Es*) is both in front of the analyst and inside him. In a marked difference from *Totem and Taboo*, yet still following its trajectory, Freud brings this confounding to the fore in *The Uncanny*—and not only in footnotes. This uncanny confusion becomes now the essential marker of psychoanalysis's "scientific" method.

Final Dislocations: Literature, Perspective, and the Uncanny Other Place

This blurring of the traveling "Freud's" ego leads, not surprisingly, to further confusions in his attempt to "differentiate" a single "source" of the uncanny. Freud claims now that uncanny feelings issue from two different returns of the familiar: of repressed "infantile complexes" and of surmounted "primitive beliefs." To complicate matters, he senses that the distinction between these two has become increasingly "hazy."[93] In the midst of this haze, "Freud," the explorer, leaves the railway and even "real life" for the "fertile province" of literature: the realm of the outlier uncanny feelings that he had earlier excluded (*SE* 17:249).

An inveterate explorer, "Freud" has allowed himself to be "tempt[ed]" into this strange province and then to "drift" through it, before realizing—like the heroes of popular adventure literature—that he is not the first. He now sees everywhere the markings of the original explorers, the "students of aesthetics." There is thus "nothing new" for him to discover (*SE* 17:251).[94] Far from reaching a unique "source" of the uncanny—like the untouched upswelling of the Nile—he makes the uncanny discovery that the uncanny's source is always what has already been discovered. Having reached his goal, yet still disenchanted by this troubling sameness, he stops speaking of his heroic-seeming journey and instead aims merely to explain "certain instances" that have "contradicted our theory." For this, he remains in this already discovered fringe aesthetic territory that, as he hinted at the beginning, is as off-to-the-side (*abseits*) and apparently insignificant as uncanniness itself: it contains only small literary problems. In this *abseits* literary realm, the subdued "adventurer" pursues an apparently trivial question that does not seem to have relevance beyond literature: why do some stories depicting repressed complexes create "uncanny effect[s]" while others do not (17:251–52)?

Like the question of uncanniness, however, this one turns out not to be *abseits* at all. By dealing with form, not content, Freud's question presents the dilemma of modernity's sciences of man—anthropology and psychoanalysis—in a deliberately *ethnographic* fashion: how does one "write" about (other) "people"? Because this "how" inheres in *perspective*, Freud senses that literature might supply the answer. Why, Freud asks, do we not get an uncanny feeling from Herodotus's story about a master thief and a princess, even though the princess probably does get this feeling? Because we remain in the "superior" position of the thief, Freud insists, and do not "put ourselves" (*uns versetzen*) into the princess's unknowing point of view. The same impasse appears in similar stories, which, because of their form, keep us at an "ironical" distance—and so do not allow us to share the characters' flawed perspectives. Uncanniness does not appear because our empathy is blocked. This purely formal effect—"independent" from "subject matter"— demonstrates what literature can teach the human sciences about how to write about other people (*SE* 17:252; *GW* 12:269).

Not surprisingly, Freud's literary point here echoes almost verbatim the psychoanalytical one that he had made at the beginning: the healthy doctor, he said, needed to *sich hineinversetzen*" into the minds of neurotics in order to understand the uncanny. Strachey renders "sich hinein*versetzen*" as "translate himself into [that state of feeling]" and "uns *versetzten*," in this literary discussion, as "put ourselves in [the place of the princess]" (*SE* 17:220; *GW* 12:230). This implies the motion of one mind into another, as in the non-reflexive *versetzen*, which is often translated as to "relocate" or "displace" (not in the technical psychoanalytic sense), as in: "We do not displace ourselves into her" (*wir versetzen uns nicht in sie*) (*SE* 17:252, trans. rev.; *GW* 12:269). This non-displaced "we" is not only the reader but also the anthropologist, who, as Freud claimed in *Totem and Taboo*, misinterprets savages because he remains in his own "mental constellations" instead of "feel[ing] [his] way into" the other's "modes of thinking."[95] The psychoanalyst, conversely, sees this as his job: he *must* displace himself into the mind of the neurotic—surrendering his "superior," ironic perspective until his attention "hovers" harmoniously with the other's (*SE* 12:111, trans. rev.). This (literary) method, Freud hinted in *Totem and Taboo*, is what will make psychoanalysis, not anthropology, the new science of man. Anthropology's nineteenth-century armchair titans could not produce accurate images of savages because they, like nineteenth-century literary narrators, stayed too far from their "characters." They pronounced on them from afar; they did not let themselves be "displaced." Through this critique of detachment, Freud paves the way for Malinowski's new anthropology and the further narrative experiments of literary modernism.

This collapse of distance is not without its risks, as Freud learned in the process of writing *The Uncanny*. After the analyst-traveler displaces himself into the other—the neurotic, the savage, the homosexual—he must figure out how to retrieve himself. This is not easy in a foreign world that turns out to be almost the same as one's own. When Freud goes looking for the savage in *Totem and Taboo*, he finds one that resembles the Viennese-Jewish scientist himself; from the ensuing fright, he invents a fairy tale about the absolute primitive. When he goes searching for the "source" of uncanniness in *The Uncanny*, he translates himself into the minds of savages and neurotics but often stays there too long to bring himself back cleanly. It is wrong to claim, as Brickman does, that Freud succeeds in separating a "primitive," "aboriginal" id from his own "enculturated" European ego.[96] Not that he does not try. But precisely this failure to reestablish a "superior" scientific "we" troubles all of *Totem and Taboo* and then becomes the main topic of *The Uncanny*. Here, Freud realizes that the "other's" relative indistinguishability from "us" *is* the source of uncanniness.

In *The Uncanny*'s third-to-last sentence, Freud writes, "We understand this," suggesting that we know that fairy tales are not meant to create uncanny feelings. But what else do "we" understand, now that we have read Freud's *The Uncanny*? Do we understand that "we" sometimes do not displace ourselves into "her" (and "him" and "it")? Do we understand that we often refuse this displacement because we fear how hard it will be to reclaim ourselves? And, most important, do we understand that this fear is often moot because our "we"—the scientific plural—is always already displaced, never fully separate from its "primitive" third-person object? As Freud demonstrates during his invention of the uncanny, the psychoanalytic "we" is not purely scientific but rather consists of the "I" (the scientist) working together with "him" (the neurotic patient). If we view *The Uncanny* as a literary text, we likewise see how a narrator, Freud, speaks in a "we" that encompasses himself, his first-person "adventurer" protagonist ("Freud"), and the third-person neurotic. At the end, these three voices have become so intertwined that the narrator can no longer separate himself. He cannot take the narrative high ground and tell us what he has learned. Unlike Hegel's spirit and the "Freud" from *Interpretation of Dreams*, this fully displaced narrator simply fades away, exiting the stage without a sublation.

This explains why *The Uncanny* goes out with a whimper: a disconnected two-sentence paragraph about "silence, solitude and darkness," three uncanny fears whose sources Freud had earlier claimed were *not* in repression. All that "we" can know about these three is that we are never safe from them: they issue from a "childhood fear" (*Kinderangst*) from which most of us will "never become quite free." This temporally faraway "source" of the uncanny—childhood fear—is, for Freud, different from "infantile complexes" (*infantile Komplexe*) as well as from their eternal pendant, the beliefs of "primitive man."[97] But like both of them, it, too, is always in us. We cannot escape "its" darkness. In the next, final sentence, Freud's embattled "we," like his "I" before it, disappears completely—vanishing into a world without human subjects: "Psychoanalytic research has dealt in another place [*an anderer Stelle*] with this problem" (*SE* 17:252, trans. rev.; *GW* 12:268). "Psychoanalytic research" might seem to grant Freud a "superior," authoritative point of view, but it simultaneously effaces both his adventurer's "I" and his scientific "we." Because Freud refers us to another, unnamed essay by him, "psychoanalytic research" again doubles, triples, even quadruples him. Freud is the narrator "we," the doctor/adventurer "I," the neurotic "he," and now the "it" of psychoanalytic research, which displaces "Freud" further, onto an "other" text.

Where is this other text? Freud gives no hint. He deliberately refrains from identifying it, as he otherwise does so regularly throughout his oeuvre (as in "cf. my book, *Totem and Taboo*"). Strachey claims that Freud is referring to a footnote in *Three Essays on the Theory of Sexuality* (which interprets the childhood fear of the dark as the fear of separation from loved ones at bedtime). Even if Strachey is right, this reference does not produce an answer. When Freud revises this footnote from *Three Essays* in 1920, he refers us to yet another "*andere Stelle*": his 1917 *Introductory Lectures on Psychoanalysis* (which now associates the fear of darkness with hysteria). But "even there," Freud admits, "it must be confessed, the question is not finally cleared up" (*auch nicht die endgültige Aufklärung erreicht worden ist*) (*SE* 7:224n1; *GW* 5:126n1). This problem at the end of *The Uncanny*—the still-missing source for uncanniness—cannot be solved. Like Freud's double in the train, the uncanny's "dark" source remains resistant to attempts at "enlightenment" (*Aufklärung*).

What is this dark *andere Stelle*? It is definitely not the "obscure," "unplumbable," "unknown" space from *Interpretation of Dreams*, which, as Freud demonstrates throughout his speculations on the uncanny, inheres only in our fantasies: the longed-for "source" in a wondrous Dark Continent waiting to tell us who we are. In *Totem and Taboo* and, especially, *The Uncanny*, Freud discovers a savage at this source that is so much like "us" that it cannot grant us this desired differentiation. The primitive *Er*'s illicit similarity with our civilized *Ich* troubles us, just as it disturbs Haggard's heroes and the adventurer, Freud. This horrifying almost-sameness *is* Freud's *andere Stelle*, which now offers us new insight into Freud's global modernity. The world, Freud insists, is not as strange as it seems. This is what makes it uncanny. Freud's sobered "conquistador" has finally located the real booty: the familiar-foreign things that, like the neurotic soldier from "Inexplicable" and Leo's dead African self from *She*, follow us home from our adventures. They are not exotic strangers but rather "the same—the same—," which is why they arouse our "dread and horror" (*SE* 17:219).

Chapter 4

✦

Exotic Europe

Modernist Ethnographies (Mann, Hofmannsthal, Musil)

Jacques' *Hot Land*, Hesse's *Robert Aghion*, and Freud's *The Uncanny*—all conceived during the swan song of German and Austrian colonial power— agreed on one major point: that the distance between Europe and its other had contracted so radically that it endangered Europe's identity. As discussed in my introduction, "high" modernist literature shared these texts' obsession with uncanny similarity and their formal slipperiness. Travel writing, science, and high modernism worked together, I contend, to create uncanniness as a concept. Just after travelers lamented the end of alterity along the Amazon and the Ganges, modernism and psychoanalysis made the opposite—but uncannily the same—claim: the exotic other infiltrated Mann's Venice, Kafka's Central European bedroom, Freud's Viennese study, and Hofmannsthal's and Musil's Alps. By announcing that the jungle had become just like Europe, adventure literature forced high culture inward, from the far-flung voyages of nineteenth-century Bildungsroman heroes toward the foreign at the hearth.

Modernism learned more from travel writing than just this need to look inward. It learned also the *ethnographic perspective*, which the modernists now turned toward the West, to reveal just how strange this West really was. Modernism's ethnography covered Europe's cities and, even more pointedly, its fringes in the East and the South. I think of course of Dracula's Transylvania[1] and especially of the many border regions appearing in German and Austro-Hungarian literature: Mann's Venice, long viewed as the threshold between Occident and Orient, the *porta Orientis*; Hofmannsthal's Carinthian hinterlands; Musil's outlandish Tyrol; the nightmarish Ukraine described by Freud's Rat Man; and the forsaken quarry just outside Joseph K.'s nameless city in *The Trial*, where he is brought for execution.

These foreign-seeming realms on Europe's peripheries distinguished Austrian and German modernism from their British and French counterparts, which, like the postcolonial theory that sprang from them, maintained a clearer division between center and periphery. *Mitteleuropa*'s proximity to the "Orient," conversely, confused these categories. Where did the imperial homeland end and the East begin? Did the "Occident" stop somewhere in eastern Poland? In the Ukraine? Near the Rat Man's brutal Austrian military station "in the East," just outside of Przemyśl?[2] How can we talk about the West when this "East" is continually shifting? When it is both somewhere out there yet already here: in the Tyrol, in Galicia, in Carinthia, in the Slavic neighborhoods of "our" home cities? In the texts I examine here, Mann, Hofmannsthal, and Musil pose precisely these questions, and they do so at the levels of both content and form. They present a European geography in which the periphery always creeps in on the center. In formal terms, they experiment with perspective, especially free indirect style, in order to ask *the* ethnographic question: "How do we write about (other) people?"[3] And they ask: how much harder is this in an era when "we" and our "other" have become less distinguishable than ever before?

All the Way to the Tigers? Exotic Venice

Like the travel stories *Hot Land* and *Robert Aghion*, also written or pub-lished in 1911, Thomas Mann's *Death in Venice* begins with a desire for foreign ecstasy.[4] Like Hesse's Aghion, Jacques' narrator from *Hot Land*, and even Conrad's Marlow, Aschenbach longs for someplace "exotic and without associations" (*das Fremdartige und Bezuglose*), someplace "incomparable" (*das Unvergleichliche*) where he can "forget" himself and "escape."[5] He originally imagined finding this in a "primitive wilderness" (*Urweltwildnis*) of "islands" (*Inseln*) and "morasses" (*Morästen*). He fantasizes of a "moist, lush [*üppig*], and monstrous" tropical swamp, where "the eyes of a lurking [*kauerndend*] tiger sparkle between the gnarled stems of a bamboo thicket [*Bambusdickichts*]" (*DV* 5, trans. rev.; *FA* 2.1:504).

Although Aschenbach eventually decides not to go "all the way to the tigers" and instead to Venice, his Venice takes on the exotic qualities of this earlier fantasy (*DV* 6). Most importantly, an "Asiatic cholera" straight from the "Ganges delta" infests Venice's ports, rising, in a direct repetition of Aschenbach's earlier words, from "morasses" (*Morästen*) in the "lushly [*üppig*] uninhabitable primitive island wilderness [*Urwelt- und Inselwildnis*]," where "the tiger lurks [*kauert*] in bamboo thickets [*Bambusdickichten*]" (*DV* 53, trans. rev.; *FA* 2.1:578). This imagery appears again later, in Aschenbach's dream, repeating the Amazonian "circle dances" filmed in that same year by the renowned German ethnographer Theodor Koch-Grünberg: half-naked women in fur skirts moan and shake tambourines above their thrown-back heads; hairy-skinned men "girdled with hides" pump their arms and thighs while banging cymbals and beating on drums; and the entire human and ani-mal swarm emits a howl with a "drawn-out cry of *uuu* at the end [*gezogenem u-Ruf am Ende*], a cry that was sweet and savage [*wild*] at the same time" (*DV* 56–57, trans. rev.; *FA* 583).[6] These savages invade Aschenbach's psyche, and, as they do, Venice itself becomes wild, suggesting that Aschenbach has indeed now made it "all the way to the tigers." Venice takes on the literal meaning of *porta Orientis* when its murderous criminality and prostitution achieve "oriental" proportions (*DV* 55; *FA* 580). Whereas Jacques, Nolde, and Hesse journeyed to the ends of earth only to find "savages" sporting European haircuts and clothes, Mann's hero apparently finds real primitiveness intact on Europe's "oriental" fringe.

As in this adventure literature, Mann's outlandish Venice, too, promises an exotic virginal love object: an adolescent Slavic boy with never-shorn honey-colored hair, bare feet, slender legs, a downy spine, smooth armpits, and a weak high voice.[7] When watching this boy emerge from the sea for the first time, Aschenbach thinks of more than just the oft-cited "young god"; he sees also the embodiment of the "beginning of time" and "origins of form," reminiscent of Freud's—and Nietzsche's and Vico's—ethnographies of the genesis of humanity (*DV* 28). Like the beloved girl from *Robert Aghion*, this boy speaks an alluringly incomprehensible tongue, a "harmony to his ear" (*DV* 36). And the lover's name itself is colorfully unintelligible: Is it Adgio or Adgiu? Tadzio or Tadziu? Its "drawn-out cry of *uuu* at the end" (*gezogenen u-Ruf am Ende*) has something "savage" (*Wildes*) about it, prefiguring verbatim the "savage" howls that will eventually infiltrate Aschenbach's dream (*DV* 28, 56; *FA* 2.1:539, 583). This outlandish Slavic boy inspires Aschenbach to an act of "intercourse between a mind and a body" that leaves him feeling worn out as if after a "debauch" (*Ausschweifung*). And not just any debauch. As Aschenbach claims in the following chapter, his encounter with Tadzio is the first of many such "exotic" debaucheries (*exotische Ausschweifungen*), the kind that contemporary adventure travelers sought vainly in the overrun jungles of India, Brazil, and the South Seas (*DV* 39, 47, trans. rev.; *FA* 556, 568).[8]

Uncanny Venice: The Repetition of the Same

But Mann ultimately makes the same point as did his more popular counterparts, in both content and form: the exotic world is, unfortunately, not as strange as it appears. Even a cursory reading of *Death in Venice* reveals how Aschenbach tragically recognizes everything in Venice; repetition structures the plot. His initial decision to leave Venice, for example, reminds him of his premature departure after a visit years ago: "now for the second time the place had made him ill, . . . for the second time he had had to flee for his life." When he decides not to leave and to return to his original hotel, these repetitions continue: he receives a new room that eerily "almost precisely resembled the first." And shortly before his death, Aschenbach returns disoriented to a little square that he had wandered into before, now eating the poisoned strawberries that lead to his death. In an "uncanny" prefiguring of

Freud's wording when he returns three times to the same spot in an Italian city a few years later, Aschenbach "recognized it" (*DV* 60).

More haunting than these overt repetitions are the more subtle ones that Aschenbach does not notice. Most important is the reappearance, in two different Venice characters, of the stranger Aschenbach had seen in Munich, a consonance hinted at by repeated words. The Venice gondolier borrows from his Munich predecessor a thin build, red facial hair, a straw hat, and, using the same words, a "short, turned-up nose" (*kurz aufgeworfene Nase*) above "pulled back" (*zurückgezogen*) lips that "bared" (*entblößte*) white teeth.[9] The Venetian street musician doubles the Munich man even more clearly, sharing his red hair and general physiognomy as described in the same words: like the Munich man, he is "thin" (*mager*), "snub-nosed" (*stumpfnäsig*), has "bared" (*entblößte*) teeth that are prone to "grimaces" (*Grimassen*). He, too, has a "gaunt" (*hager*) neck rising from a "sports shirt" (*Sporthemd*) to reveal a "naked" (*nackt*) "Adam's apple" (*Adamsapfel*). This musician even has the Munich man's "imperious" (*herrisch*) and "savage" (*wild*) "furrows" (*Furchen*), connecting both of them to the dream-world primitives who "howled" (*heulte*) "savagely" (*wild*), just as the musician now "howls" (*DV* 50, 51, 52, trans. rev.; *FA* 2.1:572–73, 575). What these repetitions signify—be it the devil, death, or a collective unconscious—is less important than the fact that they are repeated and, what is more, that Aschenbach does not realize that they are being repeated. We get, here, the sense of a second voice in *Death in Venice*, of a narrator letting us know that Aschenbach's journey is even more repetitive than the exoticist Aschenbach had feared.[10]

This narrator's quiet criticism reappears when Aschenbach insists that this savage musician *is* "strange" and "exotic" (*fremdartig*), despite his un-exotic familiarity. Even Aschenbach's very use of the root *fremd*- recalls the earlier depiction of the Munich man (as *fremdländisch*) and of Aschenbach's own desire (for "*das Fremdartige*") (*DV* 51, 4, 13; *FA* 2.1:574, 503, 516). The Venice musician is not as strange as he seems, the narrator tells us, and this is what is really frightening, even if Aschenbach does not yet take notice. This familiarity within the "*Fremdartige*" deepens when we consider that all three of these "exotic" characters—Munich man, gondolier, street musician—are foreign in the exact same way. At the beginning, middle, and end of the novella, the narrator uses an identical lexical and rhythmic scheme to describe all of them: "not of . . . stock" (*nicht . . . Schlages*). These "foreign" men are, at three distinct points in the text, "not of Bavarian stock [*nicht bajuwarischen Schlages*]," "not of Italian stock [*nicht italienischen Schlages*]," and "not of Venetian stock [*nicht venezianischen Schlages*]" (*DV* 4, 18, 50; *FA* 502, 525, 573).[11] Such uncanny narrative repetitions form a steady counter-discourse to Aschenbach's fantasy of "incomparability."

This narrative counter-discourse becomes especially clear through Aschenbach's blinkered view of Tadzio. While Aschenbach celebrates the boy's exoticism—his incomprehensible Slavic words, his resemblance to a Greek god, his virginal purity—the narrator lets us know of the boy's underlying similarity to Aschenbach. Tadzio's Slavic background, for example, recalls Aschenbach's own "exotic" (*fremd*) Eastern European heritage: the boy's obvious ill health echoes Aschenbach's recurrent sickness as a child; Tadzio's flirtation with Aschenbach suggests that they have matching desires; and Tadzio even mimics the older man's facial expressions.[12] As with the lexical repetitions of "turned-up nose," "bared teeth," and "naked Adam's apple," these plot echoes undermine Aschenbach's fantasy of a *fremdartige* Venice, even though he is not yet aware of this.

Strange Hours! The Narrator's Uncanny Intercourse

Like his counterpart in *Robert Aghion*, this narrator does not emerge unscathed from this uncannily recognizable world: he, too, becomes part of this uncanniness, most notably through his growing similarity to his own character. Just as Aschenbach resembles Tadzio, the narrator now resembles Aschenbach, midway through the third chapter, if only because he takes on the latter's point of view through focalization and free indirect style.[13] Aschenbach sets his eyes on the beautiful Tadzio, and the narrator simultaneously drops the distancing mechanisms prominent in the first two chapters (generalizations, epithets, attributions).[14] These typical signs of free indirect style had already appeared at isolated points in the first two chapters, but they intensify here when Aschenbach sees Tadzio and surrenders his own position of distanced observer. Aschenbach wonders with concern about his new love-object, and the narrator wonders with him, making us ask which one of them thinks, "Was he [Tadzio] in poor health?" When Aschenbach's loss of luggage leads him to return to Tadzio, the narrator again shares his character's perspective, astounding him at his good luck in everything: "And by the way . . . could it really be that he felt a strong breeze off the ocean to complete his bliss?" Once more, in the fourth chapter, they marvel together at the allure of Venice: "What a fine place to stay, indeed, combining the charms of a refined southern beach resort with the cozy proximity of the wondrous, wonder-filled city!" (*DV* 22, 33, 35).

Here we see how Mann's formal strategy coincides with his story's "uncanny" content. On the level of content, everything Aschenbach sees resembles everything else, just as Aschenbach is secretly more similar to his "exotic" beloved than he thought. Formally, the generally ironic narrator now finds himself closer to Aschenbach than *he* had ever imagined. Through this perspectival slippage, *Death in Venice* becomes what, in Freud's reading, Herodotus's "ironic" Rhampsinitus story cannot be: uncanny (Freud, *The Uncanny, SE* 17:252).

This perspectival intimacy culminates when Aschenbach falls in love. Now rigorously eschewing all epithets or attributions, the narrator joins Aschenbach in admiring the boy's body: the honey-colored hair, downy back, symmetrical chest and ribs, and the translucent blue-veined hollows of his knees. What follows is the novella's longest sustained example of free indirect style, a remarkable series of unattributed exclamations and interrogations in which the narrative and figural voices become nearly indistinguishable:[15]

> What discipline, what precision of thought was expressed in the stretch of this youthfully perfect body! But was not the rigorous and pure will that had been darkly active in bringing this divine form into the clear light of day entirely familiar to the artist in him? Was this same will not active in him, too, when he, full of sober passion, freed a slender form from the marble mass of language, a form he had seen with his spiritual eye and that he presented to mortal men as image and mirror of spiritual beauty?
>
> Image and mirror! His eyes embraced the noble figure there on the edge of blue, and in a transport of delight he thought his gaze was grasping beauty itself, the pure form of divine thought, the universal and pure perfection that lives in the spirit. (*DV* 37)

This description demonstrates how Aschenbach's falling in love has done more than make the arrogant, distanced narrator suddenly identify, as Dorrit Cohn argues, with his character.[16] This fall has also knocked the narrator from his detached structural perch into the position of an object: a character. He has gone from being a dissociated observer of his character's exoticist naivete to a participant who, before the eyes of the reader, shares his character's decadent fervor.

This closeness unsettles the narrator, who immediately attempts to reassert his separateness. He describes Aschenbach through distancing, often critical epithets: "the aging artist," "the impassioned onlooker," "the lonely author," "the traveler" and "the stricken one" (*der Heimgesuchte*) (*DV* 37–39, trans. rev.; *FA* 2.1:553–55). But the narrator is protesting too much, and his manufactured detachment is short-lived. When Aschenbach later uses Tadzio's body to inspire his writing, the narrator again joins in the rapture, dropping all epithets and attributions, and feeling together with Aschenbach the "Strange hours! Strangely enervating effort! Strangely fertile intercourse between a mind and a body!" But the narrator again quickly gains distance, chastising Aschenbach for his intellectual "debauch" without noticing that he should also be chastising himself (*DV* 39). Given the narrator's moral contradictions, it is not surprising that he ends this scene with his most strident condemnation of Aschenbach yet. Aschenbach deliberately eschews an opportunity to speak with Tadzio, and the narrator claims that Aschenbach does so out of perverse exoticism: because "the aging one" does not want "disillusionment" and is "in love with his own intoxication" and his "desire for licentiousness," he maintains a contrived distance from his beloved. The narrator concludes with a moralistic denunciation: "For it is licentiousness to be unable to wish for a salutary disillusionment" (*DV* 39–40, trans. rev.).[17] By not seeing how he should be directing the same sobering speech to himself, the narrator paradoxically becomes even more like the character from whom he wants to separate: he now shares the same blind spot.

After this climactic encounter between narrator and protagonist, free indirect style appears again only sparingly and, when it does, always followed by the same retaliatory buffering we saw here. Aschenbach muses already on the next page about his unexpected joy in love, and the narrator joins with him—"Where did that breath of air come from, the one that suddenly played about his temples and ears so softly and significantly like a whisper from a higher realm?"—only to distance himself immediately again from this confusingly "beguiled traveler" (*DV* 41). A few days later, in the fifth and final chapter, the protagonist and narrator ponder together the virile pleasures of worshipping Amor—"Had not [the love-god] enjoyed the highest respect among the bravest nations of the earth? Did they not say that it was because of their courage that he had flourished in their cities?"—but the narrator straight away denigrates the "infatuated thinker's train of thought" (*DV* 48). The character and narrator likewise interpret together the street musician's gestures—"He swore that he had been circumspect. One could tell"—only to have the narrator again quickly step away with the epithet of "the solitary traveler" (51, trans. rev.).

The narrator hints, however consciously, at why he continually separates himself from his character when reporting on the similar strategies of the musician performing in front of the hotel. When this musician approaches Aschenbach to collect coins, the narrator claims that this elimination of the "separation" between a performer and his audience "always tends to produce a certain embarrassment, no matter how pleasurable the performance" (*DV* 51). This intimacy, he continues, is not only embarrassing but also debilitating. Only after "reestablish[ing] a proper artistic distance" can a performer "regain" his power and become "impuden[t]" again with his audience (*DV* 52). Granted, the narrator is speaking here about the musician and his audience—not about himself and his protagonist—but does not this statement also describe his own relation to Aschenbach? When too close to Aschenbach, the narrator becomes weak (his voice almost disappears within Aschenbach's). But whenever he reestablishes "artistic distance," he can again become strong and insolent: disparaging his "stricken," "licentious," and "infatuated" protagonist. Through this impudence, the narrator gains his revenge on a character who has apparently caused his "embarrassment."

This alternation between intimate, uncanny free indirect style and distancing, critical irony reaches its apogee in the penultimate scene, just after Aschenbach decides *not* to announce the plague (which would have caused

Tadzio's family to leave) and instead pursue Tadzio at all costs. Again without any distancing markers, the narrator proclaims together with Aschenbach: "How could that tender happiness he had dreamed of a moment earlier [of telling Tadzio's family to flee] compare with these expectations [of staying near to Tadzio]? What value did art and virtue hold for him when he could have chaos?" (*DV* 56). Predictably, the narrator gains detachment from these thoughts through a series of epithets for Aschenbach: "the resisting dreamer," "the afflicted dreamer," "the lovesick traveler," and, after Aschenbach has his hair and face colored to seem younger, "the beguiled lover" (*DV* 57, 59, 38, 41). The narrator concludes this sequence with an ideological critique even more blistering than the one that followed Aschenbach's "debauch." Defeated, Aschenbach now sits at the little piazza to which he had returned by accident:

> He sat there, the master, the artist who had attained to dignity . . . . There he sat, the great success who had overcome knowledge . . . . There he sat, the author whose greatness had been officially recognized and whose name bore the title of nobility, whose style children were encouraged to emulate—sat there with his eyes shut . . . ; and his slack cosmetically enhanced lips formed occasional words that emerged out of the strange dream-logic engendered in his half-dozing brain. (*DV* 60)

Because this attack is so aggressive, critics have repeatedly drawn attention to it. Cohn influentially claimed that Mann is attempting here to alienate us from his overzealous narrator: the narrator's "moralistic" puritanism should become so extreme that it is less palatable than Aschenbach's tragic excesses. Cohn is right to insist that Mann forces us here to look critically at his narrator, who is judgmental yet not aware of his own flaws. But if Mann wanted the narrator to be as unattractively prudish as Cohn claims, why does he so often have this narrator join perspectives, uncritically, with the "repulsive" protagonist?[18] If Mann's goal were to have us reject his narrator as a moralist, then why not make him unswervingly judgmental and distanced through the entire tale? Why did Mann include so many moments of shared perspective with Aschenbach, especially the sustained one in which the narrator and the character cherish together the boy's beautiful body?

Mann's Ethnographic Impasse: How Do We Write about Others?

Mann does this, I maintain, because he is not interested in a clash of moral systems, not even in rejecting moralism in favor of tolerance, as Cohn suggests. He instead wants to investigate the problem of modern *ethnography*, in the broadest sense: What do we write about when we write about (other)

people? Do "they" even exist, especially in this modern era, when they seem
ever more like "us"? If they don't, do we create them? How much of our ethnography is fiction? And not just any fiction but an ironical fiction, in which
every narrator/ethnographer deliberately produces a gap between himself
and his "character"? What happens when this gap closes? What strategies
does the narrator/ethnographer employ to reassert distance?

Nowhere are these ethnographic questions clearer, on levels of both content and form, than in Aschenbach's aforementioned use of Tadzio's body as
a "model" for his art. Like Nolde and Pechstein with their aboriginal mod-
els in the South Seas, Aschenbach requires closeness to his object but also
distance: Aschenbach must work "in the presence of Tadzio" but not speak
with him (*DV* 39). Despite watching Tadzio "every day, even every hour,"
Aschenbach maintains an "appearance of indifference and unfamiliarity"
(*Fremdheit*) that creates a "restlessness and frustrated curiosity, the hysteria of an unsatisfied, unnaturally suppressed urge for acquaintanceship and
mutual exchange" (*DV* 42; *FA* 2.1:560).[19] John Burt Foster sees here a traditional ethnographic model of observation and erotic tension: Mann's Venice
resembles a "colonial societ[y]," in which "members of different groups"—
the Germanic Aschenbach and the Slavic Tadzio—observe "each other daily"
but "rarely speak." Against the political backdrop of an "aggressive German policy of cultural domination in the East," Foster argues, Aschenbach
upholds a "Germano-Slavic boundary" to increase his exotic frisson. Like
Mann's narrator, Foster frowns upon Aschenbach for this "entirely artificial
exoticism."[20]

By joining in the narrator's ironic critique, Foster does not analyze *Death
in Venice* as much as he acts out a position within it. And this position is
far from objective. Foster's criticism should in fact be turned on the narrator with whom Foster now tacitly sides. Like Aschenbach, the narrator, too,
engages in an "artificial" ethnographic game of attraction and repulsion. This
narrator, too, observes an "other" (Aschenbach) to whom he gets close but
not too close. He, too, feels "compelled by convention"—both literary and
social—to maintain a "strange" and "precarious" *Fremdheit*, which plays
itself out in perspectival shifts (*DV* 42; *FA* 2.1:560). And he, too, develops
a charged pattern of intimacy and exaggerated withdrawal. The narrator's
claim that Aschenbach was not "inclined to self-criticism" all too obviously
begs the question for the narrator himself and so adds another level of irony
to the story (*DV* 40).

But any such indictment of the narrator demands that we pose the same
ethnographic question to ourselves, as readers, and even to Mann. For we
stand precisely where the narrator stood before: in the "superior" ironic
position, apparently beyond the dangers of uncanny similarity.[21] Mann's subversion of the narrator's authority invites us to investigate this *mise en abyme*
of ethnography, where there is no position outside of the "field," for the
reader or for the author.[22] Given Mann's literary insight into ethnography as

a matter of *perspective*, it is not surprising that the revolutionizer of modern anthropology, Malinowski, was a great reader of literature.[23] As Malinowski argued shortly after *Death in Venice*'s publication, traditional ethnography suffered from an arrogance of distance, a distance which resembled that of nineteenth-century literary narration. The old-school ethnographer, like the traditional omniscient narrator, claimed to know all of his subject's thoughts from far away: from his desk at the British Museum. Malinowski wanted to trade this exoticizing bird's-eye perspective for a more myopic yet more revealing one: the ethnographer should get close to his subjects, live among them in a tent, and so see the world (almost) through their eyes. To describe exactly what he means, Malinowski, who once toyed with writing a Conradian colonial romance, focuses on literary perspective. The ethnographer's "final goal," he insists, is to adopt "the native's point of view," which includes "his relation to life" and "*his* vision of *his* world."[24]

This revolutionizing of perspective demonstrates Malinowski's debt not only to literature but also to Freud,[25] who hinted in *Totem and Taboo*, two years before Malinowski traveled to New Guinea, that psychoanalysis would replace anthropology as the "science of man" because it solved anthropology's problem of perspective. Instead of observing their objects through books read in the library, psychoanalysts would sit together with their neurotic patients in the same room, for hours on end (as Malinowski later did with the Trobrianders). The treatment's success rested on the analyst's ability to "displace himself" (not in the technical psychoanalytic sense [*sich hineinversetzen*]) out of his omniscient scientific position and into his patient's mind, where the analyst's "attention" would "hover" (Freud, *SE* 17:220 [*GW* 12:230]; *SE* 12:111, trans. rev.). Because this perspectival consonance had long been part of literary experimentation—but not of psychology or anthropology—Freud chooses literary examples to end his speculations on the *unheimlich*. Fiction represents our most obvious day-to-day experience of dropping our "superior," "ironic" positions in order to share, uncannily, in the emotions of the character (*SE* 17:252).

But displacing oneself into the other represents only half of ethnography's problem, whether in anthropology, psychoanalysis, or literature. Following this intimacy, the scientist-narrator has to figure out how to extricate himself. Malinowski "plunges into the life of the natives"—"is *of* it and *in* it"—but then needs to step out and see it from above; like the omniscient narrator, he must ultimately gain a "vision" of "the whole" and even "*construct* the picture of the big institution" (*Argonauts*, 22, 12, 84 [emphasis in original]). This movement in and out of others' minds sounds easy in theory, but it proves near impossible in practice. Malinowski is either too distanced from the natives—as when he first arrives—or too close, as when, after months of living in their village, he is unable to free himself "from the atmosphere created by foreign bodies" and can no longer see the village from the outside: "I saw them through their eyes (it's fine to have this ability), but I forgot to look at them with my own" (*Diary*, 163). Freud likewise plunges himself into the other's world, allowing his attention to "hover" and his unconscious to be a "receptive organ" for the patient's unconscious, yet somehow still maintaining a scientific "emotional coldness" that will allow him to see the patient's case from above ("Recommendations to Physicians Practicing Psycho-Analysis," *SE* 12:111, 115, trans. rev.). As Freud dramatizes in *The Uncanny*, this shifting from self-loss within the patient back to one's own distanced viewpoint turns out to be well-nigh impossible. This discovery undermines psychoanalysis as an objective science, yet it reveals psychoanalysis's "uncanny" methodological advantage—an advantage that anthropology can only match with Malinowski's 1922 *Argonauts* and, especially, his posthumous diaries.[26]

This impossibility of regaining distance was especially pronounced when the observer discovered that he uncannily resembled the subjects he was studying. Freud found "savages" who were like "us," or at least like our neurotics and our children, and Malinowski discovered strict rules of reciprocity, gift-giving, and "manners" similar to Europe's own (*Argonauts*, 10). More than this, both of these observers' personal histories heightened the resemblances: Malinowski admits that his "Slavonic nature"—for which he endures British condescensions while in Melanesia—is "more naturally savage than that of Western Europeans,"[27] and Freud knew from his readings of Stratz and others that his "Moorish" Jewishness was often seen as "African" and "black." This similarity to savages sometimes made Malinowski and Freud, like the narrator from *Death in Venice*, fear for their identities—as when Malinowski records how his "feeling of disorientation, which I always have in a new, unfamiliar place among natives" leads to a sense of "impotence" (*Diary*, 119). This "surfeit of native" causes Malinowski to question his own Europeanness, leading him eventually to degrade the Melanesians and retreat to the homes of colonists, as well as into drugs and alcohol (*Argonauts*, 6).[28] Freud likewise turned most virulently against his patients at the moments when they were closest to him. In his own psychological ethnography, Freud reacts toward a suddenly familiar "Dora" as Malinowski did to the "savages" and Mann's narrator did to Aschenbach.[29] This tension of attraction and repulsion lies at the heart of all three major forms of modern ethnography: anthropology, psychoanalysis, and literature.

But literature uniquely emphasizes this tension's *perspectival* nature, as *Death in Venice* demonstrates once more in its final scene, where the narrator again shares his character's viewpoint only, again, to distance himself. While dying, Aschenbach looks out at Tadzio, and then "he arose to follow him" (*machte er sich auf, ihm zu folgen*). Because this action occurs only in Aschenbach's head (the dying man can't actually have risen) and because there is no narrative attribution, the narrator and the protagonist again seem to share one voice in free indirect style. We do not read, as we do in other similar situations, "Aschenbach thought, 'I will rise and follow him,'" or "Aschenbach thought that he would rise to follow him," but rather "he arose to follow him." Immediately after this perspectival consonance, the narrator disengages again, and this time jarringly, inserting a paragraph break and, following this, his most distanced point of view since the opening sentence: "Minutes passed before anyone rushed to the aid of the man who had collapsed to one side of his chair. They carried him to his room. And later that same day a respectfully shaken world received the news of his death" (*DV* 63; *FA* 2.1:592).

Some readers see here Mann's conservative message: the narrator's salutary objectivity displaces Aschenbach's subjective derangements.[30] But because the narrator has lacked objectivity throughout, how can we now see his position as "true" and, what is more, equivalent with the author's? Are we not meant to view his opinions with suspicion? And *not* to believe that Mann endorsed this apparent shift toward moral normalization? The narrator's extreme aloofness, however polite, implies again his personal stakes. He pretends that Aschenbach is a distinguished stranger, not someone he has gotten to know so well in the course of his story. Considering the narrator's earlier remarks about "proper artistic distance," his present remoteness suggests that he has again been "embarrassed" by his intimacy with Aschenbach and needs to reassert his "ironic," "superior," non-uncanny separateness.

Caught in this dialectic of modern ethnography, the narrator repeats here its basic question: How can "I" get close to "him," understand him, even write about him, yet not become him? How can I enter into this uncanny communion, yet still extricate myself and complete the scientific project, or, in this case, the story? Mann leaves us with this dilemma, and with more: the knowledge that the ethnographic object is even less exotic than we had thought. This is ultimately why Mann does not send Aschenbach "all the way to the tigers" and why Aschenbach's fate does *not* inhere, as critics routinely claim, in his being "penetrated" by absolute difference: by the Indian cholera, by the "oriental," or by the "Slavic."[31] Rather, Aschenbach is undone by that same surfeit of familiarity that dogged the adventurers I described in chapters 1 and 2. The world's uncanniness is too much for Aschenbach, just as it is too much for his narrator.

Like Aschenbach with Tadzio, this narrator gets too close to his subject (Aschenbach) and discovers too much similarity. This causes him to reassert his separateness, most powerfully and awkwardly in the final scene, when he looks upon Aschenbach "respectfully," but as a stranger. Mann's narrator thus mirrors Hesse, who discovered, also in 1911, that his beloved East Indians uncannily resembled him and his fellow Europeans. This knowledge was likewise too much for Hesse, who, after writing his brilliant meditation on this (*Robert Aghion*), began to regard the Indians as abstract, idealized exotics. *Death in Venice* teaches us the same thing that Hesse learned: the "other" does not exist, at least not in the form or the place we had imagined. But Mann offers us something beyond Hesse's idealizations in his post-*Aghion* writings. By foregrounding a perspectival *mise en abyme*, he teaches us to reflect on why we construct such idealizations and, more important, why we can no longer sustain them—regardless of where they occur. Ethnography, Mann tells us, is always getting closer to home, whether we like it or not. The ethnography of the West begins here.

Exotic Austria

Aschenbach's initial quest for an exotic space within Europe—a place "without associations"—began, fittingly, even nearer to home than Venice. He traveled over Vienna to the Austro-Hungarian port cities of Trieste and Pola, where Austria still had a naval base when Mann wrote *Death in Venice* in 1911–12. From Pola, Aschenbach sailed to an Adriatic island just off the Istrian coast, where he found "locals dressed in colorful rags" speaking in "wildly exotic accents." Although Aschenbach quickly decides to leave—the Austrian hotel clientele annoy him—it is worth noting that he first considers Austria itself to be sufficiently "exotic" (*fremdartig*) for a journey toward the "incomparable" (*DV* 13, trans. rev.; *FA* 2.1:516–17). Vienna indeed serves as a textual premonition of Venice: before dying in the latter, Aschenbach gets sick, as a young man, in the former (*DV* 8).

Austria is exoticized here and throughout Mann's work, and with good reason: the sprawling empire on Bavaria's southern border contained over ten different languages and ethnic groups.[32] What is more, the Austro-Hungarian Empire, unlike Germany's, did not extend abroad. In this sense, Germany was to Austria what Britain and France were to Germany. Even if Germany's imperial age was short and it also had inner-European holdings (Polish Silesia, Estonian East Prussia, French Alsatia, etc.), it nonetheless still had overseas colonies with non-European "others": Africans, New Guineans, Samoans, and Chinese. Austria's "primitives" were *only* in its own backyard, always contiguous with the imperial homeland: Czech Bohemia, Slovakia, Slovenia, Croatia, Bosnia, Tyrolean Italy, Polish and Ukrainian Galicia.

Given this murky position both inside and outside of the "Occident," Austria-Hungary became *the* site for discovering an "other." What travelers could no longer find in the *Urwald* of Asia or Africa, modernists now located in *Mitteleuropa*. This was true for Mann and even for some non-Germanic writers but especially for the Austrians. I think of Kafka, Freud, Meyrink, Musil, and particularly of Hugo von Hofmannsthal, who wrote that the Orient and the unconscious are already in Vienna, which is what makes it so uncanny: Vienna is "Europe's old gateway to the Orient [*porta Orientis*]" also to "that mysterious Orient, the empire of the unconscious."[33] Hofmannsthal consequently sets his only novel, about a journey to exotic regions, not in one of the faraway countries to which he traveled (Morocco, Greece, Scandinavia, etc.) but in a surprisingly primitive *Mitteleuropa*. Hofmannsthal began the main part of his writing on *Andreas*, which he never completed, in 1912, just one year after Jacques published *Hot Land*, Hesse traveled to India, Freud began *Totem and Taboo*, and Mann started *Death in Venice*.[34] Europe was at the brink of war, and Austria's control over its surrounding regions was more fragile than ever.[35] At this crucial moment, Hofmannsthal stages this historical, eighteenth-century journey from Vienna to Venice that, for the entire first half, gets derailed by a detour to a strangely primordial village nestled in Austria's own Carinthian Alps.

Hofmannsthal's Foreign Carinthia

This village becomes the eponymous hero's—Andreas von Ferschengelder's— heart of darkness. His project of "collect[ing] the peculiarities and oddities of foreign lands and customs," of "see[ing] foreign peoples" and "observ[ing] foreign customs," begins right here, not far from his Viennese home.[36] As if entering a faraway Middle Eastern country, he hires a translator-servant, Gotthelf, who describes himself with the Arabic-based word for guide-interpreter: a "dragoman." Gotthelf knows not Arabic, Turkish, and Persian, but rather the essential, exotic foreign languages of the Carinthian region: "Slovenian," "Wälsch" (Walhaz), "Ladinisch" (Rheto-Romantic), and "Italian" (*A* 23, trans. rev.; *SWK* 30:47).[37]

And Gotthelf, too, speaks in dialect, adding to the journey's distinctively foreign feel. His diction is so unusual that today's German and Austrian readers must depend on the critical edition's glossary for a translation into High German. Gotthelf uses strange words such as "Roßtäuscher" (horse-trader), "gefingertsten" (most sly), "Bräundl" (horse), and exaggerates otherwise common Austrian bastardizations of French ("Pikeur" = "Picqueur," and "Atout" = "à tout prix") (*A* 23–25; *SWK* 30:47–48; gloss at *SWK* 30:417). As Hofmannsthal wrote just after completing this main fragment of *Andreas*, such colloquial Austrian was especially "colorful and unusual" in Andreas's late eighteenth century but "even today [1914]" remained an oft-incomprehensible "thing of its own," especially in rural regions such as Carinthia (*SWK* 30:414). As Andreas enters these hinterlands, his mother tongue fittingly seems increasingly foreign. The woman-child he falls in love with, Romana, speaks German with a slight accent—"die Leut" and "dies sei sein Sach gewesen" (*A* 40; *SWK* 30:57)—and her parents' diction is outlandish enough to again demand a glossary. At one point, for example, the parents mention wishing that they could die at the same time; they envy the old pair that got swept to their death together down a flooded mountain gorge: "mitsammen hätt sies in einen Tobel hinuntergerissen" (translated into High German: "zusammen hätte sie es in eine enge Bergschlucht hinuntergerissen") (*A* 48; *SWK* 30:61). Such phrases combine with their superstitious Catholicism to render Romana and her family exotically attractive to Andreas.[38] He resembles here Aschenbach, who likewise glorified Tadzio's Polish words and his family's ardent Catholicism.

Like *Death in Venice*, *Andreas* presents a Europe that initially seems to be teeming with the, quite literally, virgin territories no longer available in Jacques' or Hesse's jungle. Already in Venice Andreas encounters a fifteen-year-old selling her virginity, and, in the Carinthian flashback, the metaphors of virginity and territory are intertwined. Andreas searches for "maids and millers' daughters" with the "roundest, firmest bosoms" among pristine "willows and hazels," stones "gleam[ing] livid," and "water green" (*A* 27–9, 30, 31–32). This territory leads Andreas to the Finazzer family farmstead, where he falls in love with Romana, who is "still a child" and certainly a "virgin" [*Jungfrau*] (*A* 34, 37, trans. rev.; *SWK* 30:53, 55). He watches her speak "innocent[ly]" through lips transparent as "pure blood" about her six siblings who died in childbirth. This observation concludes his obsessive repetition of her language of purity: "innocent boys," an "innocent girl," "innocent twins," all "innocent children in Paradise" (*A* 42, 37, 36, trans. rev.; *SWK* 30:58, 55, 54). Andreas's fixation transfers from bodies to landscapes and back: the skies have a "piercing clearness and purity"; the entire countryside is "innocent and pure"; and Romana is as natural as an "animal" (*A* 41, 39, 38). Romana lies around barefoot in hay piles, and Andreas describes her repeatedly—as Aghion did Naissa—as a shy "deer" (*A* 38, 64, 66, 70, 73). It is as if Andreas had journeyed into a backward *Urwald* that was purer than Hesse's Indonesian jungle with its logging companies, European sexual predators, and dying species. In Carinthia, Andreas gets what Hesse can not find in the tropics: a paradise where the roosters gleam like "Indian birds," the primitive girls really are virgins, and the traveler can be the first man to set eyes on these animals and these girls.[39]

Romana's primitiveness brings with it another exotic aspect: a capacity for incest without guilt. Her grandfather married four times, she tells Andreas, and always to a relative: "there was nothing like Finazzer blood." Romana's mother and father were also "of one blood," half-sister and half-brother, brought up in the same home (*A* 40–41). Freud insisted contemporaneously that incest was always uncannily unsettling, even in the most primitive cultures, but Hofmannsthal suggests that Freud forgot to look in his own backyard: among the isolated gentry of Carinthia.[40] Romana finds nothing wrong with the relationship of her parents, who love one another precisely *because* they are siblings. This closeness is a model for her future marriage: "she would not have it any other way" (*A* 41). Andreas, too, finds this incest untroubling, such that he calmly imagines Romana together with her own youngish father: "the handsome man might have been her betrothed" (*A* 45). And Andreas ultimately fancies joining this circle of inbreeding. Hearing the Finazzer parents snuggling in bed, he recalls hiding in his parents' wardrobe and listening to them in bed when he was a boy; this ersatz *Urszene* leads him to imagine that the Finazzers *are* his parents. This allows him to complete his fantasy of being Romana's "brother" and so becoming attractive to her; they can now repeat her parents' successful incest love story (41). As uncanny as this almost-same love ought to be, it has no such effect on Andreas, who experiences it only as liberating. Like the heroes of contemporary adventure literature, he sees this world as a paradisiacal long-lost "home." He insists that it is more "*heimlich*"—in the original, positive sense of "homey"—than his native city of Vienna (*A* 50; *SWK* 30:62).

The Street of Mirrors: Uncanny Carinthia, Uncanny Vienna

But Andreas soon makes the terrifying discovery that Carinthia, like Aschenbach's Venice, is not as exotic as he had hoped. In the subsequent dream, he discovers how "*heimlich*" always contains within it the "horror" of imploding into its opposite. The dreaming Andreas chases Romana, no longer purely "peasant" but half "urban," to Vienna. He follows her to his childhood street—the "Spiegelgasse" (street of mirrors)—where he sees reflections everywhere of his boyhood traumas. Pursuing her into an entryway, he runs into the catechist he had feared as a child. This catechist grabs him with his familiarly "dreaded little podgy hand," and Andreas flees, only to run into another feared figure from his youth. A "loathsome" boy, who once whispered to Andreas what he did "not want to hear," presses against his cheek. Andreas shoves his way free to pursue Romana, whose clothes are torn and feet are bare, but his path is blocked again, this time by a relic from his own childhood sadism: the cat whose back he had broken and which had taken so long to die. As this half-dead creature creeps before him, Andreas hears screaming and enters his former Spiegelgasse home, going into that same wardrobe from which he used to listen to his parents in bed. The screaming continues. Andreas realizes only now that the screamer is Romana and that he can do nothing to help her: his parents' "many worn-out clothes," these "clothes of too many years, which had not been given away" are packed too tightly around him for him to move (*A* 52–54; *SWK* 30:64–65).

When Andreas wakes, he discovers that someone is screaming in real life: not Romana but the young maid with whom Gotthelf had begun an affair. Half-naked, tied to the post of a burning bed, the woman claims that Gotthelf first bound her, then set the bed afire and taunted her through the window as the flames grew. After this, Gotthelf poisoned the family dog, stole Andreas's horse and money, and fled. Andreas walks through this carnage half "unconscious," "like a sleepwalker," and Romana appears before him half-dressed and barefoot, just as she had in the dream, looking at him with "boundless horror." He senses that the Finazzers' groom likewise eyes him suspiciously, and Andreas remembers the saying, "Like master, like servant," which now chillingly "reverses" itself—*umkehr[en]*—in his mind. As when the word "*heimlich*" turns into its opposite and back again, this reversal terrifies

Andreas. He begins to wonder whether things actually are both themselves and their opposites: whether he, the dignified master, has also committed the servant's vulgar brutalities in his sleep. This confusion unsettles also another set of seeming opposites: dream and reality. Andreas, who had apparently only *dreamt* of violence, stands before the Finazzers "as if drenched in blood" (*A* 56–57, trans. rev.; *SWK* 30:67).

I recount this dream and its aftermath because they emphasize a paradigmatic reversal at the heart of the uncanny encounter: the hero's exotic fantasy gives way, traumatically, to familiarity. Like popular adventurers and Freud's neurotic dreamers, Andreas journeys to an unspoiled "faraway country" where he imagines he will experience "pure" love. But, as Freud warned, such voyages and such love often become uncanny: when the new woman reminds the traveler of the original woman, and the new genitalia remind him of the place where he "lived once upon a time." Andreas's Carinthian dream literalizes this return. Romana leads him directly back to his mother's sexualized body: to the wardrobe where he had, as a child, listened to his parents in bed. But this return is uncanny not only because, as Freud argues, it reminds Andreas of whence he came. It reminds him also that his mother's genitalia are a site of repetition themselves. Other children may have come from here, and men, if only his father, have been here before. Because Andreas wants to disavow this, he denies his mother's sexuality throughout (she was never "close" to his father), just as he denied Romana's by protesting her "innocence" (*A* 49).[41] He fittingly rejects any possibility of his mother's erotic pleasure, even in his adult dream: the screaming he hears from his parents' wardrobe can only signify "horrible" (*gräßlich*) pain, as if "a living creature were being butchered by a murderer" (*A* 53; *SWK* 30:65).

But the dream suggests that Andreas knows very well what he "does not want to know." The screaming that Andreas hears from his parents' wardrobe follows, in the same sentence, his earlier view of the equally "horrible" (*gräßlich*) mixture of pain and pleasure in the dying cat's face: the mélange of "sensual gratification and death agony." This unconscious suggestion of his mother's ecstasy, through the doubled "*gräßlich*," suggests that Andreas's return to the *Urszene* is twice unsettling. His desire for Romana's "faraway place" leads him back to the very first faraway place, his mother's genitalia, which now turn out to be the site of *unheimlich* phallic repetition. Both Romana and his mother have already "had her man," and enjoyed it (*A* 45; *SWK* 30:60). When Andreas hears a combination of pleasure and pain emanating from his mother's room, he immediately thinks of Romana, who originally had caused him to dream about his mother. And in a final turn of the screw, Andreas wakes to discover yet another woman likewise caught between gratification and agony: half-dressed and tied to smoldering bedposts, after a love affair gone wrong.

This uncanny mother/lover is ultimately a screen, as she is in adventure literature, for the sexually threatening masculine figures that appeared earlier in the dream: the grabby catechist and the sensual boy. Romana disappears physically from Andreas's dream already at this point, leaving him alone with the catechist's lecherous hands and the boy's horrible secrets. And Andreas moves already here from sexual predator to prey: he no longer chases Romana but runs from this man and boy. As if to prevent an uncanny gender reversal, in which the man Andreas becomes the woman, the dream-Andreas shoves these two figures away and returns to the sites of his own sadistic power (the mangled cat) and his heterosexual desire (his mother's body). Through this combination of violence and heterosexuality, Andreas re-allies himself with the brutal servant Gotthelf, who, at this very moment, is torturing the girl.

But Andreas only seems here to reestablish his masculinity; he wakes to discover that he remains in danger of becoming a woman. Even though Andreas still calls himself "master," he knows that Gotthelf has bullied him since their first meeting. Andreas now fears this "*Umkehrung*" (reversal) of the master/ slave relation because it will place him in the sexually submissive position (*A* 57; *SWK* 30:67). And Andreas's fear appears, as did his mother's, also as desire; throughout the story, Andreas has run to Gotthelf every time that Romana tried to seduce him—just as Robert Aghion repeatedly returned to Mister Bradley. Andreas both wants and does not want to be Gotthelf's "maid," tied to the bed, screaming in a mixture of pleasure and pain. In this sense, Andreas further resembles the heroes of *Hot Land*, *Robert Aghion*, and *Death in Venice*. They all traveled to an apparently feminized Dark Continent only to discover there the European phallus—the catechist's, the lad's, Gotthelf's—as well as their own uncanny fear of and desire for it. In this final *Umkehrung*, Andreas's orifices present themselves as the text's last unspoiled territory. With his mother and Romana long taken, he is indeed the only virgin left.

The Other Stage: Uncanny Narration

As in *Robert Aghion* and *Death in Venice*, the form of *Andreas* mirrors its plot—specifically through the changes in perspective that Hofmannsthal, like Hesse and Mann, deliberately introduces.[42] *Andreas*, too, begins with a detached third-person narrator, who, from the first sentence onward, separates himself firmly from his protagonist: "'That's just fine,' thought young Herr Andreas von Ferschengelder on the 7th September 1778."[43] Already in this compact opening phrase, the narrator's detachment is clear: quoted interior monologue ("'That's just fine'"), a distancing adjective ("young"), the character's full name ("Herr Andreas von Ferschengelder"), and a date that Andreas would never announce to himself ("7th September 1778"). This distancing reappears throughout the early part of the novel in various forms, including another case of interior monologue and, ostentatiously, a first-person letter (*A* 32, 20). The narrator remains removed from Andreas, just as Andreas, at this point, is separated from the action around him.

But as Andreas moves deeper into the Carinthian valley, he, like Aghion and Aschenbach before him, jumps onto that "other" stage of libidinal investment, most obviously during his dream.[44] Prompted by his desire for Romana, he dreams of erotic violence and perhaps even commits some in real life, as a "sleepwalker." His leap from observing subject to impassioned object, watched by the reader, constitutes an uncanny confusion of categories that disturbs the entire narration: the narrative "I" and figural "he" virtually collapse. The narrator announces his terror at viewing, together with Andreas, the crippled cat: "it was the cat whose back he had once broken with a cart shaft, and which had taken so long to die. And so it was not dead, after all these years!" (*A* 53). The unattributed exclamation typical of free indirect style—"after all these years!"—reveals the same conflation of narrator and character present in *Death in Venice*. Andreas is "embarrassed" by his behavior, and the narrator—like his counterpart in *Death in Venice*—is embarrassed by his intimacy with this violent character (Andreas) (*A* 58). Again like his counterpart in *Death in Venice*, this narrator separates himself perspectivally, by projecting the story, unbeknownst to Andreas, into a narrative future. He announces that, despite the tragedy on the Finazzer farm, Andreas will still have to remain there for "two more days," a fact that Andreas could never have known (59). This awkward temporal shift mirrors the larger crisis within the text: both Andreas and his narrator have lost their distance from their apparent "others" and are now clumsily attempting to reestablish this.

What follows is a nervous narrative back-and-forth that lasts for the remainder of the novel's main fragment. Over and over, the narrator's perspective shifts from the distanced third person to free indirect style and back again, sometimes even mid-sentence. Already on the following day, the narrator slips back into this style, when Andreas remembers torturing, in addition to his cat, his childhood dog. The narrator offers no distancing mechanisms, as if he were reexperiencing the killing together with Andreas: "It seemed to him that he raised his foot and struck the creature's spine with his heel. . . . The little dog fixed its eyes on him, wagged its tail, and died. He was not sure whether he had done the thing or not . . . ." The narrator begins this final sentence still in free indirect style, then shifts awkwardly in mid-sentence to narrative detachment, through the present tense: "He was not sure whether he had done the thing or not—but it issues from him" (*es kommt aus ihm*) (*A* 63–64; *SWK* 30:71). Whereas the narrator stayed in the past while reliving the crime with Andreas ("he was not sure whether he had done the thing or not"), he moves to the present when re-distancing himself from the murder ("it issues from him"). The narrator begins this sentence as an actor on the stage—together with Andreas—but completes it as an analyzing scientist: *es kommt aus ihm*. It is no coincidence that the narrator chooses here the pronoun "*Es*," if we consider Hofmannsthal's fascination with the dangerously fluid borders of the ego/I (*Ich*) as depicted in *Andreas*'s main source text:

Morton Prince's psychiatric study, *The Dissociation of Personality* (1906).[45] Precisely when Andreas's primitive unconscious appears most brutally, the narrator's implied "*Ich*" must call it "*Es*" (id/it) and, in so doing, claims an unbridgeable distance from "it."

But this narrator, like the "hovering" Freudian analyst, cannot dally unscathed with the other's primitiveness: "Es wandelt niemand ungestraft unter Palmen" (No one walks with impunity beneath palm trees).[46] Just when Andreas starts to feel sovereign again, enjoying a budding sense of an "adventurer's ego" (*abenteuerliches Ich*), he notices that he is being watched: "All at once he felt that a person [one of Finazzer's farmhands] was really close by, watching him [*ihn*]. So even this was poisoned [*vergellt*]!" (*A* 65, trans. rev.; *SWK* 30:71).[47] And this shift from heroic subject to object doubles the narrator's own. The narrator, too, moves now from his bird's-eye perspective to that of his objectified character. The unattributed exclamation—"So even this was poisoned!"—shows how he has again joined perspectives with his figure and so become trapped in the very plot he is trying to describe. He descends from a distanced, implied *Ich* into the netherworlds of the third-person unconscious object: "I" becomes "him."

Andreas now lies despondently on the grave of the poisoned dog, contemplating his fate in interior monologue, which constitutes an unusually major break between narrator and character, and also the beginning of Andreas's self-discovery: "Here! He [Andreas] said to himself. Here! All this wandering about is futile, one cannot escape oneself. One is dragged hither and thither, they sent me [*mich*] all this long way—at last it comes to an end somewhere—here!" The attribution ("he said to himself") and the first person of interior monologue ("me") separate the character from the narrator and so reestablish the border of the narrator's implied "I." This separation holds, with few exceptions, for the remaining four paragraphs of the Carinthia section and so correlates with Andreas's own project of self-realization, which gains momentum: he senses a world "behind the real one" that is not "so empty and desolate" (*A* 65; *SWK* 30:72). The narrative perspective, moreover, continues to mirror the plot. At the end of this paragraph, Andreas again uses the otherwise rare first person to muse about the mysteries of his identity, in interior monologue, leaving the narrator also comfortably separate from his character: "Then he [Andreas] was amazed at himself: Where do I [*Ich*] come from? And he felt as if another man were lying there" (*A* 65–66, trans. rev.; *SWK* 30:72).

In this single paragraph, we see the connection of form and content writ large. The narrator gains distance from his character through internal monologue at the same time that this character, with his newfound *Ich*, advances his project of self-discovery. In this sense, both the character and the narrator mirror the traditional exotic adventure hero *and* the psychoanalytic patient. The narrator and character descend into the frightening obscurity of the third person—the id/it of "*es kommt aus ihm*"—experiencing there the dissociation that Morton Prince describes. But they emerge from this with the psychological booty: a terrifying truth—the murder of the dog—that allows the ego/I (*Ich*) to solidify, now apparently free from dissociation. Freud describes this heroic-psychological voyage, likewise, as a grammatical journey—in and out of the unbearably "real" third-person underworld: "Wo Es war, soll Ich werden" ("where *It/Id* was, there *I/Ego* shall come to be") (Freud, *New Introductory Lectures on Psychoanalysis*, SE 22:80; GW 15:86).[48]

The Adventurer's Ego, the Bird's-Eye View, and Andreas's Exotic Unity

Andreas's project of self-realization continues in the subsequent wish-fulfillment dream, when he claims to discover the exotic Carinthia for which he had so longed: the utopian world "behind the real one." He follows Romana again but this time vehemently not to the uncanny Spiegelgasse. She leads him into an ancient forest that—like the *Urwald* in the adventure stories from chapters 1 and 2 above—consists of concentric circles. He ventures "deeper and deeper" into the woods, ever farther from civilization, until reaching a "middle" where everything is "darkest and most luminous." At the heart of this radiant obscurity is an even deeper "middle": a little island meadow around which water flows and where Romana sits. She no longer mirrors Andreas's mother from the Spiegelgasse but grants him his earlier fantasy of exotic "foreign customs": having "fallen asleep haymaking," she now stumbles barefoot into a "heap of hay," and resembles, like Hesse's East Indian Naissa, a "wounded doe" (*ein verwundetes Reh*) (A 66; SWK 30:72–73). Even when she turns inexplicably violent—cracking him on the head with a hay rake—this image grants him "joy" and a sense of being "blessed": this rake-wielding peasant still fits into his fantasy of the "pure" human animal. She does not threaten his identity like the urban Romana from the first dream, who led him to his mother. This Romana's backward brutality pleases Andreas's newfound *abenteuerliches Ich*; it transports him away from his parents' "street of mirrors" to the apparent no-place of exotic utopia.

After waking, Andreas now experiences the real Carinthia as if it were still part of his dream. Romana appears to him as she did there: barefoot in the hay. His joy in her "foreignness" (*Fremdes*) grows when he discovers that he, like Aschenbach with Tadzio, cannot communicate with her; they kiss, but they do not speak (A 70–71, trans. rev.; SWK 30:74–75). Andreas's triumphant transformation of this "real" world into a dreamscape culminates in his announcement that he will become the star of his own dream story: he will remain in Carinthia and take Romana as his bride. He relates this heroic fantasy again, fittingly, in the *Ich* of internal monologue: "Andreas thought lightning-fast, Let's say I [*ich*] stay here, have the luggage taken down; tell the farmhands I've changed my mind?" Although his newfound confidence dissolves in further questions, related fittingly in the third person of free indirect style, his "*Ich*" returns by the end of this paragraph. He regains his poise and decides indeed to leave, but only in order to gain an Odyssean maturity before returning to Romana: "Time must pass, I [*ich*] cannot stay here, but I can come back, he thought, and soon, as the same and as an other [*als der gleiche und als ein anderer*]" (*A* 71, trans. rev.; *SWK* 30:75). Andreas realizes again the challenges necessary for becoming an "adventurer's ego": he must first descend into the third-person "other" before he can emerge as an "I."

In the last paragraph of the Carinthia episode Andreas rides away, still clinging to this fantasy. Despite the series of uncanny disappointments in the Alpine valley, he now sees only pristine wonders of "nature." Repeating the word "pure" three times, he reminds us of his initial fantasies about Romana and the Finazzer farm. Like Jacques' protagonist and Hesse on the Pedrotallagalla, Andreas reserves his greatest wonder for the "mightiest" mountain peak within view; behind it hides a sinking sun and, he insists, the mysteries of unknown worlds. Near its summit wheels an eagle, with which Andreas identifies. Although not at the peak of the mountain himself, Andreas magically takes on the bird's perspective. He felt as if nature's "power," "uprising," and "crowning purity" had "risen from his own being." He, too, can suddenly "see everything" in the world below: the "mountain gorges," the "village," the "Finazzer valley and the farm," and the "graves of Romana's sisters and brothers" (*A* 72; *SWK* 30:76).

Taking on the eagle's point of view, Andreas becomes like his own narrator, who now likewise firmly separates himself from his character through a series of attributions: "he felt," "it was borne in upon him," "he looked into himself." Both the narrator and the character feel themselves to be distanced and omniscient again. Both sense that they can see everything from above, including Romana, whom Andreas yet again compares to a "deer" (*A* 73). In a perfect marriage of content and form, Andreas completes his exotic fantasy. He is as all-knowing and detached as his narrator; both of them have the eagle's perspective, which brings with it power. Andreas, specifically, sees himself swooping like the bird of prey over the beautiful peasant fauna, and he, too, gears up for a lust-attack on the fawn-like Romana (*A* 72–73). Through what Freud would call Andreas's "superior," ironic relation to the valley, he interacts with it while maintaining his distance and its exotic strangeness.

At the core of this beautifully foreign fantasy is again Romana. Andreas's perceived concentric circles of strangeness zoom inward—"circles dissolved into circles"—until all that remains is her "living being, a center, with a paradise about her." Andreas now has his longed-for vision of "unity," the same one that Hofmannsthal once suggested for the novel's full title: *Andreas, or the United*. This unity demands a purge of uncanny repetitions and familiarities and, on the formal level, a separation of narrator and character as well as a character with a bird's-eye perspective. "The parted are united," Andreas knows, only when they are viewed "from high enough." The paradox in this closing fantasy is that Andreas's longed-for unity can *only* occur when he is far away from it. As Andreas knows, his proximity to Romana and her valley led only to uncanniness and the need to be "parted" again. That Andreas does not notice this contradiction speaks to his stubborn exotic delusions, which remain with him through to the final sentence of the Carinthia segment: "It was the happiest moment of his life" (*A* 73).

I have recounted *Andreas*'s Carinthia flashback in detail because it demonstrates how closely Hofmannsthal's modernist text follows the three moments of the "uncanny encounter" I have described in adventure stories. *Andreas* begins with the encounter itself: the horrifying experience of the familiar in a world that ought to be utterly strange and, what is more, virginal. Andreas' beloved peasant-child, Romana, turns out be more sexually sophisticated than he; all the local girls have "had their man" by the time they are fifteen; and Romana's parents in bed remind Andreas, uncomfortably, of his own. These repetitions become manifestly uncanny in his first dream, when the exotic Romana leads him back to "everything that had ever caused him pain and fear": his childhood home, the bedroom of his mother, the cat he tortured, and the male figures that incited his homosexual desire and fear. Exotic Carinthia thus brings him back, like a malevolent "mirror," to his native Spiegelgasse, where he is now forced to "relive all the troubled and false situations of his life as a child" (*A* 52).

Following this horror of recognition, *Andreas* produces the second paradigmatic stage: anger. Even before this dream, Andreas becomes furious with Gotthelf for disabusing him of his virginity fantasy; a "fire" sprang to his throat then, tempting him "to strike the fellow across the mouth." At the time of the dream, Andreas likewise avenges himself on Romana, who has brought him back to his frightening childhood, by setting her home afire, either as his "sleepwalking" self or as his alter ego, Gotthelf. And, finally, *Andreas*, like *Hot Land*, creates the third stage of the uncanny encounter: stubborn hope. Andreas insists that there still might be a virginal barefoot peasant girl living out there, untouched by traveling cosmopolitans, on the other side of his personal "Range of Wonder." When Andreas finally leaves the Finazzer farm, he carries with him this vision of a "doe" (*Reh*) living in a world behind the "real" one, still waiting to be observed, hunted, and penetrated: waiting, that is, to make him inestimably "happ[y]" (*A* 73, trans. rev.).

Venice Again: Doubling, Anthropology at Home, and Returning to the Spiegelgasse

Unlike many contemporaneous adventure stories, however, *Andreas* does not end here. Following the Carinthia flashback, one-third of the extant main fragment remains. The action returns to Venice, where Andreas immediately sees his exotic hopes extinguished. Like Carinthia, Venice began by promising him a virgin, but it, again like Carinthia, unmasks her as uncannily sexually sophisticated: Zustina, a schemer, runs the lottery for her own body. And Andreas meets a cast of characters who blur not only into each other but also into their Carinthian predecessors, leaving him, and us, often unable to distinguish one person from the next or even one section of the story from the next. As we learn from Hofmannsthal's notes on the Venice section, Andreas sees here only the "desperate confusion of all things" (*A* 136). The "Maltese Knight" replaces Gotthelf as Andreas's alter ego and the object of his homoeroticism; the beautiful Nina transforms into Romana before Andreas's eyes; and Gotthelf's face inexplicably reappears.[49] Andreas, too, feels himself splitting off into an *unheimlich* doppelgänger, into what he calls his "other" self (*"wie anders stand er dort vor ihr"*) (*A* 104; *SWK* 30:95). In this hallucinatory world, Andreas has "double" vision. He loses the differentiating bird's-eye view he had gained, however deceptively, in Carinthia and now sees the world stereoscopically and myopically from Venice's alleys, narrow canals, and claustrophobic sitting rooms.

Andreas's crisis again corresponds to a formal one. The narrator, too, loses his ability to view things from a distance and again elides his perspective with his character's. Although the narrator occasionally separates himself from Andreas again through interior monologue,[50] he generally joins Andreas's perspective through free indirect style in this closing section of the main fragment, and emphatically so on the penultimate page. Sensing that Nina wants to kiss him, Andreas backs away from her, upset by the way she eerily dissolves into other characters. The narrator shares his fright by employing free indirect style's trademark unattributed exclamation, in which his perspective blurs with Andreas's: "He was utterly confused. How could he grasp what was so simple and so near! He did not think of the woman over whom he was leaning, but in a lightning flash he saw the mother, the father, the sister, the brothers" (*A* 107, trans. rev.). Although context implies that Andreas means Nina's mother—not his own—his pointed use of "the" instead of "her" ("corrected" in the English translation) suggests that he is confusing not only the members of Nina's family. Could this new lover, like Romana, also return him to his mother? Is he again in the haunted wardrobe of his childhood Spiegelgasse? Might he never escape?

What Andreas learns here is the impasse of modern ethnography, the kind he had wanted to practice by "collect[ing] the peculiarities and oddities of foreign lands and customs": these "oddities" inevitably resemble the same ones from home. Everything looks like everything else, such that the ethnographer eventually loses his separateness from all things "native." As Andreas senses in the main fragment's final paragraph, anthropological "secrets" (*das Geheimnisvolle*) are not elsewhere, in some distant foreignness, but right here, in ethnography's "present": in an empty Venetian square, to which Andreas "return[s]" in more ways than one (*A* 108–9; *SWK* 30:97). He is returning also to the square to which Aschenbach had already returned in *Death in Venice* just nine months earlier.[51] More than this, he, like Aschenbach, prefigures Freud's return to the same spot in "an Italian town" a few years later. The three scenes are uncanny in themselves and also uncannily similar: Aschenbach, Andreas, and "Freud" all walk along "narrow" streets toward a "deserted" spot which they have all seen before.[52]

Anthropology begins at home, in both literature and life. Its mysteries "repeat" themselves "in the form of a circle," as Andreas knows (*A* 108). Every time he steps back into the circle, these secrets double yet again. Every journey returns Andreas to the Spiegelgasse, to both the uncanny mother and the eerily familiar men in the stairwells: the catechist, the loathsome boy, and even Andreas's own narrator, who continually "confuses" himself with Andreas, comes too close for comfort, and then escapes again. The final, formal doubling constitutes the impasse of ethnography. Both Andreas and the narrator seem to sense this, as does Hofmannsthal. It spells the end of Andreas's—and the narrator's—anthropological "collecting" as well as of the story itself, which already repeats Mann and prefigures Freud. *Andreas's* main fragment breaks off here, in 1913, and Hofmannsthal never again writes a sustained paragraph on it.

Hofmannsthal's Imperial Appendix: Notes on the Great Austrian Novel

But this does not mean that Hofmannsthal stopped writing *Andreas*. As the 1982 critical edition revealed, Hofmannsthal wrote between 1913 and 1927 several hundred notes for *Andreas* covering 120 pages (double the size of the sustained fragment I have been discussing here).[53] These notes are patchy and unsystematic, but, especially in the post-1918 sketches, they show us Hofmannsthal's master plan: to reverse the novel's existing centripetal momentum by launching Andreas into far-flung landscapes. After Andreas swirls inward toward the uncanny Spiegelgasse with nowhere to turn, Hofmannsthal, as if sensing the desperation of the trapped traveler, projects Andreas outward to the outlandish spaces of Persia, West Africa, and Egypt. The Maltese Knight's Persian tale, for example, which includes private audiences with the Shah and the Sultan, occupies Andreas so obsessively that he reads until his lamp runs out of oil (*SWK* 30:172–76). After this, Hofmannsthal refers to Andreas's own journeys, either actual or planned, to "a large West African city" and to Cairo, where he will watch the Knight negotiate with Mohammed Ali on the Austrian-led construction of a canal at Suez (30:196, 202).

Significant is Hofmannsthal's decision, at the end of his 1919–25 notes on Andreas's and the Knight's "oriental" journeys, to change Andreas's birth date from 1756 to 1809.[54] In so doing, Hofmannsthal brings Andreas from the Theresian to the Metternich era, during the height of Austria's international standing in the exotic capitals of the "Levante": Tehran, Constantinople, and Cairo.[55] This chronological shift gains importance when one considers Hofmannsthal's moment of writing: just when the real Austria loses its empire, Hofmannsthal finds refuge in a mighty past, where his hero furthers Metternich's *Orientpolitik* in Cairo. As the Knight tells Andreas, "Your Europe must become like your Lower Austria—and so must the entire world!" (*SWK* 30:172). It is as if Hofmannsthal felt the same uncanny psychogeographical tightness after 1918 that Andreas felt in 1912–13. For Andreas, everything—Romana, the Finazzer parents, Gotthelf, Nina—circled back to the Spiegelgasse, but at least he experienced this within the broader Austrian empire that still included northern Italy, the Balkans, Bohemia, and so on. But Andreas's author is trapped, after 1918, in the Austrian rump state, left with nothing but the landscape of self-reflection. Whereas many of his contemporaries used this smallness to explore home even more intensively—Austrian modernism's prototypical *unheimliche Heimat*—Hofmannsthal uniquely launches his hero outward, onto a spectacular travelogue of self-discovery.[56]

The fact that Hofmannsthal expands his novelistic geography only after the Austrian defeat in 1918 contradicts Jakob Wassermann's classic reading in his afterword to *Andreas*'s first book edition (1932). Not knowing the extent of Hofmannsthal's unpublished post-1918 notes, Wassermann argues that Hofmannsthal stopped writing *Andreas* during the war—which turned out not to be true—and, what is more, that he stopped writing *because* of Austria's downfall.[57] With the "national idea" on which *Andreas* was based now "dead," Hofmannsthal's novel could not be finished. The "shredding to bits of the monarchy" left this "most Austrian" of Hofmannsthal's works likewise in "pieces" (as "*Stückwerk*"). Had Austria won the war and expanded its empire, Wassermann concludes, Hofmannsthal's novel would have been completed.[58] In this sense, Wassermann anticipates Edward Said's theory of aesthetic imperialism: the expansive genre of the novel requires the grand colonial narrative.[59] But Hofmannsthal's post-1918 notes tell us the opposite. Hofmannsthal's story can only grow—in terms of plot and geography—at the moment Austria shrinks.

Because recent Hofmannsthal scholars have eschewed "political" readings of *Andreas*, they have not come any closer than Wassermann did to understanding the stakes of Hofmannsthal's decision to release his hero into the great wide world after 1918.[60] In my view, Hofmannsthal's post-1918 expansion suggests that he, like Andreas, imagines a new geographic space saving him, as an author: he hopes for an exotic "Range of Wonder" that will grant his character an imperial ego and himself a finished Bildungsroman. Just before Andreas decides to travel to Cairo, Hofmannsthal tells us that it will be Andreas's "salvation" to "learn to see the world, great and free" (*SWK* 30:209). Andreas will, according to Hofmannsthal's notes, visit West Africa and Egypt, meet Mohammed Ali, and, after this, complete his *nostos* by returning to Austria, marrying Romana, and having many children.

Hofmannsthal even jots down the exact birth dates of their offspring, as if outlining an expansive multi-generational novel on a par with Tolstoy, Dickens, and Balzac (*SWK* 30:180).

Hofmannsthal's very last 1927 notes on *Andreas* reveal, just two years before he dies, the scale of his ambitions. He again defines his epic's "essential subject" (*Grundmotiv*) as Andreas's "unity" with Romana, and points toward a larger social, political, and metaphysical unity, as reflected in his above-mentioned suggested full title, *Andreas, or the United* (*SWK* 30:217). Hofmannsthal then goes on to outline the details of this vast unifying scope. *Andreas* "must be a compendium," which will include the dizzying entirety of social, existential, and political life: "political philosophy," including its "most subtle ramifications in biology"; the interrelation of the "phases of life"; the experience of the "professions" and their effect on humanity; the "inequalities and tensions" within "the social"; the ontological question, "Toward what do humans live?"; discussions of various "medical intuitions"; and, finally, "the sources of national peculiarities and strengths" (*SWK* 30:218). Twenty years after his first sketches for *Andreas* and shortly before his death, Hofmannsthal thus insists that his neglected notes will become the still-missing great Austrian novel: nothing short of a compendium of modern life. As he told his friend Walther Brecht, his epic will remind the world of Austria's former "prestige" to the "east, south, west, and north." Through this novelistic scope, Austria itself will again appear "vivid and great" (*SWK* 30:375).

The disjuncture between the novel's ambitions and its actual state are striking. Following his completion of the main *Andreas* fragment in 1913, Hofmannsthal never added another sentence to it, but he filled notebooks with hundreds of loosely connected notes that eventually comprised more text than the sustained fragment. The novel becomes less a compendium than a *Verzettelung* (dispersal), reminiscent of Thomas Bernhard's prototypical Austrian "loser," Wertheimer, who clutters every corner of his Alpine lodge with "notes" (*Zettel*) about what he vaguely calls the "human sciences."[61] Unlike Wertheimer's loserdom, though, Hofmannsthal's is politically poignant, revealing what Said would call his "investment" in empire, albeit in the inverse direction predicted by Said.[62] As Austria shrinks, Hofmannsthal's geographic imagination grows, and his notes proliferate. And this imagination grows unlike Said's traditional novels or empires: without organization or profit. Whereas Andreas's uncle once sailed "down the Danube," became an imperial noble, and founded a dynasty, Andreas's colonial ambitions scatter impotently, as do his author's notes about them (*A* 183, 150–51; *SWK* 30:120, 115).

In the end, we are left with a relation between the novel and Austrian imperial politics that neither Wassermann nor Said could have predicted. The failure of the novel coincides with the failure of empire, yes, but not as Wassermann had claimed. Hofmannsthal does not stop working on his novel; he simply works on it differently. The defeat of Austria produces not the cessation of Hofmannsthal's writing but rather its dispersion: both geographically (into the "Orient") and literally (into truncated notes in various sketchbooks). In this sense, Hofmannsthal's description of Andreas is also a depiction of himself. Just as Andreas reacts to claustrophobic tension (inner-Austrian tourism, incestuous returns to the declining imperial capital, and the cruel wardrobes of "home") with fantasies of geographical escape, Hofmannsthal responds to the suffocation of his stalled novel and contracting empire with topographic inflation. Like the popular adventure heroes of their day, Hofmannsthal and Andreas react to *unheimlich* shrinking with exotic breakout fantasies. Only the "Levante" can save them. The result is *Andreas*'s hysterical dispersion: a manic expansion that mirrors imperialism and the traditional novel, albeit without the organization and profit of either. Protagonist, author, and reader are left with just shards of the compendium that might have been as "vivid and great" as Austria itself. Fragments of Persia, Egypt, and West Africa appear before our eyes, but then they disappear, at the combined vanishing point of Hofmannsthal's notes and Austria's history.

Musil's Exotic Fersana Valley: Are You Still a Virgin?

Hofmannsthal's main 1912–13 *Andreas* fragment prefigures another Alp story that combines adventure tropes with modernist self-reflection: *Grigia*, which Robert Musil began in 1915 while stationed on the Italian front near the Fersana town of Palai, and which was published in 1921, to Hofmannsthal's praise.[63] Like popular adventure stories and *Andreas*, *Grigia* creates a series of concentric circles of apparent foreignness. The outer circle is Europe itself, represented by the protagonist's—Homo's—home city. Then comes the Alpine Fersana region, then the town of "P.," where Homo joins a mining expedition and, in the center, the insular German-speaking village deep in a nearby valley.

Like *Andreas*'s Carinthia, this village seems, at first glance, utterly exotic. It is "pre-historic" (*vorweltlich*), filled with "ramshackle cottages," "deer stray[ing] in the scrub," and "steep lanes disappearing into the meadows" (*FW* 17–18; *GW* 6:236). Its inhabitants, too, are remarkably primitive. Speaking an impenetrable Germanic dialect reminiscent of Carinthian, these villagers leave Homo, as well as the contemporary German reader, "rack[ing] his brains" for their words' meanings: "Geh aua!" signifies something like "Come a-up!"; "Wos, Teufi, do geh hea" resembles "Hey, you devil, come a-*here*!"; and "I glock an bei Ihm!" seems to mean "I'll bell thee!" (*FW* 34, 31, 33; *GW* 6:247, 245, 247 [emphasis in original]). As with Homo's literary relatives—Hofmannsthal's Andreas and Aschenbach from *Death in Venice*—this incomprehensibility does not frustrate but excites him.[64] He fetishizes his lover's "magical language": a nose is, for her, a "neb" (*Nos*); legs are "shanks" (*Schenken*); and an apron is "apronses" (*Schürze*). Homo ultimately exoticizes her name, deciding to call her the same thing she calls one of her cows: Grigia.

As Aschenbach did with Tadzio, Homo muses lovingly over the word, deciding to pronounce it "with a long 'e' and an aspirated 'Dscha' ": Greedscha.[65]

"Greedscha" and the other village women remind Homo of animals, as if
they—like Romana—were discovered in a forest or a jungle. Grigia resembles her own cow, then a "dor-beetle," then a "squeal[ing]" pig, and even a
"maddened horse" (*FW* 30–31, 35, 39). The other women appear equally
savage, mimicking remarkably the African laborers from Conrad's *Heart of
Darkness*: one woman's eyes stare emptily ahead and lips hang open, as she
joins a row of "silent beasts of burden" wearing baskets loaded with goods
for the mining company, numbly setting "one foot before the other."[66] These
women wear clothes that have "come down through the ages" as well as
shoes like "primitive dug-out canoes," reminding Homo of denizens of faraway lands: they walk like women "in Japan" and sit on the dirt path and
pull up their knees "like Negroes." Toward the end, a woman even stares at
him with a "bony face like an Aztec's" (*FW* 21, 22, 37). In the barn where
Homo first makes love to Grigia, the sour smell of the hay is "like the Negro
drinks that are made of fermented fruits and human saliva," and his entire
journey takes on this flavor of an expedition to a heart of darkness: "One
had only to remember that one was living among savages here [*daß man hier
unter Wilden lebte*]" (*FW* 36; *GW* 6:249).

Like the "savage" African and Asian worlds sought out by contemporary
adventurers, Homo's Fersana promises "virgin" territories—here in the center
of Europe. Homo looks up to the village's unspoiled snow-covered pastures
and feels the air "pregnant" with the snow's imminent melting. "Pregnant"
corresponds with "virgin" in Homo's fantasy both geographically and sexually: the earth is expectant but nonetheless untouched, containing hidden
gold produced out of the ground itself; the women, too, are "pregnant" but
still virgins, pregnant, he senses, with the possibility of their pregnancies (*FW*
17, 18). Although most of these women turn out not to be virgins, Homo
begins his story fascinated with the prospect. He flirts with a fourteen-year-
old "child" who wears an ancestral kerchief and primitive "shoe-boats." Her
virginity and anachronistic rusticity recall the "innocent" Romana, as does
the girl's hay "rake" (*Rechen*), suggesting, through the homophone *rächen*,
that this girl, too, could exact "revenge." Like Romana, this girl appears,
in Homo's fantasy, as pristine as the valley's flora and fauna: "'Come in
the hay,'" Homo says to her, "simply because 'the hay' suddenly seemed as
natural to him as fodder is to cattle" (*FW* 22; *GW* 6:239). The girl, too, is
"natural," uncivilized, and virginal, and, like all of the women Homo meets,
initially defenseless against his mining party, which "held sway like gods."
Homo senses, like Conrad's Kurtz, that the local women worship him: "One
met with love because one had brought blessings." This status allows him,
here, to pursue his virginal desires impudently, getting straight to the point
with a peasant woman he meets right after this fourteen-year-old: "Are you
still a virgin?" Homo asks (*FW* 18–19, 22).

Uncanny Fersana: Re-Opening the Mines

But Homo's virgin fantasies are troubled by hints that this Fersana village—
like Jacques' Brazil, Hesse's Indonesia, Mann's Venice, and Hofmannsthal's
Carinthia—might not be as strange and virginal as it seems. As we learn
already on the opening page, Homo and his team are only to "*re*-open the old
Venetian gold-mines" (*FW* 15, my emphasis). Outsiders have already left their
marks on this village, rendering it no longer virgin but instead, in Homo's
words, "*unheimlich*." Eerily mixing the known and the unknown, this village can only be described through a curious amalgamation echoing Freud's
just-published *The Uncanny*: it is "*fremd vertraut*" (foreign-familiar).[67] The
village's pre-historic traditions and Luther-era interiors are shot through with
the flotsam of the "new age": "cheap, shiny cupboards," "oleographs," and
"jokey postcards." The women's kerchiefs give Homo the sense of "bygone
centuries," but at the same time they are cheap and mass-produced, printed
with "factory-made pattern[s]" (*FW* 20, trans. rev., 21). Confronted with
this global modernity in a world that ought to be insularly primitive, Homo
is "bewildered," and he notices, like a critical anthropologist, that his own
team's presence contributes further to this transformation (*FW* 23). "Ever
and again, there was a gramophone," brought along by Homo's mining team,
transmitting the voice of the international American opera star Geraldine
Farrar (who had made a sensational debut in Berlin in 1901) (*FW* 29).

Sexual practices are likewise curiously modernized. Because the village is
poor, its men generally go to America for several years to make money and
return with the bad habits of "urban brothels." The women, too, become
sexually free, taking lovers while their men are away. This leads to what
Homo calls an "extraordinar[y]" confusion of sexual property, illustrated
by an anecdote about a man who returns from America and claims falsely
to be a village woman's husband. This woman astoundingly appears not to
notice, and the man moves in with her, only eventually to leave her and repeat
the act in the next village. He does this over and over again until finally
being apprehended. Homo implies that these women actually knew that this
swindler was not their husband—something "did not quite correspond"—yet
they still let him into their beds; this is simply "what these women were like"
(*FW* 20–21). As in Jacques' Brazilian jungle and Hofmannsthal's Carinthia,
the young women are not virgins, and the European man is omnipresent.
This swindler recalls Jacques' rapacious German "Wolf," whose ubiquitous
phallus disturbed travelers' fantasy of an untouched Dark Continent. Like
Jacques' Brazil, Musil's Fersana is "homo" both sexually and culturally. The
major in his own mining company, Homo reveals later, has made the rounds
of Grigia's body well before Homo has (*FW* 30).

Homo's worries about the village's virginity causes him to focus obsessively on it, beginning already with his interrogation of the peasant woman.
She responds to his initial query with "Yes, of course," and then he continues:

> "You're still a virgin!" he repeated, and laughed.
>
> She giggled.
>
> "Tell me!" he said, drawing closer and playfully shaking her chin. . . .
>
> "Was once, of course!"

The woman's coyness—first she is a virgin, then she is not—excites Homo but most of all "bewilders" him. Like the adventure travelers of his day, Homo finds this uncanny non-virgin territory disorienting. He now questions the "natural[ness]" of the entire village, wondering whether the villagers have staged their innocent rusticity for him all along. The fourteen-year-old with the rake on her shoulder resembles not only Hofmannsthal's Romana but also a character from a "comic opera." The almost-virgin peasant woman is, similarly, "Valkyrie-like." The latter is so clearly "acting" that Homo notes her "theatrical[ity]." He senses that his life in this village is hallucinatory: "no longer part of reality, but a play" (*FW* 22–23). And he worries that the "savages," like the Ashanti in Freud's Vienna, are only giving him, the paying tourist, what he wants.

This suspicion gains momentum throughout the story, eventually encompassing even the livestock: the village horses "group themselves somehow, apparently at random, in a perspective, so that it looked as if it were done according to some secretly agreed upon principle." Each cow's spine, hind legs, and curving tail form a clef, until the entire group resembles "a scattering of treble signs" (*FW* 26, 27). However beautiful, these apparent stagings produce anxiety in the belated traveler: How much of the village's primitiveness is simply "brilliantly and passionately acted" (23)? Is Homo a victim of his own exotic desire and thus easy prey to an "aesthetic joke" (34)?

But Homo's worry that the village's authenticity is staged does not hold. Like earlier adventure heroes, he disavows his uncanny misgivings and returns to fantasies about Fersana's pure, expectant earth, and again connects this to virginity. The "fairy-tale wood of ancient larches," he muses, holds hidden gems resembling that other "secret of nature": the "tender scarlet flower" inside of a woman. He fantasizes obsessively that this "place" in the woman's body is like a private cache in the earth: "hidden away" only for him, "only for one man," for "no other man." "No one" could touch it, Homo continues, or even see it, lest Homo "should die" (*FW* 23–24). Although Homo is musing here about his wife, not the village women, his statement spells out the psychological stakes of his obsession with virginity: exclusivity. Without exclusivity, he will surely perish, just as the mining expedition will die without sole mineral rights. Homo insists that this secret "place" in the woman's body corresponds to "living crystals" buried within the earth, reminiscent of Freud's 1905 fantasies about the virginal "Dora" (*FW* 23).[68] Disavowing the women's earlier lovers *and* the mines' previous colliers, Homo manages to uphold his fantasy of being first.

Uncanny Narration: Free Indirect Style,
Homós, and Europe's Third Person

These denials lose power when Homo surrenders his safe observer's position and accepts his "theatrical" role as sexual conquistador. As in *Robert Aghion*, *Death in Venice*, and *Andreas*, this leap onto the story's erotic stage generates a narrative shift. In remarkable consonance with these earlier texts, *Grigia* opens with a distanced third-person narrator making gnomic pronouncements: "There is a time in life when everything perceptibly slows down, as though one's life were hesitating to go on or trying to change its course. It may be that at this time one is more liable to disaster" (*FW* 15). Such declarations detach the narrator from the character, as do other mechanisms that persist through the first third of *Grigia*: repeated attributions such as "Homo said," direct speech, and the extensive use of "one" (*man*).[69] But when Homo jumps from observer to actor—at the moment when he is about to betray his wife—the narrator loses this distance, and the text, like its predecessors, enters into a formal crisis.

It is at this point that the narrator joins Homo's perspective, through free indirect style's unattributed interrogations, which virtually efface the difference between figure and narrator: "Was there anything more unreal than that one human being [i.e., Homo's wife] should for him be different [*etwas anderes*] from all other [*anderen*] human beings?—that among innumerable bodies there was one on which his inmost existence was almost as dependent as on his own [*eigenen*] body?" (*FW* 24; *GW* 6:241). Homo's doubt about the "difference" (*etwas anderes*) of all "other" (*anderen*) bodies serves as a transparent justification for deceiving his wife, but it also, more troublingly, erodes the fantasy of difference that had energized his entire exotic quest. Because all women are interchangeable (none is *the* pristine "scarlet flower"), they devolve into a series of indistinguishable "innumerable bodies." Their difference from one another dissolves as does eventually their difference from Homo's body. If all other (*anderen*) bodies are alike, is one's own (*eigenen*) body even still unique? As in *Death in Venice* and *Andreas*, *Grigia*'s form echoes here its plot by announcing the traveling ego's loss of distance from its objects through free indirect style: the narrator's implied *Ich* blurs with the character's *Er*.

This blurring is compounded by the village's uncanny modernity, especially its preponderance of urban men, mostly from Homo's own mining team. Like Hesse in India, Homo spends most of his time not with exotic women but with European men: "a literary man of independent means, a business man, a former inspector of prisons, a mining engineer, and a retired major" (*FW* 28). Every evening they sit together in a cramped vicarage and listen to Geraldine Farrar records until they are filled with voluptuousness and sensuality ("*Wollust*"). With no obvious outlet for this *Wollust*, they, like Jacques' protagonist, become angry, blaming each other for turning this exotic world into that "same standardized unit of the soul which is Europe" (FW 29; GW 6:244). They engage in violent arguments about trivialities, leading Homo to flick a fly into the face of the phallic major, whose rapaciousness has troubled Homo's virginity fantasies (FW 30). Like the "Wolf" from Hot Land, the major could furthermore turn his phallus on Homo. If the eigene male body can become like the andere female one, then Homo could end up as the object of a phallic exchange. In his charged arguments with the major, he becomes "homo" more than in the Latin sense of "man." He becomes also "the same" (homós in Greek), in two ways: like the other team members, he is one of those "same" standardized psychic units of Europe, and, what is more, his libido is now directed toward his same gender (the other men). The team's anxiety about these homogeneities generates the energy of their internal violence.

This violence moves rapidly from the other team members to the natives. Just as Bonsels goes from hating the English to attacking an Indian "half-breed," Homo's mining team vacillates from harassing one another and dreaming of "war" to brutalizing the locals (FW 29). The mining is "not progress[ing] according to plan" because predecessors have stripped away the gems, just as they have destroyed the village's innocence, leaving behind modern "rubbish," false virgins, and staged rusticality (25, 20). Unable to punish their absent predecessors for hybridizing the locals, Homo's team attacks the now "foreign-familiar" inhabitants themselves: through psychological torture (false hangings of petty thieves); terror-inciting guard dogs ("there were as many dogs as men"); and a blatant disregard for the workforce (a peasant's broken leg provides welcome "variety" [Abwechslung] for the management) (FW 25–27, trans. rev.; GW 6:241–43). Bereft of their longed-for virgin territory, the team gains its revenge in colonial fashion. Their violence is not simply about robbing the victims of their resources. It is also meant to render them absolutely primitive, as Homo's team does systematically: deliberately ignoring the village men's sophisticated knowledge of the mines (leading to Homo's eventual demise) and disregarding their legal conjugal rights (we don't even know that Grigia has a husband until the final scene). The invaders attempt to enforce alterity. Like the valley's minerals and the vaginas, its men, too, must remain primordial.

Directly following Homo's first description of this violence, the narrator temporarily halts free indirect style and returns to a detached perspective: "All these were things Homo saw for the first time in his life" (FW 28). Although this sentence seems to absolve Homo on the grounds of naivete, it, more important, pardons the narrator from experiential complicity. The narrator now posits an enlightened first-person perspective (Ich) separate from Homo's irrational third person (Er). The narrator insists that this third person, both Homo and Europe's "standardized" it (Es), is responsible for the violence. The entire sentence cited in part above reads: "It [Es] was every-where that same standardized unit of the soul which is Europe" (FW 29; GW

6:244). The narrator's implied ego (*Ich*) proclaims distance from this dangerous unconscious (*Es*), and, in so doing, continues modernism's ethnography of the West, but in his own naive manner: he does not consider himself to be part of it.

This formal self-separation pertains throughout the narrator's anthropologizing of Europe. When Homo watches flies suffer and die on flypaper, for example, the narrator employs the scientific distance of direct speech, remaining far from Homo's sexual anxiety and mounting hostility: "Homo murmured to himself: 'Kill and yet feel the presence of God; feel the presence of God and yet kill?' And with a flick of his forefinger he sent the fly right into the face of the major opposite, which caused another incident" (*FW* 30). This violent homoerotic "incident" is of pathological-anthropological interest to the narrator. Like his counterpart in *Death in Venice*, he uses his new formal distance to criticize his protagonist ideologically: Homo is irrationally aggressive. After Homo later becomes the "lover of a peasant woman," the narrator does the same, employing a sovereign external viewpoint and the generic pronoun "one" (*man*) to express his critique: "One may have principles . . . . Or one has no principles, or perhaps they have slackened somewhat, as was the case with Homo" (*FW* 34; *GW* 6:248). The narrator's perspective here is more distanced from Homo's than at any point since the opening sentence. He has dissociated himself from his savage fellow European "third person"—the primitive European *Er/Es*—which must nonetheless still be lurking somewhere within him (and us).

The Disinterested, Ethnographic Eye

As if mimicking his narrator's self-distancing, Homo, echoing Andreas, now also steps back from the village to gain a bird's-eye perspective. He climbs to the "nearest height" and watches a girl bale hay, which gives him a sense of freedom and power: he feels as if he were "lifted loose" on a "swing," "far away" from the world. From this vantage point, he can manipulate the theatricality that had once "bewildered" him. The girl becomes, in his vision, an aesthetic object: a "polka-dotted doll under the enormous glass bell of the sky." She is exotically non-human—a doll and, later, a "dor-beetle"—and is excitingly strange. He frames her as he would an exotic photograph, using visual clichés from nineteenth-century agricultural eroticism:[70] "Very sensually she [*sie*] lay on her belly across the bale and reached underneath it" (*FW* 35; *GW* 6:248). By turning her into a picture, Homo can keep her third person (*sie*) safely away from him. Like the narrator, he protects his "*Ich*" in the bargain. This girl, unlike the earlier not-virgin "Valkyrie," cannot threaten him with the mixing of the *anderen* with the *eigenen*.

This new lofty point of view has its roots in eighteenth- and nineteenth-century discourses of aesthetic distance, which merits a digression because it bears on *Grigia*'s formal politics. The eighteenth-century "disinterested" gentleman "of landed property" was viewed, as Homo and the narrator now see themselves, as objective: his rental income supposedly freed him from the biases of daily life. Through his "elevated," remote viewpoint, this disinterested gentleman combined aesthetics with power.[71] It was only a short step from here to Hegel's 1807 "master," who enjoyed objects purely, as "sheer negativity," because he separated himself absolutely from them.[72] This master in turn inspired a dense nineteenth-century nexus of power and visual detachment, culminating in Nietzsche's 1886 "pathos of distance," where the ruling classes ceaselessly "looked down" on subjects and tools, with their "elevation" allowing them to reach "ever higher" and "more comprehensive" visions.[73] This aesthetic distancing forms the philosophical background of modern anthropology, when "armchair" anthropologists took Nietzsche's detachment to the point of absurdity: they observed exotic others without ever even leaving their homes. Remaining at the figurative height of their British Museum desks, they simply read other travelers' accounts of the primitive beyond. From the eighteenth-century disinterested gentleman through to this fin de siècle anthropologist, then, observers gained authority through distance, supplying the ethnographic setting for Musil's wartime story.

Staying as far away from his objects as would a nineteenth-century anthropologist, Homo paints a contradictory picture of the world: everything is present except for the observer himself. And Homo gains his power precisely through this self-effacement. Like Hegel's master, he begins by separating himself from the objects of his world, including "his own body," and this self-distancing allows him to dispense with the fear of death. He realizes calmly that "he was soon to die, only he did not yet know how or when." Because he "has had to reckon up with his life" and is waiting "only for death," he is now "weightless and free," "health[ier]" than ever before. But there is a dialectical undercurrent to this weightlessness. By accepting death, he loses the very "ego" (*Ich*) that he had hoped to gain, and is left instead only with the "airy outlines" of his self (*FW* 34, trans. rev.; *GW* 6:248). This nothingness corresponds to his increasing absence from life. He stays away from the village, observing it only from above and painting a picture that includes everything except his own vanishing body. We see the mountain meadows, the hay, and the girl, but not the spying hero. By gaining power through self-erasure, he both exalts and undermines himself in the style of the "master," whose existential bankruptcy had already been suggested by Hegel.[74]

Going Native (and Staying There)

Neither the narrator nor Homo remains at this self-obliterating distance. Like Freud and, later, Malinowski, Homo and his narrator ultimately surrender, at least temporarily, their anthropological detachment. By the end of this same paragraph, Homo returns to the village's stage, wondering again in free indirect style, together with his narrator, about the bale the girl is carrying: "The bundle was much bigger than the bright slender little human animal that was carrying it—or was that not Grigia?" The grammatical "stroke of thought" (*Gedankenstrich*, or dash) preceding the "or" collapses Homo's perspectival separateness in one stroke. He recognizes the particularity of the once abstract "girl"—Greedscha!—and his erotic investment in her. This emotional contact spawns a physical one: he tumbles headlong back down into the hay-stooks with the natives. Once there, he sees another artful grouping of women that, as he gets closer, gives him a "sudden fright." Realizing that he now truly "belongs to them [the villagers]," he feels excited but also terrified: "in this life he was leading there was no longer any certainty of time and place." Things seem "alien" in a way they did not before. He sways drunkenly through the village, sleeping with Grigia in hay piles that smell like sour "Negro drinks" (*FW* 35–36).

Resembling the modern anthropologist and the psychoanalyst, Homo relinquishes here his ego and goes native, at least for the moment: he "displaces himself" (*sich hineinversetzen*) into his exotic subjects, as Freud had instructed (Freud, *SE* 17:220; *GW* 12:230). He will "liv[e] among savages" in order to emerge with the ethnographic goods: both the truth about the savages and his "adventurer's ego," for which Andreas had longed. Although this primitive world is not as explicitly different as he had hoped, its lack of absolute difference now in fact makes it truly strange. Its bodies are similar to his and yet not. His perspective is almost the same as theirs but not quite. This uncanny foreign-familiarity causes unexpected fright and eerie enjoyment. Homo is "intoxicated" by the devastating pleasures of self-loss, reported to us in the free indirect style of a narrator who likewise loses himself in this perspectival consonance with Homo (*FW* 36).

Unlike the successful anthropologist or psychoanalyst, Homo surrenders any plans to reemerge from this native world. He commits the cardinal sin of all post-Odyssean travelers: he forgets his *nostos*. Entering an old mineshaft with Grigia at the end to make love, he finally seems to have become one with the primitives: he lacks even "the civilized man's need to investigate [the shaft] first by the light of a match" (*FW* 38). When Grigia's vengeful husband rolls a boulder in front of the shaft's entrance to besiege them, Homo makes one last attempt to separate himself—again, as "a civilized man"—but then gives up. He has lost all sense of time, has accepted his "destiny," and, most important, relinquishes his fantasy of finding a "new self [*Ich*]": his "whole life" now slips away from him (*FW* 40, 40, 34, 40; *GW* 6:251, 252, 248, 252). Fading in and out of sleep and growing ever weaker, he wakens to realize that Grigia has escaped without telling him ("Grigia was gone"): "He smiled; telling him nothing of the way out [*Ausweg*]; meaning to leave him behind, as proof for her husband . . . !" (*FW* 40, trans. rev.; *GW* 6:252 [ellipsis in original German]). This unattributed exclamation followed by an ellipsis represents the most striking use of free indirect style in the entire story, demonstrating how the character and the narrator have lost their subjectivity together. Just as Homo left his bird's-eye perch to die with Grigia in the savage "darkness," the narrator too has surrendered his critical distance from Homo.[75] The narrator and Homo descend together. No match is struck; they slip, as one, into obscurity.

Within this ego dissolution, Homo registers not anxiety but only pleasant regression. He presses himself onto his hands and knees, and crawls, childlike, deeper into the shaft, where he sees a sliver of light. Realizing that this probably marks the crevice through which Grigia escaped, he nonetheless chooses not to follow it. Why not? Comparing the shaft to a womb, critics have argued persuasively that Homo does not escape because he has reached his paradisiacal maternal goal, as it also appears in other Musil texts.[76] Such a return places Homo firmly in the fin de siècle tradition uniting regression and exotic travel. As the poet and critic Alfred Kerr exultantly claimed in 1911, Europe's poetic *Ur*-mother could only be found in the Orient's "blood" and "umbilical cords."[77] Robert Müller's European adventurers in his 1915 *Tropics: Myth of the Journey* likewise called the tropics a "womb" that allowed one to return joyously to the "mystery of mothers."[78] Such narratives were so widespread that they caught the attention of early psychoanalysis. Alfred Winterstein, an early Freud student, argued that exotic travel expressed the desire to "penetrate . . . mother earth" to see what she has been withholding.[79] Carl Jung likewise claimed that travelers were always searching, without knowing it, for the object that they would never find: "the lost mother."[80]

Freud added a twist to Winterstein and Jung, pointing out that travelers sometimes in fact did find this lost object, but they should have been warned against wishing for it. Freud's neurotic patients found "something uncanny" about the female genitalia, leading Freud to cite the witticism, "Love is homesickness." When his patients dreamt of faraway countries and said to themselves, "this place is familiar to me, I've been here before," Freud continued, this place was the "mother's genitals or her body," where "each one of us lived once upon a time and in the beginning" (*SE* 17:245). But Homo now seems to be immune to this Freudian uncanny, just as he repressed the other uncanny details that had troubled him earlier. Like Kerr's and Müller's heroes—but unlike Aschenbach and Andreas—Homo represses these in order to return happily to the maternal body's *Urwald*.

It's the Gettin' Back That's Hard: Literary Ethnography, the Way Out, and the Last Mohicans of Love

Many interpretations of *Grigia* end here, with Homo's regressive death. But stopping here—and debating whether Musil takes a critical stand toward this regression[81]—means neglecting the final sentence, which elucidates the stakes of the entire story. At this moment, after Homo surrenders his *Ausweg* ("way out") and quietly dies, the narrator secures his own *Ausweg*. Like his counterpart from *Death in Venice*, he reacts to Homo's death coldly, forgetting his earlier intimacy with him. He underscores his remoteness with the same formal tactics used by the narrator from *Death in Venice*: a paragraph break followed by a final, curt sentence, related through distanced auctorial narration: "At this same hour, all efforts having failed and the futility of the undertaking having been recognized, Mozart Amadeo Hoffingott, down in the valley, gave orders for work to cease" (*FW* 41).

The few readers to discuss this sentence interpret it as most scholars do the finale of *Death in Venice*: as a return to an "objective," god-like voice ("god"—*gott*—is nestled within Hoffingott) and, as such, a criticism of Homo's dangerous hallucinations. As Karl Eibl writes, Homo dies because he has "continually move[d] further away from reality"; his death signals "reality's revenge," and the narrative voice, both here and at the beginning, reveals Musil's insistence that every "spiritual expedition" into the unusual be tied back to "normal behavior" (*das gewöhnliche Verhalten*).[82] But Eibl makes the same mistake as did earlier readers of *Death in Venice*. He conflates the author, Musil, with the narrator, and so echoes Jost Hermand's similarly faulty reading of *Grigia* in comparison with *Death in Venice*.[83] Even at the moments when Eibl admits that this voice is the narrator's, not the author's, he tacitly accepts the narrator's claims of "neutrality"—thereby allowing the narrator an impartiality that makes him seem more like an omniscient author and less like a character caught up in the story he is telling. Eibl does not see that Musil, like Mann, constructs his narrator as a *character*, and, what is more, as a flawed character whose weaknesses Musil subtly exposes throughout.

When this distance between Musil and his narrator becomes clear, we see how this story, like *Death in Venice*, is not about whether we should judge the main character's denial of "reality," nor is it about whether we should accept Musil's "ambivalence" regarding this denial.[84] Rather, the story becomes a meditation on reality itself, especially within the framework of ethnography. *Grigia* asks, with *Death in Venice*: how can we speak of reality, when its describer (the narrator) has already shown himself to be as "intoxicated" as the subject he observes? As *Grigia* demonstrates through the perspectival blurring of free indirect style, this observer of reality has become as "savage" and irrational as his object. And the narrator cannot deny this simply by asserting objectivity in the last sentence. "Reality" has not triumphed. *Grigia* instead takes this term to task, through a second-level ethnographic insight that overturns the truism that we can never really understand other people. Homo indeed seems to know this other, just as the narrator seems to know Homo; both are apparently not afraid to lose themselves in this other, to "go native." The problem occurs when they try to disengage. They can never reestablish a scientific, "disinterested" position, and we are left only with the "reality" of this perspectival mix. *Grigia* makes this argument even against some of Musil's own essayistic claims, demonstrating how, contrary to interpreters too wedded to authorial assertions, *Grigia*'s non-rational (*nicht-ratioïde*) fictional world is more powerful than even Musil surmised. "The great danger with which fiction threatens our world" is not always re-containable within Musil's "ratioïde" essayistic standards of "*das gewöhnliche Verhalten.*"[85]

Like *Death in Venice*, *Grigia* thus theorizes the *perspectival* impasse that literature exemplifies for psychoanalysis and anthropology: after the analyst/ethnographer/narrator transports himself into "the native's point of view," how does he get out? Grigia's husband enters a dangerous mine shaft earlier in the story and aptly remarks that the getting in is easy: "it's the gettin' back that's hard" (*das Zruckkemma is halt schwer*) (FW 39; GW 6:251). Homo learns this by going ever "deeper" into the villagers' lives, to the point of madness, until he does not even want to "return to life." It is as if Freud, after "displacing" himself into the minds of his neurotics, chose to remain in this Conradian "darkness."

But *Grigia*'s narrator, like the real Freud, does not want to remain in this other world, so he separates himself from his gone-native character. The difficulty of this reveals itself in *Grigia*'s clumsy finale, as it did in *Death in Venice*'s. Musil's narrator, like Mann's, disavows any connection to the character he has accompanied through the story, not even mentioning his name, as if the appellation could contaminate him. Musil's narrator, too, might become "homo," the "same" as all the other savages: the villagers, the gone-primitive Homo, and the mad, homoerotic miners. This narrator, too, is in danger of becoming, like the "uncanny white man" in Jacques' jungle, *ver-rückt*: geographically "disarranged" *and* "crazy." Musil's ending speaks neither about "reality" nor non-reality, but about this "sudden fright" of closeness, from which the narrator vainly and awkwardly attempts to remove himself. The "futility of the undertaking" refers also to this *ethnographic dilemma*, for which *Grigia* offers not a solution but, like *Death in Venice*, further questions: How do we represent others? How do "we" *feel with* "them"—*mitleiden*—yet not become so fused with them that we can no longer find a way out?

Grigia's only response to these questions is to show us *how* the narrator fails. The narrator institutes a literal "deus" ex machina: the "hope" for a "God" (*Hoffin-gott*) who can, like the perfect ethnographer, gain absolute knowledge of the other yet still remain safely distant. Like all *dei ex machina*, this one offers an easy solution that only emphasizes the problem's insolubility. Hoffingott simply "orders work to cease" (literally, to "break off" [*Abbruch*]), at which point he, together with the narrator, breaks off from the entire story. The result is an unconvincing escape: the "failure" and "futility" of the mining project become symbols for the story's failure—but a failure that is ultimately illuminating. It shows us how literature, with its unstinting attention to perspective, can shed a light on ethnography that ethnography cannot shed on itself. Literature, especially literature's failure, becomes the workshop for learning about the impossibility of writing about others.

This "failure" also moves literature beyond literature in a second sense: by speaking to its own moment of globalization. Ethnography has always been impossible, *Grigia* suggests, but is especially so in the era of the apparent end of alterity, when the "object" becomes so similar to the subject that the latter's identity hangs in the balance. It's not the "getting in" that's hard but, as Freud and Malinowski also sensed, the *"Zruckkemma."* How do we write about the other when "he" is so uncannily close to "us"? This became the pressing question for ethnography—whether anthropological, psychoanalytic, or literary—around 1900, when travelers discovered that the apparently exotic other shockingly resembled "us." Modernism and psychoanalysis transferred this encounter to Europe's fringes, in the initial hope that this would produce a new exotic object. But the new "other" proved, too, to be uncanny. Creating a virtue of necessity, the modernists made this foreign-familiarity their métier. Whether in the Alps or among the "aboriginal population of the mind," they now show us yet another set of "homos": European "natives" who appear to be just like us, but not quite.

Over a decade later, Musil will spin this internalization of travel even tighter, in the second, 1932 volume of his landmark *The Man without Qualities*, when he sends his hero—Ulrich—into the foreign-familiar territory of his sister's bedroom. Incest becomes here uncanniness's final concentric circle, even though Ulrich, like Hofmannsthal's Finazzers and Mann's Walsungs, finds this center not uncanny at all; it becomes pleasingly exotic. Ulrich and his sister are the "last Mohicans of love," taking a "journey to paradise": deep into the "other condition" (*anderer Zustand*).[86] Ulrich represses incest's uncanniness and replaces it with the erotically foreign, *anderer Zustand* of the Mohicans. This exoticist repression has its pendant, as I will discuss in the epilogue, in the contemporaneous mysterious reversal within the word *"Blutschande"* (incest) itself, which took on, in the 1920s, its second meaning of "race-defilement."[87] *"Blutschande's" unheimlich* linguistic turnabout tells us—as does *Grigia*—much about language's relation to history, hinting at the political unconscious beneath Musil's portentous title of this volume's opening book: *Ins Tausendjährige Reich*, meaning "Toward the Millennium" and, in Nazi speeches of the 1930s, "Toward the Thousand-Year Reich."[88]

Epilogue

Toward a Theory of Uncanny Violence

Scholars who concur on little else agree on the source of modernity's violence: it stems from our fear of difference. The other produces in us a "terror" that makes us want to "kill" him. Powerful arguments have been made supporting this theory, and it is persuasive in some situations.[1] But, as I have argued throughout this book, the fact that this theory generally goes unquestioned obscures an even more powerful cause of violence in modernity, issuing from the opposite of the fear of difference: the dread of unexpected similarity.

Freud's Narcissism of Minor Differences and Lacan's *Espace Vital*

Freud touched on this idea briefly already in 1918, in his essay on the "Taboo of Virginity": "It is precisely the minor differences in people who are otherwise alike that form the basis of feelings of strangeness and hostility between them. It would be tempting to pursue this idea and to derive from this 'narcissism of minor differences'" a general theory of aggression (*SE* 11:199). Freud never gives in to this temptation to pursue the idea further. But it does continue to haunt him, appearing three years later in "Group Psychology and the Analysis of the Ego" (1921):

> Of two neighboring towns each is the other's most jealous rival; every little canton looks down upon the others with contempt. Closely related races keep one another at arm's length; the South German cannot endure the North German, the Englishman casts every kind of aspersion upon the Scot, the Spaniard despises the Portuguese. (*SE* 18:101)

The same supposition emerges once more in *Civilization and Its Discontents* (1930), where Freud refers back to these earlier iterations:

> I gave this phenomenon the name of "the narcissism of minor differences," a name which does not do much to explain it. We can now

see that it is a convenient and relatively harmless satisfaction of the inclination to aggression, by means of which cohesion between the members of the community is made easier. In this respect the Jewish people, scattered everywhere, have rendered most useful services to the civilizations of the countries that have been their hosts. (*SE* 21:114)

Nine years later in *Moses and Monotheism* (1939), Freud again connects this narcissism of small differences to anti-Semitism:

[Jews] are not fundamentally different, for they are not Asiatics of a foreign race, as their enemies maintain, but composed for the most part of remnants of the Mediterranean peoples and heirs of the Mediterranean civilization. But they are nonetheless different, often in an indefinable way different, especially from the Nordic peoples, and the intolerance of groups is often, strangely enough, exhibited more strongly against small differences than against fundamental ones. (*SE* 23:91)

Even if Freud no longer dismisses this aggression as "harmless," he does not yet grasp its full implications and remains confused about its causes ("strangely enough"). Moreover, he never tells us why this narcissism of minor differences should be a fitting term to explain this hostility. Freud thus develops a *sociological* hypothesis (cultural/ethnic similarity produces aggression) without creating a *psychoanalytic* theory to elucidate it (i.e., how "narcissism" causes violence). And he never gets a further chance. Later that year, just following the Nazi invasion of Poland, he dies.

One goal of this epilogue is to reinvigorate Freud's half-constructed concept, which has fallen into neglect.[2] Although fragments of Freud's "narcissism of minor differences" (rarely credited as such) appear in late twentieth-century anthropological philosophy and sociology, these usages, like Freud's, are undertheorized. Notable here is René Girard, who argued in 1972 that the modern erasure of social differences produces a frightening "monstrous double" that majority groups first scapegoat and then annihilate. His theory of violence does not acknowledge Freud's but reads like it: "It is not [cultural] distinctions but the loss of them that gives birth to fierce rivalries and sets members of the same family or social group at one another's throats." And later: "It is not the differences but the loss of them that gives rise to violence and chaos."[3] Pierre Bourdieu follows in 1979: "Social identity lies in difference, and difference is asserted against what is closest, which represents the greatest threat."[4] Zygmunt Bauman likewise claims a decade later that, when the "alien" resembles the "native" too much, he "threatens to penetrate the native group and fuse with it—if preventative measures are not set out."[5] Building on Girard and Bourdieu, Anton Blok exceptionally cites Freud's theory of minor differences to explain outbreaks of violence and genocide against African Americans in the antebellum American South, Croats/Serbs/Muslims in the Balkans, the Burakumin in Japan, and the Tutsi in Rwanda.[6] But Blok, like his predecessors, fails to fill the major explanatory gap left by Freud. Can one even say with confidence, as Bourdieu does, that similarity "threatens" identity? Could not similarity instead confirm identity as when, for example, colonial powers force aboriginals to assimilate into the invading culture?

To answer this question, we must return to Freud's *The Uncanny*, specifically to his claim that the most ominous of similar others—the double—was not originally threatening. It functioned first, both ontogenetically and phylogenetically, as an "insurance against the destruction of the ego, an 'energetic denial of the power of death'": the "'immortal' soul was the first 'double' of the body." As children, we get comfort from our alter egos—imaginary friends and dolls—just as, in our phylogenetic past, we gained strength by preserving our dead in lasting materials. This ancient consolation in doubles springs, Freud concludes, from a normal and necessary self-love: from that primary narcissism that "dominates the mind of the child and of primitive man" (*SE* 17:235).

Only when this once-comforting double reappears later, out of context, does it turn into its opposite: an "uncanny harbinger of death." The double jolts us backward into an earlier ontogenetic or phylogenetic stage, when the ego had not yet clearly distinguished itself "from the external world and from other people." In this earlier phase of primary narcissism and animism, we believed in the life of all things and saw no difference between the animate and the inanimate, the self and the other, inside and outside; there was no disparity between the surrounding objects and "me." Returning to this stage after apparently surmounting it fills us with dread: we fear that our hard-fought ego, that fortress of the self, will be hurled back into a mire of indifferentiation. For this reason, the second "self" that once reassured us appears as thoroughly *unheimlich*. It is my "I" before I was an "I," anciently familiar to me but now feeling like something foreign that threatens my psychological survival (Freud, *SE* 17:235, 236).

This is how uncanny doubling creates anxiety, but why should this lead to aggression? Freud hints at an answer in his playful anecdote about traveling alone in a sleeping compartment in a train (discussed in chapter 3): after a jolt causes the door of his adjoining bathroom to swing open, Freud sees an elderly gentlemen enter, apparently by mistake. Freud jumps up to "put [the man] right" but discovers, to his dismay, that the intruder was actually Freud's own reflection in the mirror: "I can still recollect that I thoroughly disliked his appearance." After first claiming that this dislike was insignificant, Freud reconsiders and asks whether his dislike was not perhaps "a vestigial trace of the archaic reaction which feels the 'double' to be something uncanny?" (*SE* 17:248n1).

Freud's instinctual aversion and even aggression for his double (jumping up to "put him right") prefigures Jacques Lacan's 1949 lecture, "The Mirror

Stage," and, more important, his neglected, related lecture from the preceding year, "Aggressiveness in Psychoanalysis."[7] When the child (mis-)recognizes his own image in the mirror, Lacan argues, he feels jubilation but also hostility, and this "aggressiveness" reappears in adulthood when the subject encounters others who seem too similar to himself.[8] Lacan gives the example of the psychoanalytic patient who sees "in his analyst an exact replica of himself" and feels an "excess of aggressive tension." If "experienced in the strange/uncanny form [*le mode d'étrangeté*] characteristic of the apprehensions of one's *double*," this sense of being the same as his analyst can create an "uncontrollable anxiety" on the part of the analysand.[9] But Lacan, like Freud, does not explain how such anxiety and "aggressive tension" in an intrapersonal situation could make the leap to group violence. Why does it not remain in the private realm (e.g., insults toward one's analyst)? And if it does enter the social world, why not as Freud's "harmless satisfaction" of put-downs, as in English jokes about the Scottish? What gives this innocuous-seeming form of creating group cohesion its martial turn?

Lacan hints at a possible answer in the final pages of "Aggressiveness in Psychoanalysis," where he argues that we have become paranoid and violent because, in modernity, we sense that our living space is always shrinking. We can no longer mark ourselves off spatially from others, and this translates into a psychic fear of indifferentiation similar to Freud's uncanniness. In reaction, the ego transforms itself into what Lacan calls a "fortified camp"; the twentieth-century worry that the map's last blank spaces are filled produces social rivalries analogous to the ego's protection of this fortress: "Already in the 'living space' [*l''espace vital*'] in which human competition grows ever keener, an observer of our species from outer space would conclude we possess needs to escape with very odd results."[10] This 1948 connection of psychological space to Nazi desires for *Lebensraum* (both present in "*espace vital*") elucidates what Lacan means by the "odd results" of our desire to escape. He means wars and not only the Nazi one, but also the 1914 imperial one, partially caused by the Germans' anxiety about finding their "place in the sun" within overcrowded colonies. Only through a war with the older imperial powers could Germany produce *Lebensraum*, both in the European east and in the colonial south. In so doing, Germany hoped to cure its malady of being a "people without space" (*Volk ohne Raum*)—by which it still felt afflicted at the start of World War II.

Lacan takes this trajectory to its logical conclusion three paragraphs later when he claims that our "instinct of self-preservation" now develops into "the temptation to dominate space [*l'espace*]," the home of those critical observers from "outer space" that Lacan had mentioned earlier.[11] As Lacan certainly knew, this war for interstellar space (*Weltraum*) had already begun. The original Nazi flight into space in 1942 paved the way for several later 1940s U.S. missions. These culminated in 1947, just one year before Lacan delivered this lecture on aggression, in the first interstellar launch of living beings (fruit flies).

Given the overlap between Freud's uncanny and Lacan's mirror stage, it is striking that Lacan never used the term *unheimlich* in either "The Mirror Stage" or "Aggressiveness in Psychoanalysis,"[12] and that Lacanian theorists never make the connection between the uncanny and Lacan's theories of aggression.[13] The *"Heim"* (home) from *unheimlich* is, after all, the missing link between the ego's "fortified camp" and the state's expansion of its national home. As Freud insists in *The Uncanny*, we must understand neuroses as proceeding from this conflict within "home," originally configured as the vagina—that "former *Heim* of all human beings"—which seemed, to men, like a too-familiar faraway country. And just as misogynistic violence follows this overproduction of genital familiarity (in Hoffmann's "The Sandman," Freud's exemplarily uncanny story, Nathanael tries to throw the maternal Clara from the steeple), social violence stalks the too-familiar other. As I have argued in this book, such uncanny violence reached new heights at the beginning of the twentieth century, when the globe's last blank spaces were mapped, making it ever harder to find a marked-off "living space" as well as people who were not uncannily similar to "us." "We" discovered everywhere versions of ourselves that we could not "escape" and thus lashed out against the other, who was actually our mirror image. (Nathanael, of course, eventually kills himself.) Lacan, like the former head of NASA,[14] correctly predicts that this battle will continue in "outer space," but Lacan cannot yet see how it will infect our crowded cyberspaces. Governments create dead cyber "zones" to disable virtual crowds engaging in civil disobedience; they battle within computing "clouds"; and they replace adversaries' "home" pages with uncannily exact copies.

The Uncanny Exotic World, *Tropenkoller,* and Malinowski

Throughout the preceding chapters, I have examined how such uncanny encounters began around 1900, with voyagers arriving at the ends of the earth only to find hauntingly familiar others. This produced feelings of eerie surprise and shock, followed by anger and the impulse toward violence. Consider again Jacques, Nolde, Bonsels, and Hesse. They feel revulsion for the natives who seem too close to them: the "pants-wearing niggers" (*Hosennigger*), the British-Indian "cross-breeds" (*Mischlinge*), and the "slavish Malaysians" who speak better English than their German visitors.[15] This irritation manifests itself first as verbal abuse and then as physical violence: Jacques' narrator slanders "brutally" the German girl who has become so Brazilian that she can barely speak German; Bonsels slaps the Indian *Mischling* for reminding him too much of his own mimetic aspirations to be British; and Hesse's Mister Bradley hits servants who apparently do not know their racial and political place. Each perpetrator is gripped by a mysterious force that, as Bonsels claims, cannot be explained or, for Jacques' protagonist, occurs "half consciously" (*Heißes Land*, 174); experts assumed that it was a malady—"tropical rage" (*Tropenkoller*)—so widespread that the German parliament debated it in the 1890s.[16] It was not the Indian's, the Moroccan's, or the Herero's alterity that led the British, French, and Germans to fits of *Tropenkoller* but their similarity, as produced through the unrivaled mixing of identities in the first era of globalization. Colonialism created its own "darkest fantasy" by bringing so many different peoples in close contact.[17] The European was now haunted by the *Mischling*: the uncanny double whose mimicry reminded the European of the fragility of his own identity.

Malinowski famously claimed that anthropology destroyed its object the moment it discovered it, but he revealed an even more crucial truth after his death, in his diaries. *Tropenkoller* (Malinowski uses the German term) was part and parcel of the founding of modern anthropology; it turned out that Malinowski, the supposed great understander of the natives, cursed them violently and even hit one of them in the jaw.[18] Whether defending Malinowski or criticizing him, his readers generally agree with the traditional theory of violence outlined above: that Malinowski's aggression stemmed from a fear of difference. He had been living for too long within the foreignness of "a Neolithic people" and within a "form of life not merely different but incompatible with his own."[19] Malinowski himself, however, offers a different explanation. Not the absolutely foreign other but the uncannily similar one disturbs him most: "The half-civilized native in Samarai is to me something a priori repulsive" (*Diary*, 111).

Although Malinowski does not explain why, it is worth considering that these "half-civilized" others might have reminded him of himself—just as Freud might have seen his "Moorish" Jewish face in the "primitives" from *Totem and Taboo*. Malinowski once said that, as a Slav, he was more "savage" than his western European counterparts. What is more, he was constantly aware that his British colleagues treated him as something in between themselves and the natives. He sensed everywhere their "anti-Austrian-Polish attitude," and he often felt that he had to "bootlick" them in the same way that the Trobrianders did (*Diary*, 172, 167). Malinowski remembers feeling "afraid" when a British administrator paid an unexpected visit to the village where Malinowski was living; he felt as powerless as one of the natives, subject to an arbitrary and humiliating "customs search" (187). In these moments, Malinowski is torn between his "strong hatred for England and the English" and his desire—like the German Bonsels in India—to mimic these British (218). Malinowski eventually fantasizes about becoming a professor in England, where he will attend "lectures, receptions, etc." with the imagined English wife whom he has not yet acquired (204).

This position between savagery and civilization explains Malinowski's unusual rage toward natives who do not know their place: who aim—like this "penniless Pole" now living among them—to become "half-civilized."[20] Malinowski recalls telling "coarse jokes" to a group of villagers, when, out of the blue, one of them disapproves. Malinowski curses this "bloody nigger" and long remains furious: he cannot believe "that this nigger had dared to speak to me in such a manner" (*Diary*, 272). This "manner" reveals what Malinowski has long been trying to hide among the English and what he fears he has exposed through his dirty jokes: his own Slavic, less-than-civilized—"coarse"—nature.

Malinowski's in-between position similiarly creates his anxiety that he might become permanently like "them." In spring 1918, after almost four uninterrupted years in the antipodes, Malinowski finds himself lusting after a Trobriand girl and wishing that he could become "a savage" so that he could possess her. Later that day, still excited by this sight, he fondles another native girl, and so gets closer to becoming what he had wished for. Malinowski's gradual becoming-savage reveals itself at this moment linguistically, too, as untranslatable Kiriwinian terms increasingly infiltrate his already "savage" Polish: "In the village I sat a moment on the *pilapabile*, and I pawed a pretty girl in the *lauriu*." By the end of the day, Malinowski's closeness to the natives turns to anger. This anger aims to separate him, physically, from them and, metaphorically, from his own burgeoning wildness: "Resolve: absolutely never to touch any Kiriwina whore" (*Diary*, 255–56).

Instead of using Malinowski's diaries to judge him, we should view them, with the later Clifford Geertz, as the "backstage masterpiece of anthropology, our *The Double Helix*."[21] Malinowski's recording of his own *Tropenkoller* reveals the entire dilemma of early twentieth-century ethnography—of writing about other people—*in nuce*: ethnography is born out of the same frustrating "dying-away" of the differences between "us" and "them" that ethnography diagnoses (Malinowski, *Argonauts*, xv). This frustration is also writ large in that other ethnography: literature. Hesse's 1913 Mister Bradley, for example, disparages the Indians not least because he sleeps with them and so needs to stave off the apparent contamination he has brought on himself. Kafka's 1914 penal colony officer protects himself from this danger, first, by disparaging the natives and, later, through violence. Only our military "uniforms," he insists, tell us who we are. Only they keep us from forgetting "home" (*Heimat*), which we are always in the process of forgetting. Like Goethe's Ottilie, Kafka's officer knows that wandering too long "beneath palm trees" can be dangerous: we begin to resemble the people we are oppressing and might even desire secretly to take their place.[22] Here we see a radicalization of Homi Bhabha's claim that, by mimicking the colonizer, the "native" disturbs the colonizer's identity.[23] For Kafka, this disturbance of the colonizer's identity goes so far that the trajectory of mimicry reverses itself: the colonizer now starts to imitate the native he is torturing, to the point of placing himself beneath the torture machine.[24] It is the more brutal colonial version of the same ethnographic desire that excites, saddens, and frightens Malinowski: "I was sorry I was not a savage" (*Diary*, 255).

Uncanny Europe, the Familiar Unconscious, and World War I

As the difference between Europe and its other became increasingly less apparent at the fin de siècle, writers began to look elsewhere for the "real" alien: both in science fiction, which first appeared around 1900 (prefiguring Lacan's observers from "outer space"), and in the inner-European modernist tales I discussed in chapter 4.[25] Like the Martians, however, the inner-European strangers proved to be less foreign than the travelers had expected and hoped: Aschenbach's Venetian street musician looks exactly like the backpacker from home; Andreas's primitive Carinthian Romana brings him back hallucinatorily to his own mother; and Homo's primordial Alpine "savages" turn out to be uncannily modern.

Unsettled by these similarities, the modernist protagonists—like Freud—eventually stage a final journey toward the last concentric circle of strangeness: the unconscious, in Freud's words, "the aboriginal population of the mind." But this mental aborigine turns out, too, to be uncannily known and, what is worse, tied to the same foreign-familiar European geography as was the internal stranger. The heroes' visions return them to the spaces that they thought they had forgotten, as if they were absolutely unknown spots on a map, but they turn out to be the most recognizable of all: Andreas's childhood Spiegelgasse and the primal scene; Aschenbach's Munich home as well as the mythic origins of the world; and the body of Homo's wife in the city together with the Ur-mother in the cave. These spots are hauntingly foreign-familiar in both the ontological and topographic—"ontopological"—senses.[26] They are at once "our" European home cities, which, like Aschenbach's Venice, sometimes resemble exotic places, and the greatest mysteries of our being, which we both know and do not know. Just as the outlandish East is more familiar to us than we thought, we know more about the hidden aspects of existence than we admit. As Hofmannsthal writes, it is precisely the presence of the Orient *and* the unconscious within his home city of Vienna—the topographical Orient and the ontological one ("that mysterious Orient, the empire of the unconscious")—that renders Vienna *unheimlich*.[27]

Just as Malinowski and the fin de siècle exoticists were angered by this too-similar other in faraway lands, the modernist protagonists are irritated by them within their Orientalized yet still familiar "unconscious" Europe. And this irritation leads to aggression: Aschenbach exposes his uncanny Slavic love-object to the plague instead of giving up his "exotic debauch"; Andreas becomes a bird of prey, circling over his beloved Carinthian "deer," Romana; and Homo's mining team turns violently against its "foreign-familiar"

Germanic kinsmen. Homo's team displaces brutality generally reserved for the colonies onto Central Europe: psychological torture; guard dogs; and a cruel disregard for the village's "savage," yet Germanic, workforce.

As the protagonists try to differentiate themselves from these foreign-familiar "natives," the authors represent this struggle through narrators who shift back and forth between distanced third-person narration and free indirect style—as if they, too, were caught within the ethnographic tension they are describing. Like these narrators' characters and like Malinowski, the narrators cannot maintain a position outside of their investigations. At the moment their protagonists lose themselves within the minds of the natives, the narrators lose themselves within their gone-primitive protagonists. And just as the protagonists react violently toward these too-familiar others, the narrators mistreat their protagonists: ridiculing them and—especially in Mann and Musil—callously renouncing all connection to them at the end. As readers, we begin to see the geopolitical background for the *mise en abymes* of modernist irony and perspectival experimentation.

This figural and narrative violence in Mann, Hofmannsthal, and Musil occurs in the southern and eastern edges of Germanic Europe (northern Italy, Carinthia, the Fersana valley), which reminds us of the same periphery where World War I began. The Great War notoriously did not start where expected: neither at an extra-European colonial hot spot (such as Morocco, where the French and Germans twice almost came to hostilities) nor along the usual battle line (the French-German border). Rather, the flashpoint was Europe's paradigmatic internal colony: the Balkans, that same southeastern fringe of the Austro-Hungarian Empire that Aschenbach had first visited in search of an exotic world only a train ride away. Without discounting the many political causes of the war, it is worth noting this uncanny psychological one: like the East Indians for England, the Slavs were, for Austria, *Mischlinge* whose mimicking of the colonizers menaced the colonizers' identity. More threateningly than the Indians, these Slavs lived in contiguous territory or even within the empire itself (*Andreas*'s Carinthia, for example, still today holds a large Slovenian minority). This mixing made the need for differentiation even more urgent. This unconscious psychic component helps to explain Austria's extreme response to Slavic nationalism in 1914: the desire to eradicate the contaminating "Tschusch,"[28] who resembled too much the Austrian and whose own homeland was uncannily next to, and within, the fatherland.[29]

The Uncanny Jew

Was this violent 1914 uncanny encounter also this encounter's swan song? Did the end of the first great era of globalization spell the end of the uncanny as a lived experience and, in terms of my book, of its usefulness as a diagnostic tool? As I have argued throughout, "*das Unheimliche*" is, like any other concept, historical: it has a birth and, presumably, a death.[30] The word didn't even take on its modern meaning until around 1800, did not appear in philosophical discourse until the 1830s, and did not burgeon as a concept until the early twentieth century.[31] Was this concept's life as short as many others' in our sped-up modernity? Does it die already shortly after Freud pronounces it in 1919? Does it lose its relevance through the postwar nationalist re-enforcements of difference: the collapsing of multiethnic empires, the drawing of new state borders, and the politicization of nation-based "race" theory? Does uncanny global similarity give way, in 1919, to a recrudescence of the fantasy of absolute difference?

The initial answer appears to be yes, especially in the lands where the concept of the *Unheimliche* first appeared so powerfully—Germany and Austria—for three reasons. First, Germany and Austria shrank geographically and so had fewer colonial "others": no more hybridized Africans in German South-West Africa, and also many fewer Silesian Poles, Bohemian Czechs, Lower Styrian Slovenes, and so on. Second, Germans and Austrians were able to travel less, due to the devaluation of their currencies, the introduction of passports, and the new borders between their countries and Poland, Czechoslovakia, Hungary, and Yugoslavia.[32] Third, Germans and Austrians compensated for this lost physical mobility by reading more and more adventure literature; in this way, they replaced the living uncanny other within or near their borders with an imaginary exoticized (non-uncanny) one.[33] Considering these developments, the first postwar year—1919—seems to mark the end of the uncanny era and the reinstitution of an "exotic" or "marvelous" one: a return to a world before steam transportation, middle-class tourism, and modern colonialism, when Europeans imagined themselves to be separate from a wondrous world that was still waiting to be discovered. The other seems here to reappear in his ancient absolute alterity, as different from the German as the "barbarian" was from the Greek.[34]

But a closer look reveals that the uncanny encounter did not disappear in this moment that Freud delineated it. As it did in modernist fiction, it simply internalized into Europe, moving closer to Europe's centers. Incipient decolonization brought Indians to London and North Africans to Paris, and, more important for this study, the "decolonization" of the German and Austrian ghettoes—beginning already in the mid- and late nineteenth century—brought Jews to the gentile neighborhoods of Berlin, Frankfurt, and Vienna.[35] The Jews' success in mainstream German society increased especially in the interwar period,[36] and their often perfect mastery of High German rendered them uncannily similar: Germany's doppelgänger. With this in mind, it is no coincidence that, after a spike around the time Freud published *The Uncanny* in 1919, the general usage of the word *unheimlich* increased again in the 1930s, reaching an all-time high in the 1940s.[37]

As Hannah Arendt argues, German "philo-Semites" from the late nineteenth century onward took refuge from the Jew's threatening similarity by glorifying the assmiliated Jew's other: that "strange and exciting" Jew, who still carried with him the scent of the ghetto.[38] Already in 1871, Bismarck had happily imagined the "Gentile stallion" pairing off with the "Jewish mare," and this attitude culminated in what Arendt called the interwar era's "morbid lust for the exotic, abnormal, and different," especially in the form of the Jew, whom the philo-Semites "mysteriously and wickedly loved."[39] But, like the colonized Africans and Slavs before him, this "exotic" Jew could never remain as strange as his masters demanded. Malinowski's anthropological paradox held: the other is never truly outlandish precisely because "we" have come too close to him. Just as Malinowski's Trobridian savage became Europeanized through modern anthropology, so too did this "strange and exciting" ghetto Jew become unexciting through the breakdown of his internal colony and his increased contact with non-Jews.

For this, the Jew earned the gentile's fear and hatred. Whereas assimilation had once appeared to be his only mode of survival, it now became his "crime."[40] When the Jew's exotic state disappeared, he threatened German identity just as the uncanny Slav had threatened Austria's. Both resembled too much their would-be masters. From the beginnings of emancipation onward, Jews became increasingly similar in language, culture, and even, due to intermarriage, physiognomy. Georg Simmel refers to this anxiety-inspiring assimilated Jew in his 1908 "Excursus on the Stranger," which prefigures Freud's speculations on "the narcissism of minor differences" by presenting us with a "stranger" who is frightening also because he is "near."[41]

Because the Jew did not remain exotic, Jewish difference infamously had to be manufactured.[42] Society called upon "science" to create difference where there was none, which explains the explosion of German and Austrian race theory in the late nineteenth century.[43] Whereas earlier religious anti-Semites had proposed that Jews should simply surrender their Jewishness through assimilation, the new racial anti-Semites defined Jews as essentially different. In this battle between different forms of anti-Semitism, Eugen Dühring argued in 1881 against Heinrich von Treitschke, a pro-assimilation, religious anti-Semite. For Dühring, Treitschke had missed the centrality of race: "A Jewish question would still exist even if every Jew were to turn his back on his religion and join one of our major churches." Assimilation, Dühring argues, does not solve the "Jewish question" but rather exacerbates it. When the Jew becomes "German," he becomes impossible to identify: "It is precisely the baptized Jews who infiltrate furthest, unhindered in all sectors of society and political life."[44]

Dühring's racial anti-Semitism notoriously influenced the Nazis and, before this, found a common voice in the French anti-Semite, Edouard Drumont, who wrote in *Jewish France* (1886), "A Mr. Cohen, who goes to synagogue, who keeps kosher is a respectable person. I don't hold anything against him. I do have it in for the Jew who is not obvious."[45] This non-obvious Jew threatens especially German and Austrian identity, which was already more fragile than England's or France's because of the Germans' and Austrians' oft-cited belated nation-building.[46] The young Hitler is, for example, "agitated" (*aufgeregt*) by a fin de siècle world in which Jews have become so "Europeanized" that he does "not see them" and even sometimes takes them "for Germans."[47] When no one can tell the difference between the two, the Jew becomes "German," and, more worrisome for Dühring (and Hitler), the German becomes "Jewish."[48] This double mimicry produces an abyss of identity leading to an empty "Germanness" at the bottom. The Jew imitates a German who defines himself as being different from the Jew, who has, in the meantime, become more "German" than the German himself.

The increasing fear of this identity void reveals itself in the 1891 nationalist Pan-German League, which originally allowed for the membership of fully assimilated Jews but in 1912 declared race to be an underlying principle.[49] Proto-Nazi anxieties about the loss of German particularity led to similar race-based ideologies and more attempts to create Jewish difference—eventually through propaganda.[50] Nazi anti-Semitic discourse focused on the ostentatiously foreign ghetto Jew, complete with ringlets, beard, caftan and kippah, even though such a figure was rare in 1933 Germany. Propaganda films, especially the notorious *Der ewige Jude* (*The Eternal Jew*), compared this Jew, living in miserably backward circumstances, with vermin and parasites. Scholars have traditionally claimed that this othering was intended to increase the Germans' preexisting fear of racial difference and so prepare them for the annihilation of these non-human "pests."[51] But this argument forgets the crucial scene in *Der ewige Jude* where a series of Jews with beards, sidelocks, caftans, and kippahs transform before the viewers' eyes—through a camera blur—into clean-shaven, short-haired, hatless men in European suits and ties (figure 26). The voice-over warns that "the Jew" always tries to "hide his origins when he is among non-Jews" and that Jews are uncannily adept at "insinuating themselves into Western civilization" (*sich in die westliche Zivilisation einzuschleichen*); this is why they pose such a "monstrous [*ungeheure*] danger."[52] As opposed to such an *unheimlich* "German"-seeming Jew, the caftan-wearing ghetto Jew—the other who is "obvious"—becomes soothing for the anti-Semite.

Hitler is similarly relieved when he sees for the first time, with "open eyes," a Jew who does not look like a German: an "apparition in a black caftan and black hair locks." This sight allows him to ask the question which he has been longing to ask and to which he already knows the answer: "Is this a Jew?" or "Is this a German?" But this fake interrogation covers up the real one that had troubled Hitler in Linz and his first days in Vienna: how can one decide who is a Jew when Jews look so much like Germans? Hitler is happy when this confusing visual situation clears up: when he can replace the unidentifiable Jew—the monstrous double—with the brazenly foreign caftaned one. Hitler can now see the caftaned Jew behind all Jews: "Wherever I went, I began to see Jews, and . . . [they] lost all resemblance to Germans"; Hitler's visual "uncertainties" (*Schwanken*) magically disappear.[53] The recognizable Jew,

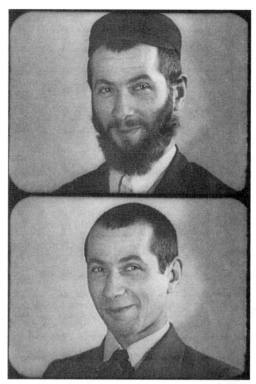

Figure 26. A Jewish man whose "beard, skull cap, and caftan" make him "recognizable to all" transforms, before the viewers' eyes, into a "German"-seeming gentleman "insinuating [himself] into Western civilization" (from the Nazi propaganda film *Der ewige Jude* [1940])

who gives Hitler the key to seeing Jews everywhere, is less dangerous than the hidden one, who can infiltrate German culture and, as Hitler recounts, confuse Germans' identity. The staying power of this uncanny fear reveals itself—two years after the war ended—in a similar remark by the Nazi jurist and legal philosopher, Carl Schmitt: "The real enemy is precisely the assimilated Jew."[54]

Blutschande

The ambivalence surrounding the exotic "caftaned" Jew—who is called vermin by the Nazis and found "strange and interesting" by the philo-Semites—comes into relief in the early twentieth-century development of the term *Blutschande* (literally, "blood disgrace"). Originally meaning any "great disgrace" and then specifically "incest," it took on its Nazi sense of "race defilement"—particularly, sex between Jews and Germans—in the 1920s. *Blutschande*'s semantic metamorphosis resembles the one made a century earlier by "*heimlich*" in that both terms develop toward ambivalence. They transform into their opposites, specifically by moving from signifying something familiar to something foreign. *Heimlich*'s meaning progresses from "familiar"/"known" to "mysterious"/"dangerous" just as *Blutschande*'s shifts from sex with the same (one's family members) to sex with the apparent opposite (the Jew).[55] Like *heimlich*, then, *Blutschande* contains a hidden meaning of familiarity within its etymology.

Like *heimlich*, *Blutschande* forgets this familiar semantic past. The early Nazis who spread the new usage acted as if it had been born fully formed, without a history. They did not bother to differentiate it from its established meaning, even though "incest" remained the only definition of *Blutschande* in Nazi-era dictionaries and encyclopedias.[56] Hitler, for example, claimed already in 1925, as a matter of course, that Vienna's "racial conglomeration" and "mix of peoples" was the "embodiment of *Blutschande*."[57] This repression of *Blutschande*'s earlier meaning in incest was exposed, inadvertently, in the title of the first published (1921) Nazi tract on the topic, which refers to *Blutschande* as "unconscious": *Eine unbewußte Blutschande—der Untergang Deutschlands: Naturgesetze über die Rassenlehre (An Unconscious Blutschande—Germany's Decline: Natural Laws on Race Theory)*. Not only are the Germans "unconsciously" mixing their race, as the authors insist; the authors themselves are unconsciously forgetting *Blutschande*'s familiar past in incest. *Blutschande*, like *heimlich*, bears what Freud calls the *un-heimlich* "mark of repression": it forgets its own lexical past.

This repressed semantic familiarity corresponds to a contextual one: the "homeliness" of the object—the Jew—to which *Blutschande*'s new meaning refers. Just as men repress the familiarity of the *heimlich* female genitalia in order to not think of whence they came, so does the Nazi repress the familiarity of the assimilated Jew. In so doing, the Nazi paradoxically resembles his apparent opposite: the philo-Semite, who likewise "forgets" the Jew's similarity and insists on his "exotic" difference.[58] Although the anti-Semite and the philo-Semite have opposed goals—forbidding contact on the one hand and gaining it on the other—both deny energetically the same fact: that the Jew is not as strange as he ought to be.

This overdetermined relation to the too-similar Jew helps to explain the unique explosion of German-language stories about "incest" (*Blutschande*) at the same time that the new meaning of *Blutschande* ("race-defilement") was invented. These narratives span German literature "high" and "low," as a partial listing reveals: Kurt Münzer's *The Road to Zion* (*Der Weg nach Zion*; 1907), Hugo von Hofmannsthal's *Andreas* (1907–27), Georg Trakl's "Blood Guilt" ("Blutschuld"; 1909), Thomas Mann's "Blood of the Walsungs" (1921 [1906]), Frank Thiess's *The Devil's Shadow* (*Die Verdammten*; 1922), Leonhard Frank's *Brother and Sister* (*Bruder und Schwester*; 1929), and the second volume of Robert Musil's *The Man without Qualities* (1932).[59] Christina von Braun correctly notes a likely reason for this upsurge of incest stories:

that "brother-sister" intercourse was a metaphor for the "brotherly-sisterly" relations of Jewish and non-Jewish Germans in the early twentieth century. But Braun ends up concluding the opposite, that these incest writings were produced by non-Jewish Germans to cement, however unconsciously, an inward-looking anti-Semitic Wagnerian tribalism that excluded Jews. Braun makes here a category error, at the same time that she grants too much power to the anti-Semitic fantasy: the German sister is not the "mirror image" of the German brother, just as the assimilated Jew is not the "antithesis" of the German—no matter how much the anti-Semite wants this to be true.[60] Regardless of the anti-Semite's disavowals, the Jew and the sibling/sister continue to occupy the same category: both are almost the same but not quite.

This tension around the almost-same Jew—and around the double meaning of *Blutschande*—is writ large in Mann's "Blood of the Walsungs," where the incestuous siblings actually *are* assimilated Jews (parodically named Siegfried and Sieglinde). Although critics disagree about whether Mann's Wagnerian Jews constitute reproductions or ironic reversals of anti-Semitic stereotypes,[61] the effect of this story on Mann's contemporaries was undeniable: a pre-publication scandal in 1906 caused Mann to withdraw the story and finally publish it only in 1921. Literary historians usually claim that the 1906 scandal erupted solely because of the biographical relation between the fictional family and Mann's Jewish in-laws,[62] but one cannot underestimate the effect that Mann's connection of incest fantasies to assimilated Jews had on German society in general. Through Mann's Jewish Siegfried and Sieglinde, he literalized the long-standing idea that assimilated Jews *were* Germans: in the form of the latters' younger, mimicking siblings. What is more, Mann's Wagnerian Jewish twins brought into relief the fear that the "pure" Jewish race was the monstrous double of that other "chosen people," the "pure" German one. By injecting incest into this sibling relationship, Mann reveals its hidden sexual subtext: the ambivalent desires of both the anti- and the philo-Semites.

From this perspective, the story of Ulrich and Agathe in *The Man without Qualities* becomes not a typically pro-German incest narrative but a diagnosis of the desire for and fear of the uncanny other in the early twentieth century. Musil's Ulrich forgets the *Unheimlichkeit* of sex with his sister at the same time that the Germans—whether anti- or philo-Semitic—repressed the *unheimlich* similarity of the "exotic" Jew; only in this way was the German free to love (or hate) the Jew with abandon. Far from celebrating Agathe's pure Germanness, Ulrich stylizes her (and himself through her) as a "Mohican." As do the philo-Semites with their "strange and exciting" Jews, Ulrich becomes magically "at home in the uncanny," which is now no longer uncanny at all. The once almost-same other—the sibling, the Jew—becomes radically foreign, the representative of a possibly utopian "other state," the un-*Heim*. The dangerous political-racial implications of this fantasy are, although never stated, evoked in the title that Musil gave to this section, *Ins*

Tausendjährige Reich, a phrase that Nazi writers began using in the 1930s to give a religious, millenarian quality to Hitler's reign.

Because both the anti- and the philo-Semite manufacture absolute difference to hide their fear of (and desire for) the almost-same, their projects become intertwined: the anti-Semite does the philo-Semite's work for him by repeatedly declaring the Jew's radical alterity. But because this declaration never suffices (for either of them), the anti-Semite's stereotypes become increasingly extreme. The philo-Semite's titillating Jewish brother or sister—first disguised as Bismarck's alluringly animal Jewish "mare"— now transforms into the beast, the rat, and the bacterium.[63] When even this stereotyping proves insufficient, the exoticizing proceeds further. As Arendt claims, it is not surprising that philo-Semites participated vigorously in the Shoah, for they needed to "purge themselves of secret viciousness, to cleanse themselves of a stigma which they had mysteriously and wickedly loved." But this secret love is, contra Arendt, not a love for an outsider or "scapegoat"; it is a love for the illicitly close sibling.[64] This shameful desire causes the philo-Semite, like the anti-Semite, to push the Jew to an even further, final stage of alterity: the total otherness of death, as captured within the double meaning of the German word *verschieden* (both "different" and "dead").[65]

The Sleeper and the War on Terror

This attempt to rid Europe of foreign-familiarity does not succeed. Even if every Jew had been murdered, another "Jew" would appear, in the form of Simmel's uncanny stranger who is endemic to global modernity. The most striking reappearance of this "Jew" in our present era is the Arab "sleeper": an apparent enemy of the state who is frightening precisely because of his similarity to "us."[66] He might not look like a traditional European, but he does resemble millions of other citizens in today's multicultural West, rendering him, like the nineteenth-century assimilated Jew, non-"obvious": capable of invisibly "infiltrating" all "sectors of society and political life." His paradigm is Mohammed Atta, the urban-planning student from Hamburg who led the September 11, 2001 attacks on New York and Washington. Atta strolled through Portland's airport security as an impeccably dressed, Westernized Arab businessman, sporting a smart shoulder bag and a first-class ticket (figure 27). Like the majority of the attackers, Atta had been living in the West for years and had become indistinguishable from the masses of other assimilated immigrants studying around him.

Like the emancipated European Jew, this Westernized Arab creates an identity void for the West: he resembles "us" in language, culture, and, through mixed marriages, physiognomy. "We" again have no other against which to define ourselves; we can no longer know how we are distinct, and so are thrown back into the uncanny bog of psychic indifferentiation. In this mire,

Figure 27. Mohammed Atta exiting airport security on the morning of September 11, 2001

our aggression turns against both this similar "other" and, like Freud in the train, ourselves, for we now understand that anybody can be the enemy. We see ourselves, too, as suspects, whether we are of Arab descent or not. Like the next Atta stepping toward the security detector, each of us senses the possibility of the terrorist within or, at the very least, within the person before or after us. This is not to deny the cruel reality of racial profiling for Arab travelers. It is rather to say that the phenomenon of the sleeper has awakened the West to the realization that the security forces might be right: the terrorist is not somewhere out there, in a wildly exotic East, but right here, in our cities and towns, and even in "us," these citizens of the multicultural West. This is why everyone must be shaken down. And this is why we submit so readily to these inspections. Not primarily because, as we sometimes say, "we need to check even the innocent to keep everyone safe," but because we know that the terrorist is potentially within us; we, too, are guilty.

The West's reaction to this uncanny blurring of identities resembles the Nazi reaction to the assimilated Jews' "infiltrations." Like Nazi propaganda, Western news responded to 9/11 by constructing an "Arab" who, like the ghetto Jew, is absolutely different. Following the initial televised repetitions of Atta striding confidently and familiarly through airport security, the news replaced this image—which we never see anymore—with his utterly foreign pendant: the toothless, turbaned Taliban peasant in the dusty Afghanistan hills. This "savage" other, his archaic bazooka somehow aimed at us, plays the same role as the re-ghettoized Jew from Nazi films. He gives us our longed-for *different* enemy, living somewhere way out there, in a poppy field, not right here, in our midst, in casual business attire, on his way to a meeting. This disavowal of the terrorist's uncanny similarity bears itself out in the absurd Western defense strategies after 9/11: the rigorous tightening of external borders around America and "fortress Europe" (the externalization of the ego's "fortified camp"), as if we did not know what we know. It is too late to close the borders. The terrorist is already inside, studying in Hamburg or taking flight lessons in Florida. The obviousness of this repressed truth can be measured in the level of violence used to deny it, most clearly in the American-led military response. The targets produced a comforting fairy tale: that the enemy is out among the relentlessly exoticized Taliban or in some other faraway country led by a crazy dictator, not already in our midst, or even in ourselves.

These U.S.- and NATO-led wars demonstrate the wider stakes of the argument presented in this book: our violent fears issue not from alterity but from similarity. We want the terrorist to look different; our anxiety occurs when he does not. We fear the Arab student in Germany and the Virginia-born U.S. army officer of Palestinian parents (Nidal Malik Hasan) and, even more viscerally, the "white" terrorist: the Californian teenager who fought for the Taliban (John Walker Lindh), the Unabomber Ted Kaczynski, Timothy McVeigh, and, more recently, the masked British-accented ISIS fighter ("Jihadi John") who sounded "white" while narrating his beheading of two American journalists. The most powerful example comes from Norway, where, following the 2011 mass murder in Utøya, mainstream European broadcasters assumed that the culprit was an "Islamist"—a dangerous other—only to discover that he was one of "us," Europe's own monstrous double: a white Norwegian from Oslo named Anders Breivik. These concentric circles of likeness make us wonder, with worry: If the white Europeans are now terrorists, too, who is not one? Do we not all harbor a terrorist within? If yes, is this terrorist not likewise an uncanny return? To our "savage" selves? And to our aggression toward a primeval father who shows his phallic might in bankers' skyscrapers?[67] Or toward an ancient distorted image of ourselves in a mirror? Do we recognize "him" in both our ontogenetic and phylogenetic pasts? Is "he," too, almost like "us" but not quite? Like the ideologues of *Blutschande*, we attempt to create a radically different terrorist to disavow this nagging sameness, which we both fear and desire.

This explains one of the greatest peculiarities of the Breivik trial: that the prosecution—not the defense—attempted to define Breivik as insane,[68] as somehow truly "different," as suggested by the German and Dutch meanings of his first name. This disavowal of Breivik's similarity to "us" demonstrates how today's uncanny moment resembles the one around 1900, except within an even tighter concentric circle. We are still fascinated with this uncanniness, even as it cripples our attempts to react rationally to our fears. And when we are not undone by it, we are reminded of the continued imperative to grapple with it. This recognition, too, haunts us.

Introduction

1. Drawn before the widespread use of triangulation, before the invention of Ramsden's surveying instruments, and before the Enlightenment's insistence on cartographic accuracy, Crusoe's 1720 map is the most obviously fictional of the three. Completely pictorial, it lacks the scientific markers of verisimilitude—place names, scale bar, compass rose—partially present in "New Switzerland" (1812–13) and compulsory by the time of *Treasure Island* (1883). Crusoe's map was narrative (depicting scenes from the novel), not geographic: without scale or direction, Crusoe's "Island of Despair" remained unnavigable for fantasy travelers like me.

2. As Jorge Luis Borges aptly points out in his "On Exactitude in Science," absolute completeness is impossible, unless one maps the world at the same size as the world; that is, at a scale of 1:1.

3. See Demhardt, "Kolonialkartographie," 65.

4. See Demhardt, "Kolonialkartographie," 65; and Kain, *Cartography in the Nineteenth Century.*

5. On the ascendance of surveyor-travelers in the late nineteenth century, see chapter 8, "Die Vermessung der Welt" (Surveying the World), in Brenner, *Reisebericht,* esp. 445.

6. On Stanley's "discovery" of the source of the Nile at Lake Victoria in 1875 (confirming John Hanning Speke's earlier speculation) and on Stanley's later connections to Leopold and the Congo, see Stanley's *Autobiography,* as well as later critical biographies: Hall, *Stanley: An Adventurer Explored*; and Bierman, *Dark Safari.*

7. For political geographers' interpretation of this mapping, see Painter and Jeffrey, *Political Geography,* 23; and Gallaher, *Key Concepts,* 5.

8. Scott, *Last Expedition,* 543–44. Two days after this, Scott reached the Pole itself, where he discovered Amundsen's abandoned tent, with a Norwegian flag atop (figure 10).

9. Wegener, *Erinnerungen eines Weltreisenden,* 126, 135–36.

10. Zweig, "Gwalior," 110.

11. Only two other monographs have focused on many of the same texts from these first two groups (i.e., not on Freud's writings). Wolfgang Reif's classic survey argues that early twentieth-century German-language exotic novels described escapist, compensatory efforts to create "utopian" spaces far from industrialized Europe (*Zivilisationsflucht und literarische Wunschräume,* esp. 10–16, 28–30). Jennifer Gosetti-Ferencei's attempt to avoid all "politically charged" readings, including Reif's, explains away the violence at the heart of many of the travelers' encounters—leaving instead only anodyne "transformations" that "may

be positively realized" (*Exotic Spaces*, esp. 4–5). My book picks up where Reif left off: with the traveler arriving at the longed-for "utopia"—only to discover that it has, during this first globalization, become frighteningly and threateningly familiar.

12. Bhabha, *Location of Culture*, 86 ("Of Mimicry and Man"), 74–75 ("Other Question"); see also "Of Mimicry and Man," 91. For more on the appropriateness of "uncanniness" (not "hybridity") as a critical tool, see Zilcosky, "Hermann Hesse's Colonial Uncanny."

13. Freud, *The Uncanny* (1919), in *Standard Edition*, 17:220 (*Standard Edition* cited hereafter in text as *SE*); Sigmund Freud, *Gesammelte Werke*, 12:231 (hereafter cited in text as *GW*).

14. Originally published as *Heiße Städte* (*Hot Cities*), *Heißes Land* (*Hot Land*) went through twelve editions, making it—albeit not a "best seller"—a book that sold quite well, even within the already high-selling genre of travel writing. See Scholdt, *Der Fall Norbert Jacques*, 172.

15. See Derrida's critique of Levi-Strauss in *Of Grammatology*, 101–7.

16. Clifford, *Routes*, 18–19.

17. Greenblatt, *Marvelous Possessions*, 132.

18. This is not to say that Cortez and Columbus were not interested in exploitation—this was of course the purpose of their journeys—but rather to say that the popular understanding of exotic travel's realpolitik was much clearer in 1900 than in 1500, primarily because of the liberal press's coverage of colonial atrocities.

19. Behdad, *Belated Travelers*, esp. 1–17.

20. See Bongie, *Exotic Memories*.

21. Ewers, *Indien und Ich*, 162, 164.

22. Nolde, *Welt und Heimat*, 91.

23. Hesse, *Sämtliche Werke* (hereafter cited in text as *SW*). The references here are from "Tagebuch der Indonesienreise," *SW* 11:336, "Abend in Asien," *SW* 13:218, "Architektur," *SW* 13:229, "Palembang," *SW* 13:254, and "Tagebuch der Indonesienreise," *SW* 11:376.

24. Nolde, *Welt und Heimat*, 119.

25. *Deutsches Wörterbuch von Jakob und Wilhelm Grimm*, vol. 10, columns 873–80 (*heimlich*); vol. 24, columns 1055–59 (*unheimlich*), http://woerterbuch netz.de/DWB/.

26. See Weber, *Legend of Freud*, 20.

27. Locke, *Essay Concerning Human Understanding*, 1:31–32.

28. Castle, *Female Thermometer*.

29. On the uses of *unheimlich* in the Late Middle Ages to describe neutrally something unfamiliar and foreign ("*nicht vertraut*" and "*fremd*") and in the sixteenth and seventeenth centuries to connote witches and ghosts ("*Hexenmeister*" and "*Gespenster*"), see *Deutsches Wörterbuch von Jakob und Wilhelm Grimm*, vol. 24, columns 1056, 1058, http://woerterbuchnetz.de/DWB/.

30. The Grimm dictionary locates only three isolated written uses of *unheimlich* in this sense before 1800: in a 1793 letter of August Wilhelm Iffland, a 1781 letter of Goethe, and in Goethe's play *Götz von Berlichingen* (1773); the remaining texts listed by Grimm that employ this usage were all written after 1800 (*Deutsches Wörterbuch*, vol. 24, column 1057).

Although Laurie Ruth Johnson confirms this virtual absence of the word "uncanny" before 1800, she nonetheless echoes Castle's claim that "the uncanny was first conceptualized in-depth in the late eighteenth century"—thereby mistaking an accumulation of "themes" that we might today "call uncanny" (in texts where "the word 'uncanny' does not appear") with the production of a concept (*Aesthetic Anxiety*, 35, 79, 85, 63).

31. A Google Ngram search of "unheimliche" reveals that this word was almost never used in the eighteenth century, then came into general usage in the course of the nineteenth century (from near zero usage in 1805 to a temporary peak in the 1860s, then further upward after 1900). I chose "unheimliche" to capture some of the adjectival and some of the nominal usage; the purely adjectival "unheimlich" and the purely nominal "Unheimliche" reveal similar curves.

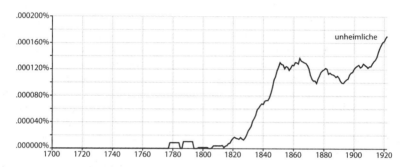

Considering that Castle is referring to the English context, it is worth noting that a similar trend appears with "uncanny" in English texts: moving from almost no appearances in the eighteenth century (near zero usage in 1796) to precipitous growth throughout the nineteenth century.

32. Schelling actually unromantically advocated that the uncanny really *ought* to stay suppressed. For Schelling, culture needed to overcome the uncanny as a first step toward a proto-Nietzschean rebirth of ancient poetry: Homer was only possible because the "uncanny principle which dominated earlier religions had been suppressed" (*Philosophie der Mythologie*, 515). Anthony Vidler cites this but does not remark on the conflict between Schellingian suppression and romantic Freudian unearthing, concluding that Schelling "summarize[s] the idea of *unheimlich* as evoked by the romantics" (*Architectural Uncanny*, 26–27).

33. Marx, *Das Kapital*, in *Marx Engels Werke*, 23:241; see Weber, *Legend of Freud*, 234–35. For more on Marx and uncanniness, see Mehlman, *Revolution and Repetition*, 8; and Royle, *The Uncanny*, 4. For an overview of nineteenth-century discussions of the uncanny in Nietzsche, Kierkegaard, and Marx, see Masschelein, "Unheimlich / das Unheimliche," 258.

34. Jentsch's phrase is "psychische Unsicherheit," which Freud later wrongly calls "intellektuelle Unsicherheit" (Jentsch, "Zur Psychologie des Unheimlichen"; Freud, *The Uncanny*, SE 17:223; GW 12:245).

35. Otto, *Das Heilige*, 19 (see also 16–18). On the relation between Otto's and Freud's "uncanny," see Dawson, "Otto and Freud." On the broader connections between the psychoanalytic and religious-philosophical notions of the uncanny, see Prawer, *The "Uncanny" in Literature*, 13–17.

36. Reik, *Der eigene und der fremde Gott*, 161–86 (on surmounted animistic beliefs) and 187–219 (on infantile complexes).

37. Heidegger, *Sein und Zeit*, 250–51.

38. Heidegger, *Einführung in die Metaphysik*, 115–16.

39. Weber correctly remarks that Heidegger's uncanny focuses more on power than does Freud's, but Weber ultimately allies Heidegger's and Freud's theories—as theatrical multipliers of "perspective"—and thereby underemphasizes their radical difference (*Legend of Freud*, 22, 31). Wolf Kittler correctly notices that Heidegger's uncanny, unlike Freud's, is "a call from afar into the far away," but Kittler concludes that Heidegger, not Freud, gets it right ("Stéphane Mallarmé," 246). This underestimates the power of "home" in modern *Unheimlichkeit*—for how can we speak of uncanniness in the twentieth century without the Freudian traffic between strangeness *and* "homeliness," between foreignness and a familiarity that "ought to have remained secret" but did not?

40. The popular use of uncanny themes (begun in Romantic and Gothic stories) was in full swing by 1900, but the conceptualization of the uncanny (even the use of the term "uncanny"/ "*unheimlich*") was still in its infancy. For the popularity of the uncanny in the eighteenth and nineteenth centuries, see Castle's *Female Thermometer*; Vidler's introduction to *Architectural Uncanny*; and Dolar, "'I Shall Be with You.'" Anneleen Masschelein likewise argues that "the uncanny" was conceptualized only *after* its nineteenth-century popularity, but she goes even further, claiming that it did not become an "actual" concept until the post-structuralists discussed it in the 1970s (*Unconcept*, 4, 6). Masschelein's claim underemphasizes the importance of several major thinkers independently choosing to write about the uncanny between 1906 and 1927 (Jentsch, Rank, Otto, Freud, Reik, Heidegger), speaking already to a concentrated attempt at theorization in the early twentieth century.

41. While reading this material on the uncanny, I was struck by the similar relation of a burgeoning concept ("the marvelous") to travel writing four hundred years earlier. My point about the European fin de siècle thus adopts Stephen Greenblatt's idiom for the Age of Discovery: the "conceptualization of the marvelous was already under way" but not "fully articulated" when travelers began writing their "marvelous" accounts; these "helped (along with many other factors) to provoke its conceptualization" (*Marvelous Possessions*, 19).

42. Vidler sees the roots of modern uncanniness specifically in the nineteenth century's "urban estrangement" and new "rent system," which causes people, as Marx writes, to live "in *someone else's* house." This *Unheimlichkeit*, he argues, culminates in the twentieth century, especially in the displacements of the "two 'postwars'": the 1919 of Freud's *The Uncanny* and, then, 1945 (*Architectural Uncanny*, 4–5, 9).

43. See Lloyd Smith, "Phantoms of *Drood* and *Rebecca*," 285. The use of "Unheimliche" increased significantly from 1893 to its second peak, in 1922, just three years after *The Uncanny*'s publication (see Google Ngram in note 31 above).

44. Freud mentions "uncanniness" in passing in *The Interpretation of Dreams* (1900) and "Bemerkungen über einen Fall von Zwangsneurose" (1909), but he only begins to develop it as a critical term in *Totem and Taboo*. Post-structuralist readers have ignored this first elaboration in *Totem and Taboo*, perhaps because

Freud does not even mention there the favorite explanations of the uncanny—"repression," "castration anxiety," "intellectual uncertainty"—but rather insists on the uncanny's "phylogenetic" origin: in the return of primitive beliefs that we thought we had surmounted. On the importance of phylogenesis in Freud's early conceptualizations of the uncanny, see Masschelein, *Unconcept*, 27–35; on the neglect of phylogenesis in post-structuralist uses of the Freudian uncanny, see Masschelein, "Unheimlich / das Unheimliche," 248–50.

45. By the 1990s, the cultural-theoretical use of "uncanny" was so trendy that Martin Jay devoted a chapter to "The Uncanny Nineties" in *Cultural Semantics*. The descriptions of 9/11 as "uncanny" are too numerous to list, but a sampling is: Hoffmann, *Unheimlich Vertraut*; Connolly, "Psychoanalytic Theory"; Heischman, "Uncanniness of September 11th"; Nayar, "Uncanny to the Sublime"; Liao, *Uncanny Terror*; and Royle, *The Uncanny*, vii–viii. Additional contemporary, popular uses of the concept include the comic book series "The Uncanny X-Men" and, in the field of human aesthetics, "The Uncanny Valley."

46. Neither of the two existing monographs on the uncanny has done this. Royle's *The Uncanny* offers a brief history of the concept in his introduction and then presents a series of mini-chapters—mostly revisions of lectures—loosely related to "uncanny" themes. Masschelein's *The Unconcept* does not discuss the uncanny's birth years in the early twentieth century, focusing instead on its second flowering in late twentieth-century literary theory (especially the 1970s and 1980s).

47. The most important of these 1970s essays following Derrida's footnotes (in "La double séance") are by Hélène Cixous (1972), Samuel Weber (1973), and Neil Hertz (1979). For an overview of these and other essays, see Masschelein, *Unconcept*, 95–131; and Bartnaes, "Freud's 'The Uncanny,'" 33–39.

48. In the final paragraph of his essay, Weber argues—"without being able to do more than indicate a possible line of research"—that it would be vital to investigate "the historical status of the Unheimliche" ("Sideshow," 1133).

49. On Victorian lost-world fiction, see Deane, "Imperial Barbarians."

50. Freud, *Complete Letters of Freud to Fliess*, 398 (hereafter cited in text as *FLF*).

51. Freud refers to female sexuality as the "dark continent" in "The Question of Lay Analysis" (*SE* 20:212; *GW* 14:241) and to the unconscious as the "aboriginal population of the mind" (*psychische Urbevölkerung*) in "The Unconscious" (*SE* 14:195; *GW* 10:294). Nineteenth-century philosophical precursors to Freud's idea of this "savage" unconscious included Jean Paul, who described the unconscious as our "true inner Africa" (*dieses wahre innere Afrika*) (*Selina*, 1182). See Lütkehaus, *"Dieses wahre innere Afrika,"* 7–45.

52. Kafka, "Bericht für eine Akademie" ("Report to an Academy"), 313. For the popular sources of Kafka's "A Report to an Academy," see Bauer-Wabnegg, *Zirkus und Artisten*; and Zilcosky, *Kafka's Travels*, 108.

53. Huyssen argues that recent scholars have exaggerated his original point about the break between high modernism and mass culture; he insists that he always considered the divide to be primarily only a "powerful imaginary" ("High/Low in an Expanded Field," 366–67). But Huyssen in fact claimed that "in modernism art and literature retained their traditional nineteenth-century autonomy from every day life." He also upheld Peter Bürger's distinction between

high modernism and the "historical avant-garde": the former "insisted on the dignity and autonomy of literature" while only the latter "attempted to break the political bondage of high culture through a fusion with popular culture and to integrate art into life" (*After the Great Divide*, 163, 167). For critiques of Huyssen's 1986 position on the examples of the Parisian avant-garde and T. S. Eliot, respectively, see Gendron, *Montmartre and the Mudd Club*, esp. 85–86 and Chinitz, *T. S. Eliot*, esp. 4–5, 81–82.

54. Kafka's first-person narrator from a 1909 fragment claims to have already read a "book about Red Indians" when he was only seventeen, and, three years later, Kafka presented a friend with the boys' book, *With the Xinqú Indians*, which describes Karl von den Steinen's 1887–88 expedition to a South American tribe that was already then on the verge of extinction (Kafka, "Fragments," 221; Zilcosky, *Kafka's Travels*, 181, 257n26).

55. For the internalization of the quest narrative in Romanticism, see Bloom, "Internalization of Quest-Romance," 3–24.

56. Malinowski, *Argonauts*, xv.

57. As Charles Grivel points out, travel notes generally come to be regarded as footnotes to the main oeuvre ("Travel/Writing," 256). T. S. Eliot refers to "the new (the really new) work of art" in "Tradition and the Individual Talent" (1919), 50.

58. As mentioned above in relation to Bloom's "Internalization of Quest-Romance," the Romantics also turned travel inward, but with two main differences: (1) Romanticism maintained a strong canon of travel writing proper, and (2) Romanticism's quest inward preceded full-blown imperialism and so was not clearly marked, like modernism's, by the flight from the uncanny encounter—and its concomitant political disappointments.

59. On the move of travel literature to *Trivialliteratur* in the late nineteenth and early twentieth centuries, see Hamann and Hermand, *Impressionismus*, 154–92; and Brenner, *Reisebericht*, 519–35 (esp. 535, on the genre's "de-literarization").

60. With this fin de siècle domestic anthropologizing in mind, Paul Rabinow's 1986 call to arms seems belated and superfluous: "We need to anthropologize the West: show how exotic its constitution of reality has been" ("Representations Are Social Facts," 241).

61. On free association as the analysand's attempt to return to "primitiveness" and on Freud's joking reference to patients as "negroes," see Brickman, *Aboriginal Populations*, 174–99.

62. Mann, *Tod in Venedig*, in *Große kommentierte Frankfurter Ausgabe*, 2:578 (*Frankfurter Ausgabe* cited hereafter in text as *FA*). The English translation is from *Death in Venice*, ed. and trans. Clayton Koelb, 53 (hereafter cited in text as *DV*). For more on the uncanniness of Mann's Venice (and of Venice in general), see Geyer-Ryan, "Venice and the Violence of Location," esp. 143–45.

63. Although some well-known critics insist on the exceptionalism of Austrian modernism (Schorske, *Fin de Siècle Vienna* [1980]; Le Rider, *Modernité viennoise et crises de l'identité* [1990]), I am arguing here for a border-crossing German-language culture—popular writing, travel reports, modernist literature—through the free flow and marketing of texts, whether "high" or "low," between Germany and Austria.

64. Musil, *Grigia*, in *Gesammelte Werke* 6:235 (*Gesammelte Werke* cited hereafter in text as Musil, *GW*). The English translation of *Grigia* is in Musil, *Five Women*, 15–41, here 17 (trans. rev.) (hereafter cited in text as *FW*).

65. Edward Said, of course, discovers colonial traces in domestic literature but primarily in the early nineteenth century, especially in Jane Austen (*Culture and Imperialism*, 80–97). By the end of the nineteenth century, however, the split between explicitly exotic (Conrad, Forster) and apparently domestic (Joyce, Woolf) British literature becomes more pronounced.

66. The other exception is the exoticized working-class neighborhoods in Paris and London, but this exoticizing occurred in most Western cities, including Vienna and Berlin (see *Berlin Alexanderplatz*), New York, and even mid-sized American cities. On middle-class touristic accounts of nineteenth-century urban poverty in London, New York, and Pittsburgh, respectively, see Schwarzenbach, "*Terra Incognita*"; Bramen Tirado, "The Urban Picturesque"; and Slavishak, *Bodies of Work*.

67. As I discuss in chapter 2, these peculiarities of the German/Austrian case open up questions that test basic tenets of postcolonial theory: how do Prussia's and Austria's long traditions of internal colonialism unsettle postcolonialism's assumptions of what is "European" and what is "other"? Were not Sarajevo, Prague, and western Poland also "colonies"? What about the history of Eastern European Jewish families like the Freuds and the Kafkas, who, in the course of the nineteenth century, came under the sway of an eastward-spreading German culture? In what ways did Germans and Austrians imagine themselves to be not only colonizers but *colonized* (first, by Napoleon and then, after World War I, by French troops in the Rhineland)? These and other questions point to ways in which a deeper study of German-speaking colonial discourse might challenge some of the basic center/periphery assumptions of postcolonialism, as presented in, for example, the classic *Post-Colonial Studies Reader* (Ashcroft). See Berman, "German Colonialism"; and Klotz, "Global Visions."

68. Andre Gunder Frank claims that "globalization" began with the rise of trade between southern Mesopotamia and the northwestern Indian subcontinent in the third millennium B.C., while others claim that it began in ancient Greece, the Roman Empire, the Age of Discovery, or the Enlightenment. But modern globalization—marked by massive industrialization, economies of scale, urban population growth, and imperialism—first exploded in the mid- to late nineteenth century, as John Maynard Keynes argues already in 1919. As Paul Krugman points out more recently, economic historians generally refer to these decades before the First World War as the "First Global Economy" (Frank, *ReOrient*; Keynes, *Economic Consequences of the Peace*, 16–17; Krugman, "Government vs. The Market," 39).

69. See www.uncontactedtribes.org/evidence.

70. After being proposed by Alfred Penck in 1891, the project's specifications were agreed upon at international conferences in London and Paris in 1909 and 1913, respectively, but then never completed.

71. Even this map, as Borges well knows, does not produce "exactitude": the age-old cartographic problem of projecting a sphere (the earth) onto a plane persists.

72. The complexity of the question of when a digital image seems "real" (i.e., when it can fool the human eye) is writ large in the debate about the Mac's *retina display*: Does the display equal what we "really" see at 300 pixels per inch (as Steve Jobs argued)? Or only at 477 (Raymond Soneira)? Or at 900 (John Brownlee)? Or is there ultimately no density at which the image will correspond to the world? See Brownlee, "Why Retina Isn't Enough," http://www.cultofmac .com/173702/why-retina-isnt-enough-feature/.

73. On front and back spaces (as well as "staged" back spaces) in the tourist experience, see MacCannell, *Tourist*, 91–107. Maxine Feifer argues that some late twentieth-century "post-touristic" travelers react ironically and playfully to this uncertainty, and Eric Ames claims to see this irony already in early twentieth-century travelers (which leads him to criticize MacCannell) (Feifer, *Going Places*; Ames, *Carl Hagenbeck's Empire of Entertainments*, 120–22; see also Urry's use of "post-tourism" in *Tourist Gaze*, 91). Although some irony in relation to touristic authenticity was certainly present at the fin de siècle and is even more so now, the *Rough Guides* and their successors speak to the stubbornness of the first-contact fantasy, even when we are faced with its obvious impossibility: the guide promises to get you off the beaten track even as it brings you there together with others clutching the same hope (and the same book). On the paradoxes of alternative tourism, see Nouzeilles, "Touching the Real."

74. Percy, *Message in the Bottle*, 52. See the discussion of Percy in Culler, *Framing the Sign*, 163–64.

75. Survival International's "uncontacted" tribe indeed turned out to have been already contacted, even if it did still live isolated from civilization. The subsequent debate almost led to a lawsuit by Survival International against the British journalist who called their claim "fake," only later to apologize. See the 2008 article in http://www.pressgazette.co.uk/node/42019.

76. Rosaldo, *Culture and Truth*, 69–70. Dean MacCannell similarly equates modern travelers' exotic nostalgia with their desire for "naturalness" (*Tourist*, 3). For more on Rosaldo and MacCannell, especially in relation to literary modernism, see Kaplan, *Questions of Travel*, 33–40.

77. MacCannell, *Tourist*, 3.

78. See Besser, "Tropenkoller," and note 16 in my epilogue.

79. On women travelers in general, see Robinson, *Wayward Women*; Polk and Tiegreen, *Women of Discovery*. For books and anthologies with wide representations of German-speaking women travelers, often with other European travelers, see Potts, *Aufbruch und Abenteuer*; Arenz and Lipsky, *Mit Kompass und Korsett*; Czarnecka, *Der weibliche Blick*. On German and European female travelers from the late nineteenth and early twentieth centuries, see Schestokat, *German Women in Cameroon*; Schlieker, *Frauenreisen in den Orient*; Habinger, *Frauen reisen in die Fremde*.

80. What I call fin de siècle "anti-colonial exoticism" in many ways resembles the "anti-conquest narrative" that Mary Pratt discovered in eighteenth-century travel writing (*Imperial Eyes* 7; see also 38–85). But because the "anti-conquest narrative" flourished in the eighteenth century, before full-blown colonialism and the mapping of the world, it does not share anti-colonial exoticism's fear of global sameness. See my discussions of German travelers in chapter 1 and, especially, of Hermann Hesse in chapter 2.

81. I refer here to the "crazy" (*verrückt*) German traveler from the ending of *Hot Land*, whom I discuss—together with the implications of the word *verrückt*—in chapter 1 (Jacques, *Heißes Land*, 228).

Chapter 1

1. For Kafka's relation to exoticism, see Zilcosky, *Kafka's Travels*. For Musil and Benn, see Noyes, "Hottentotts, Bastards, and Dead Mothers," esp. 331–35. For Schnitzler, see Boehringer, "Fantasies of White Maculinity." For Mann, see Elsaghe's *Imaginäre Nation*. For Freud, see Brickman, *Aboriginal Populations*; and Khanna, *Dark Continents*.

2. I borrow phrasing here from Stephen Greenblatt, who made a similar discovery when reading *Mandeville's Travels* "simply as background to an attempt to understand Columbus": "As I often find, the background refused to be subordinated to the foreground" (*Marvelous Possessions*, 26).

3. See Scholdt, *Der Fall Norbert Jacques*, 172. Jacques is best known, still today, as the author of the Doctor Mabuse novels, eventually filmed by Fritz Lang; a connection between the Mabuse novels and Jacques' exotic writings appears in his never-finished 1930 novel, *Mabuse's Colony*, which takes place in the fictional Brazilian city of Eitopomar.

4. See Huyssen, *After the Great Divide*, esp. 163, 167.

5. In Hesse's case, I think of *Steppenwolf*, which takes place in a nameless *mitteleuropäische* city, within whose "Magic Theater" Hermine and especially the South American Pablo take on exotic roles.

6. Mann, *Briefe 1889–1936*, 269 (Mann's praise of Jacques); Rose-Marie Bonsels, *Bonsels im Spiegel der Kritik*, 113 (Mann's praise of Bonsels); Benjamin, *Gesammelte Schriften* 3:383–86 (Benjamin's review of Dauthendey); Born, *Kafkas Bibliothek*, 41 (Kafka's copy of Jacques' *Pirath's Island*).

7. Kellermann, *Spaziergang in Japan* [*Stroll through Japan*], 130; for another description of fragments of Europe in Japan, see 212–13.

8. Zweig, "Gwalior," 110.

9. For the cartographic history of Africa from the mid-nineteenth century through to World War I, see Demhardt, "Kolonialkartographie" and Demhardt, *Entschleierung Afrikas*. See also Nicklisch, "Nilquellen."

10. Jacques, *Heißes Land*, 11. *Hot Land*'s hero often seems to be Jacques himself, but the book's more clearly fictional, experimental aspects—including the intrusion of a third-person story with a protagonist with a different name—warn against a simple equation of author and hero.

11. Conrad, *Heart of Darkness*, 10.

12. The twenty-eight uses of "heimlich[keit]" that I found in *Hot Land* are the illuminated deck of the narrator's ocean liner (*Heißes Land*, 11); a monastery organ from home (15); the French coast at dawn (20); the heavy sweetness of a hot coastal city (26); a Brazilian woman's sparkling naked arm (55); the dock workers in Santos (73); the South American stars (87); the psychological struggle of a beautiful Brazilian girl (90); the "Negro" who steers the protagonist upriver (124); twinkling church domes (128); the greenish evening light (141); a squirrel on a coastal ship (151); a German in São Francisco do Sul (155); the consent of this German's Brazilian lover (155); the hand signal of another German (161); the dust before a Creole woman's eyes (161); houses in palm gardens (167);

sand on an Itajahi street (168); conversations among German colonists (186); the wishes and gestures of these colonists (188, 189); a mysterious "door" in the jungle (202); the glowing of the stars (210); a longed-for answer (210); the shining of a jungle river (212); the breaking of glass (213); the hopes of the German colonists (222); and blood (225).

13. Jünger, *Afrikanische Spiele*, 9; see also pages 5 and 8. Although only published in 1936, *Afrikanische Spiele* (*African Diversions*) describes events that take place in 1913. For Freud's readings in adventure literature, see my chapter 3.

14. On this fantasy of blank spaces ("den weißen Flecken der Landkarte") in Jünger, see *Afrikanische Spiele*, 6.

15. When describing female sexuality as the "dark continent," Freud uses the English term, suggesting that he senses himself to be in the position of an imperial adventurer from the British Empire ("Question of Lay Analysis," *SE* 20:212; *GW* 14:241).

16. Although Jacques' autobiographical experiences in Brazil differ markedly from his protagonist's in *Hot Land*, Jacques records similar feelings in his memoir: "The girls from these Negro huts slipped into the beds of the others, and the blood-mixtures became ever more varied, ever more fluid, evaporating with a sharply corrosive, volatile smell like chloroform" (*Mit Lust gelebt*, 141).

17. Freud suggests here that the doubling of the phallus signifies both castration and a protection against castration: Dream language is "fond of representing castration by a doubling or multiplying of the genital symbol [*des Genitalsymbols*]," but Freud sees in this the counterpart to the "invention of doubling as a preservation against extinction" (*The Uncanny*, *SE* 17:235, trans. rev.; *GW* 12:247). Freud implies a closeness of this uncanny phallic doubling to castration when, in an 1899 letter to Wilhelm Fliess, he labels the very idea of "replacement" (*Ablösung*)—doubling in the broadest sense—as "*unheimlich*" (*FLF*, 358, trans. rev.; *Briefe an Fliess*, 392); I follow here Rizzuto's translation of *Ablösung* as "replacement," not as "demise" or "redemption" (*Why Did Freud Reject God?*, 198–200).

This fear of a multiplying, replacing phallus recalls "little Hans," the co-inventor of Freud's castration theory, who never expresses anxiety about having his penis cut off but rather about the plethora of "widdlers" around him—especially the horses', whose size exposes the smallness of his own (Freud, "Analysis of a Phobia in a Five-Year-Old Boy," *SE* 10:34).

18. The term "uncanny white man" (*der unheimliche Weiße*) stems from Captain Maximilian Bayer's popular account of the German massacre of the Herero in 1904 (*Im Kampfe gegen die Hereros*, 78).

19. See Schwarz, "Bastards," esp. 375.

20. For the relation of Freud's uncanny sexual mother to German colonialism, see Noyes, "Wo sind die Mütter?," esp. 371–72.

21. In "Medusa's Head" (1922), Freud "confirm[s]" his claim from *The Uncanny* (1919) that there is a "technical rule according to which a multiplication of penis symbols signifies castration," at the same time that he hints again at the symbol's flip side: the multiplication simultaneously aims toward a "mitigation" of absence (*SE* 18:273–74). Multiplication thus ambivalently both produces and soothes the fear of castration. For more on Medusa's head in relation to plenitude, castration, and uncanniness, see Dolar, "'I Shall Be with You,'" 12–13.

22. As opposed to most theorists of anxiety, Lacan tells us—in his rare remarks on "the uncanny"—that anxiety results *not* when something is missing: not the "lack" is frightening but the "lack of a lack" (*"le manque vient à manquer"*). For this (as well as Lacan's only comments on the uncanny), see his seminar on "Anxiety" (*Séminaire livre X*, 53, see also 67). *"Horror plenitudinis"* is Dolar's phrase from "'I Shall Be with You,'" 18.

23. For a similar parody, see the writings of a third Jacques (Derrida), who points out that the Lacanian "phallus"—this "privileged signifier"—is somehow always everywhere ahead of time ("Purveyor of Truth," 98).

24. Complementing this discourse of the "new life" is the contemporaneous one of the "new man" ("der neue Mensch"), which was also important for Jacques. See Scholdt, "Proklamation des Neuen Menschen," 180.

25. By having his traveler read books about travel while traveling, Jacques prefigures the similarly self-reflexive "postmodern" trend in later travel writing. In Philip Glazebrook's book about Turkey, for example, he loses himself in travelogues to the point of ignoring the events of his own trip; he concludes that he need never have left home at all, "except to travel to the London library" (*Journey to Kars*, 240; see Zilcosky, "Writing Travel," 5).

26. Dauthendey, *Raubmenschen*, 113–14, 130, 277–81. (*Raubmenschen* fictionally reworks Dauthendey's 1897 journey to Mexico); Keyserling, *Reisetagebuch eines Philosophen*, 563; Jünger, *Afrikanische Spiele*, 125, 184, 189, 211. For more on Jünger's unexpected discoveries of the "familiar" (*vertraut*) in Africa, see Mergenthaler, *Völkerschau—Kannibalismus—Fremdenlegion*, 207–8. Other notable uncanny encounters, other than those already mentioned above, are Robert Müller's 1919 exotic South Seas island, which is a "bastion of Europe" filled with "European content," including natives wearing Western clothing, and Elisabeth Krämer-Bannow's 1913 *unheimlich* "anxiety dream," based on her actual South Seas experience: the Samoans' and Palauans' magnificent thatched-room houses transform into shacks made of finished European planks, and the people themselves, wandering in their naked "beauty," are suddenly covered with "European rags" (Müller, *Inselmädchen*, 21, 22, 13; Krämer-Bannow, "Heimatschutz in die deutschen Kolonien!" 13).

27. Greenblatt likewise notes the "odd relation" for the Spanish conquistadors between the Eucharist and "Aztec cannibalism," which eventually became for the Spaniards the marker of "absolute difference" precisely because it was the "most intimate and uncanny parallel" (*Marvelous Possessions*, 136).

28. As Susanne Zantop points out, this fantasy of being "better colonialists" extends back to the eighteenth century, long before Germany even had colonies (*Colonial Fantasies*, esp. 2–9).

29. Zweig is of course not blind to the pressure of Europeanization even on Gwalior, as his comical decription of Gwalior's Westernized maharaja reveals, but he nonetheless insists that the pure India still exists, "to this day," albeit not for long; like so many of his contemporaries, Zweig stylizes himself explicitly as the "last man" ("Gwalior," 110).

30. Pechstein, *Erinnerungen*, 59, 60, 61, 64. As Jill Lloyd writes, Pechstein arrives in Angaur, the most southern island of the Palau group, only to discover immediately an "established European colony" (*German Expressionism*, 200).

31. The model for these German stories of concentric circles of authenticity was Gauguin's 1901 *Noa Noa* (his book about his first stay in Tahiti), which was ever-present for fin de siècle German travelers. Gauguin describes here his painstaking journey from a contaminated coastal town, to the interior of the island, to the "interior" of his lover's "hut," to the interior of her body, through which he can finally "enter into mysteries which hitherto remained inaccessible to me"— including the mystery of "her race" (*Noa Noa* 70–71). As Peter Brooks points out, this pure Tahiti was a fiction; European influences were everywhere. Gauguin simply bracketed them: "In the absence of paradise found, he had to invent it. *Noa Noa* is very much the record of that invention" ("Gauguin's Tahitian Body," 65).

32. In addition to Zweig, Bonsels, and Pechstein, see also Kellermann, who likewise begins by experiencing uncanny moments of European contamination but then claims to have reached an untouched spot where he is the first white man: "Europeans stumble rarely upon this coast; I was the first white passenger upon the 'Morning Sun'" (*Spaziergang in Japan*, 236).

33. See Alloula, *Colonial Harem*. See also Mitchell's discussion of Alloula in *Colonising Egypt*, 26.

34. For Bonsels's claims to know Hindi and Kannada, and to speak fluent English, see *Indienfahrt*, 40 (Kannada), 96 (Hindi), 144 (Hindi, Kannada), 153 (Kannada), 165 (English). On Bonsels's actual language skills, which limited his access to Indians, see Vridhagiri Ganeshan's afterword to *Indienfahrt* (1989), 312–13, 316–17.

35. Bonsels always quickly brushes aside his meetings with missionaries, as if they did not play an important role in his Indian landscape (see *Indienfahrt*, 165, 180, 187, 215).

36. See Lloyd, *German Expressionism*, 200–201.

37. Ibid., 207–8. As Peter Brooks writes, the Maori culture of Tahiti "had been pretty well eradicated" even long before Gauguin arrived in 1891 ("Gauguin's Tahitian Body," 61).

38. Lloyd, *German Expressionism*, 203–4.

39. Frenssen, *Peter Moors Fahrt nach Südwest*, 111.

40. Hesse, "Pedrotallagalla," *SW* 13:276; "Fluß im Urwald," 10:176.

41. Bonsels continues with a description of this Indian/German "Heimat": "The elder bloomed on the fence, rain had fallen, and the air was cool and moist. High on the gable of a farmhouse, a blackbird sang in the fading sunlight, and the clear sweetness of its voice filled the quiet country with happiness" (*Indienfahrt*, 217).

42. Freud, *The Uncanny*, *SE* 17:245.

43. For more on the traveler's attempt, however unconscious, to overcome melancholia by not noticing uncanniness, see Zilcosky, *Kafka's Travels*, 29–34.

44. See Noyes, "Wo sind die Mütter?" 369, 371–72. Other fin de siècle combinations of spatial and temporal regression (to an *Urwald* that is simultaneously the mother's body) occur in Gerhart Hauptmann's 1912 *The Island of the Great Mother* and Robert Müller's 1915 *Tropics* (*Tropen*). In the latter, the tropical world is explicitly the "womb," to which the traveler returns. Müller, *Tropen*, 169.

45. Hesse, "Pedrotallagalla," *SW* 13:277–78.

46. Freud, *Future of an Illusion*, *SE* 21:17; *GW* 14:338. Diane Jonte-Pace's reading of this passage exemplifies a common misunderstanding of the relation between *heimisch*, *heimlich*, and *unheimlich*: "religious beliefs offer a home in

the uncanny, a *Heim* in the *unheimlich*, a sense of familiarity in the unfamiliar." Later in the same paragraph, she equates *heimisch* with *heimlich*, defining both as "familiar or 'homey,'" and then opposes both to *unheimlich*, or the "unfamiliar" (*Speaking the Unspeakable*, 70). As Freud made clear at the beginning of *The Uncanny*, *heimlich* is not equivalent to *heimisch* or to any other comforting idea of home: *heimlich* develops lexically toward "ambivalence" and its own opposite. Yet *heimlich* and *unheimlich* are not actual opposites: the latter is more like a "subspecies" of the former (*SE* 17:226).

47. Bhabha, *Location of Culture* ("Of Mimicry and Man"), 85–92.

48. On tropical rage, see note 16 in my epilogue. Bonsels finds himself at the point of such rage many times in India: "a very small level of excitement sufficed to cause my already almost boiling blood to bubble over" (*Indienfahrt*, 163).

49. The narrator symptomatically asserts that India is a radically exotic "foreign [*fremd*] flower," "colorful and voluptuous" like the *Urwald*—peopled by "untouchable" figures from "fairy tales" (Bonsels, *Indienfahrt*, 172, 173).

50. See Deleuze and Guattari's claim that the psychotic often escapes the neurotic Oedipal apparatus through his generational "extension" toward the grandparents (*Anti-Oedipus*, 94); contrary to Deleuze and Guattari, this psychotic escape takes, in the case of Bonsels and of Hesse's fictional Robert Aghion (in my chapter 2), a regressive—not revolutionary—direction.

51. Bonsels befriends an anti-British Indian nationalist, Mangesh Rao, who, just before being murdered, inspires Bonsels to remember his own nationalist, anti-British responsibilities in Europe: "there were duties and obligations awaiting me in another land . . . . I remembered that this man [Rao] . . . had spoken portentously of the hopes and imminent glory of my own people, and I felt the strength of his faith glowing in my conscience like a legacy" (*Indienfahrt*, 213). At the time Bonsels publishes these words (1916), he is already serving the German war effort, writing propaganda as a correspondent in Galicia (and, later, in the Baltic States).

After Bonsels turned to nationalism here, he did so again during the Nazi period (reminiscent of Nolde and Jacques). Although Bonsels, as a neo-Romantic, was initially unpopular with the Nazis (many of his works were burned in 1933), he eventually gained entry to the Reichsschrifttumskammer through its president (and Bonsels's friend), Hans Johst. In 1943 Bonsels published a novel, *Der Grieche Dositos*, which he sent to the Nazi minister of the interior, Wilhelm Frick, along with a note emphasizing its anti-Semitic aspects. See Werner A. Fischer, "Mehr als der Vater der Biene Maja," *Die Zeit* 47, November 17, 1978.

52. Bonsels, *Indienfahrt*, 162 ("paradise"). For the Germans as "better colonialists," see Zantop, *Colonial Fantasies*, and also *Indienfahrt*, where Bonsels meets an Indian who claims to prefer him over the British because he is so "friendly" (69).

53. As Thomas Kohut writes, this "traveling Kaiser" (*Reisekaiser*) is a "narcissistic extension" of the German people; he needs "to appear to be everywhere," especially in the colonial arena (*Wilhelm II and the Germans*, 172). For more on the *Reisekaiser*'s apparent "omnipresence," see Sombart, "The Kaiser in His Epoch."

54. On Kafka's love of pulp travel writing (including a book by Jacques) and his never-realized plan to write a series of travel guides called "On the Cheap," see Zilcosky, *Kafka's Travels* (for "On the Cheap," see 7, 227n61).

55. The shift to the third person begins one-third of the way through the book (on page 76) and lasts through page 99. On Jacques and Expressionism, see Scholdt, "Expressionismus."

56. Captain Maximilian Bayer reports on this "unheimlicher Weiße": a German officer who, during the massacre of the Herero in 1904, plucked out his own glass eye in order to intimidate the Africans (*Im Kampfe gegen die Hereros*, 78).

57. According to Martin Green, adventure books for boys created the "energizing myth" of eighteenth- and nineteenth-century imperialism (*Dreams of Adventure, Deeds of Empire*, xi). For the influence of such boys' books on Kafka, see Zilcosky, *Kafka's Travels*, chapters 4 and 5.

58. Jacques' support of German expansionism started in the pre–World War I colonial period and continued after the 1911 publication of *Hot Land*, with his pro-German 1914–15 writings from London and Paris. In 1917 he published the best-selling *Pirath's Island* (*Piraths Insel*), a fantasy of a German traveling to a faraway island and establishing his personal empire. One contemporary called *Pirath's Island* Germany's great colonial novel—its *Odyssey*—written while Germany still had a chance to defeat England and France and annex their colonies. Despite Jacques' 1920s pro-colonial pamphlets (which supported a gentler form of colonialism), he did not initially side with the Nazis in the 1930s. He was married to a Jewish woman (who emigrated in 1939) and was even banned from the Reichsschrifttumskammer. He furthermore served two weeks in a Gestapo prison (in 1938), for reasons never made clear. But following Germany's 1940 westward expansion, Jacques began cooperating by propagandizing in Luxembourg, later claiming that he had hoped, by engaging with the Nazis, to spare even a few innocent lives. He returned to southwest Germany near the end of the war, was arrested by the French occupiers, and sent back to Luxembourg to be tried for treason. The trial never took place on the grounds that Jacques had been a German citizen at the time of his crime; his only punishment was a lifetime ban from Luxembourg. See Scholdt, *Der Fall Norbert Jacques*, 195–96, 231, 246–47, 161n1, 387–88; Jacques, *Mit Lust gelebt*, 473; and Scholdt, afterword to *Mit Lust gelebt*, 568–69.

59. Lukács mentions "primitive awe" in his criticism of Kafka but also of modernism in general; his "fascist demagogy" refers directly to the Expressionists ("Ideology of Modernism," 36; "Expressionism," 317). For a summary of the 1930s "Expressionismusdebatte" (Expressionism Debate), in which Lukács played a major role, see Bogdal, "Kunst, Kunstwerk," 1410–11.

60. Ettlinger, "German Expressionism," 200, 201.

61. Lloyd, *German Expressionism*, 214 ("racial difference"); for a comparison of Nolde and Pechstein, see 213 and 234. On Pechstein's atelier and costume parties, see Otterbeck, "Ästhetik," 65.

62. As is typical for Nolde, the political message of *The Missionary* (one of his "mask" still lifes) is complex: his "missionary" is actually a Korean wayside figure; but by holding a Bible and proselytizing to an African (a woman from the Yoruba region of Nigeria), this figure nonetheless evokes aspects of European missionarism. See King, *Emil Nolde*, 76.

63. Lloyd, *German Expressionism*, 234.

64. In his 1904–18 *Essai sur l'exotisme* (published posthumously in 1955), Victor Segalen champions a "universal Exoticism, essential Exoticism" that he

claims is anti-colonial (*Essay on Exoticism*, 70). On Segalen's anti-colonialism, see 35, 56, 66, 68.

65. For examples of this generally untested truism that formal complexity runs counter to fascism, see Andreas Huyssen's "Fortifying the Heart—Totally," where he connects "fascinating fascism" to "B-literature," especially to Ernst Jünger's "pre-modernist" "narrative omniscience"; conversely, Huyssen claims, "complex modernist" narration sucks the narrator and protagonist "into the unfolding spectacle" and so resists fascism's "spell of mythic horror" (*Twilight Memories*, 143). See also Russell Berman's "Written Right Across Their Faces," 115, where he claims that "fascist modernism" is a form of writing that facilely "transforms the world into a visual object" and is thus "solely descriptive."

Chapter 2

1. Jacques is Hesse's anonymous "friend" and "walking pal" in Hesse's 1906 feuilletonistic piece, "Fastnacht" (Shrove Tuesday), *SW* 13:117. See Jacques, *Mit Lust gelebt*, 90–91; and Werner Dobras, "Raufhändel mit Hermann Hesses Wanderkamerad Norbert Jacques," *Lindauer Zeitung*, July 2, 1977.

2. On Hesse's 1904 move to the Lake Constance farmhouse, as well as his relocation to a larger, but still rustic house in 1907, see Freedman, *Hesse: Autor der Krisis*, 163; Zeller, *Hermann Hesse*, 59; and Böttger, *Hesse: Leben, Werk, Zeit*, 123.

3. Cited in Ball, *Hesse: Leben und Werk*, 105.

4. Hesse's diaries from his Indonesian journey are collected as "Tagebuch der Indonesienreise" in *SW* 11:329–88. Throughout the first three sections of this chapter, I cite primarily from these notes, with occasional references to essays that Hesse wrote either while still in Indonesia or in the months immediately following his return.

5. Zweig, "Gwalior," 110. We see this general fin de siècle disappointment in India, especially among German travelers, pointedly in Hanns Heinz Ewers's chapter "Europa in Indien" ("Europe in India") from *Indien und Ich*, 126–31.

6. Hesse, "Tagebuch der Indonesienreise," *SW* 11:365, 366–67, 367–68, 370, 370–71.

7. Even the few moments of apparent authenticity among the Chinese in Singapore—an "authentic" Chinese theater, an "authentic Chinese laugh"—are disturbed by "imitations" of Europe (Hesse, "Tagebuch der Indonesienreise," *SW* 11:370, 365).

8. Hesse, "Tagebuch der Indonesienreise," *SW* 11:376, 377, 378, 381, 382 (see also 379–80).

9. Jünger, *Afrikanische Spiele*, 137. This "same place" was often coded as "foreign" even within Europe. The Paris brothel that Kafka and Max Brod visited in 1911, for example, was rendered exotic through "palm trees" (Brod, "Reise," 129), and similarly exoticized domestic brothel scenes appear in Hesse's *Der Steppenwolf* and Flaubert's *L'Éducation sentimentale* ("chez la Turque"). For this foreignness of European brothels in Kafka and Flaubert, see Zilcosky, *Kafka's Travels*, 59–60. For the foreignness of most brothel experiences, whether in Europe or abroad, see Dietmar Schmidt's afterword to *Gebuchte Lust*, 250–53. For the brothel visit as a trope of exotic travel, see Reif, "Exotismus," 445.

10. Kellermann, *Spaziergang in Japan*, 71; Keyserling, *Reisetagebuch eines Philosophen*, 563; Brod, "Reise," 96; Jünger, *Afrikanische Spiele*, 136; Kafka, "Reise," 159.

11. Hesse, "Tagebuch der Indonesienreise," *SW* 11:341, 343, 372, 376, 380.

12. Falkwitz—*SW* 11:336; Gehrmann—337; Kulsens, Delbrück—337; Tschudi, Suhl—338; Klung—339; inebriated Englishman—341; snoring Dutchman—343; young Dutch civil servant—345; Hiese—345; Hasenfratz—346; Dutch civil servants—347; Schlimmer (married couple), Beckmann—352; Kiefer—353; Nägeli—359; Brunner—360; a Swiss—361; Suhl, Brandt—364; lunch with an old Swiss—365; Bébier—366; tipsy young Englishmen—366; Tiffin, Pertile—367; Portuguese or French "Missionspatres"—369; Malchow, Müller—371; a Bavarian, Ellon—372; Rosenbaum—373; Swiss chemist, man from Zurich—376; German hotel manager—380; Leuthold, Andreae, Baumann—382; Winker ("Swabian"), Kriegs—384; Freudenberg—384; Weisflog—386; old Englishman from New Zealand—386.

13. Jünger, *Afrikanische Spiele*, 138; Freud, *The Uncanny*, *SE* 17:237; Bonsels, *Indienfahrt*, 100.

14. Brod, "Reise," 129; Kafka, "Reise," 182.

15. Lacan, *Séminaire livre X*, 53 (*"le manque vient à manquer"*).

16. The original version of *Robert Aghion* (written in 1912) is published together with the other texts from the original 1913 *Aus Indien*, as well as some India-related additions (including Hesse's 1911 diaries) in the expanded collection, *Aus Indien: Aufzeichnungen, Tagebücher, Gedichte, Betrachtungen und Erzählungen*. Hesse later published a slightly revised version of *Robert Aghion*, which now appears in *SW* 8:26–58. I cite from this latter version, except when referring to passages from the original *Aus Indien* text that were later deleted.

17. Stelzig, *Hesse's Fictions of the Self*, 114, 117.

18. Mileck, *Allure of the Orient*, 142.

19. Böttger, *Hesse: Leben, Werk, Zeit*, 169, 170.

20. As discussed in my introduction, the discourse on the uncanny preceding Freud's famous 1919 essay includes Ernst Jentsch's 1906 "On the Psychology of the Uncanny," Otto Rank's 1914 "The Doppelgänger," and Rudolf Otto's 1917 *Das Heilige* (translated as *The Idea of the Holy*); Freud cites Jentsch and Rank several times in *The Uncanny*.

21. The penultimate quotation in this paragraph ("orderly and respectable colonialism") was deleted from the revised version of *Robert Aghion*; it can be found in *Aus Indien*, 279.

22. Böttger, *Hesse: Leben, Werk, Zeit*, 169.

23. This exclamation was later deleted; it can be found in *Aus Indien*, 279.

24. Bhabha, *Location of Culture* ("The Other Question"), 74.

25. See also Freud's reference in the preceding section of *The Uncanny* to *The Student from Prague*, where the protagonist's mirror image walks out of the mirror and performs deeds that the protagonist claims to renounce (*SE* 17:236n1).

26. The German government had no federal laws relating to interracial marriage (*Mischehen*), but bans against them—unique among European colonial empires of the day—were decreed by the German colonial administrations in South-West Africa (1905), East Africa (1906), and Samoa (1912). The 1912 Reichstag debate, initiated by the Social Democrats to criticize the Samoa prohibition, resulted in

a resolution to introduce a bill that would "safeguard" the validity of *Mischehen* in the colonies; but the Federal Council (Bundesrat) vetoed this resolution (*Verhandlungen des Reichstags*, 1648–52, 1724–37, 1740–47 [May 2, 7, and 8]). See Essner, "'Wo Rauch ist'"; Wildenthal, *German Women for Empire*, 79–130; Schwarz, "Mischehendebatte"; Kundrus, *Moderne Imperialisten*, 219–20.

27. Victor Segalen contemporaneously championed "Universal Exoticism" as that which produces the ability to "conceive otherwise" (*Essay on Exoticism*, 16; see also 70, 19). See my chapter 1, n. 64.

28. On the significance of sex in late nineteenth-century anti-hybridity racial theories, which set the ideological stage for the German parliament's 1912 debate, see Robert Young, *Colonial Desire*.

29. Lacan never uses the term "*unheimlich*" in either "The Mirror Stage as Formative of the *I* Function" (1949) or the closely related "Aggressiveness in Psychoanalysis" (1948). He discusses it only in his seminar on anxiety, where he hints at a connection between uncanniness and aggression through the frightening "hôte" (both "host" and "guest") who is "not the *Heimlich*" and has "already passed into the hostile" (*Séminaire livre X*, 91).

30. In this sense, he resembles the apparently unobtrusive narrator of Thomas Mann's contemporaneous *Death in Venice* (1912), who, as we shall see in chapter 4, likewise turns out to be a character himself.

31. On theatricality as "uncanny," see Weber, *Legend of Freud*, 7.

32. Ibid., 17.

33. Weber correctly notes that this story is, for Freud, told by children of both sexes (from the boy's point of view) (ibid., 5). But only the male child experiences the story's full anxiogenic threat to identity.

34. On the centrality of offspring to activating "hybridity"-based racism, see Young, *Colonial Desire*, xi–xii.

35. Even *Aghion*'s earliest critics made this assumption, beginning with Albrecht Oepke in *Moderne Indienfahrer und Weltreligionen*, 14. For later, similar claims, see Böttger, *Hesse: Leben, Werk, Zeit*, 169, 172; Mileck, *Allure of the Orient*, 142–43; and Boulby, *Hesse: Mind and Art*, 70.

36. Nolde, *Welt und Heimat*, 119.

37. Deleuze and Guattari, *Anti-Oedipus*, 94.

38. On this "traveling Kaiser" as a "personal symbol" of the German nation, see Kohut, *Wilhelm II and the Germans*, 155–76.

39. Kafka, "In der Strafkolonie," 204.

40. Bayer, *Im Kampfe gegen die Hereros*, 78.

41. Perhaps in an attempt to make *Robert Aghion* (and Hesse) politically defensible in East Germany, Böttger wishfully claims that Aghion chooses to manage the coffee plantation "in the interests of the natives"—even though Hesse's text explicitly states otherwise (*Hesse: Leben, Werk, Zeit*, 171).

42. On Freud's ethnography and invention of the "uncanny" method, see Zilcosky, "Savage Science."

43. After neglecting the "uncanny" in his 1980s work on the "almost the same but not quite" of colonial culture, Bhabha briefly discovers uncanniness in "Articulating the Archaic" (1990), using it aptly to describe "culture's double bind"—even if he bases this on a false binary: whereas Freud insisted that *unheimlich* was a "subspecies" of *heimlich*, Bhabha opposes the "homologous" *heimlich*

(which he mistakes for "*heimisch*") to the "differentiated" *unheimlich* (Freud, *SE* 17:226; Bhabha, *Location of Culture*, 136–37). Bhabha later makes passing mention of the uncanny in "DissemiNation: Time, Narrative and the Margins of the Modern Nation" (*Location of Culture*, 143–44) and in "World and Home," 146–47 (in revised form in the introduction of *Location of Culture*).

44. The Chinese are more "authentic" already in Hesse's diaries (*SW* 11:163–64, 365, 370–71) but become even more so in his "Memory." Whereas Hesse wrote in his diary about Chinese men watching a bad European movie, causing him to be shocked by "*Unwirklichkeit*," in "Memory of India" they become flawlessly un-Western ("noble," "dignified," and "serene") (Hesse, "Singapur-Traum," *SW* 13:230–31; "Erinnerung an Indien," *SW* 13:381).

45. Freedman, *Hesse: Autor der Krisis*, 195, 196, 197.

46. Gerhard Schepers similarly claims that Hesse "overcom[es]" his exoticism in the years following his India trip, when in fact the opposite is true: Hesse's exoticist idealization of India increases with each passing year ("Exoticism in German Literature on Japan," 109–10).

47. Mileck, *Hesse: Life and Art*, 47.

48. Alfred Ehrenstein's 1914 review, "Hermann Hesse: 'Aus Indien,'" was published in an as-yet unidentified source and is available only in the Editionsarchiv Volker Michels (Offenbach, Germany). An excerpt appeared on the back cover of the 1982 edition of *Aus Indien*. See Below, *Hesse Bibliographie*, 1613.

49. For another incomplete, uncanny modernist journey to a mother, written just one year after the publication of Hesse's *Out of India*, see the unfinished chapter of Kafka's *The Trial* entitled "Journey to His Mother" ("Fahrt zur Mutter") (discussed in Zilcosky, *Kafka's Travels*, 82–83).

50. Jacques wrote pro-German reports from London and Paris in 1914–15, and Bonsels served as a war correspondent in Galicia and the Baltic states; see the end of my chapter 1.

51. See Hesse's famous November 3, 1914 essay in the *Neue Zürcher Zeitung*, "O Freunde, nicht diese Töne," in which he warns his fellow intellectuals against the polemics of nationalism and patriotism. In his 1917 "Memory of India," Hesse insists that the lessons of international "brotherhood" he learned in India have become even more important since the beginning of World War I (*SW* 13:381–82). Joseph Mileck correctly cautions against exaggerating Hesse's 1914 pacifism (his 1914–15 writings contained some militaristic and nationalist remarks) and points to 1917 as the year when Hesse's antiwar stance became pronounced (*Allure of the Orient*, 19–25).

52. L. D. Ettlinger argues that "Africanization" in German Expressionism was generally only thematic, not formal ("German Expressionism," 191–92). The Expressionists were indeed not as formally influenced by African art as was, say, Picasso, but one need only look at Ernst Ludwig Kirchner's *Viertageszeitenspiegel* to see the significant impact of the "formal language of extra-European art" on aspects of German Expressionism (Wanken, introduction to *Wilde Welten*, 19).

Chapter 3

1. Although David Ellison similarly claims that the "uncanny's" emergence as a governing concept is "a determining factor in the movement from Romanticism to Modernism," his aversion to "intellectual history" keeps him from describing

how this movement occurred. His opening chapters thus jump with little transition from sublimity (in Kant), to romantic irony (in Hegel and Kierkegaard), to uncanniness (in Freud's 1919 essay) (*Ethics and Aesthetics*, ix; see 3–84).

2. Vidler, *Architectural Uncanny*, 9.

3. As Hans Magnus Enzensberger wrote a century after Marx, "Liberation from the industrial world has become an industry in its own right, the journey from the commodity world has itself become a commodity" ("Theorie des Tourismus," 196).

4. See Lloyd Smith, "Phantoms of *Drood* and *Rebecca*," 285.

5. Hélène Cixous was the first to point out that *The Uncanny* exhibits many traits of a work of fiction, calling it a "strange theoretical novel" ("Fiction and Its Phantoms," 525).

6. For "Red-Indian poetry" (*Indianerpoesie*) and the *Leatherstocking* cycle, see Freud's February 7, 1884 letter to Martha Bernays (*Letters of Freud*, 113); for *Tramp Abroad*, see *SE* 17:237; for *Travels in the Interior of Africa*, see *SE* 4:131n; for "Phantom Rickshaw" and *The Light That Failed*, see Freud's letter to Fliess, October 21, 1892; for *The Jungle Book*, see *SE* 9:245–47; for *She* and *Heart of the World*, see *SE* 5:453–55. Although Freud does not write about *Ramona*, he spoke about it to one of his patients (Roazen, *Wie Freud arbeitete*, 105–6). Freud owned *Treasure Island*, as well as the German translations of *Det tabte Land* (*Das verlorene Land*), *Barrack-Room Ballads* (*Soldatenlieder*), *Claire Lenoir* (in vol. 3 of Villiers' *Gesammelte Werke*), and *Typee* (*Taipi*). See Davies and Fichtner, *Freud's Library*; and Trosman/Simmons, "Freud Library." For a discussion of some of Freud's adventure-literature reading, see chapters 4 ("Adventures of Body and Mind") and 5 ("'Just So Stories'") from Prawer, *Cultural Citizen of the World*.

Even this long list of adventure fiction—which does not include the many non-fiction books by travelers, archaeologists, folklorists, and missionaries that Freud owned or mentioned—is certainly longer. We have no record of the books that Freud read in libraries or gave away, nor do we have a list of the books that Freud mentions in his works and letters. Freud's *Gesammelte Werke* contains a bibliography of the works that Freud cites in his scientific work (*GW* 18:977–1029) but does not include the countless hidden quotations, the texts that Freud mentions but does not cite, the works that he discusses implicitly, or the works to which he refers in his voluminous letters.

7. The popular books kept in the living quarters were also available to the family's other voracious readers (including Freud's wife, his sister-in-law, Minna, and daughter, Anna, who read *The Jungle Book* to her pupils) (Lobner, "Remarks on Freud's Library," 22). See also Molnar, "Bizarre Chair," esp. 253.

8. Molnar, "Bizarre Chair," 253. For similar claims that Freud's fiction readings were primarily for "relaxation" (Jones) or "compensatory" and not vital for his work (Brückner), see Jones, *Freud: Life and Work*, 1:189; and Brückner, *Freuds Privatlektüre*, esp. 145–48.

9. Haggard, *She*, 238.

10. Grinstein, *On Sigmund Freud's Dreams*, 417.

11. Anzieu, *Freud's Self-Analysis*, 426.

12. Etherington, "Haggard, Imperialism," 76, see also 76n12.

13. Gilbert and Gubar, *Sexchanges*, 36. See also Stott, "Dark Continent."

14. Young, "Freud's Secret," 227–28.

15. Gallo, *Freud's Mexico*, 317, 319.

16. Freud, *FLF* 398 (February 1, 1900). Like Haggard's heroes at the beginnings of their journeys, Freud claims in 1913 that he will voyage intellectually to a "new territory" in order to "annex" it (in the name of psychoanalysis). In 1915, Freud similarly insists that thinkers like him must not fear "voyages of discovery to distant countries" because "it is necessary to sail the seas, it is not necessary to live" ("Claims of Psycho-Analysis to Scientific Interest," *SE* 13:172; and "Thoughts for the Times on War and Death," *SE* 14:291).

17. Freud, *FLF* 365 (August 6, 1899).

18. The generally accepted reading of Haggard's novels as misogynist and imperialist (Gilbert and Gubar, Stott, Young) or Orientalist (Gallo) often issues from equating Haggard's politics with his novels. Although Haggard's public views were clearly Conservative and "New Imperialist," his novels never described imperial wars or territorial occupation. As Norman Etherington points out, Haggard did not take his reader "with Clive to India" or "with Kitchener to Khartoum," as did many of his contempories, and, although Haggard's European characters spout plenty of imperialist prejudice (albeit no more than Kipling's or Conrad's), his "savages" are the "best and cleverest to appear in novels since James Fenimore Cooper's Mohicans" (Etherington, *Rider Haggard*, 98, 91). Haggard's plots also consistently delineate the fragility of European empires: *Heart of the World* describes a powerful hidden Aztec city and an Indian plot "to drive out the accursed Spaniards and their spawn, and to establish an Indian Republic," and *She* proposes a *Dracula*-like "reverse colonization," in which Queen Ayesha will overthrow Queen Victoria and, as Holly announces happily, "assume absolute rule over the British dominions, and probably over the whole earth" (*Heart of the World*, 21; *She*, 226; see Arata, "Reverse Colonization"). As Marianna Torgovnick writes, *She*'s male characters are unusually receptive to the idea of female authority: they "adore She and are more than willing to live under her power" (*Gone Primitive*, 263n26).

19. Young, "Freud's Secret," 227.

20. On this point, the traditional psychoanalytic and later feminist/postcolonial interpreters agree: Ayesha is the "magna mater" and the "Great Mother" (Grinstein, *On Sigmund Freud's Dreams*, 402; Gilbert and Gubar, *Sexchanges*, 18).

21. Leo's mother dies while giving birth to him in "May, 1856." This date appeared in *She*'s original serialized version (1886–87) as well as its first seven 1887 book editions, but is sometimes omitted in later versons based on Haggard's 1888 "new edition" (see *She*, 278n33).

22. Gay, *Freud*, 417; see also 157–58.

23. The dream reveals Freud's "deeper wish ultimately to return to his mother," to attain "the mother which is so clearly referred to in *She*"; this fantasy is at once soothing and "frightening" (Grinstein, *On Sigmund Freud's Dreams*, 416, 421). Freud's dream evokes the "maternal imago," a woman who is "dangerous" also "because of the prohibited and reprehensible incestuous desires she arouses in the boy"; this image is not "in the actual text of the dream" and "can only be fully grasped by reading Rider Haggard's novels" (Anzieu, *Freud's Self-Analysis*, 430).

24. One year before his Haggard dream, Freud first used the term "conquistador," this time ironically—not to describe himself but rather a catacomb-guide who announced "neurotic[ally]" that one should penetrate caves "like with a virgin; the farther you get, the more beautiful it is" (*FLF* 309 [April 14, 1898]).

25. Grinstein saw this connection between the homoerotic pairs Strickland/Ignatio, Holly/Leo, and Freud/Fliess already in 1968 (*On Sigmund Freud's Dreams*, 417), but scholars have since ignored his insight. For further homoerotic moments between Strickland and Ignatio and between Holly and Leo, see Haggard's *Heart of the World* (34, 35) and *She* (78, 97, 211). Freud discusses his own "homosexual investment" in Fliess in *Correspondence of Freud and Ferenczi*, 1:221 (see also 1:227). For more on this attachment between Freud and Fliess, see Micale, *Hysterical Men*, 253–72.

26. Gallo cites as evidence an out-of-context quotation from Maya that does not refer to this pyramid but rather to the entire ancient Aztec city, which is figuratively, Maya claims, "a great burying-place, and those who dwell in it are like ghosts who wander to and fro thinking of the things that they did, or did not do, a thousand years before" (Haggard, *Heart of the World*, 159). See Gallo, *Freud's Mexico*, 318–19.

27. Gallo, *Freud's Mexico*, 318.

28. In Freud's revision of his interpretation of this dream in *Interpretation of Dreams*, the dream-children go from being benevolent alter egos (fulfilling Freud's wish that "children may perhaps achieve what their father has failed to") to augurs of replacement and death: Freud's "gruesome" fears (*Grauen*) about his own "growing grey" (*Grauen*) and dying remind him that he might "have to leave it to my children to reach the goal of my difficult journey" (*SE* 5:454–55, 478).

29. Lacan, *Séminaire livre X*, 53.

30. As Robin Lydenberg puts it, Freud splits himself narratologically in *The Uncanny* "into controlling narrator and helpless protagonist." "Freud's Uncanny Narratives," 1079.

31. Freud uses "Quelle" four more times (*SE* 17:234, 236, 240, 252; *GW* 12:246, 249, 253, 267); Strachey translates this as "source" everywhere except for *SE* 17:252 ("proceeds from").

32. See Derrida's argument that, in *The Uncanny*, castration can "never become an originary, central, or ultimate signified, the place proper to truth." Freud has "recourse both to castration anxiety, behind which no deeper secret [*kein tieferes Geheimnis*], no other meaning [*keine andere Bedeutung*] would lie hidden, and to the substitutive relation [*Ersatzbeziehung*] itself, for example between the eye and the male member. Castration is that nonsecret of seminal division that breaks into substitution" (Derrida, "Double Session," 306n67). On this *Ersatzbeziehung* "itself," see also Cixous, "Fiction and Its Phantoms," 536.

33. For the massive influence of Darwinism, biology, and anthropology on Freud, see the classic works by Ritvo, *Darwin's Influence on Freud*; Sulloway, *Freud, Biologist of the Mind*; and Wallace, *Freud and Anthropology*. For more recent studies that chart these fields' effect on Freud's understanding of colonialism and "primitiveness," see Khanna, *Dark Continents*, and Brickman, *Aboriginal Populations*. Khanna and Brickman ultimately take opposed stances, with Khanna viewing psychoanalysis as a critique of both colonialism and the modern nation state (28) and Brickman arguing that psychoanalysis is founded

on an act of "colonial" violence that renders both the analysand and the non-European other "primitive" (73).

34. This provides a twist to Johannes Fabian's claim that nineteenth-century anthropology renders "primitives" temporally exotic by denying them "coevalness" (i.e., by placing them in a distant past) (*Time and the Other*, 25–69, 156–65). For Freud, this is true, but with the caveat that these primitives gain their revenge on Europe as ghosts: by becoming simultaneously past and uncannily present.

35. Werner Michael Schwarz, *Anthropologische Spektakel*, 16. In addition to Schwarz's excellent study of the Viennese scene, see Thode-Arora's groundbreaking, if uneven, work on the Hagenbeck exhibitions, *Für fünfzig Pfennig um die Welt*; and some of the best-researched recent works in the ever-growing literature on German and Austrian *Völkerschauen*: Besser, "Schauspiel der Scham"; Badenberg, "Zwischen Kairo und Alt-Berlin"; Mergenthaler, *Völkerschau—Kannibalismus—Fremdenlegion*; Kim, "Task of the Loving Translator"; and Ames, *Carl Hagenbeck's Empire of Entertainments*.

36. For Freud and the *Neue Freie Presse*, see Molnar, introduction to Sigmund Freud, *Tagebuch*, 12.

37. Franceschini, "Das Aschanti-Fieber" (see Schwarz, *Anthropologische Spektakel*, 147–48). A second 1897 Vienna exhibit on Africa's "Gold Coast" also featured Ashanti, including many who had participated the previous year (see Ian Foster, "Altenberg's African Spectacle," 43–44).

38. Altenberg, *Ashantee*, 14 ("We're supposed to play 'savages,' Mister, play Africans. It's totally foolish. We couldn't act like this in Africa. Everyone would laugh. Like 'men of the bush,' yes, these. Nobody lives in such huts. . . . Quite foolish. They want us to play animals").

39. Freud, *Letters of Freud*, 344; Freud, *Briefe*, 357.

40. Schnitzler, "Andreas Thameyers letzter Brief" (1902), 69, 71. On the relation of this story to the 1896 Ashanti exhibit, see Urbach, *Schnitzler-Kommentar*, 112, and, more important, Boehringer, "Fantasies of White Masculinity," esp. 86–92. A more specific possible source (unnoticed by Urbach and Boehringer) is the 1898 libel suit launched by a Viennese woman named Rudarsky after rumors flew that she had given birth to an "Ashanti" baby, whom she supposedly poisoned immediately after its birth (*Illustrirtes Wiener Extrablatt*, April 20, 1898, 9–10).

41. See, for example, the caricatures in *Kikeriki*, April 4, 1897, 1, and *Humoristische Blätter*, April 18, 1897, 8.

42. Steiner, "Als Wien frohe Feste feierte," 5; caricature entitled "Des Aschanti-Don Juan's Abschied von Wien," *Kikeriki*, October 31, 1897, 3. For an overview of the phenomenon of the *Aschanti-Kinder*, see Schwarz, *Anthropologische Spektakel*, 168–78; and Plener, "(K)ein Mohr im Hemd," 2–3.

43. Cited in the official report of the 1896 German Colonial Exhibition, *Deutschland und seine Kolonien*, 6. A more likely goal of the exhibition was to drum up business for colonial goods (see "Das Deutsche Kolonialhaus Bruno Antelmann, Berlin," *Deutsche Kolonialzeitung*, November 30, 1899, 483). For this and the subsequent examples from this paragraph about the 1896 Exhibition, see also Badenberg, "Zwischen Kairo und Alt-Berlin," 193–98.

44. *Deutschland und seine Kolonien*, 213.

45. Schott, "Deutsche Kolonial-Ausstellung," 256.

46. *Deutschland und seine Kolonien*, 37, 38.

47. Badenberg, "Zwischen Kairo und Alt-Berlin," 197–98. For more about Martin Dibobe, see Paulette Reed-Anderson, *Rewriting the Footnotes*, 44–51.

48. May wrote his fabulously popular American Indian stories without traveling to America until very late in his life (in 1908). Before that, his only sightings of Indians would have been in Germany, particularly in Dresden, at the zoo's post-1874 *Völkerschauen* and in the "Buffalo Bill" Cody Sioux-Indian shows from 1890 and 1906 (Joch, "Halbwilder Westen," 327).

49. These quotations refer to the Sarrasani Circus's "Wild-West-Show" from 1926 (Thode-Arora, *Für fünfzig Pfennig um die Welt*, 29). For similar comments about the "Buffalo Bill" "Wild West" Indian shows from 1890 and especially 1906, see Thode-Arora, 22–27; Schwarz, *Anthropologische Spektakel*, 205–22; and Joch, "Halbwilder Westen," 326.

50. Bruckner, "Spectacle of (Human) Nature," 143.

51. Freud states in *Totem and Taboo* that our "uncanny" feelings stem from our vestigial beliefs in "animism" and the "omnipotence of thoughts" (*SE* 13:86). In *The Uncanny*, he develops this claim: uncanniness results when we inadvertently stumble upon the "primitive" "residues of animistic mental activity" (*SE* 17:235, 248, 241).

52. For a review of the "comparative method" and the "recapitulation" theory, see Stocking, *Victorian Anthropology*, 150–85 (comparative method) and 219, 228–29 (recapitulation). For their importance for Freud, see Grubrich-Simitis, "Metapsychology and Metabiology," 75–107; Brickman, *Aboriginal Populations*, 44–80; and Khanna, *Dark Continents*, 67–76.

53. Gilman, *Freud, Race, and Gender*, 20–22; Boyarin, "What Does a Jew Want?," 220; Gilman, *Case of Sigmund Freud*, 13. See also Gilman, *Inscribing the Other*, 21.

54. Adam de Gurowski, *America and Europe*, 177. For the long-standing connection of Jews to "blackness" from medieval iconography to late nineteenth-century race theory, see Gilman, *Difference and Pathology*, 30–35, and *Jewish Self-Hatred*, 6–12.

55. Marx, July 30, 1862 letter to Engels, in Marx/Engels, *Briefwechsel*, 257, 259; Roth, *Spinnennetz*, 57; Kafka, *Letters to Milena,* 136; Jacobowski, *Werther, der Jude* (*Werther, the Jew*), 315; and Jacobowski, "Selbstporträt," 226. On Marx, Roth, and Kafka, see Gilman, *Jewish Self-Hatred*, 206–7, and *Freud, Race, and Gender*, 19–20. On Jacobowski, see Anderson, "'Jewish' Mimesis," 197–99.

56. Stratz, *Was sind Juden?*, 13–14. Even though Stratz disputed the stereotype of the primitive Jew, his need to make a counterargument demonstrated the stubbornness of the prevailing view. Specifically, Stratz argued that the "nigritic," "mulatto" features that race theorists saw in Jews were typical of the "third" Mediterranean branch of the "white" ("Indo-European [*indogermanisch*], Caucasian, Aryan") race, to which Jews belonged (12, 18, 11; see also 21, 25). For the general Austro-German fin de siècle anthropological construction of the Jew as "exotic" and the effect of this on Freud, see Gilman, *Case of Sigmund Freud*, 11–37.

For images in addition to the ones that I reproduce here (figures 21 and 22), see, in Stratz's *Was sind Juden?*, pages 12 (a Muslim Turk with "Jewish features"),

13 (one Fellah of "Jewish stamp"), 14 (a Berber of "Jewish type"), and 15, 16, 17, 18, and 20 ("exotic" Jews). For a list of the books owned by Freud, including *Was sind Juden?*, see *Freud's Library / Freuds Bibliothek*, ed. Davies and Fichtner.

57. "Fetisch-Tanz," *Kikeriki*, October 8, 1896, 2. On the anti-Semitic press's tendency to connect the Ashanti with Jews, see Foster, "Peter Altenberg und das Fremde," 340; Schwarz, *Anthropologische Spektakel*, 177–78; and Besser, "Schauspiel der Scham," 201.

58. On the eastern Jew as "primitive" and "barbarian," see Gilman, *Jewish Self-Hatred*, 99 and 270–86. See also Klein, *Jewish Origins*, esp. 12–13 and 16–18 (on the Viennese Jews' attitudes toward the *Ostjuden*) and 48–55 (on Freud's attitude toward the *Ostjuden*). As Klein writes, "Jews already living in Vienna . . . began to feel the uncomfortable pressure of association, especially if they were living in or near the refugee quarters of the Leopoldstadt. From this point on [the 1870s] Jews resented the unassimilated *Ostjud*" (12).

59. This trope of Africa as a dead land appears not only in anthropology but also in the writing of the most popular German colonial author, Hans Grimm, whose protagonist in *Dina* speaks of Africa as "the dead land" (*Dina*, 24). See Noyes, "Wo sind die Mütter?," 371.

60. Gutzkow, "Julius Mosens Ahasver," 166; Schopenhauer, "On Jurisprudence and Politics," 264; Heine, *Poetry and Prose*, 601; Moses Hess, *Revival of Israel*, iv; Pinsker, "Auto-Emancipation," 163–64; Ha'Am, "Pinsker and Political Zionism," 186–87. For more on these writers and on the "uncanny Jew" in general, see Shapiro, "Uncanny Jew," esp. 63–69. On Gutzkow, see Rose, *German Question/Jewish Question*, 199; on Heine, see Newman, "Death of Judaism," 466–67.

61. Amy Newman claims that the nineteenth-century "Egyptian craze" resulted in an emphasis on "the Egyptian origins of Judaism" and the idea "that the uncanny persistence of the Jewish corpse after the death of Judaism might be attributable to a process of 'mummification' " ("The Death of Judaism," 467).

62. During his self-analysis, Freud remembers his young mother referring to him, as a boy, as the "little Moor" because of his "tangle of black hair" (*Interpretation of Dreams, SE* 4:337n).

63. Freud, *SE* 17:219, trans. rev.; *GW* 12:252 (*"unterscheiden"* for "differentiate").

64. Kafka, "Reise," 159 ("single"); Brod, "Reise," 96 ("doctor's office").

65. Cixous, "Fiction and Its Phantoms," 537.

66. Freud, "Notes upon a Case of Obsessional Neurosis," *SE* 10:215n2. The Rat Man not only fears rats but senses that the rat is a "living likeness of himself" (10:216). Because the rat is *"unheimlich,"* it resembles "taboo" itself, whose meaning, like *heimlich*'s, "diverges" uncannily "in two contrary directions" (toward both "consecrated" *and* "unclean") (*Totem and Taboo, SE* 13:18).

67. Freud emphasizes that rats are underground creatures, living "in sewers," and the Rat Man seconds this: he imagines that a rat has dug its way into "his father's grave" to nibble on the corpse (*SE* 10:214, 215).

68. Khanna likewise remarks on this footnote's subversive qualities but then does not discuss it further, claiming that it does not "disturb the main text" (*Dark Continents*, 74–75).

69. Malinowski, *Argonauts*, xv.

70. Bloom, "Reading Freud," 320.

71. Brickman, *Aboriginal Populations*, 53.

72. *International Dictionary of Psychoanalysis*, 3:1815.

73. Despite the tireless scholarly research into the texts Freud mentions in *The Uncanny*, "Inexplicable" has been neglected—even in a volume devoted to Freud's reading practices, *Reading Freud's Reading* (Gilman). The only (brief) references to "Inexplicable" have been by Hugh Haughton, introduction to Freud, *The Uncanny*, iii; Robin Lydenberg, "Freud's Uncanny Narratives," 1082; Royle, *The Uncanny*, 135–40; and Iurascu, "Freud-the-Father, Ernst-the-Son."

74. Moberly, "Inexplicable," 577.

75. Since the 1930s, scholars have related Freud's *The Uncanny* to Villiers' "uncanny" *Claire Lenoir*—without noticing that Freud actually owned this book and without discussing the colonial-cannibalist storyline that contributes to *Claire Lenoir*'s uncanniness: a gigantic black man emerges from a swamp in the Marquesas Islands (rumored in the nineteenth century to be the home of cannibals), then decapitates an English traveler and runs off with his head. See Bergler, "Psycho-Analysis of the Uncanny"; Weber, "Sideshow," 1123–31; Bartnaes, "Freud's 'The Uncanny,'" 34. On nineteenth-century fears of cannibalism on the Marquesas Islands, see Philbrick, *Heart of the Sea*. On the uncanniness of cannibalism, see Royle, *The Uncanny*, 205–12.

76. Iurascu insightfully makes this connection between "Inexplicable" and Freud's wartime worries about his sons but then goes on, through the pun on "Ernst," to focus instead on the relation of *The Uncanny* to Max Ernst's 1923 *Pietà ou la révolution la nuit* ("Freud-the-Father, Ernst-the-Son").

77. Freud first published *The Uncanny* in 1919 but claimed that it had been in "a drawer" for years (*SE* 17:218). Remarks about the "uncanny" in "Notes upon a Case of Obsessional Neurosis" (1909) and, especially, *Totem and Taboo* (1912–13) suggest that Freud indeed was occupied with this idea well before *The Uncanny*'s publication (*SE* 10:162; 13:86).

78. Freud, *Correspondence of Freud and Ferenczi*, 2:64.

79. For a detailed treatment of this dream, see Lehmann, "Freud's Dream of February 1918."

80. For the typical symptoms of the war neurotic in the First World War, see Fischer-Homberger, *Traumatische Neurose*, 105–69; and Lerner, *Hysterical Men*, 61–85.

81. On Freud's knowledge of the military-psychiatric history of handling war neuroses, see his official report for a postwar inquiry into military-psychiatric malpractice, which addressed specifically the use of extreme electroshock therapy to convince soldiers, thought to be malingerers, that the front would be less "painful" than the military hospitals ("Memorandum on the Electrical Treatment of War Neurotics," *SE* 17:213).

82. Kafka, "Großer Plan der Kriegsfürsorge," 494.

83. In between *Totem and Taboo* and *The Uncanny*, Freud read about this doubly dangerous son in Reik's "Couvade and the Psychogenesis of the Fear of Retaliation," which appeared first in 1914 in *Imago* and then as a chapter of Reik's *Ritual*, for which Freud wrote the introduction—in the same year that he published *The Uncanny* (on the dangerous son, see especially *Ritual*, 77–78).

84. See Iurascu, "Freud-the-Father, Ernst-the-Son."

85. See Lerner, *Hyterical Men*, 182.

86. The *Oxford English Dictionary* notes the first usage of "queer" to mean "homosexual" (noun) in an 1894 letter by the Marquess of Queensberry, the archenemy of Oscar Wilde (further cementing the connection to "Wilding"). As an adjective, this usage appeared first in the *Los Angeles Times* in 1914, three years before the publication of "Inexplicable" (*OED Online*, http://www.oed .com). "Queer's" etymological movement toward its modern meaning around 1900 replicates that of *heimlich*, albeit in reverse: "queer" goes from signifying "strange" to "familiar" (through the uncanny love of the "same").

87. Abraham, "Erstes Korreferat," 38–39.

88. In five separate letters to Wilhelm Fliess between the summer of 1897 and the winter of 1899, Freud writes of his "fear of the next train accident," of his "railway phobia," and of the general "travel anxiety" that he calls "my own hysteria." Freud traces this hysteria, which he eventually claims to "overcome," back to seeing his mother naked in a train when he was two years old. Because Fliess has "witnessed one of my finest attacks of travel anxiety," Freud insists on Fliess's secrecy (*FLF* 262, 268, 269, 285, 358, 392).

89. Freud, *Correspondence of Freud and Ferenczi*, 1:221 (see also 1:227). On Freud's train phobia, his hysteria, and his "homosexual investments," see Micale, *Hysterical Men*, 260–68.

90. Freud, *Interpretation of Dreams*, SE 4:337n. Shortly before writing *The Uncanny*, Freud examines a lithograph of himself and senses something "foreign" (*fremd*) in his own "Jewishness"; this foreignness within the familiar is, as Gilman notes, a prime example of the "uncanny" (Freud, *Letters of Freud*, 313 / *Briefe*, 318; Gilman, *Case of Sigmund Freud*, 55).

91. In a technical essay on psychoanalytic practice published in the same year as the first part of *Totem and Taboo*, Freud warns that the close connection between the analyst's and the patient's unconscious creates the danger of leaving the analyst psychologically vulnerable and even "helpless" ("Recommendations to Physicians Practicing Psycho-Analysis," *SE* 12:115).

92. Weber, *Legend of Freud*, 17.

93. Freud claims here that primitive beliefs are "based on" infantile complexes, suggesting a hierarchy, but if this is true, then why does Freud's most important infantile complex—the castration complex—appear nowhere among the "savages" in his own genesis tale, *Totem and Taboo*? Why do Freud's own primitives believe in the omnipotence of thought and even desire oedipally to kill their fathers, yet not fear castration?

94. Specifically, Freud claims that everything here is *"längst bekannt"*—"long familiar" (not "nothing new")—suggesting, in an intratextual play, that he has indeed reached his goal of getting to the source of the uncanny (*GW* 12:267); for, as Freud had warned us earlier, his journey will not bring great discoveries but will lead only back to what is "known of old and long familiar" (*das Altbekannte, Längstvertraute*) (*SE* 17:220; *GW* 12:230).

95. Using Freud's own descriptors from this entire passage, we see that he covertly praises psychoanalysis's solution to each of the four problems faced by anthropology: the psychoanalyst, unlike the anthropologist, revolutionarily combines "observ[er]" and theoretician in one; he *expects* "false and misleading

information" from his patients and perseveres for "many years" in order to gain, unlike the anthropologist, access to his subject's "most intimate details"; the psychoanalyst knows that memory and history have "distort[ed]" his patient's "original ideas," which themselves are always only retroactive "constructions"; and, most important, he recognizes that his own "mental constellations" will inevitably obstruct his attempts to "feel [his] way into" his patient's "modes of thinking" (*SE* 13:102n1–103n1).

96. Brickman, *Aboriginal Populations*, 206.

97. As Freud points out earlier in *The Uncanny*, the childhood "fear" (*Angst*) of, say, darkness or silence differs from the clinical infantile complexes ("infantile Komplexe") that include castration—leading Freud to presume that infantile complexes are *not* the source of this type of uncanny fear (*SE* 17:246–49; *GW* 12:260–64).

Chapter 4

1. For the figuration of Transylvania as a colonial region, see Arata, "Reverse Colonization," 627–34.

2. When the Rat Man's captain speaks of "a specially horrible punishment used in the East," he seems to be suggesting a farther "East," but his speaking occurs already in "the East": near "P——," which, as we learn from Freud's originally unpublished notes, is Przemyśl, a military town at the southeastern edge of today's Poland, at the border of Ukraine (Freud, "Case of Obsessional Neurosis," *SE* 10:166, 10:170, 10:170n1).

3. As Roy Pascal correctly points out, only the modernists realized the full "potential resources" of free indirect style, even though its usage extended back to the early nineteenth century (in Goethe, Austen, Büchner) and then, in midcentury, to Flaubert, who became the modernists' most important precursor (*Dual Voice*, ix, 37–66, 98–112).

4. Mann began writing *Death in Venice* in 1911 and published it in 1912. For the history of the writing and publication of *Death in Venice*, see Mann, *FA* 2.2:360–74.

5. *DV* 13, trans. rev., 6; *FA* 2.1:516–17, 505–6. In Conrad's *Heart of Darkness*, Marlow has a "hankering" after "blank spaces," especially "the biggest—the most blank, so to speak": in the heart of Africa (11). For a comparison of *Death in Venice* and *Heart of Darkness*, see Laura Otis, who claims that both "express and question imperial mentality" (*Membranes*, 165–66). For further correspondences between *Death in Venice* and *Heart of Darkness*, see McIntyre, "Psychology and Symbol"; and Vidan, "Conrad and Thomas Mann."

6. Generally read as Mann's attempt to depict the Dionysian aspect of ancient Greek culture, this scene's connection to what Thomas Schwarz calls the "cartography of the Dionysian" is often neglected. For the relation of this scene to Koch-Grünberg's groundbreaking 1911 film of a tribal "circle dance" along the Amazon, see Schwarz, "Tropenenthusiasmus"; and Schwarz, *Robert Müllers Tropen*, 136.

7. Mann, *DV* 28, 21, 22, 26, 37, 27.

8. Even though Tadzio is aristocratic, there is a hint of colonial power relations throughout the story, not least because Germany in 1912 still held large parts of Poland, and the Germans there employed rhetoric from the extra-European

colonial realm to justify their expansionism (see Kopp, *Germany's Wild East*). In terms specific to *Death in Venice*, John Burt Foster argues that Aschenbach's relation to Tadzio echoes interactions in "colonial societies" and that Aschenbach deliberately "uphold[s] and maintain[s] the Germano-Slavic boundary" ("Why Is Tadzio Polish?" 201). Russell Berman similarly contends that Aschenbach views his relation with Tadzio in a colonial fashion: the child of "Prussian officials in Silesia," Aschenbach shows no sympathy for Tadzio's incipient "Polish patriotism" ("History and Community in *Death in Venice*," 269).

9. The German varies in the two passages, albeit only slightly: both characters have the exact same "*kurz aufgeworfene Nase*"; the Munich man has "pulled back" (*zurückgezogen*) lips whereas the gondolier "pulled his lips back" (*zog er … die Lippen zurück*); the Munich man's "white" teeth are "bared" (*bloßgelegt*) whereas the gondolier "bared his white teeth" (*entblößte seine weißen Zähne*) (*DV* 4, 18, trans. rev.; *FA* 2.1:503, 525).

10. I disagree here with Dorrit Cohn, who claims that Mann's narrator is as unaware of the repetitions as is Aschenbach, basing her claim on the fact that the narrator never comments on the repetitions ("Second Author," 192). But given the narrator's general taciturnity in comparison to other Mann narrators (e.g., Zeitblom in *Doktor Faustus*), it does not follow that his silence necessarily corresponds to his lack of awareness.

11. The narrator again hints at the story's underlying uncanniness when he refers to the triad's middle figure—the gondolier—as "*unheimlich*," even if Aschenbach cannot understand why. Aschenbach begins by romanticizing the gondolier as an exotic "criminal" who will dispatch him "to the house of Aides" but then understands the more uncanny truth: only dressed up in the clothing of death, this gondolier turns out to be an ultra-familiar scammer who recognizes in Aschenbach the naive double of thousands of other German tourists (*DV* 19; *FA* 2.1:525). The narrator's uncanny lexical repetitions furthermore haunt his descriptions of Venice, which Aschenbach imagines to be "beyond associations" and—because of the cholera—"oriental," while the narrator hints that this disease is utterly familiar: the "lush" (*üppig*) birthplace of cholera echoes literally Aschenbach's opening exotic fantasy as well as Venice itself, Venice's gondolas, the "oriental temple" of San Marco, and Aschenbach's creativity, which are all described as *üppig* (translated as "luxurious" [twice], "voluptuously," and "indulgent") (*DV* 47, 17, 45, 22; *FA* 568, 524, 566, 531). What is more, the "oriental" cholera originates from a swamp, recalling again Aschenbach's initial desire and also Venice itself, known for its "stagnant smell of sea and of swamp [*Sumpf*]" (*DV* 31–32; *FA* 545). Finally, the "crouching" or "lurking" (*kauern*) tiger, too, is already in Europe, in the simmering resentments of the underclass: the second-class Italian passengers in Pola and a beggar in Venice all "*kauern*" near Aschenbach, as if ready to pounce (*DV* 14, 46; *FA* 518, 567).

12. *DV* 7, 8, 50, 52; *FA* 2.1:508, 509, 572, 576. See Foster, who likewise cites resemblances between Tadzio and Aschenbach, including the first two mentioned here ("Why Is Tadzio Polish?" 200–201). Susanne Widmaier-Haag argues similarly that Aschenbach identifies narcissistically with Tadzio in *Lächeln des Narziß*, 93, 187, 190.

13. The beginnings of my formal argument echo Dorrit Cohn, who claimed convincingly in 1983 that *Death in Venice*'s narrator is a distinct character (a

"second author"), not simply a mouthpiece for the author's intentions, and that this narrator "shar[es]" Aschenbach's perspective when the narrator starts to slip into free indirect style ("Second Author," 179, 185).

14. Already in the famous first sentence, the narrator establishes distance with a typically removed nineteenth-century realist style ("On a spring afternoon in 19—, . . ."), and, throughout the first two chapters, he employs adjectives and epithets that describe his protagonist externally: Aschenbach becomes "the waiting one" (*der Wartende*), "the author," "the patient artist," and "the creator" (*DV* 4, 7, trans. rev.; *FA* 2.1:502, 507). This narrative distance culminates at the end of chapter 2 with an extreme example of distanced third-person narration, beginning with "Gustav von Aschenbach was a man of slightly less than middle height" (*DV* 12).

15. I say "nearly" because I agree with Cohn's point that the narratorial and figural voices never actually become one (contra Wayne Booth and George Szanto); rather, the very presence of the third-person pronoun precludes such a complete unity (Cohn, *Transparent Minds*, 112).

16. Cohn, "Second Author," 185.

17. Cohn likewise discusses the narrator's criticism of Aschenbach in some of these quotations but does not point out, as I do, the psychology behind this narrative structure of attraction and repulsion ("Second Author," 183–87).

18. Cohn, "Second Author," 192, 189.

19. Aschenbach must maintain this distance especially because, as mentioned above, Tadzio resembles him so closely. A relationship with this narcissistic double would signify the "return home" (*Heimkehr*) and to "himself" (*in sich*) that Aschenbach dreads (*DV* 55, trans. rev.; *FA* 2.1:581). Aschenbach now sees the possibility of his relationship to Tadzio signifying an uncanny return: toward Socrates, toward August von Platen, toward Aschenbach's own sickly boyhood. Like Brazil for Jacques and India for Hesse, Venice becomes a disturbingly homo-home. Rife with masculine repetitions—of the Munich stranger, the made-up old man from Pola, and the young Aschenbach as Tadzio—Venice is the opposite of a feminine Dark Continent. It teems with phalluses, culminating in the "gigantic" "obscene" dream "symbol" that haunts the text's final pages. This symbol finally renders Aschenbach "*heimgesucht*"—"stricken"—but literally "sought out at home" (*DV* 57; *FA* 2.1:584). Itself a repetition (*DV* 24, 38, 56; *FA* 533, 555, 581), the word "*heimgesucht*" leads to the text's final two repetitions: stricken by "*heim*," Aschenbach lets himself be made up like the old man in Pola and then lands in a little piazza he knows he has been to before. These fateful homecomings coincide with *der Heimgesuchte*'s fatal infection: already feverish, he sits down here with the contaminated strawberries.

20. Foster, "Why Is Tadzio Polish?" 195, 201.

21. Freud, *The Uncanny, SE* 17:252.

22. In this sense, *Death in Venice* is a literary prefiguration of today's critical anthropology, which has long argued that the "field" must be expanded to include the anthropologist him or herself. See Clifford, *Routes*, 20–21, and "On Ethnographic Self-Fashioning," 160–62. For a critical view of this anthropological "I-Witnessing," see Geertz, *Works and Lives*, 73–101.

23. Malinowski records a massive amount of novel-reading in his 1914–15 and 1917–18 diaries from Melanesia. In his first two months alone, he reads

an unnamed Rider Haggard novel (7), Thackeray's *Vanity Fair* (16), Guy de Maupassant's short stories (22), *Romance* by Joseph Conrad (coauthored with Ford Madox Ford) (27), Victor Cherbuliez's *L'Aventure de Ladislaus Bolski* (28), and *Golden Legend*, a popular late medieval book by Jacobus de Voragine (28). Malinowski despises people who are "incapable of finding a glimmer of poetry in certain things," yet understands his own novel-reading as a nasty addiction: "I couldn't tear myself away [from *Vanity Fair* and *Romance*]; it was as though I had been drugged"; "I promised myself I would read no novels. For a few days I kept my promise. Then I relapsed"; "Reading novels is simply disastrous" (16, 17, 31). This tension between Malinowski's voracious novel-reading and his never-successful attempts to stay away from this "drug" continues—sometimes with even greater intensity—throughout the entire 300-page diary.

24. Malinowski, *Argonauts*, 25 (emphasis in original). On Malinowski's plan to write a colonial novel, see his *Diary*, 211–12. On the influence of fiction, especially Conrad, on Malinowski's ethnographic style, see Stocking, "Empathy and Antipathy"; Payne, "Malinowski's Style"; Clifford, "On Ethnographic Self-Fashioning"; and Thompson, "Anthropology's Conrad."

25. That Malinowski knew Freud's work before writing *Argonauts of the Western Pacific* (1922) is evidenced by his mention of Freud in his 1917–18 diaries (*Diary* 245, 290; see also 274, 282). On Malinowski's (and anthropology's) ambivalent relationship to Freudian psychoanalysis, see Stocking, "Anthropology and the Science of the Irrational."

26. On Freud's uncanny method, see Zilcosky, "Savage Science," esp. 468–71. On Malinowski as the inventor of anthropology's radical perspectival paradox—between, on the one hand, erasing "the affective distance between the observer and the observed" and, on the other, rendering this distance "near absolute"—see Geertz, *Works and Lives*, 83.

27. Malinowski, *Argonauts*, 21. On Malinowski having to endure the English colonists' "anti-Austrian-Polish attitude," see *Diary*, 172; and Charles Seligman's 1916 letter on behalf of Malinowski (cited in Michael Young, *Malinowski*, 439).

28. On Malinowski's mistreatment of natives, see my epilogue. For examples of his retreats to the colonists' homes and his use of arsenic (as a stimulant) and of brandy, sherry, and beer (too numerous to list exhaustively here), see his *Diary*, 76–78, 89, 92, 97–98, 135. For the two sides of the furious debate about Malinowski's legacy immediately following the posthumous (1967) publication of his diary, see Clifford Geertz ("Under the Mosquito Net") and Hortense Powdermaker ("Agreeable Man"). For an overview of this debate, see Stocking, *Ethnographer's Magic*, 49–50.

29. For Freud's identification with Dora and his own femininity, as well as his rejection of this (and of her), see the articles by Neil Hertz, Toril Moi, and Madelon Sprengnether in *In Dora's Case*; Bernheimer summarizes this point in his introduction: "Resisting . . . his identification with her [Dora], Freud rejects as other and aberrant the feminine side of himself" (17).

30. Jost Hermand claims that Mann in *Death in Venice* (like Robert Musil in *Grigia*) identifies with his narrator, and that he commendably and deliberately keeps narrative distance, through strategic diction, from his protagonist's "mood-charged excesses or emotional derailments": both authors "approach the object of their analyses—decadence and Expressionism—only to a certain degree,

absorbing and comprehending them yet simultaneously dissociating themselves" ("Musils *Grigia*," 179, 179–80).

31. For Laura Otis, Aschenbach is "penetrat[ed]" by a "foreign invader": the germ-based "disease" that comes from the "Ganges-Delta." Yahya Elsaghe similarly claims that Aschenbach suffers from the violent puncturing of Mann's imagined "cordon sanitaire" between Germany and Austria-Hungary. And Foster argues that *Death in Venice* depicts the destruction of the cultural "boundary" between Aschenbach's Germany and the "Slavic East" (Otis, *Membranes*, 164–65; Elsaghe, *Imaginäre Nation* 39–52; Foster, "Why Is Tadzio Polish?" 207).

32. Yahya Elsaghe aptly describes the exotic aspects of Mann's Austria-Hungary, especially in *Death in Venice* and *The Magic Mountain*—even if he then goes on to argue unconvincingly that these exotic descriptions exemplify Mann's particularly "German" xenophobia (*Imaginäre Nation*, 39–60).

33. Hofmannsthal, "Wiener Brief [II]," 195. On Hofmannsthal's and Freud's concepts of the unconscious within their fin de siècle Vienna context, see Urban, *Hofmannsthal, Freud, und die Psychoanalyse*. On Vienna and the "Orient," see Elsaghe, *Imaginäre Nation*, 42.

34. Hofmannsthal started making scattered notes on this still untitled narrative already in 1907, but he only began the sustained text on September 12, 1912. See Hofmannsthal, *Andreas*, in *Sämtliche Werke: Kritische Ausgabe*, 30:7–38, 40n1 (hereafter cited in text as *SWK*).

35. 1912 was a tense year not least because it came on the heels of the Second Moroccan Crisis from the preceding summer: the Germans had sent gunboats to threaten French supremacy in Agadir, leading many to believe war was imminent. These tensions loom over the opening of Mann's *Death in Venice*, which he wrote in 1911–12: "in 19—, a year that for months glowered threateningly over our continent" (*DV* 3; *FA* 2.1:501).

36. Hofmannsthal, *Andreas*, trans. Marie D. Hottinger, 20, 51 (hereafter cited in text as *A*); original German in *SWK* 30:45, 63.

37. "Wälsch" referred to "foreign" in general, often in relation to the Romance languages, probably here to the French spoken by minorities in Switzerland and Austria; "Ladinisch" meant "Rheto-Romantic" but today denotes "Ladin," a subgroup of the Rheto-Romantic languages spoken by the Ladin people in and around South Tyrol (today, in northern Italy) (see *SWK* 30:417).

38. On the family's exotic-seeming Catholicism, see *A* 36, 37, 44, 49; *SWK* 30:54, 55, 58, 61.

39. Hofmannsthal, *SWK* 30:58. The reference to "Indian birds" was left out of the English translation (but should have been included at *A* 42).

40. Freud describes the "primitives'" incest taboos in his *Totem and Taboo: Some Resemblances between the Mental Lives of Savages and Neurotics*, which he began writing in 1911, just before Hofmannsthal started the main *Andreas* fragment.

41. To the reader, Romana appears as not at all "innocent": she is bestially erotic (suckling from a goat), physically free and flirtatious with Andreas (pulling him toward her for "the first kiss of his life"), and open about her desire for inbreeding (*A* 39–40, 44).

42. In the course of working out his perspectival strategy, Hofmannsthal considers the whole gamut of narrative possibilities, from omniscient third-person

to first-person "Schnitzlerian" stream-of-consciousness (*SWK* 30:130 [note 131], 197 [note 319]).

43. The English translation wrongly cites the date as the "17th," not the "7th" (*A* 11; *SWK* 30:40).

44. Samuel Weber describes the uncanny's "other scene" in dreams as "irreducibly theatrical," in *Legend of Freud*, 7.

45. On the importance of Prince's investigation into the borders of the ego/ *Ich* for *Andreas*, see Alewyn's groundbreaking "Andreas und die 'wunderbare Freundin.' "

46. Goethe, *Wahlverwandtschaften*, 457.

47. "Abenteuerliches Ich" appears in the German original but not in the English translation, where it should come right after "before the Empress. . . ." (*A* 64, ellipsis in English translation).

48. As Lacan points out, one could also read Freud's *Ich* as *not* emerging heroically from its encounter with the *Es* but rather remaining forever in that other place ("where *Es* was"), whose unbearable truth destabilizes "the moorings of [man's] being"—precisely what happens, as I describe later in this chapter, to Hofmannsthal's Andreas (Lacan, "Instance of the Letter," 435, 438).

49. At their first meeting, Andreas is immediately attracted to the Maltese knight: "every limb of his body was aware of every other, and, as flame quivers on flame, imprinted deep within him was the image of the tall figure which, in easy assurance, in gracious civility, bent slightly towards him." Andreas then has the uncanny sense that he has "seen him [the knight] before," and a letter apparently addressed to the knight seems, as the knight claims, to "belong to you [Andreas]" (*A* 87–88). For Nina and Gotthelf, see *A* 103 and 107, respectively.

50. Hofmannsthal penciled an interior monologue into the margin of this final "Venice" part of the manuscript ("have I ever seen him [the knight Sacramozo] before? How else could his image have been impressed on me in one moment? I can learn about him from myself!"), but this monologue was misleadingly inserted without comment into the main text of the English translation; the German edition includes it, appropriately, only as a footnote (*A* 87–88; *SWK* 30:85n1).

51. Hofmannsthal wrote this description of the Venetian square on August 29, 1913 (*SWK* 30:95n2, 307); *Death in Venice* was published in two 1912 installments of *Die neue Rundschau* (October-November), and twice in book form in 1913 (in February by Fischer and later that spring by Hyperion) (*FA* 2.2:373–74). Hofmannsthal would certainly have read *Death in Venice*, given his friendship with Mann, the novella's immediate impact on the literary scene, and the likelihood that Mann borrowed parts of Aschenbach's biography from Hofmannsthal's own. For more on the relationship between Mann and Hofmannsthal, see their letter exchange: Hofmannsthal / Mann, "Briefwechsel." On the contemporaneous reception of *Death in Venice* and the parts of Hofmannsthal's biography that appear in Aschenbach, see *FA* 2.2:381–90 and 407–8, respectively.

52. Mann: *DV* 59, 60; *FA* 2.1:586, 587; Hofmannsthal: *A* 90, 108; *SWK* 30:86, 97; Freud: *SE* 17:236; *GW* 12:249. In the German original, Hofmannsthal and Freud employ the exact same words ("*eng*" [narrow] and "*menschenleer*" [deserted]); Mann uses synonyms ("*schmal*" and "*verlassen*").

53. Hofmannsthal's unpublished 1913–27 notes for *Andreas* can be found in *SWK* 30:98–218 (the first few notes are undated, so they might come from late

1912). Because not all of these notes are contained in the English translation of *Andreas* (111–83), I cite only the German edition.

54. In the main 1912–13 fragment, the story begins in 1778, when Andreas is twenty-two years old, resulting in a birth year of 1755 or 1756. In Hofmannsthal's subsequent notes, he first shifts this slightly forward to 1757 and then, in the 1925 note, all the way to 1809. *SWK* 30:40, 51, 120, 207; for the Knight's "oriental" journeys, see 164, 195.

55. Hofmannsthal gave this reason for shifting eras in a conversation with Walter Brecht (*SWK* 30:374–75).

56. "*Unheimliche Heimat*" (uncanny home) is the name W. G. Sebald uses to describe modern Austrian literature in his book of the same title. See also Sebald's essay on *Andreas*, "Venezianisches Kryptogramm."

57. The 1932 edition for which Wassermann wrote the afterword contains only the main fragment and some of Hofmannsthal's 1913–18 notes; the only reference to the existence of post-1918 notes is a nebulous single sentence at the end of this edition's explanatory remarks (Hofmannsthal, *Andreas oder die Vereinigten*, 184).

58. Wassermann, afterword to Hofmannsthal, *Andreas oder die Vereinigten*, 177–78.

59. Because of narrative's vital connection to the "imperial quest," it is "not surprising that France and (especially) England have an unbroken tradition of novel-writing, unparalleled elsewhere" (Said, *Culture and Imperialism*, xxii).

60. This dismissal of historical-political readings such as Wassermann's is exemplified by Mathias Mayer, who claims that serious "scientific investigations" of *Andreas* could only begin after the 1930s "political" readings by Hofmannsthal's contemporaries had been overcome. These "scientific investigations" have generally ignored *Andreas*'s relation to Austria's political moment, focusing instead on "text-immanent interpretations," "the analysis of new sources," "problematizing the 'Bildungsroman' model," "the analysis of the modern character of the novel," and "*geistesgeschichtliche* and psychoanalytical approaches." Mayer, "Hofmannsthals *Andreas*," 102 (for reprints of the early, pre-1954 criticism of *Andreas*, see 105–97); Mayer, afterword to *Andreas* (2000), 133 (for a summary of the post-1954 criticism, see 133–36).

61. *The Loser* is the English title of Thomas Bernhard's *Der Untergeher*.

62. "The great cultural archive, I argue, is where the intellectual and aesthetic investments in overseas dominion are made" (Said, *Culture and Imperialism*, xxi).

63. On Hofmannsthal's praise of *Grigia*, see Hermand, "Musils *Grigia*," 180.

64. Hermand points out *Grigia*'s thematic similarities to both *Andreas* and *Death in Venice*, but he only relates *Grigia* to each of them individually, never connecting the three narratives. He cites the equally exotic Alpine regions of Fersana and Carinthia (*Grigia, Andreas*), the "descent into the unconscious" (*Grigia, Death in Venice*), the apparent authorial distance from the "exotic-jungle-like" objects of analysis (*Grigia, Death in Venice*), and the deliberately non-"synthetic" narrative in which the reader repeatedly "loses the thread" (*Grigia, Andreas*) ("Musils *Grigia*," 172, 175, 179, 180–81).

For the specific importance of *Death in Venice* for *Grigia*, see Musil's 1918 diaries, where he begins sketching the framework of *Grigia* and then quotes a sentence from *Death in Venice* that applies to the ecstasy-seeking of both Aschenbach and Homo: "When one is beside oneself there is nothing more abhorrent than returning to one's senses—*Death in Venice* p. 129—psych[ology] of ecstasy." Musil, *Tagebücher*, 1:346 (this sentence appears in chapter 5 of *Death in Venice*, *DV* 55). For further Musil diary entries about *Death in Venice* during the years of *Grigia*'s composition (1918–21), see *Tagebücher*, 1:477, 478 and 2:307n181.

65. Musil, *FW* 33, 30, trans. rev.; *GW* 6:247, 245; the latter phrase is not included in the English translation. Hermand noticed this similarity between Tadzio and "Greedscha" in "Musils *Grigia*," 175.

66. Consider this full passage from *Grigia* in relation to one from *Heart of Darkness*, respectively:

> And the big basket on each woman's back would be loaded until her knees gave and the veins in her neck swelled. When one of those pretty young women had been loaded up, her eyes stared and her lips hung open; then she took her place in the column and, at a sign, these now silent beasts of burden slowly began to set one foot before the other up the long, winding track into the heights. (*FW* 19)

> Six black men advanced in a file, toiling up the path. They walked erect and slow, balancing small baskets full of earth on their heads, and the clink kept time with their footsteps. . . . All their meagre breasts panted together, the violently dilated nostrils quivered, the eyes stared stonily uphill. They passed me within six inches, without a glance, with that complete, deathlike indifference of unhappy savages. (*Heart of Darkness*, 19)

67. Musil, *FW* 17, trans. rev.; *GW* 6:235. In 1919, Freud investigated, similarly, how "das Vertraute unheimlich . . . werden kann" (Freud, *SE* 17:220; *GW* 12:231).

Although Musil made notes for *Grigia* in 1915 while on the Italian front and again in 1918, he did the bulk of his writing on *Grigia* in 1921, two years after Freud published *The Uncanny*. On the history of *Grigia*'s composition, see Arntzen, *Musil-Kommentar*, 126–27.

68. When discussing Dora's dream of a "jewel-case" (*Schmuckkästchen*), Freud tells her that *Schmuckkästchen* is a popular term for the female genitalia; Dora's only response is, "I knew that *you* would say that" (Freud, *SE* 7:69; *GW* 5:231 [emphasis in original]; see also *SE* 7:77; *GW* 5:240; and "Introductory Lectures on Psycho-Analysis," *SE* 15:156; *GW* 11:158). On Freud's counter-transferential desire for Dora through his identification with the man whom Freud claimed she loved, see Lacan, "Presentation on Transference"; and Sprengnether, "Enforcing Oedipus."

69. For attributions and direct speech in *Grigia*, see, for example, Musil *FW* 22–23; *GW* 6:238–39 (*GW* includes the narrator's ironic reference, missing from the English translation, to "Doktor Homo"). For the repeated use of "one" (*man*), see *FW* 17–19; *GW* 6:237.

70. I think, for example, of Thomas Hardy's *Tess of the D'Urbervilles* (1891), whose Tess produced, not surprisingly, an ethnographic prototype for Malinowski's Ur-woman. See Elbert, "Malinowski's Reading List."

71. Barrell, *English Literature in History*, 33, 38.

72. Hegel, *Phenomenology of Spirit*, 116.

73. Nietzsche, *Beyond Good and Evil*, 201. Although Nietzsche asserts elsewhere that modern "disinterestedness" remains firmly within the moralizing herd instinct, his vision of the pre-historic nobility nonetheless resembles Barrell's description of the disinterested gentleman: both lay claim to a supra-human, in Nietzsche's words, "self-surmounting" point of view that should be extraordinarily "distanced" and "comprehensive" (*Genealogy of Morals*, 26, 201).

74. As Hegel writes, "[The master's] truth is in reality the unessential consciousness and its unessential action" (*Phenomenology of Spirit*, 117). Alexandre Kojève famously expands this point to argue that the master's "truth" becomes the slave (and the slave's labor), such that, by the end of the master/slave dialectic, the master loses and the slave wins: "In the long run, all slavish work realizes not the Master's will, but the will—at first unconscious—of the Slave, who—finally—succeeds where the Master—necessarily—fails" (*Introduction to Hegel*, 30).

75. This narrative switch occurs mid-sentence. The narrator first refers unusually to Grigia as "Lene Maria Lenzi"—thereby insisting on the auctorial perspective—only to change abruptly to Homo's perspective: "the darkness all around was thick as a wall" and, in the next sentence, "with Grigia clutching his sleeve" (*FW* 39).

76. On the mineshaft as womb, see Magill, *Literarische Reisen*, 74, 77, 94; and Hermand, "Musils *Grigia*," 176. The return to the womb is further suggested by echoes of "Grigia's" opening mother-father-son triad. At the outset, Homo is the outsider in this triad because his wife and son leave on a trip without him. But when he enters the shaft in the end, he takes the position of the Oedipal son: winning the mother's (Grigia's) love at the expense of the excluded father (Grigia's husband). The other Musil texts to which I refer are *Der Mann ohne Eigenschaften*, where the incest narrative has been interpreted as a desire to "return to the womb," and *The Confusions of Young Törless*, where, at the end, the hero "inspects the quietly perfumed smell rising from the waist of his mother" (Henry and Mary Garland, "Mann ohne Eigenschaften," 556; Musil, *GW* 6:140).

77. Kerr, "Jagow, Flaubert, Pan," 222.

78. Müller's hero senses that he has experienced the lush heat of the tropics before, but only in dimmest memory: "Where, where had I gone through this tropical condition, this scene of will-less growth, where, where?"; later he refers to the tropics as that "great race [sex, *Geschlecht*] of primal nature, mother and whore at once," which eventually leads him to the "mystery of mothers." Finally, toward the end, when wandering into a deserted grotto, his fellow adventurer, Slim, claims to have discovered "The second womb! . . . When you miss the first one, you can still live here in the spare!" (*Tropen*, 15, 23, 24, 169).

79. Winterstein, "Zur Psychologie des Reisens," 502.

80. Jung, "Wandlungen und Symbole der Libido," 249.

81. Most critics stop here, debating whether this is an unhealthy and dangerous regression (Hermand, Bedwell, Reif, Aue, Eibl), a salutary "return to the archaic, to writing from the 'absorbed fantasy of the silent child'" (Kaiser and Wilkins), or an "ambivalent" approach toward the "other condition" (Magill). Hermand, "Musils *Grigia*," 179–80; Bedwell, "Musil's *Grigia*," 125; Reif, *Zivilisationsflucht und literarische Wunschräume*, 76; Aue, "Ablehnung romantischer Vorstellungen"; Eibl, "*Drei Frauen*," 114, 137, 145–46; Kaiser and Wilkins, *Robert Musil*, 108, 115; Magill, *Literarische Reisen*, 92–97.

82. Eibl, *"Drei Frauen,"* 114, 145–46, 137.

83. Eibl claims that the narrator's essayistic tone at the outset is a mouthpiece for Musil's own concepts of "theory and example" from *Skizze der Erkenntnis des Dichters* and that the narrator's general "intervening" (*eingreifen*) into the story is Musil's attempt to show that "the author"—not the narrator—"is *doing* something here" (Eibl's emphasis) (*"Drei Frauen,"* 104, 137, 138). Hermand commits the same error, claiming that, in *Grigia* and *Death in Venice*, both Musil and Mann (not their narrators) deliberately "dissociate themselves" from their protagonists' emotional excesses ("Musils *Grigia,"* 179-80).

84. Magill, *Literarische Reisen*, 92.

85. In "Skizze der Erkenntnis des Dichters" (1918) and "Ansätze zu neuer Ästhetik: Bemerkungen über eine Dramaturgie des Films" (1925), Musil argues that art, unlike science, has the goal of shedding light on the *"nicht-ratioïde"* (non-rational) world but that art must nonetheless, unlike mysticism, remain connected to the "normal condition" (*Normalzustand*) and *"das gewöhnliche Verhalten"* (Musil, *GW* 8:1028, 1154). Based on these two essays, Eibl's reading of *Grigia* assumes too smooth a transfer of authorial statements about literature into literature itself. Moreover, Eibl underestimates how Musil's creation of the *"nicht-ratioïde"* world of *Grigia* might have, however temporarily, weakened his ability to return unscathed to the *Normalzustand* (Eibl, *"Drei Frauen,"* 137). The "great danger" of fiction stems from Foucault, "What Is an Author?" 118.

86. The *"anderer Zustand"* (other condition) appears so often in Musil's work that he abbreviates it as "aZ." For one example of the relation of "aZ" to the apparent "crime" of "sibling love" in *The Man without Qualities*, see *Man without Qualities*, *GW* 5:1841. For the "last Mohicans of love" and for Ulrich and Agathe's planned erotic "journey to paradise," see *Man without Qualities*, *GW* 4:1094 and 5:1536.

87. Although *"Blutschande"* is initially used in this second sense already in 1833 in F. L. Jahn's *Merke zum Deutschen Volksthum*, Jahn's text is an outlier. This second sense only came into broader usage in the 1920s, beginning with the 1921 publication of the proto-Nazi brochure, *Eine unbewußte Blutschande—der Untergang Deutschlands: Naturgesetze über die Rassenlehre*, followed by *Mein Kampf* (1925/26) and Alfred Rosenberg's influential *Der Mythus des 20. Jahrhunderts* (1930). See Schmitz-Berning, *Vokabular des National-Sozialismus*, 118–20.

88. See Schmitz-Berning, *Vokabular des National-Sozialismus*, 607.

Epilogue

1. The quotations are from Maurice Blanchot ("the need to kill the Other") and Jean-François Lyotard ("terror"). Julia Kristeva similarly argues that anti-Semitism issues from a fear of the "abject": the "mark of maternal, feminine, or pagan substance" aligned with Jewishness (Blanchot, *Infinite Conversation*, 129; Lyotard, *Heidegger and "the jews,"* 21–22; Kristeva, *Powers of Horror*, 185, 186). Beyond post-structuralist philosophy, this same argument—that xenophobia stems from fears of difference—holds the day. Consider just a few prominent examples: the anthropologist Victor Turner argues that "structural differentiation, both vertical and horizontal, is the foundation of strife and factionalism, and of struggles in dyadic relations between incumbents of positions or rivals for positions." The novelist and sociologist Albert Memmi similarly claims that

racism is a fear of "differences" based on the primitive dread of everything "unknown." Christian Delacampagne, a cultural theorist, claims that racism is a "refusal of difference." The sociologist Joseph Gabel puts a fine point on it: "racism is essentially heterophobia" (Turner, *Ritual Process*, 179; Memmi, *Racisme*, 208; Delacampagne, *Figures de l'oppression*, 145; Gabel, "Racisme et alienation," 432). For a critical summary of some of these "heterophobia" theories, where "half-truths of common sense . . . become truths," see Taguieff, *Force of Prejudice*, 19–22, 50.

2. For a rare use of Freud's theory of the narcissism of minor differences during his lifetime, see Reik, "Über Differenzierung," in *Der eigene und der fremde Gott*, 238–56. Reik devotes two different chapters in this book to the "uncanny," but he never connects the uncanny to the narcissism of small differences.

3. René Girard, *Violence and the Sacred*, 161, 49, 51. Given Girard's focus on the threatening "double" (78–79, 159–66), it is striking that he never mentions Freud's "uncanny" or Lacan's "mirror stage." Perhaps Girard sensed an uncanny closeness, which would explain his strong reaction against both Freud (169–92) and Lacan (who "failed to discover" the theory of mimetic desire before Girard because Lacan was blinded by "his linguistic fetishism" [185]).

4. Bourdieu, *Distinction*, 479.

5. Bauman, *Modernity and the Holocaust*, 64–65.

6. Blok, "Narcissism of Minor Differences."

7. The lectures "L'Agressivité en psychanalyse" ("Aggressiveness in Psychoanalysis," 1948) and "Le stade du miroir comme formateur de la function du *Je*" ("The Mirror Stage as Formative of the *I* Function," 1949) were both first published in 1966, in *Écrits*; Lacan had already delivered an earlier, never-published version of the latter at the Fourteenth International Psychoanalytical Congress at Marienbad in 1936.

8. Lacan, "Mirror Stage," 79.

9. Lacan, "Aggressiveness in Psychoanalysis," 89, trans. rev.; "Agressivité en psychanalyse," 109 (emphasis in original). The major English translators differ on whether to translate "*étrangeté*" as "uncanny" (in the 2002 Bruce Fink translation cited here) or as "strange" (Alan Sheridan's 1977 rendering in *Écrits: A Selection*). Although the word "*étrangeté*" generally appears somewhere in French translations of the term "*unheimlich*" (following Bonaparte's original *L'Inquiétante étrangeté*), the possibilities of translating *unheimlich* into French are so varied—more so than in English—that French writers generally use the German word if they mean to refer to it, as Lacan does in his seminar on "Anxiety": "l'horrible, le louche, l'inquiétant, tout ce par quoi nous traduisons, comme nous pouvons, en français, le magistral *unheimlich* de l'allemand" (*Séminaire livre X*, 90).

10. Lacan, "Mirror Stage," 78 (fortified camp); "Agressivité en psychanalyse," 122 (l'"espace vital"); "Aggressiveness in Psychoanalysis," 100, trans. rev. Fink overtranslates Lacan's "l'espace vital" by inserting the German term: "Already in the *Lebensraum* ('living space') in which . . . ." Although I do not dispute that Lacan is referring also to Nazi *Lebensraum*, he deliberately does not include the German in his original, leaving open the lability, alive in the French term, between the psychological and the social-political meanings: between "personal space" and *Lebensraum*.

11. Lacan, "Aggressiveness in Psychoanalysis," 100; "Agressivité en psychanalyse," 123.

12. Lacan discusses Freud's "uncanny" only in his seminar on anxiety, where he gives the slightest nod toward a theory of uncanny violence, through the anxiogenic "*hôte*" (both "host" and "guest") who is "not the *Heimlich*" and has "already passed into the hostile" ("Cet hôte, c'est déjà ce qui était passé dans l'hostile") (*Séminaire livre X*, 91).

13. The rare Lacanian critic to discuss the uncanny—Mladen Dolar—focuses on "anxiety," not on aggression ("'I Shall Be with You,'" 13–15). Lacanian theorists of aggression, meanwhile, generally claim that it springs from the Other's radically different *jouissance*, not his uncanny similarity. This leads to theories of violence akin to the ones of Blanchot, Lyotard, and Kristeva cited above: extreme alterity, not *unheimlich* familiarity, produces violence. Žižek, for example, argues that our aggression is directed precisely *not* toward our "imaginary double/*semblant*" but rather toward "the Other," that "monstrous, impenetrable Thing" and "bearer of a monstrous Otherness" (Žižek, "Neighbors and Other Monsters," 162).

14. "NASA's Griffin: 'Humans Will Colonize the Solar System,'" *Washington Post*, September 25, 2005. For the importance of this fantasy in populist politics, see Newt Gingrich's speech during the 2012 Republican presidential primary, in which he advocates creating American colonies in space (Joel Aschenbach, "Newt Gingrich's Plan for a Moon Base: Is It Science Fiction?," *Washington Post*, January 26, 2012).

15. On the "slavish Malaysians," see Hesse, *SW* 13:254.

16. Besser, "Tropenkoller," 301. *Tropenkoller* was a widely used term in popular discourse, too, as evidenced by the publication of two novels about *Tropenkoller* (in 1894 and 1904, respectively). Although there were of course similar problems of sadistic violence in the English and French colonies, the term "*Tropenkoller*" only appears in German, suggesting a particularly German context. The closest English and French cognates—"tropical neurasthenia" and "*soudanité*"—refer only to the ill health of the traveler, not to his rage (Besser, "Tropenkoller," 307–8).

17. "Darkest fantasy" is Robert Young's term (*Colonial Desire*, 98).

18. Malinowski, *Diary*, 215 ("Tropenkoller"). For Malinowski's cursing and rage at the Melanesians—the examples of which are too numerous to list fully here—see *Diary*, 216, 250, 261, 279, as well as the scenes that I describe in the main text below.

19. Powdermaker, "Agreeable Man," 36 (in Malinowski's defense); Geertz, "Under the Mosquito Net," 12 (a criticism of Malinowski).

20. Young, *Malinowski*, 450.

21. Geertz, *Works and Lives*, 75 (Geertz reverses here his own critical take on the diaries from his 1967 "Under the Mosquito Net").

22. A slightly bastardized version of this Goethe text (see chap. 4, n. 46) was cited already in the 1894 German parlimentary debate about "Tropenkoller" (Besser, "Tropenkoller," 301); Kafka, "In der Strafkolonie," 204, 219.

23. Bhabha, *Location of Culture* ("Of Mimicry and Man"), 85–92.

24. On this "reverse mimicry," see Zilcosky, *Kafka's Travels*, 117–19.

25. Although science fiction arguably has its roots in Lucian's second-century *True History*, it only takes its modern form in the second half of the nineteenth

century, with Jules Verne's books about the moon and the depths of the sea. And it only becomes widely popular in the early twentieth century, culminating in the 1926 founding of *Amazing Stories*, the first magazine devoted solely to science fiction (then still called "scientifiction"). See Ashley, *Time Machines*.

26. "Ontopology" is Jacques Derrida's neologism from *Specters of Marx*. For the relation of "ontopology" to Aschenbach's Venice, and to Venice in general, see Helga Geyer-Ryan, "Venice and the Violence of Location," 146–49.

27. Hofmannsthal, "Wiener Brief [II]," 195.

28. "Tschusch" is a perjorative Austrian term for Slavs, which emerged in the second half of the nineteenth century. Its etymology is unclear, but it probably developed out of a similar-sounding Slavic term used by workers in the Balkan territories occupied by Austria-Hungary. The connection to colonial discourse is evident from the word's semantic flexibility: it refers to Slavs primarily, but also to "Oriental" people and, during the German colonial period, to black soldiers working for the Germans in German East Africa (in the slightly different form of "Tschausch") (*Österreichisches Wörterbuch*, 39th ed., s.v. "Tschusch"; *Deutsches Kolonial-Lexikon*, 3:552).

29. Given this uncomfortable familiarity of Austria and Germany's initial enemy in World War I, it is not surprising that the Austrians and Germans later attempted to make even the French and the British seem more foreign than they were. The Germans widely publicized their battles against colonial (East Indian and North African) troops, publicly displayed the black prisoners they took from the French, and collected these exotic prisoners in POW camps that served as "a *Völkerschau* without comparison!" for anthropologists. Theses POW camps mixed non-European prisoners with European ones, and the Europeans were also exoticized: "the French . . . came to occupy the same category as Algerians or Tatars" and were placed "in the same colonial position as Africans and Asians." The camps served to "shape a view of the European enemies as racial 'others,' " such that "the liberal view of Europeans as interrelated and physically indistinguishable was replaced by a nationalist perspective that defined peoples according to their racial characters" (Evans, "Anthropology at War," 199, 217, 229). This production of alterity repeated the initial anti-Slavic movement by attempting, again, to establish difference in a world in which the enemy seemed too uncannily similar: whether Europeanized Indians, Germanic Frenchmen, or Hannoverian Englishmen (whose leader was the Kaiser's own grandmother).

30. In this sense, I follow the claims of Reinhart Koselleck, who developed the study of *Begriffsgeschichte* ("history of concepts") in the 1970s. See Koselleck, *Begriffsgeschichten*.

31. Anneleen Masschelein claims that the uncanny didn't become an "actual" concept until the 1970s post-structuralist return to Freud (*Unconcept*, 4, 6), but this argument underplays the fact that, as mentioned in my introduction, several thinkers independently wrote about the uncanny between 1906 and 1927 (Jentsch, Rank, Otto, Freud, Reik, Heidegger), and that Edmund Bergler attempted already in 1934 to illustrate the value of "the uncanny" for psychoanalytic practice ("Psycho-Analysis of the Uncanny").

32. This introduction of passports in Europe after the outbreak of war was actually a reintroduction. Until the mid-nineteenth century, some form of passport was required for travel through most countries in Europe. Only the expansion of

rail travel and explosion of tourism created a breakdown of the passport system, leading France to eliminate them in 1861—after which most European countries followed suit.

33. On the "boom" (*Konjunktur*) in travel writing after the end of World War I, see Schütz, "Autobiographien und Reiseliteratur," 568. On the popularity of German-language exotic novels during and immediately after World War I—as representations of "faraway place[s]" to which one "could flee, at least in literature"—see Reif, *Zivilisationsflucht und literarische Wunschräume*, 56.

34. On this absolute "strangeness" of the barbarians for the Greeks, see Georg Simmel's "Exkurs über den Fremden" ("Excursus on the Stranger"), 770.

35. On the European Jewish ghettos as "internal colonies" that were eventually "de-colonis[ed]," see Krobb, "Reclaiming the Location," 42. Susannah Heschel similarly argues that debates surrounding Jewish emancipation in Germany constituted a "proto-colonialist enterprise" that anticipated later German colonial discourse ("Revolt of the Colonized," esp. 62–63). Jonathan Hess likewise points out various forms of "internal colonization" of Jews in Europe in *Germans, Jews*, 15, 27, 31, 43–48, 57, 87–89. Building on Heschel and on Bhabha's claim that lines between colonizers and colonized often blur, Riegert deepens the question by arguing that Jews are "agents" as well as "subjects" of empire ("Subjects and Agents of Empire").

36. On the non-Jewish Germans' jealousy of the Jews' success, see Aly, *Warum die Deutschen? Warum die Juden?*

37. For the dramatic increase in the use of this word during the Nazi period, see Google Ngram Viewer: "unheimliche." Although I briefly outline the likely reasons for this in this epilogue, this phenomenon suggests possibilities for future research.

38. Arendt, *Origins of Totalitarianism*, 65. As Arendt writes in the subsequent paragraph, educated Jews were more readily admitted into "fashionable circles" than were non-Jews of the same station but only at the price of self-exoticizing: they had "to indicate that they were Jews; under no circumstances were they allowed simply to disappear among their neighbors."

39. Arendt, *Origins of Totalitarianism*, 65, 68, 86 (Arendt incorrectly cites Bismarck as saying "German," not "gentile"). See also Pulzer, *Rise of Political Anti-Semitism*, 92.

40. Finkielkraut, *Imaginary Jew*, 70. Anton Blok likewise claims that "anti-Semitism in Germany intensified with the growing assimilation of Jews" and that the pogroms in Poland and Ukraine occurred only after Jewish emancipation. In a neglected article from thirty-five years ago, Patrick Girard insightfully connects this fear of similarity to the Freudian uncanny: "modern anti-Semitism was born not from the great difference between groups but rather from the threat of the absence of differences, the homogenization of Western society. . . . Racist passions reach a climax precisely when the psychobiological differences on which they depend no longer exist, having been belied by the facts or reduced to what Freud designates by the term *unheimlich*" (Blok, "Narcissism of Minor Differences," 46, 47; Girard, "Historical Foundations of Anti-Semitism," 71).

41. Simmel, "Exkurs über den Fremden," 770. On the connection of Jewishness to both Simmel's "stranger" and Freud's "uncanny," see Wohlfarth, "'Männer aus der Fremde,'" 20–23.

42. See Bauman, *Modernity and the Holocaust*, 57.

43. Finkielkraut, *Imaginary Jew*, 83 ("Science was charged with succeeding where the gaze had failed, asked to make sure that the adversary remained foreign"). See also Bauman, who argues that "differences now had to be created" and that post-assimilation modern Europe suddenly "needed a theory of ascription to redeem boundary-drawing and boundary-guarding concerns under new conditions which made boundary-crossing easier than ever before" (*Modernity and the Holocaust*, 58, 62).

44. Dühring, *Judenfrage*, 3–4.

45. Drumont, *France juive*, 41. Drumont's book appeared in that same year (1886) in German translation (as *Das verjudete Frankreich*) and immediately became a popular success.

46. See Paul Laurence Rose, who writes, "For nineteenth-century Germans, so unsure of their own 'Germanness,' the Jewish Question was ultimately the German Question. It was, in effect, another way of asking 'What is German': and receiving the satisfying answer—'whatever is not Jewish'" (*German Question/Jewish Question*, 41). See also Patrick Girard, who writes of Drumont's fear of the non-"obvious" Jew: "One finds similar ideas in Germany, where Jews in ritual curls and caftans were less scorned . . . than their coreligionists, the German patriots of Jewish persuasion who imitated their Christian countrymen" ("Historical Foundations of Anti-Semitism," 71).

47. Hitler, *Mein Kampf*, 56, 55.

48. Susan Shapiro discusses this German fear of "jewification," which is seen as "contagion" ("Uncanny Jew," 65).

49. See Bauman, *Modernity and the Holocaust*, 60 (on identity void).

50. Most historians agree on a significant continuity between the anti-Semitism of the Second Reich (1871–1918) and of the Nazi period. Shulamit Volkov has argued against this continuity, albeit unconvincingly, claiming that the Nazi emphasis on the spoken word produced a different kind of anti-Semitism ("Written and Spoken Word," 33–53).

51. The historian David Welch writes, "the constant analogy with rats and parasites suggested that the Jew differed from the Aryan not only in body but, more significantly, in soul, for the Jew had no soul." By depicting the Jews as "not human beings but pests which had to be exterminated," the Nazis provided the "emotional basis" for the Final Solution and "prepare[d] people for the future treatment of Jews in Germany and in the occupied territory." Welch gains an unlikely ally in Slavoj Žižek, who similarly claims that the "anti-Semitic image" successfully provokes "rage" in the "perpetrators of pogroms" (Welch, *Third Reich*, 80, 81, 82; Žižek, *Violence*, 57).

52. Höppler, *Der ewige Jude*.

53. Hitler, *Mein Kampf*, 59, 60.

54. "Gerade der assimilierte Jude ist der wahre Feind" (Schmitt, *Glossarium*, 18 [September 25, 1947]).

55. As noted in the Grimms' *German Dictionary*, the word "heimlich" develops in such a way that it eventually "obtains the meaning that 'unheimlich' . . . normally has" (*Deutsches Wörterbuch* vol. 10, column 879, http://woerterbuchnetz .de/DWB/). On the similar development of "Blutschande" in the 1920s, see Schmitz-Berning, *Vokabular des National-Sozialismus*, 118–20.

56. Encyclopedias and dictionaries of the Nazi period oddly ignored the second, racist meaning, even though these same works were rife with similar National Socialist terms—*Blut und Boden, Blutreinheit, Rassenschande* (*Blutschande*'s near-synonym)—and with references to the 1935 Nuremberg racial laws. See "Blutschande" in the major Nazi-era encyclopedia, the 8th edition of *Meyers Lexikon* (1936–42), 1:1487; and "Blut" (where "Blutschande" is a subset) in the first, 1939 volume (A–B) of the largest dictionary project of the Nazi period, *Trübners Deutsches Wörterbuch*, 1:377. For a historical overview of the other terms, see "Blut und Boden," "Blutreinheit," and "Rassenschande" in Schmitz-Berning, *Vokabular des National-Sozialismus*. Only retroactively, after World War II, did the definition of *Blutschande* as "race defilement" appear in German dictionaries and encyclopedias—marked specifically as "National Socialist usage."

57. Hitler, *Mein Kampf*, 135.

58. On the structural connectedness of "heterophobia" and "heterophilia" in racial discourse, see Taguieff, *Force of Prejudice*, 19–30.

59. For additions to this list, such as Albrecht Schaeffer's "Das Gitter" (1923) and Fritz von Unruh's *Ein Geschlecht* (1917), see Marcuse, "Inzest ('Blutschande')," 302.

60. Braun, "*Blutschande*," 138, 137, 139. Braun's claim that "the Jewish authors . . . developed no affinity for the theme of brother-sister love, which only made it all the more popular among the anti-Semites" oversimplifies matters in three ways (138). First, her too-clear division of "Jewish" and non-Jewish assumes that German-Jewish authors considered themselves, in matters of incest, to be "Jewish"—even though, in many other matters, they identified primarily as "German." Second, her connection of incest themes to anti-Semitism forces her to underestimate the topic's popularity among staunchly anti-Nazi non-Jewish Germans (e.g., Schaeffer, Frank) and among German-speaking Jews. (Freud resuscitated the myth of Oedipus's incest; Münzer created an incest story in *The Road to Zion*; and Kafka played with incestuous desire in *The Metamorphosis*. And where do we place Hofmannsthal, with his partial Jewish background and his incest story in *Andreas*?) Finally, Braun's insistence that incest is a "Christian" mythology neglects the fact that some Kabbalistic teachings found incest explicitly "pleasing to God" (Braun, "*Blutschande*," 145-46; Marcuse, "Inzest ['Blutschande']," 302).

61. For an overview of this debate, see Anderson, " 'Jewish' Mimesis," 193.

62. For just one prominent example, see Heilbut, *Mann: Eros and Literature*, 191.

63. As René Girard notes, the "brother" is often transformed into the other—the "enemy brother"—and then attacked, as in the stories of Cain and Abel, Jacob and Esau, Romulus and Remus (*Violence and the Sacred*, 61). Max Marcuse specifically connects this enemy brother ("feindlichen Bruder") to the "incest conflict" in "Inzest ('Blutschande')," 302.

64. Arendt, *Origins of Totalitarianism*, 86–87. Arendt employs the "scapegoat theory" here, even though she had criticized it earlier in the same book (5–7).

65. Christina von Braun likewise relates the double meaning of "*verschieden*" to *Blutschande*, but to make a different point: that the death of the real Jew makes "the imaginary figure, 'the Jew,' come to life" ("*Blutschande*," 144).

66. On the German Jew of the interwar period as a precursor to today's "sleeper," see Braun, "'Sleeper,'" 181–83.

67. See Jean Baudrillard's remarks on 9/11: "It is that superpower which, by its unbearable power, has fomented all this violence which is endemic throughout the world, and hence that (unwittingly) terroristic imagination which dwells in all of us. The fact that we have dreamt of this event, that everyone without exception has dreamt of it—because no one can avoid dreaming of the destruction of any power that has become hegemonic to this degree—is unacceptable to the Western moral conscience. Yet it is a fact, and one which can indeed be measured by the emotive violence of all that has been said and written in the effort to dispel it. At a pinch, we can say that they *did it*, but we *wished for* it" (*Spirit of Terrorism*, 5; emphasis in original).

68. See Borchgrevink, *Norwegian Tragedy*, 253.

Abraham, Karl. "Erstes Korreferat." In *Zur Psychoanalyse der Kriegsneurosen*, edited by Sigmund Freud, Karl Abraham, Ernest Jones, and Ernst Simmel, 31–41. Leipzig: Internationaler Psychoanalytischer Verlag, 1919.

Alewyn, Richard. "Andreas und die 'wunderbare Freundin': Zur Fortsetzung von Hofmannsthals Roman-Fragment und ihrer psychiatrischen Quelle." *Euphorion* 49 (1955): 446–82.

Alloula, Malek. *The Colonial Harem*. Translated by Myrna Godzich and Wlad Godzich. Minneapolis: University of Minnesota Press, 1986.

Altenberg, Peter. *Ashantee*. Berlin: S. Fischer, 1897.

Aly, Götz. *Warum die Deutschen? Warum die Juden? Gleichheit, Neid und Rassenhass 1800—1933*. Frankfurt am Main: S. Fischer, 2011.

Ames, Eric. *Carl Hagenbeck's Empire of Entertainments*. Seattle: University of Washington Press, 2009.

Anderson, Mark M. "'Jewish' Mimesis: Imitation and Assimiliation in Thomas Mann's 'Wälsungenblut' and Ludwig Jacobowski's *Werther, der Jude*." *German Life and Letters* 49, no. 2 (1996): 193–204.

Anzieu, Didier. *Freud's Self-Analysis*. Translated by Peter Graham. London: Hogarth, 1986. First published 1959 (as *L'auto-analyse de Sigmund Freud*).

Arata, Stephen D. "The Occidental Tourist: *Dracula* and the Anxiety of Reverse Colonization." *Victorian Studies* 33, no. 4 (Summer 1990): 621–45.

Arendt, Hannah. *The Origins of Totalitarianism*. New York: Harcourt, 1968.

Arenz, Bärbel, and Gisela Lipsky, eds. *Mit Kompass und Korsett: Reisende Entdeckerinnen*. Cadolzburg: Ars Vivendi, 2009.

Arntzen, Helmut. *Musil-Kommentar: Sämtlicher zu Lebzeiten erschienener Schriften außer dem Roman "Der Mann ohne Eigenschaften."* Munich: Winkler, 1980.

Ashcroft, Bill, Gareth Griffiths, and Helen Tiffin, eds. *The Post-Colonial Studies Reader*. London: Routledge, 1995.

Ashley, Mike. *The Time Machines: The Story of the Science-Fiction Pulp Magazines from the Beginning to 1950*. Liverpool: University of Liverpool Press, 2000.

Aue, Maximilian. "Die Ablehnung romantischer Vorstellungen von Liebe, Natur und Tod in Musils *Drei Frauen*." *Modern Austrian Literature* 9, no. 3/4 (1976): 240–56.

Badenberg, Nana. "Zwischen Kairo und Alt-Berlin: Sommer 1896: Die deutschen Kolonien als Ware und Werbung auf der Gewerbe-Ausstellung in Treptow." In Honold and Scherpe, *Mit Deutschland um die Welt*, 190–99.

Ball, Hugo. *Hermann Hesse: Sein Leben und sein Werk*. Frankfurt am Main: Suhrkamp, 1977.

Barrell, John. *English Literature in History 1730–80: An Equal, Wide Survey.* London: Hutchinson, 1983.

Bartnaes, Morton. "Freud's 'The Uncanny' and Deconstructive Criticism: Intellectual Uncertainty and Delicacy of Perception." *Psychoanalysis and History* 12, no. 1 (2010): 29–53.

Baudrillard, Jean. *The Spirit of Terrorism.* Translated by Chris Turner. New York: Verso, 2003.

Bauer-Wabnegg, Walter. *Zirkus und Artisten in Franz Kafkas Werk: Ein Beitrag über Körper und Literatur im Zeitalter der Technik.* Erlangen: Palm & Enke, 1986.

Bauman, Zygmunt. *Modernity and the Holocaust.* Cambridge, Eng.: Polity, 1989.

Bayer, Maximilian. *Im Kampfe gegen die Hereros: Bilder aus dem Feldzug in Südwest.* Edited by Nicolaus Henningsen. Cologne: Schaffstein, 1911.

Bedwell, Carol C. "Musil's *Grigia*: An Analysis of Cultural Dissolution." *Seminar* 3, no. 2 (1967): 117–26.

Behdad, Ali. *Belated Travelers: Orientalism in the Age of Colonial Dissolution.* Durham, N.C.: Duke University Press, 1994.

Below, Jürgen. *Hermann Hesse Bibliographie: Sekundärliteratur 1899–2007.* Berlin: de Gruyter, 2007.

Benjamin, Walter. *Kritiken und Rezensionen.* Vol. 3 of *Gesammelte Schriften,* edited by Hella Tiedemann. Frankfurt am Main: Suhrkamp, 1972.

Berger, Ursula, and Christiane Wanken, eds. *Wilde Welten: Aneignung des Fremden in der Moderne.* Berlin: Georg-Kolbe-Museum, 2010.

Bergler, Edmund. "The Psycho-Analysis of the Uncanny." *International Journal of Psychoanalysis* 15 (1934): 215–44.

Berman, Russell A. "German Colonialism: Another *Sonderweg?*" *European Studies Journal,* special issue: "German Colonialism: Another Sonderweg?" 16 (Fall 1999): 25–36.

———. "History and Community in *Death in Venice.*" In Ritter, *Death in Venice,* 263–80.

———. "Written Right Across Their Faces: Leni Riefenstahl, Ernst Jünger, and Fascist Modernism." Chap. 6 in *Modern Culture and Critical Theory: Art, Politics, and the Legacy of the Frankfurt School.* Madison: University of Wisconsin Press, 1989.

Bernheimer, Charles. Introduction to Bernheimer and Kahane, *In Dora's Case.*

Bernmeiner, Charles, and Claire Kahane, eds. *In Dora's Case: Freud—Hysteria—Feminism.* New York: Columbia University Press, 1985.

Besser, Stephan. "Schauspiel der Scham: Juli 1896: Peter Altenberg gesellt sich im Wiener Tiergarten zu den Aschanti." In Honold and Scherpe, *Mit Deutschland um die Welt,* 200–208.

———. "Tropenkoller." In Honold and Scherpe, *Mit Deutschland um die Welt,* 300–309.

Bhabha, Homi K. *The Location of Culture.* New York: Routledge, 1994. See esp. "Of Mimicry and Man," "The Other Question," and "DissemiNation: Time, Narrative and the Margins of the Modern Nation."

———. "The World and the Home." *Social Text* 31/32 (1992): 141–53.

Bierman, John. *Dark Safari: The Life Behind the Legend of Henry Morton Stanley.* London: Hodder and Stoughton, 1990.

Blanchot, Maurice. *The Infinite Conversation.* Translated by Susan Hanson. Minneapolis: University of Minnesota Press, 1993.

Blok, Anton. "The Narcissism of Minor Differences." *European Journal of Social Theory* 1, no. 1 (July 1998): 33–56.

Bloom, Harold. "The Internalization of Quest-Romance." In *Romanticism and Consciousness: Essays in Criticism,* edited by Harold Bloom, 3–24. New York: Norton, 1970.

———. "Reading Freud: Transference, Taboo, and Truth." In *Centre and Labyrinth: Essays in Honour of Northrop Frye,* edited by Eleanor Cook et al., 309–28. Toronto: University of Toronto Press, 1993.

Boehringer, Michael. "Fantasies of White Masculinity in Arthur Schnitzler's *Andreas Thameyers letzter Brief* (1900)." *The German Quarterly* 84, no. 1 (Winter 2011): 80–96.

Bogdal, Klaus-Michael. "Kunst, Kunstwerk." In vol. 4 of *Historisches Wörterbuch der Philosophie,* edited by Joachim Ritter, Karlfried Gründer, and Gottfried Gabriel, 1410–12. Darmstadt: Wissenschaftliche Buchgesselschaft, 1976.

Bongie, Chris. *Exotic Memories: Literature, Colonialism and the Fin de siècle.* Stanford, Calif.: Stanford University Press, 1991.

Bonsels, Rose-Marie, ed. *Waldemar Bonsels im Spiegel der Kritik.* Wiesbaden: Otto Harrassowitz Verlag, 1986.

Bonsels, Waldemar. *Indienfahrt* (1916). In vol. 3 of *Wanderschaft zwischen Staub und Sternen: Gesamtwerk,* edited by Rose-Marie Bonsels, 5–217. Munich: Langen Müller, 1980.

Borchgrevink, Aage. *A Norwegian Tragedy: Anders Behring Breivik and the Massacre on Utøya.* Cambridge, Eng.: Polity, 2013.

Born, Jürgen. *Kafkas Bibliothek.* Frankfurt am Main: S. Fischer, 1990.

Böttger, Fritz. *Hermann Hesse: Leben, Werk, Zeit.* Berlin: Verlag der Nation, 1974.

Boulby, Mark. *Hermann Hesse: His Mind and Art.* Ithaca, N.Y.: Cornell University Press, 1967.

Bourdieu, Pierre. *Distinction: A Social Critique of the Judgement of Taste.* Translated by Richard Nice. London: Routledge, 1984. First published 1979 (as *La distinction: Critique sociale du jugement*).

Boyarin, Daniel. "What Does a Jew Want?; or, The Political Meaning of the Phallus." In *The Psychoanalysis of Race,* edited by Christopher Lane, 211–40. New York: Columbia University Press, 1998.

Bramen, Carrie. "The Urban Picturesque and the Spectacle of Americanization." *American Quarterly* 52, no. 3 (September 2000): 444–77.

Braun, Christina von. "*Blutschande*: From the Incest Taboo to the Nuremberg Racial Laws." In *Encountering the Other(s),* edited by Gisela Brinkler-Gabler, 127–48. Albany: State University of New York Press, 1995.

———. "'Sleeper': Der Körper des Fremden." In *Die Machbarkeit der Welt: Wie der Mensch sich selbst als Subjekt der Geschichte entdeckt,* edited by Mihran Dabag and Kristin Platt, 172–85. Munich: Fink, 2006.

Brenner, Peter J. *Der Reisebericht in der deutschen Literatur: Ein Forschungsüberblick als Vorstudie zu einer Gattungsgeschichte.* Tübingen: Niemeyer, 1990.

Brickman, Celia. *Aboriginal Populations in the Mind: Race and Primitivity in Psychoanalysis.* New York: Columbia University Press, 2003.

Brod, Max. "Reise Lugano—Mailand—Paris" (1911). In Brod and Kafka, *Reiseaufzeichnungen*, 73–142.

Brod, Max, and Franz Kafka. *Reiseaufzeichnungen*. Vol. 1 of *Eine Freundschaft*, edited by Malcolm Pasley. Frankfurt am Main: S. Fischer, 1987.

Brooks, Peter. "Gauguin's Tahitian Body." *The Yale Journal of Criticism* 3, no. 2 (1990): 51–90.

Brückner, Peter. *Freuds Privatlektüre*. Cologne: Rolf Horst, 1975.

Bruckner, Sierra A. "Spectacle of (Human) Nature: Commercial Ethnography between Leisure, Learning, and *Schaulust*." In Penny and Bunzl, *Worldly Provincialism*, 127–55.

Castle, Terry. *The Female Thermometer: Eighteenth-Century Culture and the Invention of the Uncanny*. Oxford: Oxford University Press, 1995.

Chinitz, David. *T. S. Eliot and the Cultural Divide*. Chicago: University of Chicago Press, 2003.

Cixous, Hélène. "Fiction and Its Phantoms: A Reading of Freud's *Das Unheimliche* (*The Uncanny*)." [1972]. *New Literary History* 7, no. 3 (Spring 1976): 525–48.

Clifford, James. "On Ethnographic Self-Fashioning: Conrad and Malinowski." In *Reconstructing Individualism*, edited by Thomas C. Heller, Morton Sonsa, and David E. Wellbery, 140–62. Stanford, Calif.: Stanford University Press, 1986.

———. *Routes: Travel and Translation in the Late Twentieth Century*. Cambridge, Mass.: Harvard University Press, 1997.

Cohn, Dorrit. "The Second Author of *Death in Venice*." In Mann, *Death in Venice*, edited by Clayton Koelb, 178–95.

———. *Transparent Minds: Narrative Modes for Presenting Consciousness in Fiction*. Princeton, N.J.: Princeton University Press, 1978.

Connolly, Angela. "Psychoanalytic Theory in Times of Terror." *Journal of Analytical Psychology* 48, no. 4 (September 2003): 407–31.

Conrad, Joseph. *Heart of Darkness*. New York: Norton, 1988.

Culler, Jonathan. *Framing the Sign: Criticism and Its Institutions*. Oxford: Basil Blackwell, 1988.

Czarnecka, Miroslawa, Grazyna Barbara Szewczyk, and Christa Ebert, eds. *Der weibliche Blick auf den Orient: Reisebeschreibungen europäischer Frauen im Vergleich*. Bern: Peter Lang, 2011.

Dauthendey, Max. *Raubmenschen*. Munich: A. Langen, 1924. First published 1911.

Davies, J. Keith, and Gerhard Fichtner, eds. *Freud's Library: A Comprehensive Catalogue/Freuds Bibliothek: Vollständiger Katalog*. Tübingen: edition diskord, 2006.

Dawson, Lorne. "Otto and Freud on the Uncanny and Beyond." *Journal of the American Academy of Religion* 57, no. 2 (Summer 1989): 283–311.

Deane, Bradley. "Imperial Barbarians: Primitive Masculinity in Lost World Fiction." *Victorian Literature and Culture* 36, no. 1 (March 2008): 205–25.

Delacampagne, Christian. *Figures de l'oppression*. Paris: Presses Universitaires de France, 1977.

Deleuze, Gilles, and Félix Guattari. *Anti-Oedipus: Capitalism and Schizophrenia*. Minneapolis: University of Minnesota Press, 1983.

Demhardt, Imre Josef. *Die Entschleierung Afrikas: Deutsche Kartenbeiträge von August Petermann bis zum Kolonialkartographischen Institut*. Gotha: Klett-Perthes, 2000.

————. "Kolonialkartographie." In König, *Vermessen,* 60–65.

Derrida, Jacques. "The Double Session." In *Dissemination,* translated by Barbara Johnson, 187–236. New York: Continuum, 2004. First published 1970 (as "La double séance").

————. *Of Grammatology.* Translated by Gayatri Chakravorty Spivak. Baltimore: Johns Hopkins University Press, 1997.

————. "The Purveyor of Truth." *Yale French Studies* 52 (1975): 31–113.

————. *Specters of Marx: The State of Debt, the Work of Mourning, and the New International.* New York: Routledge, 1994.

Deutsches Kolonial-Lexikon. Ed. Heinrich Schnee. 3 vols. Leipzig: Quelle & Meyer, 1920.

Deutschland und seine Kolonien im Jahre 1896: Amtlicher Bericht über die erste Deutsche Kolonial-Ausstellung. Ed. Arbeitsausschuß der Deutschen Kolonial-Ausstellung. Berlin: Reimer, 1897.

Dolar, Mladen. "'I Shall Be with You on Your Wedding Night': Lacan and the Uncanny." *October* 58 (Autumn 1991): 5–23.

Drumont, Edouard. *La France juive: Essai d'histoire contemporaine.* Paris: Flammarion, 1886.

Dühring, Eugen. *Die Judenfrage als Racen-, Sitten- und Culturfrage: Mit einer weltgeschichtlichen Antwort.* Karlsruhe: H. Reuter, 1881.

Eibl, Karl. *Robert Musil: "Drei Frauen": Text, Materialien, Kommentar.* Munich: Hanser, 1978.

Elbert, Monika. "Malinowski's Reading List: *Tess* as Field Guide to Woman." *Colby Quarterly* 35, no. 1 (March 1999): 49–67.

Eliot, T. S. "Tradition and the Individual Talent" (1919). In *The Sacred Wood: Essays on Poetry and Criticism,* 42–54. London: Methuen, 1969.

Ellison, David. *Ethics and Aesthetics in European Modernist Literature: From the Sublime to the Uncanny.* Cambridge, Eng.: Cambridge University Press, 2001.

Elsaghe, Yahya. *Die imaginäre Nation: Thomas Mann und das "Deutsche."* Munich: W. Fink, 2000.

Enzensberger, Hans Magnus. "Eine Theorie des Tourismus." In *Einzelheiten I: Bewusstseins-Industrie,* 147–68. Frankfurt am Main: Suhrkamp, 1964.

Essner, Cornelia. "'Wo Rauch ist, da ist auch Feuer': Zu den Ansätzen eines Rassenrechts für die deutschen Kolonien." In *Rassendiskriminierung, Kolonialpolitik und ethnisch-nationale Identität,* edited by Wilfried Wagner and Ulrich van der Heyden, 145–60. Münster: LIT Verlag, 1992.

Etherington, Norman. *Rider Haggard.* Boston: Twayne, 1984.

————. "Rider Haggard, Imperialism, and the Layered Personality." *Victorian Studies* 22, no. 1 (1978): 71–87.

Ettlinger, L. D. "German Expressionism and Primitive Art." *The Burlington Magazine* 110, no. 781 (April 1968): 191–201.

Evans, Andrew D. "Anthropology at War: Racial Studies of POWs during World War I." In Penny and Bunzl, *Worldly Provincialism,* 198–229.

Ewers, Hanns Heinz. *Indien und Ich.* Munich: Georg Müller, 1919. First published 1911.

Fabian, Johannes. *Time and the Other: How Anthropology Makes Its Object.* New York: Columbia University Press, 1983.

Feifer, Maxine. *Going Places.* London: Macmillan, 1985.

Finkielkraut, Alain. *The Imaginary Jew*. Translated by Kevin O'Neill and David Suchoff. Lincoln: University of Nebraska Press, 1994. First published 1980 (as *Le Juif imaginaire*).

Fischer-Homberger, Esther. *Die traumatische Neurose: Vom somatischen zum sozialen Leiden*. Giessen: Psychosozial-Verlag, 2004.

Foster, Ian. "Altenberg's African Spectacle: *Ashantee* in Context." In *Theatre and Performance in Austria: From Mozart to Jelinek*, edited by Ritchie Robertson and Edward Timms, 43–44. Edinburgh: University of Edinburgh Press, 1993.

———. "Peter Altenberg und das Fremde." In *Reisen im Diskurs: Modelle der literarischen Fremderfahrung von den Pilgerberichten bis zur Postmoderne*, edited by Anne Fuchs, Theo Harden, and Eva Juhl, 333–42. Heidelberg: Carl Winter, 1995.

Foster, John Burt Jr. "Why Is Tadzio Polish? *Kultur* and Cultural Multiplicity in *Death in Venice*." In Ritter, *Death in Venice*, 192–210.

Foucault, Michel. "What Is an Author?" In *The Foucault Reader*, edited by Paul Rabinow and translated by Josué V. Harari, 101–20. New York: Pantheon, 1984.

Franceschini, Robert. "Das Aschanti-Fieber." *Neues Wiener Tagblatt*. October 7, 1896.

Frank, Andre Gunder. *ReOrient: Global Economy in the Asian Age*. Berkeley: University of California Press, 1998.

Freedman, Ralph. *Hermann Hesse: Autor der Krisis*. Frankfurt am Main: Suhrkamp, 1991.

Frenssen, Gustav. *Peter Moors Fahrt nach Südwest: Ein Feldzugsbericht*. Berlin: Grote, 1919. First published 1906.

Freud, Sigmund. "Analysis of a Phobia in a Five-Year-Old Boy" ("Analyse der Phobie eines fünfjährigen Knaben") (1909). In *Standard Edition* 10:1–150/ *Gesammelte Werke* 7:243–377.

———. *Beyond the Pleasure Principle* (*Jenseits des Lustprinzips*) (1920). In *Standard Edition* 18:1–64/*Gesammelte Werke* 13:3–69.

———. *Briefe, 1873–1939*. Edited by Ernst Freud and Lucie Freud. Frankfurt am Main: S. Fischer, 1960.

———. *Briefe an Wilhelm Fliess, 1874–1904*. Edited by Jeffrey Moussaieff Masson. Frankfurt am Main: S. Fischer, 1986.

———. "The Claims of Psycho-Analysis to Scientific Interest" ("Das Interesse an der Psychoanalyse") (1913). In *Standard Edition* 13:163–90/*Gesammelte Werke* 8:390–420.

———. *The Complete Letters of Sigmund Freud to Wilhelm Fliess, 1887–1904*. Edited and translated by Jeffrey Moussaieff Masson. Cambridge, Mass.: Harvard University Press, 1985.

———. *The Correspondence of Sigmund Freud and Sándor Ferenczi*. Edited by E. Brabant, E. Falzeder, and P. Giampieri-Deutsch. 3 vols. Cambridge, Mass.: Harvard University Press, 1996.

———. *The Future of an Illusion* (*Die Zukunft einer Illusion*) (1927). In *Standard Edition* 21:1–56/*Gesammelte Werke* 14:325–80.

———. *Gesammelte Werke: Chronologisch geordnet*. Edited by Anna Freud et al. 19 vols. London: Imago, 1940–87.

———. *The Interpretation of Dreams* (*Die Traumdeutung*) (1900). In *Standard Edition*, vols. 4 and 5/*Gesammelte Werke*, vols. 2 and 3.

———. Introduction to *Psychoanalysis and the War Neuroses* (*Einleitung zu Zur Psychoanalyse der Kriegsneurosen*) (1919). In *Standard Edition* 17:205–10/ *Gesammelte Werke* 12:321–24.

———. *Introductory Lectures on Psycho-Analysis (Parts I and II)* (*Vorlesungen zur Einführung in die Psychoanalyse*) (1915–16). *Standard Edition*, vol. 15/ *Gesammelte Werke*, vol. 11.

———. *Letters of Sigmund Freud, 1873–1939*. Edited by Ernst Freud, translated by Tania and James Stern. London: Hogarth, 1970.

———. "Memorandum on the Electrical Treatment of War Neurotics" ("Gutachten über die elektrische Behandlung der Kriegsneurotiker") (1920). In *Standard Edition* 17:211–16/*Gesammelte Werke* Nachtragsband: 704–10.

———. *New Introductory Lectures on Psycho-Analysis* (*Neue Folge der Vorlesungen zur Einführung in die Psychoanalyse*) (1933). In *Standard Edition* 22:1–182/*Gesammelte Werke* 15:iv–206.

———. "Notes upon a Case of Obsessional Neurosis" ("Bemerkungen über einen Fall von Zwangsneurose") (1909). In *Standard Edition* 10:153–318/ *Gesammelte Werke* 7:381–463.

———. "The Question of Lay Analysis" ("Die Frage der Laienanalyse") (1926). In *Standard Edition* 20:177–258/*Gesammelte Werke* 14:209–86.

———. "Recommendations to Physicians Practicing Psycho-Analysis" ("Ratschläge für den Arzt bei der psychoanalytischen Behandlung") (1912). In *Standard Edition* 12:109–20/*Gesammelte Werke* 8:376–87.

———. *The Standard Edition of the Complete Psychological Works of Sigmund Freud*. Edited and translated by James Strachey. 24 vols. London: Hogarth Press and the Institute of Psycho-analysis, 1953–74.

———. *Tagebuch 1929–1939: Kürzeste Chronik*. Edited by Michael Molnar. Frankfurt am Main: Stroemfeld, 1996.

———. "Thoughts for the Times on War and Death" ("Zeitgemässes über Krieg und Tod") (1915). In *Standard Edition* 14:273–300/*Gesammelte Werke* 10:323–55.

———. *Totem and Taboo: Some Points of Agreement between the Mental Lives of Savages and Neurotics* (*Totem und Tabu: Einige Übereinstimmungen im Seelenleben der Wilden und der Neurotiker*) (1912–13). In *Standard Edition* 13:ix–162/*Gesammelte Werke* 9:1–205.

———. *The Uncanny* (*Das Unheimliche*) (1919). In *Standard Edition* 17:217–52/*Gesammelte Werke* 12:227–68.

———. "The Unconscious" ("Das Unbewußte") (1915). In *Standard Edition* 14:159–215/*Gesammelte Werke* 10:264–303.

Gabel, Joseph. "Racisme et alienation." In *Praxis International* 2, no. 4 (January 1983): 432.

Gallaher, Carolyn et al., eds. *Key Concepts in Political Geography*. Los Angeles: Sage, 2009.

Gallo, Rubén. *Freud's Mexico: Into the Wilds of Psychoanalysis*. Cambridge, Mass.: MIT Press, 2010.

Ganeshan, Vridhagiri. Afterword to *Indienfahrt*, by Waldemar Bonsels. Zürich: Manesse Verlag, 1989.

Garland, Henry and Mary. "Der Mann ohne Eigenschaften." In *The Oxford Companion to German Literature*, edited by H. and M. Garland. 3rd edition, 556. Oxford: Oxford University Press, 1997.

Gauguin, Paul. *Noa Noa*. San Francisco: Chronicle Books, 2005.

Gay, Peter. *Freud: A Life for Our Time*. New York: Norton, 1988.

Geertz, Clifford. "Under the Mosquito Net." *New York Review of Books*, September 14, 1967.

———. *Works and Lives: The Anthropologist as Author*. Cambridge, Eng.: Polity, 1988.

Gendron, Bernard. *Between Montmartre and the Mudd Club: Popular Music and the Avant-Garde*. Chicago: Chicago University Press, 2002.

Geyer-Ryan, Helga. "Venice and the Violence of Location." In *The Practice of Cultural Analysis: Exposing Interdisciplinary Interpretation*, edited by Mieke Bal, 143–50. Stanford, Calif.: Stanford University Press, 1999.

Gilbert, Sandra, and Susan Gubar. *Sexchanges*. Vol. 2 of *No Man's Land: The Place of the Woman Writer in the Twentieth Century*. New Haven, Conn.: Yale University Press, 1989.

Gilman, Sander L. *The Case of Sigmund Freud: Medicine and Identity at the Fin de Siècle*. Baltimore, Md.: Johns Hopkins University Press, 1993.

———. *Difference and Pathology: Stereotypes of Sexuality, Race, and Madness*. Ithaca, N.Y.: Cornell University Press, 1985.

———. *Freud, Race, and Gender*. Princeton, N.J.: Princeton University Press, 1993.

———. *Inscribing the Other*. Lincoln: University of Nebraska Press, 1991.

———. *Jewish Self-Hatred: Anti-Semitism and the Hidden Language of the Jews*. Baltimore: Johns Hopkins University Press, 1986.

Gilman, Sander L., et al., eds. *Reading Freud's Reading*. New York: New York University Press, 1994.

Girard, Patrick. "Historical Foundations of Anti-Semitism." In *Survivors, Victims, and Perpetrators: Essays on the Nazi Holocaust*, edited by Joel E. Dimsdale, 55–77. New York: Hemisphere, 1980.

Girard, René. *Violence and the Sacred*. Translated by Patrick Gregory. Baltimore, Md.: Johns Hopkins University Press, 1979. First published 1972 (as *La Violence et le sacré*).

Glazebrook, Philip. *Journey to Kars*. Harmondsworth, Eng.: Penguin, 1985.

Goethe, Johann Wolfgang von. *Die Wahlverwandtschaften*. In *Epoche der Wahlverwandtschaften 1807–1814*, vol. 9 of *Sämtliche Werke nach Epochen seines Schaffens*, edited by Christoph Siegrist et al., 283–530. Munich: Hanser, 1987.

Gosetti-Ferencei, Jennifer. *Exotic Spaces in German Modernism*. New York: Oxford, 2011.

Green, Martin. *Dreams of Adventure, Deeds of Empire*. New York: Basic Books, 1979.

Greenblatt, Stephen. *Marvelous Possessions: The Wonder of the New World*. Chicago: University of Chicago Press, 1991.

Grimm, Hans. *Dina*. In *Südafrikanische Novellen*, 7–41. Lippoldsberg: Klosterhaus Verlag, 1975. First published 1913.

Grinstein, Alexander. *On Sigmund Freud's Dreams*. Detroit: Wayne State University Press, 1968.

Grivel, Charles. "Travel/Writing." In *Materialities of Communication*, edited by Hans Ulrich Gumbrecht and Ludwig K. Pfeiffer, 242–57. Stanford, Calif.: Stanford University Press, 1994.

Grubrich-Simitis, Ilse. "Metapsychology and Metabiology: On Sigmund Freud's Draft Overview of the Transference Neuroses." In *A Phylogenetic Fantasy: Overview of the Transference Neuroses*, by Sigmund Freud, edited by Grubrich-Simitis, 75–107. Cambridge, Mass.: Harvard University Press, 1987.

Gurowski, Adam de. *America and Europe*. New York: Appleton, 1857.

Gutzkow, Karl. "Julius Mosens Ahasver." In *Vermittelungen: Kritiken und Charakteristiken*, vol. 2 of *Vermischte Schriften*, 154–70. Leipzig: J. J. Weber, 1842.

Ha'Am, Ahad. "Pinsker and Political Zionism." In *Ahad Ha'Am: Essays, Letters, Memoirs*, translated by Leon Simon, 186–87. Oxford: Phaidon, 1946.

Habinger, Gabriele. *Frauen reisen in die Fremde: Diskurse und Repräsentationen von reisenden Europäerinnen im 19. und beginnenden 20. Jahrhundert*. Vienna: Promedia, 2006.

Haggard, H. Rider. *Heart of the World*. North Hollywood, Calif.: Newcastle, 1976. First published 1895.

———. *She*. Oxford: Oxford University Press, 1991. First published 1886–87.

Hall, Richard. *Stanley: An Adventurer Explored*. London: Collins, 1974.

Hamann, Richard, and Jost Hermand. *Impressionismus*. Berlin: Akademie-Verlag, 1966.

Haughton, Hugh. Introduction to *The Uncanny*, by Sigmund Freud. London: Penguin, 2003.

Hegel, G. W. F. *The Phenomenology of Spirit*. Translated by A. V. Miller. New York: Oxford University Press, 1977.

Heidegger, Martin. *Einführung in die Metaphysik*. Tübingen: Niemeyer, 1976. Lectures from 1935.

———. *Sein und Zeit* (1927). Vol. 2 of *Gesamtausgabe*, edited by Friedrich Wilhelm von Herrmann. Frankfurt am Main: Klostermann, 1977.

Heilbut, Anthony. *Thomas Mann: Eros and Literature*. New York: Knopf, 1995.

Heine, Heinrich. *The Poetry and Prose of Heinrich Heine*. Edited by Frederic Ewen and translated by Emma Lazarus. New York: Citadel, 1948.

Heischman, Daniel R. "The Uncanniness of September 11th." *Journal of Religion and Health* 41 (2002): 197–205.

Hermand, Jost. "Musils *Grigia*." *Monatshefte für den deutschen Unterricht, deutsche Sprache und Literatur* 54 (1962): 171–82.

Hertz, Neil. "Dora's Secrets, Freud's Techniques." In Bernheimer and Kahane, *In Dora's Case*, 221–42.

———. "Freud and the Sandman." In *Textual Strategies: Perspectives in Post-Structuralist Criticism*, edited by Josué V. Harari, 296–321. Ithaca: Cornell University Press, 1979.

Heschel, Susannah. "Revolt of the Colonized: Abraham Geiger's *Wissenschaft des Judentums* as a Challenge to Christian Hegemony in the Academy." *New German Critique* 77 (1999): 61–85.

Hess, Jonathan. *Germans, Jews and the Claims of Modernity*. New Haven, Conn.: Yale University Press, 2002.

Hess, Moses. *The Revival of Israel: Rome and Jerusalem, the Last Nationalist Question*. Lincoln: University of Nebraska Press, 1995. First published 1862.

Hesse, Hermann. "Abend in Asien" (1912). In *Sämtliche Werke* 13:215–18.

———. "Architektur" (1912). In *Sämtliche Werke* 13:227–29.

———. *Aus Indien: Aufzeichnungen, Tagebücher, Gedichte, Betrachtungen und Erzählungen*. Frankfurt am Main: Suhrkamp, 1982.

———. "Besuch aus Indien" (1922). In *Sämtliche Werke* 13:422–26.

———. "Erinnerung an Indien" (1917). In *Sämtliche Werke* 13:378–83.

———. "Fastnacht" (1906). In *Sämtliche Werke* 13:117–22.

———. "Fluß im Urwald" (1912). In *Sämtliche Werke* 10:176–77.

———. "Der Hanswurst" (1912). In *Sämtliche Werke* 13:226–27.

———. "Nacht auf Deck" (1912). In *Sämtliche Werke* 13:244–47.

———. "Die Nikobaren" (1913). In *Sämtliche Werke* 13:210–15.

———. "Palembang" (1912). In *Sämtliche Werke* 13:251–54.

———. "Pedrotallagalla" (1912). In *Sämtliche Werke* 13:276–78.

———. *Robert Aghion* (1913). In *Sämtliche Werke* 8:26–58.

———. *Sämtliche Werke in 20 Bänden und einem Registerband*. Edited by Volker Michels. 21 vols. Frankfurt am Main: Suhrkamp, 2001–2007.

———. "Singapur-Traum" (1912). In *Sämtliche Werke* 13:230–35.

———. "Spaziergang in Kandy" (1913). In *Sämtliche Werke* 13:269–72.

———. "Tagebuch der Indonesienreise" (1911). In *Sämtliche Werke* 11:329–88.

Hitler, Adolf. *Mein Kampf*. Munich: Zentralverlag der NDSAP, 1934. First published 1925–26.

Hoffmann, Felix, ed. *Unheimlich Vertraut: Bilder vom Terror/The Uncanny Familiar: Images of Terror*. Cologne: Walther König, 2011.

Hofmannsthal, Hugo von. *Andreas*. In *Sämtliche Werke* 30:7–218. First published posthumously in 1932.

———. *Andreas*. Translated by Marie D. Hottinger. London: Pushkin, 1998.

———. *Andreas (Varianten und Erläuterungen)*. In *Sämtliche Werke* 30:303–77.

———. *Andreas oder die Vereinigten*. Berlin: S. Fischer, 1932.

———. *Sämtliche Werke: Kritische Ausgabe*. Edited by Rudolf Hirsch et al. 42 vols. Frankfurt am Main: S. Fischer, 1975–.

———. "Wiener Brief [II]." In *Gesammelte Werke in zehn Einzelbänden, Reden und Aufsätze 2 (1914–1924)*, edited by Bernd Schoeller, 185–96. Frankfurt am Main: S. Fischer, 1979.

Hofmannsthal, Hugo von, and Thomas Mann. "Briefwechsel." In *Almanach: Das zweiundachtzigste Jahr*, edited by Hellmut Freund and Gerda Niedeck, 13–44. Frankfurt am Main: S. Fischer, 1968.

Honold, Alexander, and Klaus Scherpe, eds. *Mit Deutschland um die Welt: Eine Kulturgeschichte des Fremden in der Kolonialzeit*. Stuttgart: J.B. Metzler, 2004.

Höppler, Fritz. *Der ewige Jude*. Screenplay by Eberhardt Tauber. Germany, Deutsche Film Gesellschaft, 1940.

Huyssen, Andreas. *After the Great Divide: Modernism, Mass Culture, Postmodernism*. Bloomington: Indiana University Press, 1986.

———. "Fortifying the Heart—Totally: Ernst Jünger's Armored Texts." In *Twilight Memories: Marking Time in a Culture of Amnesia*, 127–44. New York: Routledge, 1995.

———. "High/Low in an Expanded Field." *Modernism/Modernity* 9, no. 3 (2002): 363–74.

International Dictionary of Psychoanalysis. Edited by Alain de Mijolla. 3 vols. Detroit: Macmillan Reference, 2005.

Iurascu, Ilinca. "Freud-the-Father, Ernst-the-Son and the Politics of the Uncanny." Unpublished conference paper, NeMLA Convention, Philadelphia, March 5, 2006.

Jacobowski, Ludwig. "Selbstporträt." In *Leuchtende Tage: Neue Gedichte, 1896–98*. 2nd ed. Minden: Bruns Verlag, 1901.

———. *Werther, der Jude*. 6th ed. Berlin: Verlag Berlin-Wien, pref. 1898.

Jacques, Norbert. *Heißes Land: Eine Reise nach Brasilien (Hot Land: A Journey to Brazil)*. Dachau: Einhorn, 1924. First published 1911 (as *Heiße Städte: Eine Reise nach Brasilien*).

———. *Mit Lust gelebt: Roman meines Lebens*. St. Ingbert: Röhrig Universitätsverlag, 2004.

———. *Piraths Insel*. Berlin: S. Fischer, 1917.

Jay, Martin. "The Uncanny Nineties." Chap. 14 in *Cultural Semantics: Keywords of Our Time*. Amherst, Mass.: University of Massachusetts Press, 1998.

Jean Paul. *Selina*. In Vol. 6 of *Werke*, edited by Norbert Miller, 1105–1236. Munich: Hanser, 1963.

Jentsch, Ernst. "Zur Psychologie des Unheimlichen." *Psychiatrisch-Neurologische Wochenschrift* 8 (1906): 195–98 and 203–5.

Joch, Markus. "Halbwilder Westen: Juni 1905: Buffalo Bill reitet im Groschenheft." In Honold and Scherpe, *Mit Deutschland um die Welt*, 320–28.

Johnson, Laurie Ruth. *Aesthetic Anxiety: Uncanny Symptoms in German Literature and Culture*. Amsterdam: Rodopi, 2010.

Jones, Ernest. *Sigmund Freud: Life and Work*. 3 vols. London: Hogarth, 1953–57.

Jonte-Pace, Diane. *Speaking the Unspeakable: Religion, Misogyny, and the Uncanny Mother in Freud's Cultural Texts*. Berkeley: University of California Press, 2001.

Jung, Carl J. "Wandlungen und Symbole der Libido: Beiträge zur Entwicklungsgeschichte des Denkens" (part 2). *Jahrbuch für psychoanalytische und psychopathische Forschungen* 4 (1912): 162–464.

Jünger, Ernst. *Afrikanische Spiele*. Munich: DTV, 1987.

Kafka, Franz. "Ein Bericht für eine Akademie" ("A Report to an Academy") (1917). In *Drucke zu Lebzeiten*, 299–313.

———. *Drucke zu Lebzeiten*. Edited by Wolf Kittler, Hans-Gerd Koch, and Gerhard Neumann. Frankfurt am Main: S. Fischer, 1994.

———. "Fragments from Note-Books and Loose Pages." In *Wedding Preparations in the Country and Other Posthumous Prose Writings*, translated by Ernst Kaiser and Eithne Wilkins, 218–413. London: Secker & Warburg, 1954.

———. "Ein großer Plan der Kriegsfürsorge verlangt Verwirklichung: Gründung einer Nervenheilanstalt in Deutschböhmen" (1916). In *Amtliche Schriften*, edited by Klaus Hermsdorf and Benno Wagner, 494–98. Frankfurt am Main: S. Fischer, 2004.

———. "In der Strafkolonie" ("In the Penal Colony") (1919; written 1914). In *Drucke zu Lebzeiten*, 210–48.

———. *Letters to Milena*. Translated by Philip Boehm. New York: Schocken, 1990.

———. "Reise Lugano—Mailand—Paris—Erlenbach" (1911). In Brod and Kafka, *Reiseaufzeichnungen*, 143–88.

Kain, Roger J. P., ed. *Cartography in the Nineteenth Century.* Vol. 5 of *The History of Cartography.* Chicago: University of Chicago Press, forthcoming.

Kaiser, Ernst, and Eithne Wilkins. *Robert Musil: Eine Einführung in das Werk.* Stuttgart: Kohlhammer, 1962.

Kaplan, Caren. *Questions of Travel: Postmodern Discourses of Displacement.* Durham, N.C.: Duke University Press, 1996.

Kellermann, Bernhard. *Ein Spaziergang in Japan.* Berlin: Paul Cassirer, 1910.

Kerr, Alfred. "Jagow, Flaubert, Pan," *Pan* 1, no. 7 (February 1, 1911): 217–23.

Keynes, John Maynard. *The Economic Consequences of the Peace.* Charleston, S.C.: BiblioBazaar, 2007. First published 1919.

Keyserling, Hermann. *Das Reisetagebuch eines Philosophen.* Stuttgart: Deutsche-Verlagsanstalt, 1932. First published 1918.

Khanna, Ranjana. *Dark Continents: Psychoanalysis and Colonialism.* Durham, N.C.: Duke University Press, 2003.

Kim, David. "The Task of the Loving Translator: Translation, *Völkerschauen,* and Colonial Ambivalence in Peter Altenberg's *Ashantee* (1897)." *Transit* 2, no. 1 (2006): Essay 60404.

King, Averil. *Emil Nolde: Artist of the Elements.* London: Philip Wilson, 2013.

Kittler, Wolf. "Stéphane Mallarmé: Brise marine, Übersetzung und Kommentar." In *FAKtisch: Festschrift für Friedrich Kittler zum 60. Geburtstag,* edited by Peter Berz, Annette Bitsch and Bernhard Siegert, 245–52. Munich: Wilhelm Fink, 2003.

Klein, Dennis B. *Jewish Origins of the Psychoanalytic Movement.* New York: Praeger, 1981.

Klotz, Marcia. "Global Visions: From the Colonial to the National Socialist World." *European Studies Journal,* special issue: "German Colonialism: Another Sonderweg?" 16 (Fall 1999): 37–68.

Kohut, Thomas. *Wilhelm II and the Germans: A Study in Leadership.* New York: Oxford University Press, 1991.

Kojève, Alexandre. *Introduction to the Reading of Hegel.* New York: Basic Books, 1969.

König, Viola, ed. *Vermessen: Kartographie der Tropen.* Berlin: Staatliche Museen zu Berlin, 2006.

Kopp, Kristin. *Germany's Wild East: Constructing Poland as Colonial Space.* Ann Arbor: University of Michigan Press, 2012.

Koselleck, Reinhart. *Begriffsgeschichten: Studien zur Semantik und Pragmatik der politischen und sozialen Sprache.* Frankfurt am Main: Suhrkamp, 2006.

Krämer-Bannow, Elisabeth. "Heimatschutz in die deutschen Kolonien!" *Der Kunstwart und Kulturwart* 19, first July issue (1913): 13–22.

Kristeva, Julia. *Powers of Horror: An Essay on Abjection.* Translated by Leon Roudiez. New York: Columbia University Press, 1982.

Krobb, Florian. "Reclaiming the Location: Leopold Kompert's Ghetto Fiction in Post-Colonial Perspective." In *Ghetto Writing: Traditional and Eastern Jewry in the German-Jewish Literature from Heine to Hilsenrath,* edited by Anne Fuchs and Florian Krobb, 41–53. Columbia, S.C.: Camden House, 1999.

Krugman, Paul. "Government vs. The Market," *The Washington Monthly* 30, no. 3 (March 1998): 39–41.

Kundrus, Birthe. *Moderne Imperialisten: Das Kaiserreich im Spiegel seiner Kolonien.* Cologne: Böhlau, 2003.

Lacan. Jacques. "Aggressiveness in Psychoanalysis" ("L'agressivité en psychanal-yse"). In *Écrits* (English), 82–101/*Écrits* (French), 101–24.

———. *Écrits*. Paris: Seuil, 1966.

———. *Écrits: The First Complete Edition in English*. Translated by Bruce Fink. New York: Norton, 2006.

———. "The Instance of the Letter in the Unconscious, or Reason Since Freud" ("L'instance de la letter dans l'inconscient ou la raison depuis Freud"). In *Écrits* (English), 412–41/*Écrits* (French), 493–528.

———. "The Mirror Stage as Formative of the *I* Function" ("Le stade du miroir comme formateur de la fonction du *Je*"). In *Écrits* (English), 75–81/*Écrits* (French), 93–100.

———. "Presentation on Transference" ("Intervention sur le transfert"). In *Écrits* (English), 176–85/*Écrits* (French), 215–26.

———. *Le séminaire livre X: L'angoisse*. Edited by Jacques-Alain Miller. Paris: Seuil, 2004.

Lehmann, Herbert. "Freud's Dream of February 1918." *International Review of Psycho-Analysis* 10 (1983): 87–93.

Le Rider, Jacques. *Modernité viennoise et crises de l'identité*. Paris: Presses Universitaires de France, 1990.

Lerner, Paul. *Hysterical Men: War, Psychiatry, and the Politics of Trauma in Germany, 1890–1930*. Ithaca, N.Y.: Cornell University Press, 2003.

Liao, Pei-Chen. *'Post'-9/11 South Asian Diasporic Fiction: Uncanny Terror*. New York: Palgrave Macmillan, 2013.

Lloyd, Jill. *German Expressionism: Primitivism and Modernity*. New Haven, Conn.: Yale University Press, 1991.

Lloyd Smith, Allan. "The Phantoms of *Drood* and *Rebecca*: The Uncanny Reencountered through Abraham and Torok's 'Cryptonymy.'" *Poetics Today* 13, no. 2 (Summer 1992): 285–308.

Lobner, Hans. "Some Additional Remarks on Freud's Library." *Sigmund Freud House Bulletin* 1 (1975): 18–29.

Locke, John. *An Essay Concerning Human Understanding*. Edited by Alexander Campbell Fraser. 2 vols. New York: Dover, 1959.

Lukács, Georg. "Expressionism: Its Significance and Decline" (1934). In *German Expressionism: Documents from the End of the Wilhelmine Empire to the Rise of National Socialism*, edited by Rose-Carol Washton Long, 313–16. Berkeley: University of California Press, 1995.

———. "The Ideology of Modernism" (1957). In *The Meaning of Contemporary Realism*, translated by John and Necke Mander, 17–46. London: Merlin, 1963.

Lütkehaus, Ludger. Introduction to *"Dieses wahre innere Afrika": Texte zur Entdeckung des Unbewußten vor Freud*, edited by Ludger Lütkehaus. Giessen: Psychosozial Verlag, 2005.

Lydenberg, Robin. "Freud's Uncanny Narratives." *PMLA* 112, no. 5 (October 1997): 1072–86.

Lyotard, Jean-François. *Heidegger and "the jews."* Minneapolis: University of Minnesota Press, 1990.

MacCannell, Dean. *The Tourist: A New Theory of the Leisure Class*. New York: Schocken, 1976.

Magill, Daniela. *Literarische Reisen in die exotische Fremde: Topoi der Darstellung von Eigen- und Fremdkultur.* Frankfurt am Main: Peter Lang, 1989.

Malinowski, Bronislaw. *Argonauts of the Western Pacific: An Account of Native Enterprise and Adventure in the Archipelagoes of Melanesian New Guinea.* Long Grove, Ill.: Waveland, 1984. First published 1922.

———. *A Diary in the Strict Sense of the Term.* Stanford, Calif.: Stanford University Press, 1989.

Mann, Thomas. *Briefe 1889–1936.* Edited by Erika Mann. Frankfurt am Main: S. Fischer, 1961.

———. *Death in Venice: A New Translation, Backgrounds and Contexts, Criticism.* Edited and translated by Clayton Koelb. New York: Norton Critical Edition, 1994.

———. *Große kommentierte Frankfurter Ausgabe.* Edited by Heinrich Detering et al. 38 vols. Frankfurt am Main: S. Fischer, 2001–.

———. *Der Tod in Venedig* (1912). In *Große kommentierte Frankfurter Ausgabe* 2.1:501–92.

———. *Der Tod in Venedig (Kommentar).* In *Große kommentierte Frankfurter Ausgabe* 2.2:360–507.

Marcuse, Max, "Inzest ('Blutschande')." In *Handwörterbuch der Sexualwissenschaft: Enzyklopädie der natur- und kulturwissenschaftlichen Sexualkunde des Menschen,* edited by Max Marcuse, 301–11. Berlin: De Gruyter, 2001. First published 1923.

Marx, Karl. *Das Kapital.* In *Marx Engels Werke,* vols. 23–25.

Marx, Karl, and Friedrich Engels. *Briefwechsel zwischen Marx und Engels: Januar 1860—September 1864.* In *Marx Engels Werke,* 30:5–434.

———. *Marx Engels Werke.* Edited by Manfred Kliem, Horst Merbach, and Richard Sperl. 43 vols. Berlin: Dietz, 1952–1969.

Masschelein, Anneleen. *The Unconcept: The Freudian Uncanny in Late Twentieth-Century Theory.* Albany: State University of New York Press, 2011.

———. "Unheimlich/das Unheimliche." In Vol. 6 of *Ästhetische Grundbegriffe: historisches Wörterbuch in sieben Bänden,* edited by Karlheinz Barck et al., 241–59. Stuttgart: Metzler, 2005.

Mayer, Mathias. Afterword to *Andreas,* by Hugo von Hofmannsthal. Stuttgart: Reclam, 2000.

———. "Hofmannsthals *Andreas*: Nachträge, Nachfragen und Nachwirkungen." *Hofmannsthal Jahrbuch* 7 (1999): 101–98.

McIntyre, Allan J. "Psychology and Symbol: Correspondences between *Heart of Darkness* and *Death in Venice.*" *Hartford Studies in Literature* 7, no. 2 (1975): 216–35.

Mehlman, Jeffrey. *Revolution and Repetition: Marx/Hugo/Balzac.* Berkeley: University of California Press, 1977.

Memmi, Albert. *Le Racisme.* Paris: Gallimard, 1982.

Mergenthaler, Volker. *Völkerschau—Kannibalismus—Fremdenlegion: Zur Ästhetik der Transgression 1897–1936.* Tübingen: Max Niemeyer, 2005.

Micale, Mark S. *Hysterical Men: The Hidden History of Male Nervous Illness.* Cambridge, Mass.: Harvard University Press, 2008.

Mileck, Joseph. *Hermann Hesse: Between the Perils of Politics and the Allure of the Orient.* New York: Peter Lang, 2003.

————. *Hermann Hesse: Life and Art.* Berkeley: University of California Press, 1978.

Mitchell, Timothy. *Colonising Egypt.* Berkeley: University of California Press, 1988.

Moberly, L. G. "Inexplicable." *Strand Magazine* 54 (December 1917): 572–81.

Moi, Toril. "Representations of Patriarchy: Sexuality and Epistemology in Freud's Dora." In Bernheimer and Kahane, *In Dora's Case,* 181–99.

Molnar, Michael. "The Bizarre Chair: A Slant on Freud's Light Reading in the 1930s." In Gilman et al., *Reading Freud's Reading,* 252–65.

————. Introduction to Freud, *Tagebuch 1929–1939: Kürzeste Chronik.*

Müller, Robert. *Das Inselmädchen.* Paderborn: Igel Verlag, 1994. First published 1919.

————. *Tropen: Der Mythos der Reise: Urkunden eines deutschen Ingenieurs.* Paderborn: Igel Verl. Literatur, 1990. First published 1915.

Musil, Robert. "Ansätze zu neuer Ästhetik: Bemerkungen über eine Dramaturgie des Films" (1925). In *Gesammelte Werke* 8:1137–54.

————. *Five Women.* Translated by Eithne Wilkins and Ernst Kaiser. Boston: Godine, 1999.

————. *Gesammelte Werke in neun Bänden.* Edited by Adolf Frisé. 9 vols. Reinbek bei Hamburg: Rowohlt, 1978.

————. *Grigia* (1921). In *Gesammelte Werke* 6:234–52.

————. *Der Mann ohne Eigenschaften.* In *Gesammelte Werke,* vols. 1–5. Original publication began 1930.

————. "Skizze der Erkenntnis des Dichters" (1918). In *Gesammelte Werke* 8:1025–30.

————. *Tagebücher.* Edited by Adolf Frisé. 2 vols. Reinbek: Rowohlt, 1983.

Nayar, Pramrod K. "From the Uncanny to the Sublime: 9/11 and Don DeLillo's *Falling Man.*" *The IUP Journal of American Literature* 4 (2011): 7–19.

Newman, Amy. "The Death of Judaism in German Protestant Thought from Luther to Hegel." *The Journal of the American Academy of Religion* 61, no. 3 (Fall 1993): 455–84.

Nicklisch, Andrea. "Auf der Suche nach den Nilquellen." In König, *Vermessen,* 52–59.

Nietzsche, Friedrich. *Beyond Good and Evil.* Translated by Walter Kaufmann. New York: Vintage, 1966.

————. *On the Genealogy of Morals.* Translated by Walter Kaufmann and R. J. Hollingdale. New York: Vintage, 1966.

Nolde, Emil. *Welt und Heimat: Die Südseereise: 1913–1918.* Cologne: DuMont, 1965.

Nouzeilles, Gabriela. "Touching the Real: Alternative Travel and Landscapes of Fear." In Zilcosky, *Writing Travel,* 195–210.

Noyes, John K. "Hottentotts, Bastards, and Dead Mothers: Hans Grimm's Topology of Female Sexuality." In *Kultur, Sprache, Macht: Festschrift für Peter Horn,* edited by John K. Noyes, Gunther Pakendorf, and Wolfgang Pasche, 323–35. Frankfurt am Main: Peter Lang, 2000.

————. "Wo sind die Mütter?: 1907: Margarethe von Eckenbrechers Erinnerungen *Was Afrika mir gab und nahm.*" In Honold and Scherpe, *Mit Deutschland um die Welt,* 367–72.

Oepke, Albrecht. *Moderne Indienfahrer und Weltreligionen.* Leipzig: Dörffling & Franke, 1921.

Otis, Laura. *Membranes: Metaphors of Invasion in Nineteenth-Century Literature, Science, and Politics.* Baltimore: Johns Hopkins University Press, 1999.

Otterbeck, Christoph. "Auf der Suche nach einer elementaren Ästhetik: Von der Holzbildhauerei der *Brücke*-Künstler zum Werk Otto Freundlichs." In Berger and Wanken, *Wilde Welten,* 57–71.

Otto, Rudolf. *Das Heilige: Über das Irrationale in der Idee des Göttlichen und sein Verhältnis zum Rationalen.* Munich: C.H. Beck, 1979. First published 1917.

Painter, Joe, and Alex Jeffrey. *Political Geography: An Introduction to Space and Power.* 2nd ed. Los Angeles: Sage, 2009.

Pascal, Roy. *The Dual Voice: Free Indirect Speech and Its Functioning in the Nineteenth-Century European Novel.* Manchester: University of Manchester Press, 1977.

Payne, Harry C. "Malinowski's Style." *Proceedings of the American Philosophical Society* 125, no. 6 (December 1981): 416–40.

Pechstein, Max. *Erinnerungen.* Munich: List Verlag, 1963.

Penny, H. Glenn, and Matti Bunzl, eds. *Worldly Provincialism: German Anthropology in the Age of Empire.* Ann Arbor: University of Michigan Press, 2003.

Percy, Walker. *The Message in the Bottle.* New York: Picador, 1975.

Philbrick, Nathaniel. *In the Heart of the Sea.* New York: Viking, 2000.

Pinsker, Leo. "Auto-Emancipation: An Appeal to His People by a Russian Jew." In *Modern Jewish History: A Source Reader,* edited by Robert Chazan and Marc Lee Raphael, 161–74. New York: Schocken, 1969.

Plener, Peter. "(K)ein Mohr im Hemd. Aschantis in Budapest und Wien 1896/97." *Kakanien Revisited,* November 6, 2001, 1–4. http://www.kakanien-revisited .at/beitr/fallstudie/PPlener1/?alpha=p.

Polk, Milbry, and Mary Tiegreen. *Women of Discovery: A Celebration of Intrepid Women Who Explored the World.* London: Scriptum, 2001.

Potts, Lydia, ed. *Aufbruch und Abenteuer: Frauen-Reisen um die Welt ab 1785.* Frankfurt am Main: S. Fischer, 1995.

Powdermaker, Hortense. "An Agreeable Man." *New York Review of Books,* November 9, 1967.

Pratt, Mary. *Imperial Eyes: Travel Writing and Transculturation.* New York: Routledge, 1992.

Prawer, Siegbert Salomon. *A Cultural Citizen of the World: Sigmund Freud's Knowledge and Use of British and American Writings.* London: Legenda, 2009.

———. *The "Uncanny" in Literature: An Apology for Its Investigation.* London: Westfield College, 1965.

Pulzer, Peter. *The Rise of Political Anti-Semitism in Germany and Austria.* Cambridge, Mass.: Harvard University Press, 1988.

Rabinow, Paul. "Representations Are Social Facts: Modernity and Post-Modernity in Anthropology." In *Writing Culture: The Politics and Poetics of Ethnography,* edited by James Clifford and George E. Marcus, 234–61. Berkeley: University of California Press, 1986.

Reed-Anderson, Paulette. *Rewriting the Footnotes: Berlin und die afrikanische Diaspora/Berlin and the African Diaspora.* Berlin: Ausländerbeauftragte des Senats, 2000.

Reif, Wolfgang. "Exotismus im Reisebericht des frühen 20. Jahrhunderts." In *Der Reisebericht: Die Entwicklung einer Gattung in der deutschen Literatur*, edited by Peter J. Brenner, 434–62. Frankfurt am Main: Suhrkamp, 1989.

———. *Zivilisationsflucht und literarische Wunschräume: Der exotistische Roman im ersten Viertel des zwanzigsten Jahrhunderts.* Stuttgart: Metzler, 1975.

Reik, Theodor. *Der eigene und der fremde Gott: Zur Psychoanalyse der religiösen Entwicklung.* Vienna: Internationaler Psychoanalytischer Verlag, 1923.

———. *Ritual: Psycho-Analytic Studies.* New York: Farrar, Straus, 1946. First published 1919.

Riegert, Leo W. "Subjects and Agents of Empire: German Jews in Post-Colonial Perspective." *German Quarterly* 82, no. 3 (Summer 2009): 336–55.

Ritter, Naomi, ed. *Death in Venice* (Case Studies in Contemporary Criticism). New York: Bedford, 1998.

Ritvo, Lucille B. *Darwin's Influence on Freud: A Tale of Two Sciences.* New Haven, Conn.: Yale University Press, 1990.

Rizzuto, Ana-Maria. *Why Did Freud Reject God?* New Haven, Conn.: Yale University Press, 1998.

Roazen, Paul. *Wie Freud arbeitete: Berichte aus erster Hand.* Giessen: Psychosozial-Verlag, 1999.

Robinson, Jane. *Wayward Women: A Guide to Women Travellers.* Oxford: Oxford University Press, 1990.

Rosaldo, Renato. *Culture and Truth: The Remaking of Social Analysis.* Boston: Beacon, 1993.

Rose, Paul Laurence. *German Question/Jewish Question: Revolutionary Antisemitism from Kant to Wagner.* Princeton, N.J.: Princeton University Press, 1990.

Roth, Joseph. *Das Spinnennetz* (1923). In *Werke*, 4 vols., edited by Hermann Kesten, 1:45–127. Cologne: Kiepenheuer & Witsch, 1975.

Royle, Nicholas. *The Uncanny.* New York: Routledge, 2003.

Said, Edward. *Culture and Imperialism.* New York: Vintage, 1993.

Schelling, Friedrich Wilhelm. *Philosophie der Mythologie.* 5th suppl. vol. of *Schellings Werke*, edited by Manfred Schröter. Munich: Beck, 1968. Lectures from the 1830s, first published 1842.

Schepers, Gerhard. "Exoticism in German Literature on Japan." In *Japanese-German Relations, 1895–1945: War, Diplomacy and Public Opinion*, edited by Christian W. Spang and Rolf-Harald Wippich, 98–116. London: Routledge, 2006.

Schestokat, Karin U. *German Women in Cameroon: Travelogues from Colonial Times.* New York: Peter Lang, 2003.

Schlieker, Kerstin. *Frauenreisen in den Orient zu Beginn des 20. Jahrhunderts: Weibliche Strategien der Erfahrung und textuellen Vermittlung kultureller Fremde (Marie von Bunsen, Alma Karlin, Ella Maillart und Annemarie Schwarzbach).* Berlin: WiKu-Verlag, 2003.

Schmidt, Dietmar. Afterword to *Gebuchte Lust: Texte zur Prostitution*, edited by Dietmar Schmidt. Leipzig: Reclam, 1996.

Schmitt, Carl. *Glossarium: Aufzeichnungen der Jahre 1947–1951.* Edited by Eberhard von Medem. Berlin: Duncker & Humblot, 1991.

Schmitz-Berning, Cornelia. *Vokabular des National-Sozialismus.* Berlin: Walter de Gruyter, 2007.

Schnitzler, Arthur. "Andreas Thameyers letzter Brief." In vol. 2 of *Das erzählerische Werk*, 66–72. Frankfurt am Main: S. Fischer, 1977.

Scholdt, Günter. Afterword to Jacques, *Mit Lust gelebt*.

———. *Der Fall Norbert Jacques: Über Rang und Niedergang eines Erzählers (1889–1954)*. Stuttgart: Heinz, 1976.

———. "Norbert Jacques, Fritz von Unruh und der Expressionismus." *Schiller-Jahrbuch* 19 (1975): 63–97.

———. "Die Proklamation des Neuen Menschen in der deutschsprachigen Literatur vom Ausgang des 19. Jahrhunderts bis zur Mitte des 20. Jahrhunderts." In *Der Traum vom neuen Menschen—Hoffnung—Utopie—Illusion?*, edited by Evangelische Akademie Baden, 22–63. Karlsruhe: Evangelische Akademie Baden, 1999.

Schopenhauer, Arthur. "On Jurisprudence and Politics." In *Parerga and Paralipomena: Short Philosophical Essays*, 2:240–66, translated by E. F. J. Payne. Oxford: Clarendon, 1974.

Schorske, Carl. *Fin de Siècle Vienna: Politics and Culture*. New York: Knopf, 1980.

Schott, Richard. "Die deutsche Kolonial-Ausstellung." In *Groß-Berlin: Bilder von der Austellungsstadt*, edited by Albert Kühnemann, 253–63. Berlin: Pauli, 1897.

Schütz, Erhard. "Autobiographien und Reiseliteratur." In *Literatur der Weimarer Republik 1918–1933*, edited by Bernhard Weyergraf, 549–600. Munich: Carl Hanser, 1995.

Schwarz, Thomas. "Bastards: Juli 1908: Eugen Fischer bringt die 'Rassenkunde' nach Afrika." In Honold and Scherpe, *Mit Deutschland um die Welt*, 373–80.

———. "Die Mischehendebatte im Reichstag 1912." *Dokilomunhak: Deutsche Sprach- und Literaturwissenschaft* 19 (2002): 323–50.

———. *Robert Müllers Tropen: Eine Reiseführer in den imperialen Exotismus*. Heidelberg: Synchron, 2006.

———. "Tropenenthusiasmus: Zur Kartographie des Dionysischen bei Thomas Mann, Robert Müller und Theodor Koch-Grünberg." *TDLV-Forum* 8 (2004): 30–34.

Schwarz, Werner Michael. *Anthropologische Spektakel: Zur Schaustellung "exotischer" Menschen, Wien 1870–1910*. Vienna: Turia + Kant, 2001.

Schwarzenbach, F. S. "'Terra Incognita'—An Image of the City in English Literature, 1820–1855." In *The Art of Travel*, edited by Philip Dodd, 61–84. London: Frank Cass, 1982.

Scott, Robert Falcon. *Scott's Last Expedition, Vol. 1: Being the Journals of Captain R. F. Scott, R.N., C.V.O.* Edited by Leonard Huxley. London: Smith, Elder, 1913.

Sebald, W. G. *Unheimliche Heimat. Essays zur österreichischen Literatur*. Salzburg: Residenz, 1991.

———. "Venezianisches Kryptogramm: Hofmannsthals *Andreas*." In *Die Beschreibung des Unglücks*, 61–77. Salzburg: Residenz, 1985.

Segalen, Victor. *Essay on Exoticism: An Aesthetics of Diversity*. Translated and edited by Yaël Rachel Schlick, foreword by Harry Harootunian. Durham, N.C.: Duke University Press, 2002. Written 1904–18; first published posthumously 1955 (as *Essai sur l'exotisme*).

Shapiro, Susan. "The Uncanny Jew: A Brief History of an Image." *Judaism: A Quarterly Journal of Jewish Life and Thought* 46, no. 1 (1997): 63–78.

Simmel, Georg. "Exkurs über den Fremden" (1908). In *Soziologie: Untersuchungen über die Formen der Vergesellschaftung*, vol. 11 of *Gesamtausgabe*, edited by Otthein Rammstedt, 764–71. Frankfurt am Main: Suhrkamp, 1992.

Slavishak, Edward. *Bodies of Work: Civic Display and Labor in Industrial Pittsburgh*. Durham, N.C.: Duke University Press, 2008.

Sombart, Nicolaus. "The Kaiser in His Epoch: Some Reflexions on Wilhelmian Society, Sexuality, and Culture." In *Kaiser Wilhelm II: New Interpretations*, edited by John Roehl and Nicolaus Sombart, 287–311. Cambridge, Eng.: Cambridge University Press, 1982.

Sprengnether, Madelon. "Enforcing Oedipus: Freud and Dora." In Bernheimer and Kahane, *In Dora's Case*, 254–75.

Stanley, Henry Morton. *The Autobiography of Sir Henry Morton Stanley*, edited by Dorothy Stanley. London: S. Low Marston, 1909.

Steiner, Gabor. "Als Wien frohe Feste feierte . . . : Gründung und Glanzheit der Vergnügungsstadt 'Venedig in Wien.'" *Illustrierte Wochenpost*. December 5, 1930.

Stelzig, Eugene L. *Hermann Hesse's Fictions of the Self*. Princeton, N.J.: Princeton University Press, 1988.

Stocking, George. "Anthropology and the Science of the Irrational: Malinowski's Encounter with Freudian Psychoanalysis." In *Malinowski, Rivers, Benedict and Others: Essays in Culture and Personality*, edited by George Stocking, 13–49. Madison: University of Wisconsin Press, 1986.

———. "Empathy and Antipathy in the Heart of Darkness: An Essay Review of Malinowski's Field Diaries." *Journal of the History of the Behavioral Sciences* 4, no. 2 (1968): 189–94.

———. *The Ethnographer's Magic and Other Essays in the History of Anthropology*. Madison: University of Wisconsin Press, 1992.

———. *Victorian Anthropology*. New York: Free Press, 1987.

Stott, Rebecca. "The Dark Continent: Africa as Female Body in Haggard's Adventure Fiction." *Feminist Review* 32 (Summer 1989): 69–89.

Stratz, Carl Heinrich. *Was sind Juden? Eine ethnographisch-anthropologische Studie*. Vienna: F. Tempsky, 1903.

Sulloway, Frank J. *Freud, Biologist of the Mind: Beyond the Psychoanalytic Legend*. New York: Basic Books, 1979.

Taguieff, Pierre-André. *The Force of Prejudice: On Racism and Its Doubles*. Translated by Hassan Melehy. Minneapolis: University of Minnesota Press, 2001.

Thode-Arora, Hilke. *Für fünfzig Pfennig um die Welt: Die Hagenbeckschen Völkerschauen*. Frankfurt am Main: Campus Verlag, 1989.

Thompson, Christina A. "Anthropology's Conrad: Malinowski in the Tropics and What He Read." *The Journal of Pacific History* 30, no. 1 (June 1995): 53–75.

Torgovnick, Marianna. *Gone Primitive: Savage Intellects, Modern Lives*. Chicago: University of Chicago Press, 1990.

Trosman, Harry, and Roger Simmons. "The Freud Library." *Journal of the American Psychoanalytic Association* 21 (1973): 646–87.

Turner, Victor. *The Ritual Process: Structure and Anti-Structure*. Chicago: Aldine, 1969.

Urbach, Reinhard. *Schnitzler-Kommentar zu den erzählenden Schriften und dramatischen Werken.* Munich: Winkler, 1974.

Urban, Bernd. *Hofmannsthal, Freud, und die Psychoanalyse: Quellenkundliche Untersuchungen.* Frankfurt am Main: Peter Lang, 1978.

Urry, John. *The Tourist Gaze: Leisure and Travel in Contemporary Societies.* London: Sage, 1990.

Verhandlungen des Reichstags: Stenographische Berichte. Legislative Period 13 (1912–18). Berlin: Verlag der Buchdruckerei der Norddeutschen Allgemeinen Zeitung.

Vidan, Ivo. "Conrad and Thomas Mann." In *Contexts for Conrad*, edited by Keith Carabine, Owen Knowles, and Wieslaw Krajka, 265–85. Boulder, Colo.: East European Monographs, 1993.

Vidler, Anthony. *The Architectural Uncanny: Essays in the Modern Unhomely.* Cambridge, Mass.: MIT Press, 1992.

Villiers de l'Isle-Adam. *Claire Lenoir.* In *Tribulat Bonhomet*, edited by P. V. Stock, 37–267. 3rd ed. Paris: Tresse & Stock, 1908. First published 1887.

Volkov, Shulamit. "The Written and the Spoken Word: Continuity and Discontinuity of Antisemitism in Germany 1870–1945." In *Unanswered Questions: Nazi Germany and the Genocide of the Jews*, edited by François Furet, 33–53. New York: Schocken, 1989.

Wallace, Edwin. *Freud and Anthropology: A History and Appraisal.* New York: International Universities Press, 1983.

Wanken, Christiane. Introduction to Berger and Wanken, *Wilde Welten.*

Wassermann, Jakob. Afterword to Hofmannsthal, *Andreas oder die Vereinigten.*

Weber, Samuel. The *Legend of Freud*. Expanded edition. Stanford, Calif.: Stanford University Press, 2000.

———. "The Sideshow, or: Remarks on a Canny Moment." *MLN* 88, no. 6 (December 1973): 1102–33.

Wegener, Georg. *Erinnerungen eines Weltreisenden.* Leipzig: Brockhaus, 1921. First published 1919 in a longer version, entitled *Der Zaubermantel.*

Welch, David. *The Third Reich: Politics and Propaganda.* New York: Routledge, 1993.

Widmaier-Haag, Susanne. *Es was das Lächeln des Narziß: Die Theorien der Psychoanalyse im Spiegel der literatur-psychologischen Interpretationen des "Tod in Venedig."* Würzburg: Königshausen & Neumann, 1999.

Wildenthal, Lora. *German Women for Empire, 1884–1945.* Durham, N.C.: Duke University Press, 2001.

Winterstein, Alfred. "Zur Psychologie des Reisens." *Imago: Zeitschrift für Anwendung der Psychoanalyse auf die Geisteswissenschaften.* Year 1, issue 1 (March 1912): 489–506.

Wohlfarth, Irving. "'Männer aus der Fremde': Walter Benjamin and the 'German-Jewish Parnassus.'" *New German Critique* 70 (Winter 1997): 3–85.

Young, Michael W. *Malinowski.* New Haven, Conn.: Yale University Press, 2004.

Young, Robert J. C. *Colonial Desire: Hybridity in Theory, Culture, and Race.* New York: Routledge, 1995.

———. "Freud's Secret: *The Interpretation of Dreams* was a Gothic Novel." In *Sigmund Freud's "The Interpretation of Dreams": New Interdisciplinary*

Essays, edited by Laura Marcus, 206–31. Manchester: University of Manchester Press, 1999.

Zantop, Susanne. *Colonial Fantasies: Conquest, Family, and Nation in Precolonial Germany, 1770–1870.* Durham, N.C.: Duke University Press, 1997.

Zeller, Bernhard. *Hermann Hesse.* Reinbek: Rowohlt, 2005.

Zilcosky, John. "Hermann Hesse's Colonial Uncanny: *Robert Aghion,* 1913." *New German Critique* 41, no. 3 (Fall 2014): 199–218.

———. *Kafka's Travels: Exoticism, Colonialism, and the Traffic of Writing.* New York: Palgrave Macmillan, 2003.

———. "Savage Science: Primitives, War Neurotics, and Freud's Uncanny Method." *American Imago* 70, no. 3 (Fall 2013): 461–86.

———. "Writing Travel." In Zilcosky, *Writing Travel,* 3–21.

———, ed. *Writing Travel: The Poetics and Politics of the Modern Journey.* Toronto: University of Toronto Press, 2008.

Žižek, Slavoj. "Neighbors and Other Monsters: A Plea for Ethical Violence." In *The Neighbor: Three Inquiries in Political Theology,* edited by Slavoj Žižek, Eric L. Santner, and Kenneth Reinhard, 134–90. Chicago: University of Chicago Press, 2005.

———. *Violence: Six Sideways Reflections.* London: Profile, 2008.

Zweig, Stefan. "Gwalior, die indische Residenz" (1909). In *Auf Reisen: Feuilletons und Berichten,* edited by Knut Beck, 105–10. Frankfurt am Main: S. Fischer, 1987.

Page numbers in italics refer to figures.